OTHER BOOKS BY FAMILY CIRCLE

To order **FamilyCircle** books, write to Family Circle Special Projects Dept.,
110 Fifth Avenue, New York, NY 10011.

To order **FamilyCircle** magazine, write to Family Circle Subscriptions,
110 Fifth Avenue, New York, NY 10011.

Project Staff
Project Editor — Ann Bradley
Book Design — Levavi & Levavi
Typesetting — Gary S. Borden, Alison Chandler
Illustrations — Helen Granger

FAMILY CIRCLE STAFF — EDITORIAL
Editor, Family Circle Books — Carol A. Guasti
Production Assistant — Susan M. Sereno
How-To Editors — Arlene Gise, Toni Scott
Photocomposition Manager — Wendy Allen

FAMILY CIRCLE STAFF — MARKETING
Manager — Margaret Chan-Yip
Project Coordinator — Judith M. Tashbook

Cover Photo — Rudy Muller

Photographers:
Paul Amato — Jon Aron — Tito Barberis — Barbara Bersell — Ralph
Bogertman — Jon Bonjour — Ron Colby — Tony Edgeworth — Ronald Harris —
Richard Jeffery — Will Landin — Leombruno-Bodi — Mort Mace — Bill
McGinn — Charles Nesbit — Ron Nicolaysen — Leonard Nones — Rudolph
Nuttgans — Karin Riley — Bob Stoller — Theo — René Velez — Ken
Whitmore — Susan Wood

Published by The Family Circle, Inc.
110 Fifth Avenue, New York, NY 10011

Manufactured in the United States of America

10 9 8 7 6 5 4 3 2 1

ISBN 0-933585-05-5

FamilyCircle

F·A·V·O·R·I·T·E
NEEDLECRAFTS

TABLE
OF
CONTENTS

INTRODUCTION

We should tell you right off that quite frankly, we love needlecrafts. There's something wonderfully satisfying about creating something by hand — and this book is dedicated to everyone who loves doing just that. But don't get us wrong: this isn't an 'experts only' book: you'll find offerings that satisfy the novice, as well as challenge the more experienced.

Take a look through the book: you'll see that each project is shown in full color, is graded according to achievement level (easy, average, challenging) and is flagged with the type of needlework involved.

The projects span the needle arts' most popular techniques: knitting, crocheting, sewing, quilting, embroidery — and more. There are also some new ideas, like knitting with scrap cloth and needlepoint rugmaking!

In the back of the book, you'll also find a step-by-step primer for knitting and crocheting, a stitch guide for needlepoint and embroidery and a Materials Shopping Guide to help you locate resources.

So jump right in and experience the joy of creating memorable handwork — and let Family Circle help you start your *own* family needlework tradition!

·1·

QUILTS & BEDSPREADS

Even if you didn't inherit a quilt from Aunt Sue or cousin Martha, you can create precious heirlooms of your own. Not only is quilting a time-honored art — but participating in it means you'll be part of a proud American tradition that began in pioneer days. Forced to recycle any precious cloth they could come by, early needlewomen devised the patterns we know and love today. Here to keep this great American tradition alive are authentic old patterns — and some new ones — for you to make and display as bed covers or wallhangings. You'll find helpful tips on cutting, piecing and construction in the how-to's. And most importantly, you'll experience a terrific sense of pride in completing a quilt that could become your family heirloom!

BOW-TIE QUILT

(Quilt, shown on the previous page, is about 98" x 112", for a double bed)

TECHNIQUE: Patchwork.

AVERAGE: For those with some experience in patchwork quilting.

Note: The quilt contains 126 blocks to cover the mattress of a double bed plus 9" to tuck under pillows, drops about 22" deep, and has a 6" top border.

MATERIALS: 15 yds. 45"-wide white broadcloth or unbleached muslin; 2⅜ yds. 45"-wide blue and 2½ yds. red printed fabrics; two 90" x 108" quilt batts (synthetic); white dressmaker's pencil; #8 or 10 quilting needle.

DIRECTIONS:
(¼" seams allowed):

1. PATTERN: Carefully draw the pattern (*see* FIG. 1) on thin, firm cardboard.

2. CUTTING: Straighten the cut ends of all fabrics and cut away the selvages. *Across the width of the blue fabric,* draw 21 rows 3½" apart, then draw down them vertically, making 3½" squares (252 altogether). Place pattern (*see* FIG. 1) in each square with edges matching and trace the cut-off corner. Cut out 252 patches. *From white fabric,* cut 252 patches, same as blue. Also from white, cut two side borders each 21" x 88", two quilt backs, each 45" x 117", one quilt back piecing 14" x 117", one foot border 21" x 99" and one top border 5" x 99". *From one edge of the red fabric,* cut off four 2" wide border strips. Across the width of the red fabric, mark off seven 2" wide rows, then draw across them vertically, making 2" squares. Cut out 126 square patches. From the remaining red fabric, cut enough 2½"-wide bias strips to make (piecing as needed) about 12 yds. of bias binding.

3. QUILT BLOCK: With right sides together, pin the short edge of a white patch *centered* over one edge of a red patch, long edges even (short ends won't match). Stitch, starting and stopping at the seamline, so seam allowances are left open. Seam another white patch the same way to opposite red edge. Seam a blue patch, the same way, to each remaining red edge. Then with edges even, seam the four long seams which remain. Press seams toward the darker fabric. Make 125 more quilt blocks the same. Seam the quilt blocks together (edges even and seams matching) in fourteen horizontal rows of nine blocks each. Seam the rows together, top to bottom (edges even and seams matching).

4. RED BORDER: Seam a red border to each long side of the quilt and trim red edges flush with patchwork. Seam a red border to the top and bottom edges and trim the red edges flush with the side borders.

5. WHITE BORDER: Seam the white borders to the red, same as Step 4.

6. MARKING: Mark the borders with evenly spaced diagonal lines, 1½" apart, lightly with a hard pencil. Draw similar lines in the opposite direction.

7. QUILT BACK: Seam the 14" quilt back piece between the two 45" pieces, stitching along the 117" edges of the fabric.

8. BASTING: Smooth out the quilt back wrong side up on a clean floor and tape down the corners. Over this spread one whole batt beside a 28" x 108" strip cut from the second batt. Butt the long edges together and sew long cross stitches (through batting only) from one to the other piece to keep them together. Center the resulting piece (118" x 108") over the quilt back (there will be some fabric extending at each edge). Centered over the batting, spread the quilt top, right side up. With long stitches baste the three layers together (still on the floor), from the center outward diagonally to each

---

TIP

About the Bow-Tie Quilt

The top section of this quilt is pieced by hand (or you can do it by machine); side panels are hand-quilted in a diamond pattern. With a finished size of 98" x 112", the quilt fits a double bed to the floor, with enough to tuck over pillows.

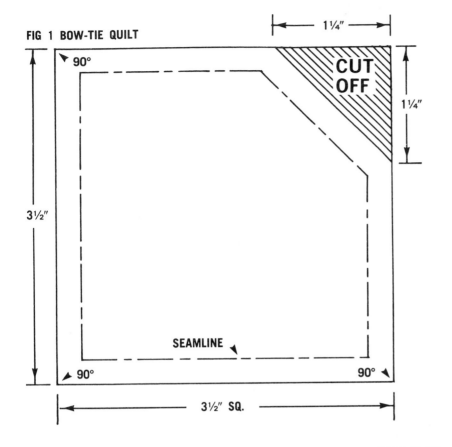

FIG 1 BOW-TIE QUILT

1¼"

CUT OFF

1¼"

90°

3½"

SEAMLINE

90°   90°

3½" SQ.

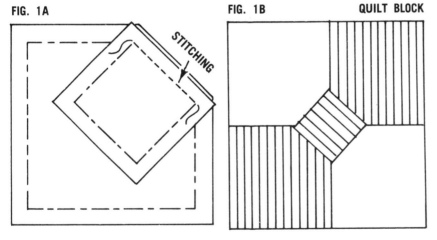

FIG. 1A

STITCHING

FIG. 1B   QUILT BLOCK

Did You Know

Our stunning bow-tie quilt in patriotic red, white and blue is inspired by an early 19th-century pattern? This light-hearted pattern has, surprisingly, been much favored by the reserved Amish. In their quilts, the bow-tie patchwork motifs can be seen worked diagonally like ours, as well as vertically or horizontally; sometimes the Amish bow-ties are set at angles forming a circle on the quilt top.

corner and straight to each side. Baste additional rows (from the center outward) about 8" apart. Untape the quilt.

9. QUILTING: For best results use a quilting frame or quilting hoop. Place the hoop at the center of the quilt to begin. Sew running stitches, about ¼" inside the blue and white seams. Continue quilting from the center toward the edges, until the patchwork section is all quilted. Then quilt the borders.

10. BINDING: Trim back and batting edges flush with the quilt top. Fold the binding (*see Step 2*) in half, wrong sides together and press. Pin it (still folded) to the quilt, right sides together and raw edges even. Stitch ⅝" from raw edges. Turn the folded edge to wrong side and slip stitch.

CAROLINA LILY QUILT

(about 88" square)

TECHNIQUE: Quilting (patchwork and appliqué).

CHALLENGING: For those with more experience in quilting.

MATERIALS: 14 yds. 45"-wide muslin (includes quilt back); 1½ yds. red and 2 yds. green 45"-wide calico; 90" square of batting; white quilting thread and needle; quilting frame or large quilting hoop.

DIRECTIONS:
(¼" seams allowed):

1. **PATTERNS:** On crisp cardboard (such as a manila folder), draw or trace patterns A through M (see FIGS. 2, 2A and 2B on pages 7 and 8).

2. **CUTTING:** *Note: To cut a "pair", trace once with pattern right side up and once right side down. From red*, cut 144 pairs of Patch A and about 10 yds. of 1"-wide strips (pieced as needed) for binding. *From green*, cut 48 pairs of Patch A, 16 pairs each of curved stems and leaves, sixteen 1" x 13" straight stems and 108 Patches J. *From muslin*, cut one 45" x 94" and two 26" x 94" quilt back pieces, four 7½" x 74" border strips and 4 Patches M, 9 quiltblocks 12½" square, 12 half-blocks (Patch K), 4 quarter-blocks (Patch L), 48 Patches B,

96 Patches C, 32 each of Patches D, E and F, 16 each of Patches G, H and I and 108 Patches J.

3. **PATCHWORK QUILT-BLOCK:** *Note: Be sure to take ¼" seams. Begin and end these seams ¼" from the raw edges; this makes it easy to seam the adjoining pieces to inside corners.* Seam a pair of red Patches A at one long edge; make 6 sets. Seam one red Patch A to a green Patch A at a long edge; make 3 sets. Seam 2 red sets and 2 mixed sets together at pointed ends to make one flower (see FIG. 3); make 3 flowers. Seam one B, two C's and one D to each flower. Seam two F's and E's between the 3 flowers.

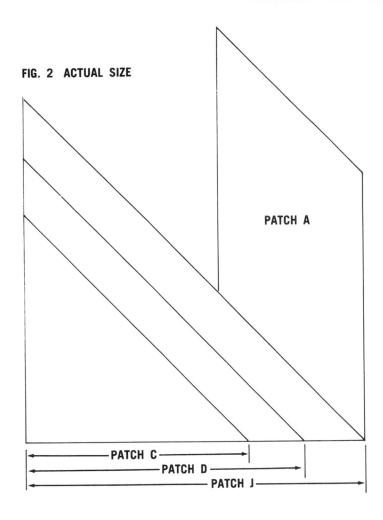

FIG. 2 ACTUAL SIZE

PATCH A

PATCH C

PATCH D

PATCH J

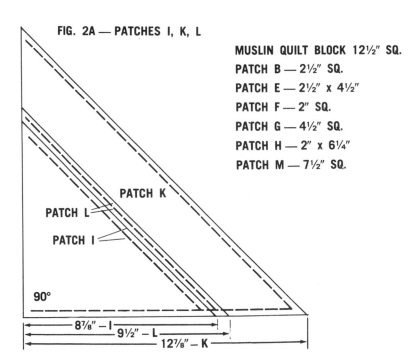

FIG. 2A — PATCHES I, K, L

PATCH K

PATCH L

PATCH I

90°

8⅞" — I

9½" — L

12⅞" — K

MUSLIN QUILT BLOCK 12½" SQ.

PATCH B — 2½" SQ.

PATCH E — 2½" x 4½"

PATCH F — 2" SQ.

PATCH G — 4½" SQ.

PATCH H — 2" x 6¼"

PATCH M — 7½" SQ.

Seam a G within the flowers; draw a diagonal line across it flush with the raw edge of the green patches; cut on the drawn line. Seam Patch H (see Fig. 3). Press the colored seam away from the muslin. Seam the whole assembly to Patch I. Make 16 quiltblocks.

4. APPLIQUÉ: On the three stem pieces, turn under ¼" at the long edges and press. Turn under the top ends and pin them to the block (see dotted lines in Fig. 3), letting the bottom ends run either under the center stem or out to the raw corner of I. Turn under the leaf edges and pin them to the block. Slip stitch all turned edges.

5. BLOCK ASSEMBLY: Seam patchwork blocks alternating with muslin blocks, to make the diagonal rows in Fig. 4; add partial blocks K or L to complete the rows. Seam the rows together, seams matching; add the two remaining Patch L's to complete the rectangle.

6. BORDERS: Seam each green Patch J to a muslin Patch J at the long edge to make a square. Seam 26 squares side by side to make a row; make 4 rows. Seam one row to each edge of the block assembly with raw ends flush; seam in an extra square to fill each corner (see Fig. 4). Seam the muslin borders (and M square) to quilt in the same way to complete the 88"-square quilt top.

7. MARKING: With a hard sharp pencil and a straight-edge, draw a quilting pattern of your

Did You Know
....
The Carolina Lily has been a favorite patchwork quilt pattern since the 1800s!

FIG. 2B

choice. On the quilt photographed, the muslin blocks were quilted in 1″ squares. The patchwork blocks were quilted in lines parallel to center stem (1″ each side of it, then ½″ away, then repeated); the borders were quilted the same, parallel to the long edge of the green triangles.

8. QUILT BACK: Seam a 26″ x 94″ muslin piece to each long edge of a 45″ x 94″ piece; press seams to one side. Spread it, wrong side up, on a clean floor and tape down the corners. On top, spread the batting, smooth it outward and trim it flush with the muslin. Centered on top, spread the quilt top. From the center outward, baste it with long stitches diagonally to each corner and straight to each edge. Baste more rows in between, about 6″ apart.

9. QUILTING: Place the quilt in a quilting frame or (starting at the center) in a quilting hoop. Sew small running stitches along the marked lines, through all layers. Trim the quilt back/muslin flush with the quilt top and baste around the edges.

10. BINDING: Bind the opposite edges with 1″-wide strips of red. Bind the remaining edges, turning under the raw ends.

TIP

A note on the Carolina Lily Quilt

. . . .

To make the Carolina Lily Quilt better fit a modern double bed, we have enlarged the quilt and made the muslin borders 4″ wider than those shown in the photograph on page 6.

FIG. 3

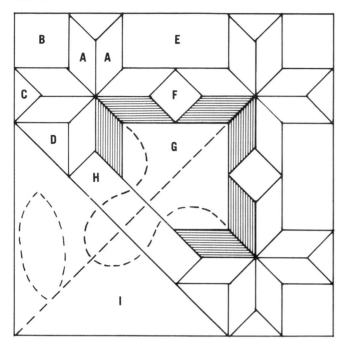

FIG. 4

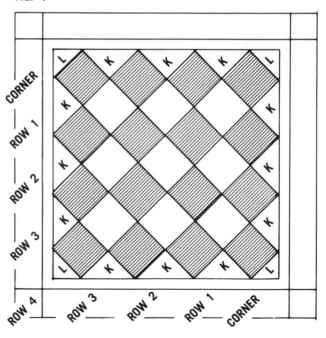

WILDFLOWER QUILT, PILLOW AND BASKET

(about 113" x 131")

TECHNIQUE: Appliqué, quilting.

CHALLENGING: For those with more experience in appliqué and quilting.

MATERIALS: (45"-wide broadcloth) 13½ yds. gold calico, 5¼ yds. solid gold, 7½ yds. each of red and ivory, 2 yds. green calico; thirty ¾" red buttons; 12 yds. of ⅜"-wide red ribbon; two 90" x 108" rolls of synthetic batting; as-

sorted scraps (broadcloth weight) for flowers; lightweight cardboard; T-square or triangle.

DIRECTIONS:
(½" seams allowed):

1. PATTERNS: Following the instructions on page 294, enlarge FIG. 6 on the cardboard. Also make cardboard patterns for FIGS. 5 and 7. Draw patterns for a 4" circle and a 3½" square. Cut out patterns. Draw basket guide *(see FIG. 5)* on folded paper, then use an awl to make the eleven

holes.

2. CUTTING: *Note: On the wrong side of the fabric, mark all pieces before cutting any. Measure carefully and draw the edges butted and on grain, with corners squared. Draw the thirty quilt blocks (two side by side) down one selvage and save the opposite selvage for the long borders. From ivory fabric, cut thirty 16" squares, two 4" x 103" top and bottom borders and two 4" x 115" side borders. From red fabric, cut seventy-one 4" x 16" bands, two 9" x 118" top*

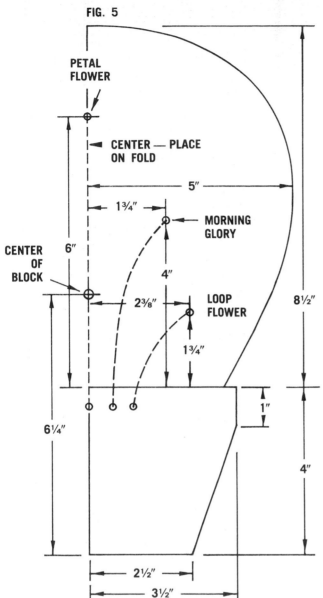

FIG. 5

PETAL FLOWER

CENTER — PLACE ON FOLD

5"

1¾"

MORNING GLORY

CENTER OF BLOCK

6"

4"

2⅜"

LOOP FLOWER

1¾"

8½"

1"

6¼"

4"

2½"

3½"

leaves and enough 4"-wide strips to make one hundred twenty ca-lyxes (Fɪɢ. 7 makes four). *From fabric scraps,* cut one hundred twenty 4" circles, sixty daisies and sixty 1" x 24" bias strips for loop flowers (for which you can substitute double-fold bias tape or ribbon).

3. Stems: Mark the center of an ivory square and place basket guide on top, centers matching and lower edges parallel. Lightly trace the outline and the holes, then remove the guide. Turn un-der and press ¼" along both long edges of a green stem strip. With the right side up, center and pin a "stem" between two dots *(see broken lines)* on the ivory block. Cut the strip to fit, make four more stems, then edgestitch.

4. Handles: Use one calico and two gold strips (each 2" x 36") for one handle. Fold each strip lengthwise, wrong side in, and press. Open, and fold in the long raw edges to meet at the center. Re-fold at center and press (to make ½" strip). Braid the strips together, and sew across the raw ends. Stretch the braid and steam it lightly. Center and pin the braid over the guide-line on a quilt block (with each end extending about an inch be-

and bottom bindings and two 9" x 127" side bindings. *From gold calico,* cut three 38" x 130" quilt back pieces, two 4" x 109" top and bottom borders, two 4" x 121" side borders, forty-two 4" squares and sixty 2" x 36" strips (for handles and baskets). *From solid gold fabric,* cut sixty 2" x 36" handle strips and thirty 2" x 42" basket strips. *From green print,* cut thirty 1" x 25" bias strips for stems, sixty 3½" squares for

FIG. 6 DAISY   1 SQ. = 1"

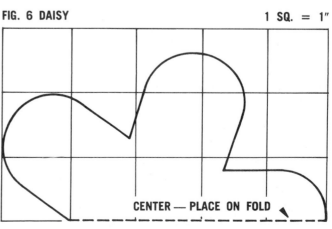

CENTER — PLACE ON FOLD

FIG. 7 CALYX STENCIL

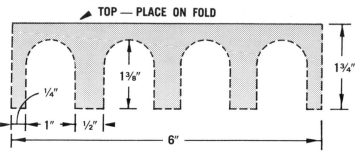

TOP — PLACE ON FOLD

1⅜"
1¾"
¼"
1"
½"
6"

low top edge of basket) and slip stitch in place.

5. BASKET: On one 2" x 42" gold and one 2" x 36" calico strip, turn under and press ½" along each long edge. Cut the calico strip into four 9" lengths and the gold strip into seven 6" lengths. With the long edges touching, place the calico strips (horizontally) below each other on a piece of cardboard and pin the ends. Weave the six gold strips through them and pin. Center the basket guide (*see* FIG. 5) over the 6" x 9" weaving, matching the top and bottom edges to calico edges. Lightly trace around the basket, remove the guide and pin strips together inside the traced lines. Turn the ends under on drawn lines and press. Pin the basket to the quilt block (over handle ends). Edgestitch through all thicknesses.

6. DAISY: With right sides together and edges even, stitch daisy front to back ¼" from edges. Trim the seam to ⅛" and clip at inner curves. At the center of the flower, separate the fabric layers between your fingers, make a 1" slash in top layer, then turn the flower right side out through the slash. Press. Using a gathering stitch, sew a circle (about 1" dia.) around the center of the flower. Pull up the gathers tightly and tack the flower center over the top edge of the middle stem and

sew a button on top.

7. CALYX: Fold the 4"-wide fabric strip in half (right sides together) matching the long edges and press. Place the stencil (*see* FIG. 7) on the fabric, matching the top edge to the fabric fold. Trace along all the broken lines. Repeat, moving the stencil along the strip. Stitch on the traced lines in one continuous line. Cut away the long raw edges ⅛" below the stitching. Cut ⅛" outside the curved edges and separate the calyxes. Turn them right side out and press. Turn in raw edges ¼".

8. MORNING GLORY: With right sides together and edges even, seam (¼") two 4" fabric circles together. Trim, slash and turn (*see* Step 6, *Daisy*). Fold circle in half, box-pleat side edges to meet in the center and tack ½" from bottom point. Insert into calyx and slip stitch to

straight edges of calyx. Tack calyx in place over top end of a medium stem. Repeat, for second flower.

9. LOOP FLOWERS: With right sides together, fold a 1" x 24" bias strip in half, matching long edges, and stitch. Turn right side out using a small safety pin. Press flat. *Note: Or, use double fold bias tape or ribbon.* Arrange the strip into a five loop flower, tacking together at the bottom edges, insert into a calyx and slip stitch together across the top of the calyx. Slip stitch the calyx over the top end of a short stem. Repeat, for the second flower.

10. LEAVES: With right sides together and edges even, fold a 3½" square of green calico in half diagonally. Stitch along the raw edges. (*See* Step 6 *to slash, turn and press.*) Fold under the points ½", matching the fold lines, and press. Make three ½" accordion pleats across the folded edge and tack the folds together at back corner. Tack the leaf to the outer edge of the short stem just above the top edge of the basket. Repeat, for the second leaf. Tack a 14" ribbon bow to the center of the top edge of the basket.

11. REPEAT Steps 3-10 to make thirty quilt blocks.

TIP *For easier appliquéing:*
. . . .

1. Trace your appliqué motif onto fabric, allowing ¼" seam to turn under.

2. With sharp scissors, make small snips all around the edges of curved outlines to allow for neater, easier turning under.

3. Fold raw edges ¼" to the back and steam iron them. Baste all around the edges following the shape of your appliqué motif.

FIG. 8 QUILT ASSEMBLY

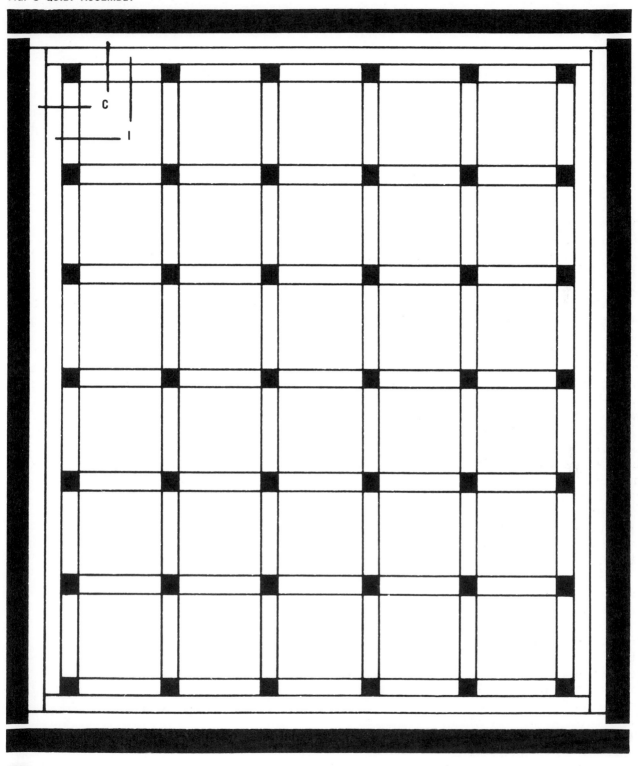

■ = RED   C = CALICO   I = IVORY

12. BLOCK ASSEMBLY: *see* FIG. 8. *Note: The cut sizes include a half-inch seam allowance. Draw the seamline on the wrong side if you wish, or use the seam guide on your sewing machine.*

a. Narrow Rows: Beginning and ending with a square, seam alternating 4″ calico squares and 4″ x 16″ red bands to make a horizontal row of six squares and five bands. Repeat, to have seven rows (*see Quilt Diagram*).

b. Wide Rows: Beginning and ending with a red band, seam alternating bands and blocks to make a horizontal row of six vertical bands and five blocks. Repeat to have six rows.

c. With right sides together and seams matching, stitch alternating narrow and wide horizontal rows together, starting and stopping with a narrow row.

13. BORDERS: *Note: The borders have been cut a little longer than you should need.* With right sides together, stitch ivory side border strips to the block assembly and trim ends flush with top edge of quilt. Stitch the top and bottom border strips to the block assembly and trim flush. Stitch the calico side borders, then the top and bottom borders, the same way.

14. QUILT BACK: Join the three calico back pieces together at the long edges to make a 109″ x 130″ rectangle.

15. ASSEMBLING QUILT: Tape the quilt back wrong side up to a flat surface. Place one batt over it, flush with the top edge, smoothing it from the center out. (The quilt back will extend about 1″ at each side edge and about a yard at the bottom.) Piece the batting layer with part of the second batt, butting the edges and catch-stitching across

them without sewing through the quilt back. Trim the batt flush with the lower edge and save the remainder for binding. Center the quilt top right side up over the batting. Beginning at the center, pin the layers together to keep them from shifting. Then hand-baste the layers together vertically, horizontally, and diagonally in lines 5″-6″ apart. Baste around the edges and trim the quilt back and batting flush with quilt top.

16. QUILTING: Quilt on all vertical and horizontal seamlines, by hand or machine. If hand quilting, a frame is helpful but not essential. If machine quilting, work from the center outward, keeping the bulk of the quilt rolled or folded and opening up only the portion you are working on.

17. BINDING: Baste a 9″-wide strip of batting (pieced as needed) to the wrong side of each binding strip. Stitch one edge of the binding to one side edge of quilt. Fold the other edge to the quilt back, turn under ½″ and slip stitch to the stitchline. Bind the opposite edge the same (*see Step 13*). Bind the top and bottom edges the same way, turning in raw ends.

18. TIE ribbons.

WILDFLOWER BASKET

TECHNIQUE: Sewing.

EASY: Achievable by anyone.

MATERIALS: *For basket:* (45″-wide fabric) 1½ yds. of gold calico and 2 yds. of solid gold; ½ yd. 40″-wide fleece; 3 yds. of 1″ cotton filler cord (from upholstery shops); ⅝″-wide fuser; styrofoam block; 10″ square of stiff cardboard; ¾ yd. of 2″-wide grosgrain ribbon. *For flowers:* green velour pipe cleaners for stems; scraps of fabric for flowers and leaves; white glue.

DIRECTIONS:

1. *See Step 1 for Quilt, omitting basket guide;* also, cut one 9¾″ cardboard circle.

2. CUTTING FOR FLOWERS: From scraps cut flowers and leaves and 1¼″ dia. back circles for the daisies.

3. CUTTING FOR BASKET: *From the solid gold fabric,* cut two 11″ circles, two 3″ x 36″ bias handle strips, twenty-eight 3″ x 6″ basket strips, one 3″ x 36″ bias strip for binding; *from gold calico,* cut one 3″ x 36″ handle strip, three 3″ x 36″ basket strips; *from fleece,* cut twenty-eight 1¼″ x 6″ strips and three 1¼″ x 36″ strips.

4. BASKET: Center and place the fleece strips over the wrong side of the 6″ gold strips. Fold the edges of the fabric over the fleece (to make a 1¼″ wide strip); fuse them together. Repeat, to have twenty-eight strips. Make three 36″ calico strips the same way. With right sides together and edges matching, pin the gold strips (evenly spaced) around one gold circle. Baste. With right sides together place the second circle on top. Stitch a ½″ seam, leaving a 10″ opening. Turn right side out and insert the cardboard circle. Slip stitch the opening.

5. WOVEN SIDES: With seams facing inside, weave one calico strip above the circle and sew the ends together on the inside. Weave two more strips and baste them through the gold strips just above the top calico edge. Trim the ends 1″ above the basting and bind with the gold binding strip.

6. HANDLE: Cut the cotton cording into three equal pieces. Press under ½″ on one long edge of each handle strip. With right side out cover one cord with calico, slip stitching the folded edge over the raw edge. Cover two more with gold. Braid them together with calico in the center. Tack the ends (opposite each other) to the bottom of the basket and up against (inside) the sides.

7. FLOWERS AND LEAVES: Make flowers and leaves (*see Quilt, Steps 6-10*). Insert pipe cleaner stems into the fold of the leaves or seams of calyxes. For the daisy, insert the stem through the center to the right side of the flower and turn the end over about ¼″. Stitch a button (over this end) to the petals. Make a small slash in the center of a back circle, pull it over the stem, then glue the circle to the back of the petals. Trim the styrofoam (about 8″ round), place it in the bottom of the basket and insert the flowers and leaves. Fill with Baby's Breath. Make a bow from red ribbon and tack it to the front of the basket.

WILDFLOWER PILLOW

. . . .

(*16″ square*)

TECHNIQUE: Appliqué, quilting.

AVERAGE: For those with some experience in appliqué and quilting.

MATERIALS: (45″-wide broadcloth) ½ yd. of ivory, 1 yd. of red, 1 yd. gold calico, ½ yd. of solid gold; ½ yd. of ⅜″-wide red ribbon; one ¾″ button; synthetic stuffing; assorted broadcloth scraps for flowers; lightweight cardboard; awl or nail.

. . . .

DIRECTIONS:

1. PATTERNS: (*See Step 1, Matching Quilt.*)

2. CUTTING: *From ivory and red fabric, cut one 16″ square each, for pillow front and back; from red, cut 5″-wide bias ruffle strips to measure 120″ when pieced; from gold calico, cut 7″-wide bias ruffle strips to measure 120″ when pieced and two 2″ x 36″ strips (one for handle and one for basket); from solid gold fabric, cut two 2″ x 36″ handle strips and one 2″ x 42″ basket strip; from green print, cut one 1″ x 25″ bias stem strip, two 3½″ squares for leaves and four calyxes; from scraps, cut two daisies, two sets of 4″ circles and two 1″ x 24″ bias strips.*

3. COMPLETE the block (*see Steps 3-10, Quilt*).

4. RUFFLES: Seam the red bias pieces together at the short ends (on grain) to make a 120″ strip. Seam the ends to make a ring. With the wrong side in and the raw edges matching, press the ring in half lengthwise. Sew gathering stitches ½″ and ¼″ from the raw edges. Fold and mark the ring into four equal parts. With right sides together and raw edges even, pin the marks to the corners of the pillow front, pull up the gathers to fit and machine baste (½″ seams).

5. REPEAT Step 4 for the gold calico ruffle, stitching it over the red one. With right sides together and edges matching, pin the red back over ruffles and stitch around three sides and four corners. Turn right side out, stuff and slip stitch the opening closed.

FLOWER MEDALLION QUILT

(about 99" x 107")

TECHNIQUE: Patchwork and appliqué quilting.

CHALLENGING: For those with more experience in quilting.

MATERIALS: (45"-wide cotton fabric) 9 yds. (for quilt back), 5½ yds. white, 4½ yds. green and 3 yds. each of pink and red; batting, pieced as needed *(See Step 10)* to make 100" x 108"; thread to match appliqués; crisp cardboard for patterns.

. . . .

DIRECTIONS:

Note: The quilt top is assembled from blocks, right triangles and bands (see Fig. 12*). Patchwork is machine seamed (½"); appliqués and quilting are hand sewn. Quilt edges are bound.*

   1. **Patterns:** Cut a large and a small triangle from cardboard *(see* Fig. 9*).* Enlarge *(see page 294)* patterns *(see* Fig. 10*)* for appliqués on cardboard and cut them out. Cut patterns for the three blocks (11" square, 9" square and 9" x 11"), making sure the corners are squared.

   2. **Cutting:** *From white fabric,* cut the following blocks — thirty-two 11" squares, twenty-eight 9" squares and twelve 9" x 11" rectangles. *From green fabric,* cut the following bands — two 3" x 21" and two 3" x 25" for central border, then two 4" x 65" and two 4" x 71" for outer border. Also cut 4"-wide bindings in the following lengths — two each 104" and 12" long and one each 100" and 88" long. *From pink fabric,* cut a 4" x 100" band, 20 large

FIG. 9

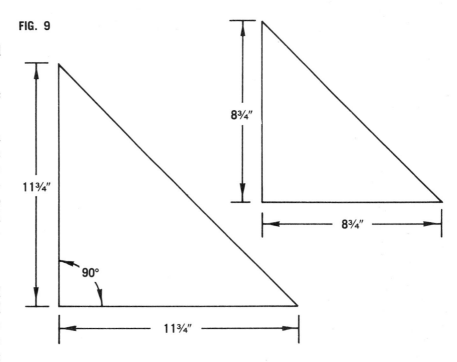

FIG. 10 APPLIQUÉS   1 SQ. = 1"

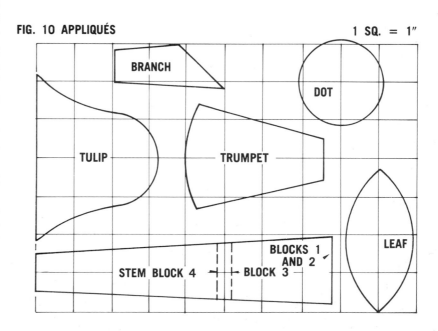

and 4 small triangles (cutting triangles with long edge on the straight grain). *From red fabric,* cut a 6″ x 100″ band and four 3″-wide bands (two 45″ and two 49″ long) for the middle border. Also cut 20 large and 10 small triangles (with the long edges on the grain). *From green fabric,* cut the following appliqués: 240 leaves, 44 long and 28 short stems, 88 branches. *From pink fabric,* cut 72 tulips. *From red fabric,* cut 64 trumpets and 28 dots.

3. APPLIQUÉ (¼″ seams allowed): Pin appliqués (avoiding edges) to the white blocks in the positions shown (*see* FIG. 11). Turn under ¼″ at appliqué edges and sew (slip stitch or running stitch) with matching thread. You need not turn under underlapping edges or lower stem edges which run into the seams. Sew stems and branches first. Finish 12 Block No. 2, 24 Block No. 3, 4 Block No. 4, 30 Block No. 1 (with diagonal stem) and 2 Block No. 1 with straight stem for lower corners (*see* FIG. 12), shortening stem as needed.

> ## Quiltmakers please note:
> Precision is a must when cutting the makings of a quilt block. Your efforts deserve nothing less than the finest and sharpest of forged steel blade fabric scissors. And, never cut anything but fabric with these special shears — using them on paper is sure to dull them.

4. BLOCK ASSEMBLY (½″ seams allowed for all patchwork): Seam four Blocks No. 1 together (*see* FIG. 12). Seam 21″ green borders to top and bottom, then 25″ borders to sides to make a 25″ square medallion.

5. SEAM three Blocks No. 2 together, then seam the strip to the bottom of the medallion, stems toward center (*see* FIG. 12). Repeat at the top. Seam three Blocks No. 2 between two Blocks No. 1 and seam the strip to the left edge of the medallion, stems toward center (*see* FIG. 12). Repeat at the right edge. Seam the 45″ red borders to the top and bottom, the 49″ borders to the sides to make a 49″ square.

6. SEAM six Blocks No. 3 together, then seam the strip (stems outward) to the bottom edge of the last squares (*see* FIG. 12). Repeat at the top edge. Seam six Blocks No. 3 between two Blocks No. 4 (stems outward) and seam the strip to the left edge. Repeat at the right edge. Seam the 65″ green borders to the top and bottom, then the 71″ borders to the sides to make a 71″ square.

7. BORDERS: To the upper right edge of a Block No. 1, seam a short edge of a large pink triangle, matching centers (*see* FIG. 13); seam a red triangle at the lower left the same way. Make 15 more strips the same. Seam five

FIG. 11 BLOCK 2 HALF PATTERN

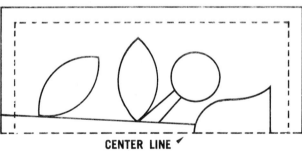

CENTER LINE

FIG. 11 BLOCK 4 HALF PATTERN

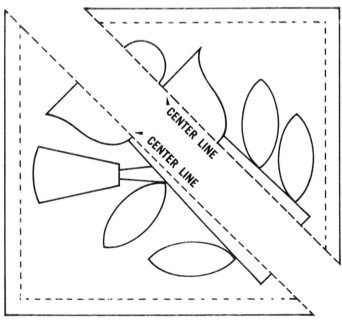

CENTER LINE

CENTER LINE

FIG. 11 BLOCK 1 HALF PATTERN

FIG. 11 BLOCK 3 HALF PATTERN

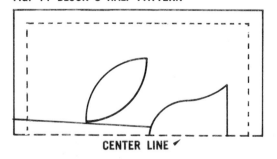

CENTER LINE

strips together for each side edge, then three for the top and three for the bottom. Add patches to each end of the strips to complete the borders (*see* Fig. 12); seam them to the patchwork at the top and bottom, then at the sides.

8. Top Edge: Seam the two 100″ bands (pink then red) to the top edges, trimming the ends flush with the side edges, if necessary.

9. Quilt Back: Cut across the quilt back fabric from selvage to selvage, to make three 3 yd. lengths. Trim off the selvages. Seam (½″) pieces together at the 3 yd. edges (seams will be parallel to top edge of quilt). Press.

10. Basting: Spread out the quilt back wrong side up on the floor and tape down the corners, to prevent slipping. Centered on top, spread out a 100″ x 108″ batting. (If piecing is needed, butt the batting edges and sew long cross stitches from one edge to the other to keep them flush). Centered over this, spread the quilt top right side up. With long stitches, baste the layers together from the center outward to each corner and each side. Add more basting rows, about 6″ apart so the three layers are well bonded before you untape the corners. Trim off the excess quilt back, leaving 3 or 4 inches extending at each edge.

11. Quilting: To quilt, sew a small running stitch through all layers, with a single thread in the needle. Quilt about ¼″ from each seam and appliqué. Enlarge the quilting pattern (*see* Fig. 14) on folded brown paper; cut it out and unfold it. Trace around it with a hard pencil on the triangles and quilt over the traced lines.

12. Finishing: Baste along the quilt top edges through all

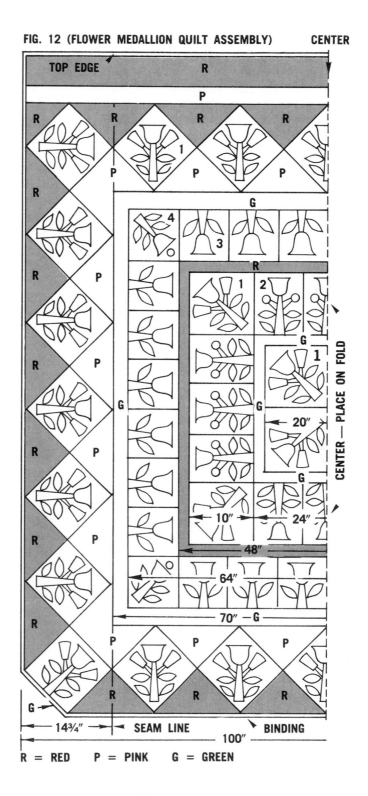

FIG. 12 (FLOWER MEDALLION QUILT ASSEMBLY)

R = RED   P = PINK   G = GREEN

FIG. 13 (FLOWER MEDALLION QUILT)

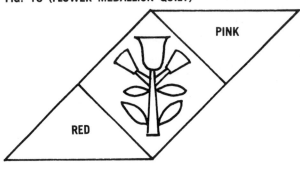

**FIG. 14 QUILTING PATTERN
(FLOWER MEDALLION QUILT)**

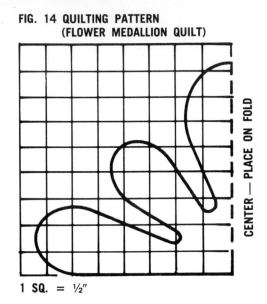

1 SQ. = ½″

layers. Trim off the batting ¼″ outside the quilt top.

13. BINDING: Fold the green binding strips in half lengthwise and press (to be used double). Pin the 100″ binding to the top edge of the quilt, right sides together and raw edges even with the batting. Stitch a ½″ seam.

Turn the folded edge to the back of the quilt and slip stitch the fold to the seamline (making a ¾″ binding). With the 88″ strip, bind the bottom edge; stop stitching ¾″ from the slanted edge; miter the corners and sew the binding by hand for about an inch up the slanted edge; then

cut off the excess binding. Bind the side edges with 104″ strips, turning under one raw end flush with the top edge and mitering at the lower edge same as the bottom. Bind the two lower corners with 12″ strips; stop stitching at the seamline, turn under each raw end in a miter and handsew.

SUNSHINE AND SHADOW QUILT

(about 81" x 102")

TECHNIQUE: Patchwork quilting.

AVERAGE: For those with some experience in quilting.

Note: In this quilt we have used thirteen fabrics. You may use more or less, as you wish, but choose the fabrics and arrange them in terms of their value (light, medium or dark) so that you will have a "sunshine and shadow" effect. To identify the

TIP | Quilting: More than just pretty

Beyond the decoration it provides, quilting has two functions — to fasten the backing, batting and top layers together and to keep the batting from developing holes or lumps after long use. Hand-quilting (that is, sewing a running stitch about ⅛" from the patchwork seams) is the most secure method. If you are using synthetic batting, the quilting rows can be as far as 3 or 4 inches apart.

lettered fabrics below, compare Fig. 1 *with the photo on page 21.*

MATERIALS: (45″-wide calico) *light shades* ¾ yd. A, 1⅛ yd. each of E and F and ½ yd. G, *medium shades* ¼ yd. B, ¾ yd. D and ½ yd. each of H and Y, *dark shades* ¾ yd. C, 2¾ yds. I, 1 yd. J, ½ yd. X and ¼ yd. Z; synthetic batting; 6 yds. 44″-wide fabric for quilt back and binding; crochet thread.

. . . .

DIRECTIONS:
(¼″ seams allowed):

1. Cutting: *From Fabric I,* cut four 4″-wide borders, two 95″ and two 74″ long. Then, on the wrong side of the fabrics, mark off the following 4″-square patches: 59 (A), 16 (B), 44 (C), 52 (D), 82 (E), 86 (F), 24 (G), 28 (H), 32 (I), 72 (J), 40 (X), 28 (Y) and 8 (Z).

2. Patchwork: Seam 21 patches (*see* Fig. 15) to make horizontal Row 1. (Notice that the last ten patches are the same as the first ten, but in the reverse order.) Make Rows 1-13 twice, Row 14 once. *Be sure to make seams exactly ¼″ from the raw edges.* Then seam the 27 rows together vertically Rows 1 at top and bottom and counting toward

FIG. 15 "SUNSHINE & SHADOW" QUILT COLOR CHART

	F											I											F
ROW 1																							
ROW 2																							
ROW 3																							
ROW 4																							
ROW 5																							
ROW 6																							
ROW 7																							
ROW 8																							
ROW 9																							
ROW 10																							
ROW 11												D											
ROW 12											D	C	D										
ROW 13										D	C	B	C	D									
ROW 14	I	D	J	I	H	G	F	E	D	C	B	A	B	C	D								I
ROW 13		A	D	J	I	H	G	F	E	D	C	B	C	D									
ROW 12		E	A	D	J	I	H	G	F	E	D	C	D										
ROW 11		F	E	A	D	J	I	H	G	F	E	D											
ROW 10		X	F	E	A	D	J	I	H	G	F	E											
ROW 9		J	X	F	E	A	D	J	I	H	G	F											
ROW 8		C	J	X	F	E	A	D	J	I	H	G											
ROW 7		Y	C	J	X	F	E	A	D	J	I	H											
ROW 6		E	Y	C	J	X	F	E	A	D	J	I											
ROW 5		F	E	Y	C	J	X	F	E	A	D	J											
ROW 4		A	F	E	Y	C	J	X	F	E	A	D											
ROW 3		B	A	F	E	Y	C	J	X	F	E	A											
ROW 2		Z	B	A	F	E	Y	C	J	X	F	E	F	X	J	C	Y	E	F	A	B	Z	
ROW 1		C	Z	B	A	F	E	Y	C	J	X	F	X	J	C	Y	E	F	A	B	Z	C	
	F											I											F

Row 14, the center row (*see* Fig. 15).

3. BORDERS: Seam a long (95″) border to each side edge of the patchwork. Seam a light (F) square to each end of a shorter (74″) border and seam the strip to the top edge of the patchwork. Repeat at the bottom edge.

4. QUILT BACK: Cut across the quilt back fabric to make two 45″ x 3 yd. pieces. Seam them side by side along a selvage.

5. FASTEN the quilt backs, batting and quilt top to a quilting frame if you have one. If you have not, spread the quilt back on the floor wrong side up and tape down the corners to prevent its moving. Centered over it spread the quilt batting (at least as large as the quilt top). Centered over the batting, spread the quilt top, right side up. Starting at the center, baste through all three layers, diagonally to each corner and straight to each edge. Add more rows of basting, about

---

> ### TIP / *Just what is tie-quilting?*
>
> The basic procedure is this: Piece together the quilt top (ours is machine-stitched), add batting, backing, then simply *tie* all the layers together at evenly spaced intervals with sturdy cotton thread or yarn. Tying is a faster process than hand-quilting and will last a reasonable length of time if synthetic, not cotton, batting is used. This is the method we used in our Sunshine and Shadow Quilt.

---

six inches apart.

6. BINDING: Trim only the batting flush with the quilt top. Trim the quilt back 1¼″ outside the quilt top; fold the raw edges over the top (for binding) and pin. Pick up the quilt, turn under the raw edges of the binding and slip stitch.

7. QUILTING: To tie, thread needle with crochet thread (Don't knot the end). Working from the quilt top, take a short stitch through all the layers, leaving a tail of thread (about 2″); then take another stitch on top. Cut the thread about 2″ from the stitch. Tie the tails of thread in a square knot, and trim the ends back to about ½″. The ties should be evenly spaced across the quilt and not too far (4-6″) apart. Tie within one quilt block, then tie at the same places on the other blocks. Remove the basting.

SWEET-
HEARTS
BEDSPREAD

(about 54" x 72"; each square about 17½" x 17½")

TECHNIQUE: Appliqué on crochet.

AVERAGE: For those with some experience in appliqué and crochet.

MATERIALS: Coats & Clark Red Heart Wintuk* Worsted Weight Yarn (3½ oz. pull skein, 212 yd.): 12 skeins #3 Off White (A), 7 skeins #732 Candy (B), 4 skeins #755 Pale Rose (C). *Fabric for appliqué* (approximate yardage depending on careful layout for cutting): ¾ yd. each Calico #3 and Solid Green #2, ½ yd. each Calico #1 and #4, ⅜ yd. each Calico #5B and Solid Pale Coral #5A. Size H aluminum crochet hook, OR ANY SIZE HOOK TO OBTAIN GAUGE BELOW; sewing thread to match fabrics; cardboard for templates.

GAUGE: 7 sc = 2"; 4 rows = 1". TO SAVE TIME, TAKE TIME TO CHECK GAUGE.

. . . .

DIRECTIONS:

CROCHET SQUARE: Make 12. With A, ch 42. **Row 1** (*right side*): Sc in 2nd ch from hook, sc in each ch across — 41 sc. Ch 1, turn. **Row 2:** Sc in each sc. Ch 1, turn. **Rows 3 through 50:** Rep row 2, *do not* fasten off at end of last row. Ch 1, turn. **Edging** (*right side*): Work 3 sc in first st

(corner made); 1 sc in next 39 sc; 3 sc in last sc (corner made); work 39 sc evenly spaced along side edge; 3 sc in corner st; work 39 sc in free lps of starting ch; 3 sc in corner st; work 39 sc evenly spaced along side edge. Join with a sl st to first sc. Fasten off. Join C in a center sc of 3 sc corner. **Rnd 2:** Ch 1, * 3 sc in center st (corner), sc in 41 sc; rep from * around. Join with a sl st. **Rnd 3:** Sl st in center sc of corner. Ch 1, turn. * 3 sc in center sc of corner, sc in next 43 sc; rep from * around. Join with a sl st. Fasten off and turn. **Rnd 4:** Join A in center sc of corner. Ch 1, * 3 sc in center sc of corner, sc in next 45 sc; rep from * around. Join

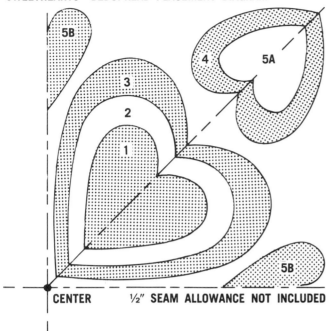

"SWEETHEARTS" BEDSPREAD PLACEMENT DIAGRAM

CENTER   ½" SEAM ALLOWANCE NOT INCLUDED

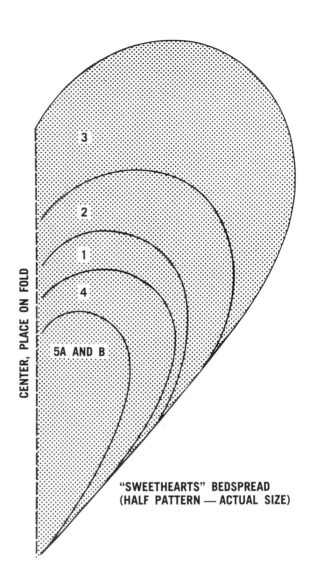

CENTER, PLACE ON FOLD

"SWEETHEARTS" BEDSPREAD (HALF PATTERN — ACTUAL SIZE)

with a sl st. **Rnd 5:** Sl st to center sc of corner, ch 1, turn. Work as for Rnd 4, with 47 sc between corners. Fasten off, turn. **Rnd 6:** Join B in center sc of corner, ch 1, work as for Rnd 4, with 49 sc between corners. **Rnd 7:** Sl st to corner sc, ch 1, turn. Work as for Rnd 3 with 51 sc between corners. **Rnd 8:** Sl st to corner st, ch 1, turn. Work as for Rnd 4, with 53 sc between corners. Fasten off. Steam each square lightly, making sure all corners form right angles. With right side facing, place a thread marker in the exact center of each square.

To Appliqué One Square:

1. On wrong side of corresponding fabric, draw 8 hearts each of Templates 1, 2, 3, 4, 5A and 5B, allowing ½" seam allowance on all sides. 2. Cut out hearts with seam allowance added (this includes front and linings of hearts for one square). 3. Pin two #3 hearts with right sides

> **TIP**
>
> ## *A note on appliqués*
> ....
> All the layered and single heart fabric appliqués on this crocheted bedspread have been constructed with backings (like tiny pillow covers). In addition to adding pretty, puffed dimension to the fabric motifs, this strengthened construction of the appliqué pieces allows for more secure attachment to the crocheted background, thus giving extra durability and easier washability to the coverlet. An heirlom to be enjoyed and *used* by a generation to come.

tog. Sew together around the entire outer edge along the drawn outline. Clip the curves and points and trim the seams as necessary. Make a small slit in the center of one side of the joined hearts; turn right side out. Steam the edges flat. **4.** When all four #3 hearts have been joined in this manner, pin them as shown on Placement Diagram with center marker on the square corresponding to the center dot on the diagram. **5.** Sew hearts in place around outer edges. **6.** Draw and cut eight #2 hearts and assemble in the same manner. Pin in place and sew onto #3 hearts. **7.** Repeat with #1 heart and continue until all hearts have been joined and appliquéd to the square. **8.** Steam lightly. **9.** Sew or sl st all 12 appliquéd squares tog — 4 squares long and 3 squares wide. **10.** Steam the seams lightly on the wrong side.

Design your own quilt!

And don't be afraid to experiment. Any line drawing can serve as an appliqué motif. If you can't draw, dream up a pattern the kindergarten paper-cutting way: Remember the lovely snowflakes that materialized from simple cuts when they were unfolded? Map some lines on a paper square which has been folded into quarters, leaving the two folded edges intact. Cut along your lines, unfold and — voila! — your very own intriguing pattern for an appliqué piece.

OUTER EDGING:
Rnd 1: With right side facing, join B in a corner, ch 1, * 3 sc in center st of corner, sc in each sc to next corner; rep from * around. Join with a sl st. *Do not turn.* **Rnd 2:** Sl st loosely in each sc around, making sure not to draw in and keep to work flat. Sl st to corner st. Ch 1, turn. **Rnd 3:** With wrong side facing, * 3 sc in corner sl st, sc in each st to next corner; rep from * around. Join with a sl st. Fasten off, turn. Join C in same st. **Rnd 4:** Ch 1, * 1 sc in next 3 sc, sl st in next sc, ch 4, sl st back in same sc for a picot; rep from * around. Join with a sl st. Fasten off. Steam the edging flat.

CANDLEWICK "DAISY" QUILT AND PILLOWS

QUILT

(64" twin, 80" double or 96" queen size, all 112" long)

TECHNIQUE: Candlewick embroidery and quilting.

AVERAGE: For those with some experience in embroidery and quilting.

MATERIALS: The following yards each of 36"-wide blue muslin-like fabric, muslin backing and synthetic batting: 7¼ yds.

TIP

A Stitch In Time

That's what we've done with this adaptation of "candlewicking", an Early American needlecraft. Instead of the traditional method of stitching candlewick on a large piece of muslin, you embroider with candlewick thread or floss on pretty pastel fabric, one square at a time. Big, speedy French Knots form the delicate patterns, as well as hold the top, backing and batting together!

FIG. 16 DAISY BLOCK - ¼ PATTERN

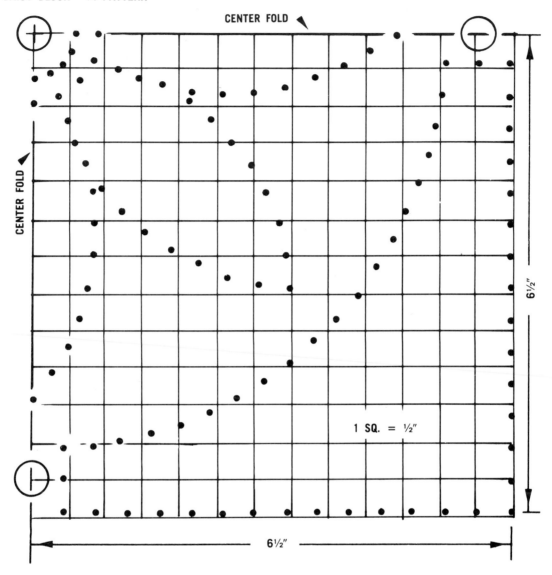

for twin, 9¼ yds. for double or 10¾ yds. for queen-size quilt; of 4-ply candlewick thread: 450 yds. for twin, 560 yds. for double or 675 yds. for queen (or of 6-strand embroidery cotton, twice as much); of fringe: 10½ yds. for twin, 11½ yds. for double or 12½ yds. for queen.

. . . .

DIRECTIONS:

(1″ seams allowed):

1. QUILTBLOCKS: For each block, cut one 18″ square of blue, one of muslin and one of batting. Make the quiltblocks, following Steps 2-5, "Daisy" Pillow *(page 29)*, except in Step 4, hand baste 1″ from each edge *through the top and batting only.* You will need 28 quiltblocks for twin, 35 for double or 42 for queen-size quilt.

2. JOINING BLOCKS: Pin two quiltblocks right sides together with edges even. *Pin both backings away from the edges.* Stitch along the basting line, through the tops and battings only, beginning and ending one inch from the cut edges. In this manner assemble seven horizontal strips of four blocks for twin, five blocks for double or six blocks for queen-size quilt. With the seams open, lay one backing flat over the seam. Turn under 1″ of the other backing and slip stitch it to the seamline, stopping one inch from the cut edges.

3. JOINING ROWS: With seams matching, sew the rows together the same way *(see Step 2).*

FIG. 17 HEART PILLOW - ½ PATTERN

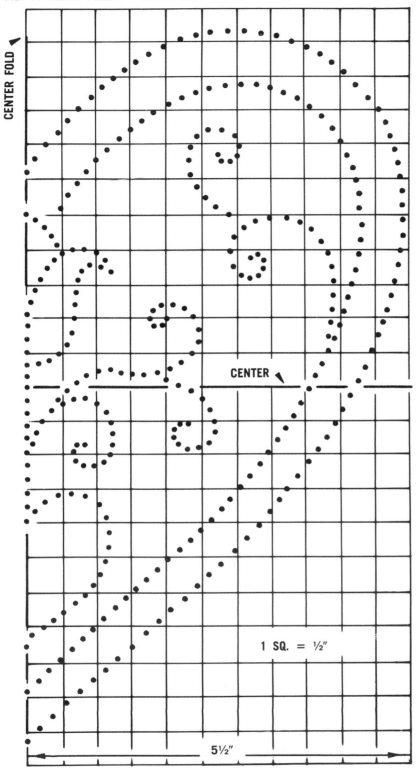

CENTER FOLD

CENTER

1 SQ. = ½"

5½"

4. FRINGE: With right sides together and fringes toward the center, stitch the fringe to the quilt edges, through the top and batting only. Turn the fringe outward. Turn under the backing and slip stitch it to the seam.

CANDLEWICK "DAISY" PILLOW

. . . .

(16" square)

TECHNIQUE: Candlewick embroidery and quilting.

AVERAGE: For those with some experience in embroidery and quilting.

MATERIALS: 1⅛ yd. 36" unbleached muslin; 18"-square of batting; 2 yds. each of piping and/or ruffled lace; synthetic stuffing; 16 yds. 4-ply candlewick thread or 32 yds. 6-strand embroidery floss; embroidery hoop.

. . . .

DIRECTIONS:

1. **CUTTING:** Cut the following 18" squares: three of muslin and one of batting.

2. **MARKING:** Fold one muslin square (pillow top) in half twice (9"-sq.) and press the folds to mark the centerlines. Fold a 14" square of tracing paper in half twice (7"-sq.) and on it enlarge (*see page 294*) the quarter-pattern (*see* FIG. 16) with foldlines matching. Trace three times (for full pattern) and pin the open paper to the pillow top, centerlines matching. Trace dots.

3. **SATIN STITCH:** Fill the five open circles with padded satin stitch (*see Stitch Guide, pages 298-299*), threading the needle with one 48" strand of candlewick thread (ends knotted to make two strands) or a length of 6-

strand embroidery floss (one end knotted).

4. Basting: Place the pillow top over the batting over a muslin square and machine baste along the seamlines (1″ from each edge).

5. French Knots: At each dot work a French Knot (*see Stitch Guide*) through all three layers. For the inside and outside circles, thread the needle as for the satin stitch. For daisy petals, use 3-plies of candlewick thread (with ends knotted to make 6 strands) or two lengths of 6-strand floss (knotted together at one end only).

6. Assembling: Stitch piping to the pillow front (right sides together, raw edges outward and seamlines matching), clipping at the corners. Stitch the ruffled lace on top the same way. Seam the pillow back on top, around three sides and four corners. Turn right side out, insert the stuffing, turn in the open edges and slip stitch.

CANDLEWICK "HEART" PILLOW

(about 12″)

TECHNIQUE: Candlewick embroidery.

AVERAGE: For those with some experience in embroidery.

MATERIALS: ½ yd. 44″-wide unbleached muslin or similar fabric; 14″ square of batting; 1¼ yd. each of piping and/or ruffled lace; stuffing; 17 yds. 4-ply candlewick thread or 34 yds. 6-strand embroidery floss; embroidery hoop.

DIRECTIONS:

1. Cutting: Cut the following 14″ squares: three of muslin and one of batting.

2. Marking: Follow Step 2 of "Daisy" Pillow, folding a 12″ square of transparent paper in half (to 6″ x 12″) and enlarging Fig. 17, page 294.

3. Embroidery: Follow Steps 4 and 5 of "Daisy" Pillow, working French Knots as in petals.

4. Assembling: Stitch the seamline ½″ outside the embroidered heart; cut ½″ outside the stitchline. Cut a pillow back the same size. Add trims and assemble (*see Step 6, "Daisy" Pillow*).

STRIPED QUILTED COVERLET, SHAM AND PILLOWS

QUILTED COVERLET AND SHAM

(coverlet, about 71" x 86";)
sham, about 25" x 28")

TECHNIQUE: Quilting.

AVERAGE: For those with some experience in quilting.

MATERIALS *(including sham):* (45"-wide fabric) about 9 yds. as- sorted prints for quilt top, 7 yds. blue print for quilt back and 4½ yds. solid blue for bands and binding; 7 yds. 40"-wide fleece interfacing.

. . . .

DIRECTIONS:
(½" seams allowed except for pressedwork, see Step 2):
1. CUTTING: *From assorted prints, cut 22" long patches in various widths (1½"-3").* **Note:** *Draw pieces (as follows) on the fleece before cutting. Piece the sham filler lengthwise to save fabric. From*

fleece interfacing cut, for the quilt, three pressedwork fillers each 22" x 82", two band fillers each 3" x 82", four 2½"-wide binding fillers (two 82" and two 73" long); then, for the sham, cut a 22" x 74" pressedwork filler and four 2½"-wide binding fillers (two 74" and two 27" long). From quilt back fabric cut, for the quilt, three pressedwork backs, each 22" x 82", and two band backs, each 3" x 82"; then, for the sham, cut a pressedwork back 22" x 74". From solid blue fabric cut, for the

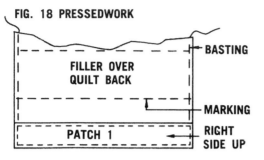

FIG. 18 PRESSEDWORK
BASTING
FILLER OVER QUILT BACK
MARKING
PATCH 1 — RIGHT SIDE UP

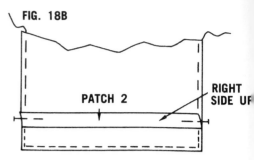

FIG. 18B
PATCH 2
RIGHT SIDE UP

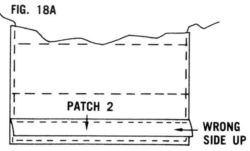

FIG. 18A
PATCH 2
WRONG SIDE UP

quilt, two bands each 3″ x 82″ and four 9″-wide bindings (two 82″ and two 73″ long); then, for the sham, cut four 9″-wide bindings (two 74″ and two 27″ long).

2. PRESSEDWORK (*1/4″ seams allowed*): Baste the fleece to wrong side of a 22″ x 82″ quilt back. Across the fleece draw guidelines about 6″ apart, parallel to the short edges. Pressedwork seams should be parallel to these lines; check as you sew. Pin a patch right side up to the left end of the fleece (three edges even) and stitch 1/4″ from all four edges (*see* FIG. 18). Pin the second patch on top, right sides together and edges matching at the ends and right-hand side (*see* FIG. 18A). Topstitch 1/4″ from the long raw edge; then press the patch outward, pinning across each end (*see* FIG. 18B). Apply the remaining patches like the second, mixing the colors and widths, until you reach the opposite end of the fleece. One of these panels makes the "sham," three make the quilt.

3. QUILT ASSEMBLY: Baste a fleece band (3″ x 82″) to the wrong side of each solid blue band. With right sides together and long edges matching, seam them between the three pressedwork panels. Trim off the seam allowance of the fleece near the stitching.

4. QUILT BACK: Turn the quilt wrong side up. With right sides together and long edges even, stitch one edge of a blue band back to the raw edges of the band front. Turn under the opposite edge and slip stitch along the

seamline covering the raw edges and the fleece. Repeat over the second band, to finish the quilt back.

5. QUILT BINDING: Fold the blue binding in half lengthwise, wrong sides together, and press. Baste a binding filler to one side of the fabric binding, with the three raw edges even. With right sides together and raw edges even, stitch an 82″ binding (interfaced edge) at each side edge of the quilt. Turn the folded edge to the wrong side of the quilt and slip stitch the fold along the

---

TIP **Mix 'n Match Stripes**
....

For the Stripe-by-Stripe Coverlet, machine quilt horizontal rows of print and solid fabrics; for the matching sham, use stripes vertically. To create the striking cotton and velveteen patchwork pillows on the Victorian settee (*see photo*), just run stripes in different directions — diagonally in chevrons, in ladder rows or 'round and 'round.

seamline, enclosing the raw edges and making a 2″-wide binding. Bind the top and bottom edges the same way, turning in 1″ at each end.

6. **Sham Binding:** Bind the same way as the quilt, long edges first.

BLUE STRIPED PILLOW

. . . .

TECHNIQUE: Quilting.

AVERAGE: For those with some experience in quilting.

MATERIALS: 12″ x 18″ each of fleece interfacing (for pillow front) and of fabric for pillow back; scraps of fabric and laces; 2 yds. bias binding; synthetic stuffing.

. . . .

DIRECTIONS:

Cover fleece with strips of assorted fabrics, using pressedwork method (*see Quilted Coverlet, Step 2*). Stitch lace, finished edge toward center, over each edge. Hand quilt. Topstitch pillow front to back, wrong sides together, leaving an opening for stuffing. Stuff. Bind raw edges.

PINK PILLOWS

. . . .

TECHNIQUE: Quilting.

AVERAGE: For those with some experience in quilting.

MATERIALS: See Blue Striped Pillow, above, plus ¼ yd. muslin.

DIRECTIONS:

1. **Draw** the seamlines on the 12″ x 18″ fleece pillow tops (*see* Figs. 19 and 19A).

2. **Trace** central diamond to fabric, cut it out ¼″ *outside traced*

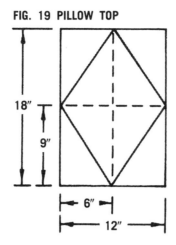

FIG. 19 PILLOW TOP

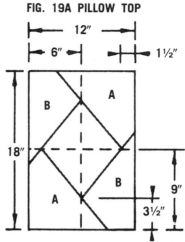

FIG. 19A PILLOW TOP

lines and sew the patch (right side up and centered) to the fleece. Sew a strip of lace along each edge of the patch (*see photo*).

3. **Large Diamond Top:** Cut two 7″ x 10″ pieces of muslin. Cut 2″ x 7″ strips of fabrics and stitch them across the muslin to make pressedwork (*see Quilted Coverlet, Step 2*). Cut each piece diagonally to make the four corner patches. Pin one to each edge of the center diamond (right sides together), stitch ¼″ from edges, then press them outward and stitch the edges to the fleece. Stitch the piping to the seamline, raw edges outward. Hand quilt.

4. **Small Diamond Top:** Trace an A-corner and a B-corner to paper; then add ¼″ seam allowance to each inside (slanted) edge. Cut two B-shapes from muslin and two A-shapes from a print. Cover B-muslins with pressedwork stripes. Seam the four corner patches to the center patch (*see Step 3*), stopping the stitching at the seamlines of the diamond. Press them outward (clipping to ends of seam). Turn under the print edges and slip stitch them over the pressedwork edges. Baste around the outside edges. Stitch

lace to the seamlines, right sides together. Hand quilt.

5. **Assembling:** With right sides together and edges even, stitch the pillow front to the pillow back around three sides and four corners. Turn right side out and stuff. Turn in the open edges and slip stitch.

STRIPED BOLSTERS
. . . .
(*about 6″ x 16″*)

TECHNIQUE: Patchwork.

AVERAGE: For those with some experience in patchwork.

MATERIALS: Scraps of print and velveteen fabrics; narrow cord or string; ½ yd. 45″-wide muslin; synthetic stuffing.
. . . .
DIRECTIONS:
(*¼″ seams allowed*):

1. **Patchwork:** *For Vertical Stripes*, seam 18″-long strips of fabric together (at the long edges) to make patchwork about 21″ x 18″. *For Horizontal Stripes*, seam 7½″-long strips together to make a piece 21″ x 18″.

2. **Pillow Cover:** Stitch the long ends of the patchwork piece together (right side facing and seams matching) to make a 21″ long tube. Turn right side out.

FIG. 20 PRESSEDWORK

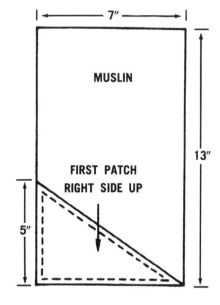

At both raw ends, turn under ¼″, then ½″, and stitch a hem casing, leaving a half inch opening.

3. INNER PILLOW: Cut 18″ x 21″ muslin; fold it in half lengthwise and stitch the 21″ edges together. Turn right side out. At each end, with longest machine stitch, sew a gathering row with strong thread. Pull up thread tightly at one end and tie a square knot; push raw edges inside. Fill muslin with stuffing; then pull up the open end the same way.

4. FINISHING: Draw a piece of string through one casing. Draw it up tight and tie a square knot. Place the inner pillow inside; then draw up the second end the same as the first. Tuck string ends inside.

RAIL FENCE PILLOW

. . . .

(12″ x 18″)

TECHNIQUE: Patchwork.

EASY: Achievable by anyone.

MATERIALS: ½ yd. 45″-wide velveteen for pillow back and piping; 2 yds. ¼″ cord for piping; scraps of fabric for pillow top; synthetic stuffing; ⅝ yd. muslin.

. . . .

DIRECTIONS:
(¼″ seams allowed):

1. PATCHWORK: Cut 2″ x 6½″ strips from four fabrics and seam them (¼″ from raw edges) side by side, to make a 5″ square block. Make five more blocks. Seam them into two rows of three blocks each, alternating the direction of the stripes *(see photo on page 34)*. Seam one row beneath the other to make the pillow top.

2. BACK AND PIPING: From the velveteen, cut a 12½″ x 18½″ pillow back and enough 1½″-wide bias strips to make (when pieced) about 2 yds. Over the cord fold the bias strip, right side out with raw edges even. Stitch along the cord, using zipper foot, to make piping. Trim seam allowance to ¼″.

3. ASSEMBLING: Stitch the piping to the pillow front, right sides together and raw edges even, clipping the seam allowance at each corner. Stitch the pillow front to the back around three sides and four corners. Turn right side out.

4. INNER PILLOW: Fold 19″ x 24″ muslin in half (to make 19″ x 12″) and stitch ½″ from the raw edges, leaving a 6″ opening. Turn right side out and stuff. Turn in the open edges and slip stitch closed.

5. FINISHING: Slide the inner pillow into the cover. Turn in

FIG. 20A

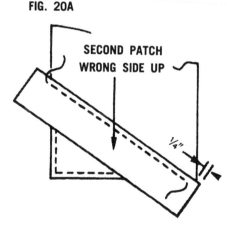

FIG. 20B

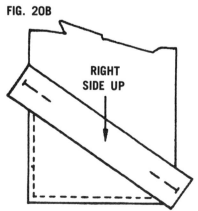

the open edges and slip stitch closed.

DIAGONALS PILLOW

(16" square)

TECHNIQUE: Patchwork.

AVERAGE: For those with some experience in patchwork.

MATERIALS: (45"-wide velveteen) ½ yd. teal blue and ¼ yd. rhubarb; scraps of cotton prints; 2 yds. ¼" cord for piping; ¼ yd. muslin; 16" square pillow form.

DIRECTIONS:

1. **PRESSEDWORK** (¼" *seams allowed*): Cut a muslin backing 7" x 13". Cut a blue velvet triangle (*see* FIG. 20) and sew it right side up over the lower left corner of the muslin, straight edges flush. Cut ten 2" x 10" strips of printed fabric and one 3" x 5" strip of blue velvet. With right sides together, long edges even and right hand end ¼" beyond the muslin (*see* FIGS. 20A *and* 20B) stitch the first strip to the muslin. Continue the same way with five print strips and end with the velvet strip. Turn the muslin side up and trim the ends of the patches flush with the muslin. Make another pressedwork panel the same way, but cut the blue triangle with the pattern turned wrong side up and sew the patch over the lower right corner (*see photo on page 34*).

2. **PILLOW TOP:** Seam (½") the two pressedwork panels together (*see photo*) to make the 13" square center section.

3. **BORDERS:** Cut four 3" x 18" strips of wine velvet. Fold each in half crosswise and mark the center. Also mark the center of each edge of the pressedwork. Pin the borders to the pressedwork right sides together, edges even and centers matching. Stitch ½" from the edges and stop ½" from the pressedwork corners (*see* FIGS. 21 and 21A). Press the borders outward. With the fabric right side up, fold one border at each corner diagonally and slip stitch it over the adjoining (underlapping) border (*see* FIG. 21B); trim the seam allowance to ½". Repeat at each corner.

4. **CUT** the blue velvet pillow back the same size as the pillow front and make 2 yds. of self binding, then finish the pillow cover (*see Rail Fence Pillow, Steps 2, 3 and 5*), inserting a 16" pillow form.

LADDER PILLOW

(14" square)

TECHNIQUE: Patchwork.

EASY: Achievable by anyone.

MATERIALS: ½ yd. 45"-wide velveteen for pillow back and piping; 2 yds. ¼" cord for piping; scraps of fabric for pillow top; 14" square pillow form.

DIRECTIONS:

1. **PATCHWORK:** From assorted fabric, cut 8" long strips in various widths (¾"-1½"). Seam the long sides together to make a "ladder" 8" x 15". To each long edge of the ladder, seam 15"-long strips to complete a 15" square.

2. **BACK AND PIPING:** From velveteen, cut a 15" square pillow back. Make piping (*see Rail Fence Pillow, Step 2*).

3. **ASSEMBLING:** Follow Rail Fence Pillow, Step 3. Insert the

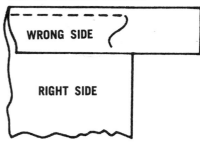

FIG. 21 MITERED BORDER

WRONG SIDE

RIGHT SIDE

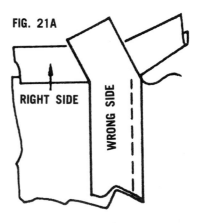

FIG. 21A

RIGHT SIDE

WRONG SIDE

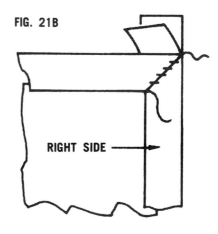

FIG. 21B

RIGHT SIDE

pillow form. Turn in the open edges and slip stitch closed.

HOW TO PRESERVE
YOUR HEIRLOOMS

Whether you own an antique lace hankie or a time-worn quilt, here's how to care for your heirloom or your own expertly crafted handwork so you can enjoy it for years to come.

HOW TO DISPLAY HEIRLOOMS

- QUILTS can be displayed for three months at a time. Then, "rest" them for four months by storing them as suggested below.
- TO PROTECT needlework, cover with glass or sheer net fabric. Leave space between the covering and the item so threads are not crushed.
- IF YOU FRAME needlework, lace or linen, always place an acid-free mat board between it and the frame backing. (Acid-free products and other special products for heirlooms are available at crafts stores or by mail — see *Where to Get Special Materials By Mail.*)
- NEVER DISPLAY an heirloom in direct sunlight or its reflected glare, near heat or under fluorescent lights.
- NEVER PLACE an object on top of an heirloom, *even one under glass.*

DO'S & DONT'S OF STORING HEIRLOOMS

DON'T keep anything in an attic or a basement — it will mildew.

DO store heirlooms in a cool area that is clean, dry, dark, and well-ventilated. Relative humidity should be about 50%.

DON'T wrap items in plastic, styrofoam, anything made from wood, such as cardboard or regular tissue paper.

DO wrap things in acid-free tissue paper; washed muslin; washed cotton or cotton/poly sheets. If your heirloom had a metal part attached to it, such as a bellpull, remove the metal, if possible, before wrapping.

DO place wrapped pieces in acid-free boxes. Or, put them in a bureau drawer lined with acid-free tissues or washed cotton or muslin sheets. For more protection, coat bureau drawers with polyurethane varnish before lining with the paper or sheets. If your home gets a lot of dust, line drawers with heavy polyethylene sheets, Mylar or fiberfill.

The best way to fold a quilt for storage: *This method prevents soil buildup, discoloration and wear along fold lines.* Fold the quilt into thirds, placing a roll of acid-free paper along and under each fold. Now fold the quilt again into thirds, toward the center. Place a roll of crumpled acid-free tissue along and under each of these two fold lines. (You can substi-

tute washed sheets or unbleached muslin for the acid-free paper).

QUILTS

- AIRING: The safest method for airing a quilt 50 years and older, is to place it in the shade on a nice, breezy day. Lay the quilt flat on the ground or on a table between two clean sheets. Leave it out for a half day. *Never hang a quilt on a clothesline*; this weakens the stitches. To air a quilt indoors: Drape the quilt over a chair for half a day.
- VACUUM-CLEANING: Materials needed: low-power, hand-held vacuum with a clean brush attachment, a piece of fiberglass screen with its edges taped. (A good size to work with is 24" square.) To do: Lay the quilt flat on a bed or other clean surface. Place the screen on the quilt; slowly and gently vacuum over the screen. Move the screen to another part of the quilt; repeat the vacuuming. When the top of the quilt is done, turn back half of it and vacuum the bed or surface under it; repeat the vacuuming on the other side. NEVER VACUUM A QUILT WITH BEADS ON IT. This method should not be used more than once a year.
- DRY-CLEANING: Wool, velvet

or silk quilts must be done by an expert cleaner who specializes in antique garments. *Note: There is no guarantee that dry-cleaning will work or that it will not damage item.*
• WET-CLEANING: Like dry-cleaning, washing a quilt should be done by an expert. It is too easy to damage it if you wash it at home.

HOW TO CLEAN AN HEIRLOOM

Many heirlooms over 50 years old look "dirty" because they develop brownish or rust spots. But these spots are not dirt. They're the result of a natural action in the fabric, and therefore usually cannot be removed. In fact, experts say these spots enhance an article as an antique. So when should you clean your heirloom? Only if it is so soiled it can't possibly be displayed, or if you've recently stained it yourself. *Note: Never attempt to take out stains with bleaches or detergents with "brighteners added."*

• WASHING LINEN OR COTTON WITH LACE EDGING, ALL-LINEN OR ALL-LACE ITEMS. *Remember:* Always avoid wringing or scrubbing items.
For a very mild cleaning for lace or linen: Soak the piece in distilled water at room temperature for a half hour. This removes foreign matter and loosens dirt. If you are washing an all-lace item, lower the item into water and take it out on a fiberglass screen with taped edges. **For extremely**

fragile or very lightly soiled items: Dissolve ¼ of a 3.2-ounce bar of Neutrogena or a small amount of a mild laundry detergent in 1 cup of distilled water at room temperature. Add 1 ounce of this solution to a gallon of distilled water. Soak item for a half hour, making sure to rinse it thoroughly afterward with distilled water.
• DRYING: Spread the item on an undyed terrycloth or a plain cloth towel and let it dry at room temperature.
• IRONING: Steam-press lace on a well-padded ironing board, placing a damp undyed cloth over the lace first. For linen, start with your iron set at cool. Continue raising the heat and testing the fabric on the wrong side until you reach the setting needed. Iron the item on the wrong side, placing a damp, undyed cloth between it and the iron. To iron embroidered linen, place it on a doubled, undyed bath towel to cushion the threads so they won't tear.
• NEEDLEWORK: Don't wash or clean needlework because the threads can be weakened and unravel or deteriorate.

SHOULD YOU REPAIR A WORN HEIRLOOM?

To conserve the value of an heirloom, experts recommend that you take it to a professional who specializes in restoring fabric antiques. He/she has the right kinds of thread, fabric, etc., and knows how to work with old, delicate fabrics.

WHERE TO GET PROFESSIONAL ADVICE

If you have questions about your heirloom, you can contact the following experts: Pan Handle Plains Museum, Textiles Department in the Conservation Center, P.O. Box 967 WP Station, Canyon, Texas 79016, 806-655-7191; Lynn Young, Director of Education, 155 Town & Country, Houston, Texas 77024, 713-465-7622; Indianapolis Museum of Art, Textiles Conservation, 1200 West 38 Street, Indianapolis, Indiana 46208, 317-923-1331; Blanche Greenstein, c/o Thomas K. Woodward, American Antiques and Quilts, 835 Madison Ave., NY., NY 10021; Texas Sesquicentennial Quilt Association, P.O. Box 5394, Austin, Texas 78763; 512-476-0548; Metropolitan Museum of Art, Conservator at The Costume Institute, 5th Ave. at 82 Street, NY, NY 10028.

WHERE TO GET SPECIAL MATERIALS BY MAIL

Acid-free paper, boxes: TALAS, Division of Technical Library Service, 213 West 35 St., New York, NY 10001 - 1996; 155 Town & Country Village, (see above); Pan Handle Plains Museum (see above); *Orvus and Ensure:* 155 Town & Country Village (see above); Conservation Materials Ltd., Box 2884, 340 Freeport Boulevard, Sparks, Nevada 89431; *Polyethylene:* Conservation Material Ltd., (see above); *Mylar:* Conservation Material Ltd. and TALAS (see above).

·2·

PILLOWS

For needlecrafters, pillows offer something very special: a small-scale stage to display a variety of your stitchery talents! What's more, pillows are the perfect size for trying out *new* skills. (Ideal if you're a novice with the needle!) Of course, we love pillows for other reasons too. As well-planned accents of color, texture and pattern, these moveable room brighteners can give any living area instant life. So try your hand at our selection — from frosty and lacy luxuries to whimsical "pet" pillows, we bet one of these cushioned treasures will find a "soft spot" in your home!

PASTEL SCRAPS PILLOWS

(Pillows are shown on the previous page.)

TECHNIQUE: Sewing, appliqué.

EASY: Achievable by anyone.

MATERIALS: 15" square each of batting, pillow top (base color) and pillow back; scraps of fabric for appliqués; synthetic stuffing.

DIRECTIONS:

1. CUTTING: On brown paper, draw a right triangle with two 8" legs; use this as a pattern to cut 4 triangles for the corner appliqués. Cut 15"-long strips of fabric — two wide (about 3½" to 4½") and two narrow (about 1½" to 2½") to form a plus sign on top. Short strips (instead of triangles) to fill in the corners (*see photo*) can be cut as well.

2. BASTE the batting to the wrong side of the pillow top, with edges even.

3. TRIANGLES: If you are using triangles, apply them first, as follows. Turn under ¼" at the long edge of each triangle and press; place it on the pillow top, right side up and raw edges even. Carefully turn it wrong side up and pin along the pressed mark; stitch on the pinline and turn the triangle right side up again. Baste the corners to the pillow top. Repeat at each corner.

4. LONG STRIPS: At each long edge of each strip, turn under ¼" and press. With right sides together, place a wide strip across the pillow top and stitch along the fold. Turn the strip right side up; turn under the long raw edge and edgestitch (if you are also using short strips, *see Step 5*). Stitch a narrow strip on top the same way. Repeat (across center on top) with the other 2 strips.

5. SHORT STRIPS: Arrange short strips so that one end is flush with an edge of the pillow-top and the opposite end will be covered with a long strip. Stitch in place, like the longer strips, seaming one edge, topstitching at the other. Proceed with Step 4.

6. STITCH the pillow-top to the pillow-back around 3 sides and 4 corners. Turn right side out and stuff. Turn in the open edges and slip stitch.

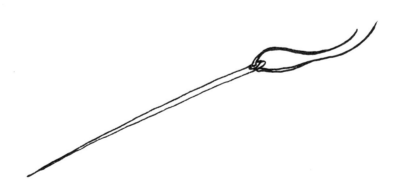

"ANTIQUE" PILLOWS

TECHNIQUE: Sewing.

EASY: Achievable by anyone.

MATERIALS: ½ yd. muslin or other pale fabric for pillow cover; gathered lace or eyelet for ruffle; synthetic stuffing or pillow form. *For appliqués:* old doilies; embroidered handkerchiefs; scraps of lace and ribbon; silk flowers; pearls; trims and appliqués.

DIRECTIONS:

1. BASIC PILLOW: From fabric, cut a pillow-top and pillow-back, each ½" larger all around than the finished size desired.

2. APPLIQUÉS: Arrange the appliqués on the top of the pillow-top, overlapping them freely. Pin, then slip stitch them in place.

3. RUFFLES: Pin ruffled lace or eyelet to the pillow top, right sides together, with finished edge toward the center and seam lines matching. Stitch, seaming the raw ends. Another wider ruffle can be sewn on top (to lie underneath when turned) if you wish.

4. ASSEMBLING: Pin the pillow-back to the pillow top (over ruffles). Seam (½") around 3 sides and 4 corners. Turn right side out and stuff. Turn in the open edges and slip stitch.

STRIKING AMISH PILLOWS

GENERAL DIRECTIONS FOR ALL AMISH PATCHWORK PILLOWS

MATERIALS: Use color-fast all-cotton fabrics. Quilting thread is usually black or white throughout these projects. A quilting needle and hoop make hand-quilting easy. A white fabric-marking pencil will show best on these colors, when you draw the quilting lines.

PATTERNS: The cutting patterns have been drawn full size, so just trace them, one pattern for each patch. They include the ¼" seam allowance.

CUTTING: Trace patterns or draw the rectangular* patches on the wrong side of the fabric with common edges, so as not to waste fabric. All edges (except the longest edge of triangles) should match the grain (lengthwise or crosswise thread) of the fabric. Two matching triangles can be drawn with a common hypotenuse to make a square. Cut out carefully on the drawn lines. *Make sure all the square corners are really 90°, by using a drafting triangle, T-square or transparent ruler (calibrated lengthwise and crosswise). Keep your pencil sharpened.

PIECING: Pin the pieces together at both ends of the seamline, then in between. When you pin the long edge of a triangle to a square, the cut edges will not match, but the seamlines (¼" from *each* edge) will. Be sure to stitch exactly ¼" deep. Press seam allowances to one (the darker) side.

QUILTING: Begin to quilt at the center. Take even running stitches with a single thread knotted at one end. Continue until the quilting is finished.

VERTICAL BARS PILLOW

(16" square — burgundy, green, yellow and black)

TECHNIQUE: Patchwork quilting.

AVERAGE: For those with some experience in patchwork.

MATERIALS: (44"-wide fabric) ½ yd. yellow, ¼ yd. burgundy, ⅛ yd. each of green and black; 18" square each of batting and muslin; 16"-square knife-edge pillow form.

DIRECTIONS:
(¼" seams allowed):
Note: Please read General Directions at left.
   1. **CUTTING:** *From yellow,* cut a 17"-square pillow-back and two 2½ x 10½ strips. *From black,* cut three 2½" x 10½" strips and four 1½" squares. *From green,* cut four 1½" x 10½" strips and four 2½" squares. *From burgundy,* cut four 2½" x 12½" borders.
   2. **PILLOW-TOP:** Alternating black with yellow, seam 5 strips side by side at a 10½" edge, then a green strip against each black edge; press seams toward black. Seam a black square to each end of two remaining green strips; seam both strips to black/yellow edges *(see photo).* Seam burgundy strips against two opposite green edges. Seam a green square to each end of the remaining burgundy strips; seam them to the other green edges.
   3. **QUILTING:** Place the pillow-top, right side up, over batting, then the muslin. Quilt *(see General Directions)* "in the ditch" of each seam. Trim muslin and batting flush with pillow-top.
   4. **ASSEMBLING:** Pin the pillow-top to the pillow-back right sides together; trim the back edges flush with the top. Seam around 3 sides and 4 corners. Turn right side out and insert the pillow form. Turn in the open edges and slip stitch closed.

HORIZONTAL BARS PILLOW

(16" square — red, green, purple)

TECHNIQUE: Patchwork quilting.

AVERAGE: For those with some experience in patchwork.

MATERIALS: (44"-wide fabric) ½ yd. purple, ¼ yd. red and ⅛ yd. green; 18" sq. each of batting and muslin; 16"-square knife-edge pillow form.

DIRECTIONS
(¼" seams allowed):
Note: Please read General Directions at left.
   1. **CUTTING:** *From purple,* cut a 17"-square pillow-back, three

2½" x 10½" rectangles and four 2½" squares. *From red, cut two 2½" x 10½" and four 2½" x 12½" rectangles. From green, cut two 1½" x 10½" and two 1½" x 12½" rectangles.*

2. Pillow-Top: At a 10½" edge, seam 2 red rectangles between 3 purple, then a shorter green one against each purple edge *(see photo)*. Seam a 12½" green strip at other two edges. Seam red rectangles to two opposite green edges. Seam a purple square to each end of remaining red strips; seam them to the other two edges.

3. Quilt along the seams and make the pillow *(see Steps 3 and 4 of Vertical Bars Amish Pillow on page 43)*.

BARS AND ARROWS PILLOW

. . . .

(16" square)

TECHNIQUE: Patchwork quilting.

AVERAGE: For those with some experience in patchwork.

MATERIALS: (44"-wide fabric) ½ yd. green and ¼ yd. each of yellow and burgundy; 18" square each of batting and muslin; 16"-square knife-edge pillow form.

. . . .

DIRECTIONS:
Note: Please read General Directions on page 43.
1. Pattern: Trace pattern *(see Fig. 1/2)* for Nos. 1 and 2 triangles. Also draw patterns for one 2½" square (No. 5 patch) and two rectangular patches (No. 3 — 1½" x 4½" — and No. 4 — 2½" x 4½" patches).
2. Cutting: *From green, cut a 17"-square pillow-back, four*

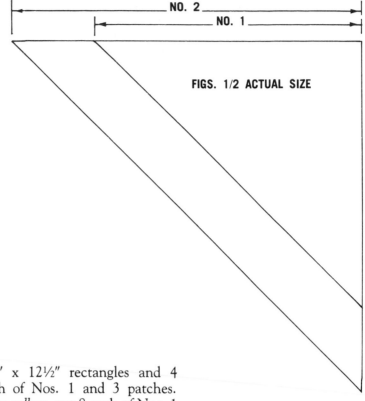

NO. 2
NO. 1
FIGS. 1/2 ACTUAL SIZE

2½" x 12½" rectangles and 4 each of Nos. 1 and 3 patches. *From yellow, cut 8 each of Nos. 1 and 3, and 2 each of Nos. 2 and 4 patches. From burgundy, cut 4 each of Nos. 2, 4 and 5.*

3. Patchwork: Seam the long side of a No. 1 to each short side of a No. 2 (yellow to burgundy arrow, green to yellow arrow). In the same colors, seam a No. 3 to each side of a No. 4. Press seams toward darker color. Seam these two units together to make an arrow *(see photo)*. Repeat, to make 6 arrows. Seam the arrows together in 2 rows of 3 *(see photo)*. Seam a green strip to two opposite edges of the central assembly. Seam a burgundy square to each end of the remaining green strips and seam them to the other edges of the arrow assembly.

4. Quilt the pillow-top and make the pillow *(see Steps 3 and 4 of Vertical Bars Amish Pillow on page 43)*.

WILD GOOSE PILLOW

. . . .

(16" square)

TECHNIQUE: Patchwork quilting.

AVERAGE: For those with some experience in patchwork.

MATERIALS: (44"-wide fabric) ½ yd. turquoise, ¼ yd. black and ⅛ yd. lavender; 18" square each of batting and muslin; 16"-square knife-edge pillow form.

. . . .

DIRECTIONS
(¼" seams allowed):
Note: Please read General Directions on page 43.
1. Pattern: Trace pattern *(see Fig. 1/2)* for Nos. 1 and 2 triangles.
2. Cutting: *From turquoise,*

cut a 17"-square pillow back, 10 No. 2 patches and four 2½" squares. *From black, cut 20 No. 1 patches and four 2½" x 12½" rectangles. From lavender, cut one 2½" x 10½", two 1½" x 10½" and two 1½" x 12½" rectangles.*

3. PILLOW-TOP: Seam the long side of each black No. 1 patch to a short side of a turquoise No. 2 patch. Seam them into 2 vertical rows of 5 each (*see photo*). Seam the 2½"-wide lavender strip between the arrows;

seam the 10½"-long lavender strips at each side edge. Seam the 12½" lavender strips to top and bottom. Seam black strips at two opposite edges. Seam a turquoise square to each end of the remaining black pieces and seam these strips to the top and bottom edges of patchwork.

4. QUILT the pillow-top and make the pillow (*see Steps 3 and 4 of Vertical Bars Amish Pillow on page 43*).

BOW TIE PILLOW

. . . .

(*16" square*)

TECHNIQUE: Patchwork quilting.

AVERAGE: For those with some experience in patchwork.

MATERIALS: (44"-wide fabric) ½ yd. purple, ¼ yd. green and ⅛ yd. red; 18" square each of

batting and muslin; 16"-square knife-edge pillow form.
. . . .

DIRECTIONS
(¼" seams allowed):
Note: Please read General Directions on page 43.

1. PATTERN: Trace patterns (*see* FIG. 3) for Nos. 1, 2 and 3 patches.

2. CUTTING: *From purple,* cut a 17"-square pillow-back, 8 No. 2 patches and four 2½" x 12½" rectangles. *From green,* cut 4 each of No. 2 and No. 3 patches, also a 4¾" square. *From red,* cut four 2½" x 3½" rectangles, 8 No. 1 triangles and also a 4¾" square. *From red,* cut four 2½" x 3½" rectangles, 8 No. 1 triangles and four 2½" squares.

3. BLOCK: Trim off the points of the purple No. 2 patches along the dotted lines (*see* FIG. 3). Seam a red rectangle between 2 purple patches along the 3½" edges, then seam the longest edges of a red No. 1 patch at each end. Make 3 more blocks the same way.

4. ROWS: Seam the green square between two pieced

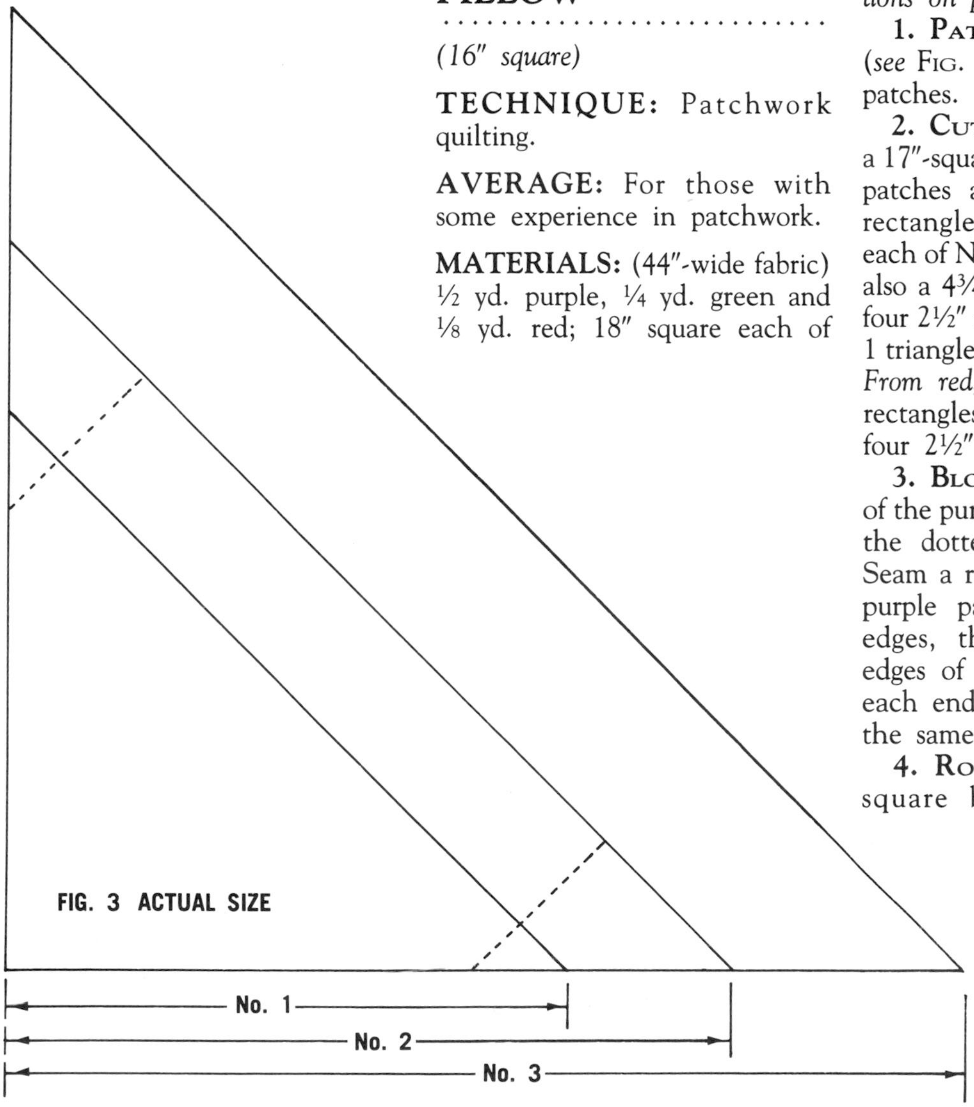

FIG. 3 ACTUAL SIZE

No. 1
No. 2
No. 3

blocks. Seam the long edge of a No. 2 block to each end, to make the center diagonal row. Seam a short edge of No. 3 triangles to opposite edges of a block. Then seam the long edge of a No. 2 block in between, to complete one corner (*see photo*). Assemble other corner the same way. Seam 1 corner to each edge of the center row to complete the square.

5. **Borders:** Seam a purple strip to the opposite edges of the patchwork square. Seam a red square to each end of the remaining purple strips, then sew that strip to the other two edges.

6. **Quilt** the pillow-top (about ¼" from seams) and make the pillow (*see Steps 3 and 4 of Vertical Bars Amish Pillow on page 43*).

CENTER SQUARES PILLOW

(16" *square*)

TECHNIQUE: Patchwork.

AVERAGE: For those with some experience in patchwork.

MATERIALS: (44"-wide fabric) ½ yd. lavender and ¼ yd. each of burgundy and black; 18" square each of batting and muslin; 16"-square knife-edge pillow form.

DIRECTIONS

(¼" *seams allowed*):
Note: Please read General Directions on page 43.

1. **Patterns:** Trace No. 2 and No. 4 patches (*see* Fig. 4)

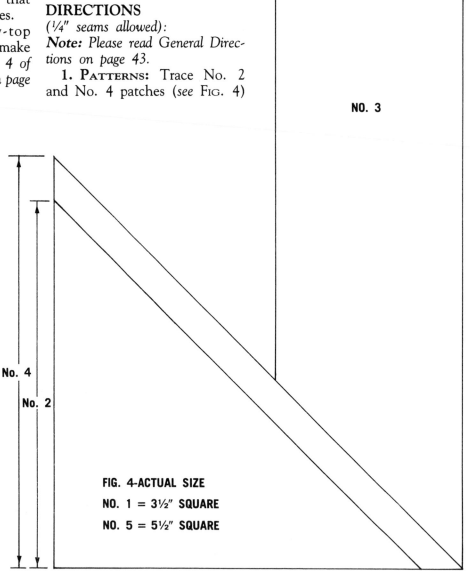

PLACE ON FOLD ◄

NO. 3

No. 4

No. 2

FIG. 4-ACTUAL SIZE

NO. 1 = 3½" SQUARE

NO. 5 = 5½" SQUARE

FIG. 5

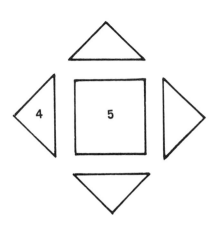

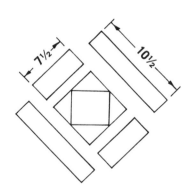

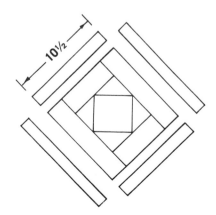

and, on folded paper, No. 3. Open up No. 3 for a full pattern.

2. CUTTING: *From lavender,* cut a 17"-square pillow-back, one 5½" square and four 3½" squares. *From burgundy,* cut 8 No. 2 and 4 No. 4 patches, then four 1¼"-wide strips (two 10½" and two 12" long). *From black,* cut four 2"-wide strips (two 7½" and two 10½" long) and four No. 3 patches.

3. PILLOW-TOP: Seam the long end of a No. 4 triangle to each side of the larger lavender square. Seam 7½"-long black strips to opposite edges, then 10½" black strips to the other edges (*see* FIG. 5). Seam 10½"-long burgundy strips to opposite edges, then 12"-long burgundy strips to the other edges. Seam

the longest edge of a black No. 3 patch to each burgundy edge. Seam a short edge of two No. 2 burgundy patches to adjoining sides of a small lavender square (*see photo*). Repeat 3 times. Seam each of these corner units to a black edge to complete the square.

4. QUILT the pillow-top and make the pillow (*see Steps 3 and 4 of Vertical Bars Amish pillow on page 43*).

Did You Know
....
That Amish quilts and pillows invariably contain a deliberate flaw so as not to claim perfection or invite vanity!

STARS AND
OVALS
PILLOW

(about 13" square)

TECHNIQUE: Counted thread embroidery.

AVERAGE: For those with some experience in counted thread embroidery.

MATERIALS: 16″ square of 18-mesh Aida cloth; 13 yds. dark and 44 yds. light coral 6-strand embroidery floss; ½ yd. white muslin; synthetic stuffing; tapestry needle; embroidery hoop.

DIRECTIONS:

1. **MARKING:** Turn under and stitch ½″ at each edge of Aida cloth. Baste vertical and horizontal centerlines.

2. **EMBROIDERY:** With three strands in needle, work a double straight cross-stitch *(see Stitch Guide, pages 298-299)* at the center. To start second star, after

FIG. 6 STAR AND OVALS PILLOW

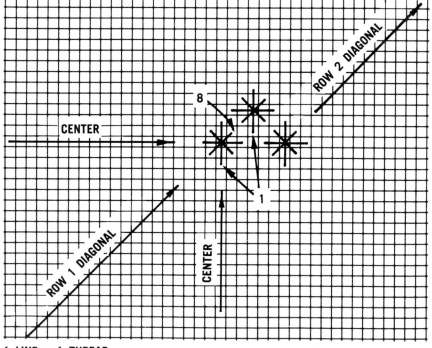

1 LINE = 1 THREAD

hole 8 pass needle under two threads to right and out again at hole 1 (*see* Fig. 6). Continue the diagonal row, working 22 stars each side of the center star. Work eleven diagonal rows each side of central row. Then fill in each corner by adding shorter rows to complete the square (23 x 23 stars). Work a border (69 stitches square) of cross stitch, in darker thread against the outer stars. Each cross-stitch is worked over two vertical and two horizontal threads. Be sure to work all the underlying stitches in the same direction (*see Stitch Guide, pages 298-299*). In darker thread, work the cross stitch border (*see* Fig. 7). Fill in the ovals with stars, beginning at centers (*see circles in* Fig. 7).

3. Assembling: Wash (if needed) and press the pillow top, wrong side up over a towel. Pin it over a matching muslin square and baste the seamline four threads away from the cross stitches. Topstitch just outside the central square.

4. Stitch the same size muslin pillow-back to the pillow-top around three sides and four corners.

5. Trapunto: Cut a short slit in the muslin (only) behind the square. Push stuffing inside, using a wooden knitting needle to raise the square shape.

6. Turn pillow cover right side out and stuff. Turn in open edges and slip stitch.

FIG. 7 STAR AND OVALS PILLOW BORDER

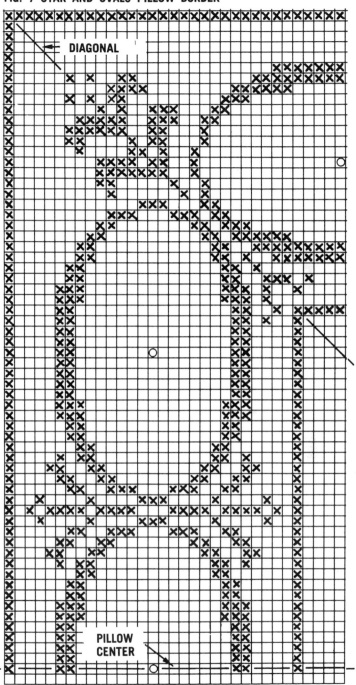

DIAGONAL

PILLOW CENTER

1 SQ. = 2 THREADS (1 CROSS-STITCH)

WOOLLY SHEEP AND "FOLK ART" CAT PILLOWS

WOOLLY SHEEP PILLOW

(18″ x 22″)

TECHNIQUE: Sewing, yarn looping.

EASY: Achievable by anyone.

MATERIALS: ½ yd. 45″-wide creamy-white wool fabric; same color wool yarn; scrap of black felt; synthetic stuffing.

DIRECTIONS
(¼″ seams allowed):

1. ENLARGE *(see page 294)* pattern *(see* FIG. 8). Cut a pair of white bodies. From black felt, cut one Ear, a pair of Faces, and 2 pairs of Feet.

2. STITCH each pair of feet together except at the top edge. Stitch the face together at the two short edges. Turn all right side out and stuff lightly; baste open edges together.

3. SEAM the top edge of each foot to a lower edge of the body back, right sides together and raw edges even. Seam the face to the body back the same way,

between black dots.

4. PIN the body front to the body back (over feet and face) right sides together and edges even. Seam all around except at the face edge, and leave another 5″ open at the back (for handwork). Turn right side out.

5. TUFTS: Make a yarn tuft, as follows: Fold yarn back and forth to make a pile of 2½″ wide loops *(see* FIG. 8A). Thread a needle with double strong thread and wrap the center of the loops *(see* FIG. 8B). Hold all the loops together in one hand and wrap the thread several times around the center. Pass the thread back and forth through the nub (*see* FIG. 8C) and tie off. Handsew the nub of the tuft to the front body only of the sheep and tack down 2 or 3 of the loops. Repeat until the front body is covered.

6. EAR: Take a ½″ pleat in the bottom edge of the ear and whipstitch the edge to the sheep, among the tufts.

7. STUFF the sheep. Turn in the open edges at the face and at the back and slip stitch closed.

"FOLK ART" CAT PILLOW

(18″ x 20″)

TECHNIQUE: Machine embroidery.

CHALLENGING: For those with more experience in machine embroidery.

MATERIALS: 24″ x 40″ white felt; three 9″ x 12″ blue felt pieces; 2 pkgs. synthetic stuffing; blue thread; embroidery scissors; white glue.

DIRECTIONS:

1. ENLARGE (*see page 294*) pattern (*see* FIG. 9, *page 52*) on transparent paper.

2. CUT a white cat front (the back will be cut later) and 2 pairs of ears. Machine embroider the cat front on the single lines (in plant, face and ears) and the borders of short lines around the cat's back and face. Press the felt, stretching slightly.

3. CUT out the blue felt pieces. Pin them to the cat front, using the pattern as a placement

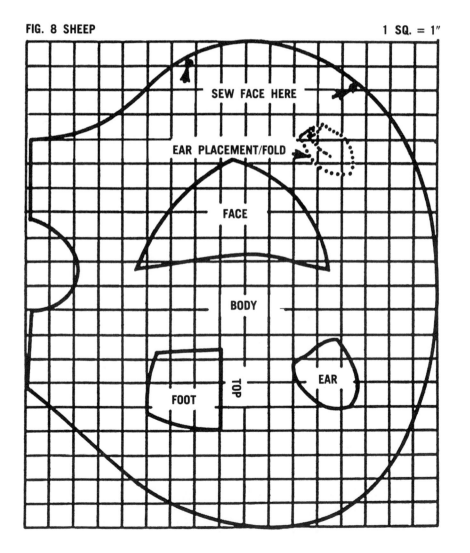

FIG. 8 SHEEP   1 SQ. = 1″

SEW FACE HERE

EAR PLACEMENT/FOLD

FACE

BODY

TOP

FOOT

EAR

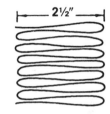

FIG. 8A

2½″

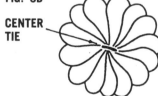

FIG. 8B

CENTER TIE

FIG. 8C

THREAD

guide. Edgestitch all but the rows of small pieces along the front legs — these are glued.

4. EDGESTITCH each pair of ears together at the side edge. Stuff them and baste open edges closed. Sew ears to head, right sides together and edges even, between lines shown.

5. PIN the cat front, wrong sides together, to the uncut white felt. Trace around the edges and

across the ear bases, then cut out the cat back. Pin the cat front to the cat back (ears upward) and edgestitch, leaving an opening for the stuffing. Stuff the cat, sew open edges closed.

FIG. 9 "FOLK ART" FELT CAT　　　　　　　　　**1 SQ. = 2"**

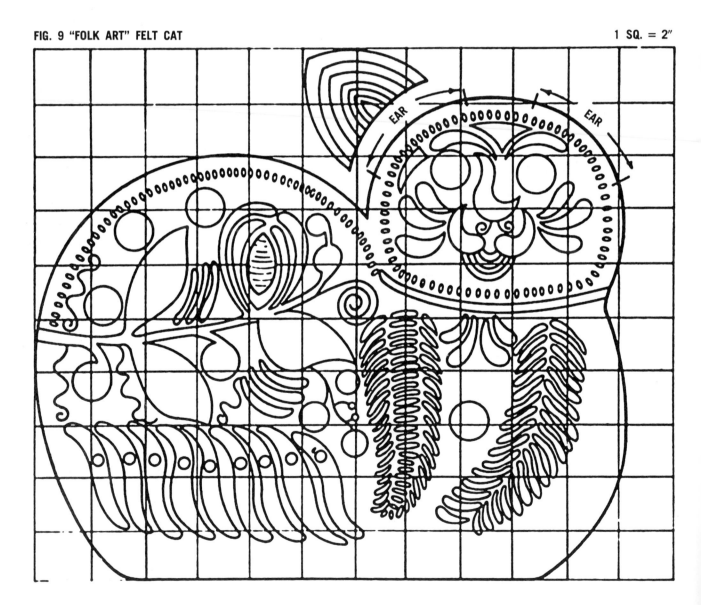

"CRAZY QUILT" PILLOWS

(13" sq. and 11" x 14", plus ruffles)

TECHNIQUE: "Crazy Quilt" patchwork, embroidery.

AVERAGE: For those with some experience in sewing and embroidery.

MATERIALS: ½ yd. 45"-wide velveteen or moiré; ½ yd. 36"-wide muslin; scraps of velvet,

> ### TIP | "Crazy" Fabrics
>
> What kind of fabric is right for a crazy quilt? Why not create a sampler of such mixes as old neckties, patterned scarves, print and solid ribbons, pretty bits of discarded lingerie, even old velveteen skirts or tops. Use your imagination — the more, the "crazier"!

FIG. 10   1 SQ. = 1"

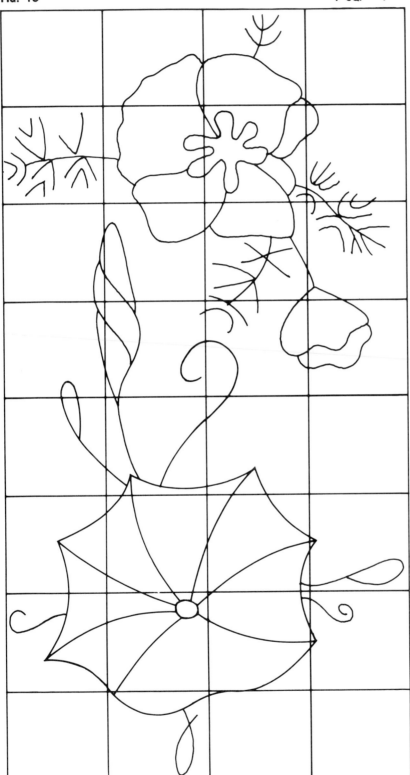

Did You Know
....
Crazy Quilts became popular in 19th-century America. While quilts began as a thrify use of scarce fabric, crazy quilts reflected the splendor of the Victorian era. Originally, they were made of silk, in opulent jewel tones. Beautiful ribbons, laces and other materials were produced especially for making these quilts. There was even a quilt completely pieced with fur — the animal's feet still attached!

silk, taffeta etc.; 1¾ yds. 2½"-wide ruffled lace; embroidery floss; *optional:* tiny beads or pearls, narrow lace or ribbon; pillow forms or synthetic stuffing.
....
DIRECTIONS
(½" seams allowed):

  1. CUTTING: *For the square pillow:* From velvet or moiré, cut a 14" square pillow-back and 3½ yds. (pieced as needed) of 2½"-wide strips for ruffle; also cut a 14" square pillow-top from muslin. *For the oblong pillow:* from moiré cut a 12" x 15" pillow-back and 3½ yds. (pieced as needed) of 2½"-wide strips for ruffling; also cut a 12" x 15" pillow-front from muslin.

  2. "CRAZY" PATCHWORK: Cut a roughly triangular patch

FEATHER STITCH

and pin it over a righthand corner of the muslin pillow-top; trim 2 corners to match the muslin edges and baste around corner, turning under the free edge. Slide one raw edge of two more patches under free edge and pin. Where the two patches meet, turn under one edge and lap it over the other raw edge. Slip stitch the folded edges through all layers. Continue adding patches across the muslin, always covering a raw edge with a turned under edge. Stitch ¼" from the pillow-top edges.

3. EMBROIDERY AND TRIMS: Outline the seams by sewing on a strip of narrow ribbon or lace or by working rows of embroidery in stitches of your choice (*see Stitch Guide, pages 298-299*), adding in small beads if you wish. Embroidery stitches can also be scattered all over the patch and a flower (*see* FIG. 10) can be embroidered

---

TIP

"Crazy" Seams

Originally, seams of "crazy" patch pieces were joined with feather stitches and other decorative embroidery. To speed up work on your Crazy Quilt pillows, you can embellish the patch seamlines by stitching over them with narrow ribbons and/or a variety of lacy novelty edgings with tiny beads.

---

in stem or outline stitch on one of the larger patches.

4. RUFFLE: Seam the short ends of the ruffle strip together to make a loop. Turn under ¼" at one long edge and stitch with zigzag stitch. With the longest machine stitch, sew a gathering row ½" from opposite edge. Pin the ruffle to the pillow-top, right sides together and raw edges flush, pulling up on the bobbin thread until the ruffle fits. Distribute fullness evenly, with a little extra at the corners. Stitch over gathering row. Stitch a strip of 2½"-wide ruffled lace over the fabric ruffle, seaming the short ends together.

5. ASSEMBLING: Pin the pillow-back to the pillow-top (over ruffle), right sides together and edges even. Seam (½") around 3 sides and 4 corners. Turn right side out and stuff. Turn in open edges and slip stitch.

CROCHETED DOILIES
ON PILLOWS

"DAISY FRILL" DOILY PILLOW TOP

(pillow is 15" in diameter; doily pillow top is 18" in diameter)

TECHNIQUE: Crochet.

AVERAGE: For those with some experience in crochet.

MATERIALS: DMC "Brilliant" crochet cotton 2 (218 yd.) balls of White; steel crochet hook, Size 6; ½ yd. of velveteen fabric for pillow; polyester fiberfill.

DIRECTIONS:

PILLOW TOP: Starting at center ch 8, join with sl st to form ring. **Rnd 1:** Ch 3, 23 dc in ring, join with sl st in top of ch 3; 24 dc (counting ch 3). **Rnd 2:** Ch 9 sk 2, * 1 tr in next st, ch 5, sk 2; repeat from *6 times, end with sl st in 4th ch of ch 9; 8 spaces. **Rnd 3:** Sl st into first ch-sp, ch 4, 6 tr in same sp, ch 3, *7 tr in next ch-sp, ch 3; repeat from *, end with sl st in top of ch 4. **Rnd 4:** Ch 4, tr in next 6 sts, ch 5, 1 sc in ch-3 sp, ch 5, * 1 tr in next 7 tr, ch 5, 1 sc in ch-3 sp, ch 5; repeat from *, end with sl st in top of ch 4. **Rnd 5:** Ch 4, 1 tr in next 6 sts, ch 4, *yo hook twice, pull up a lp in first ch-5 sp of rnd below, (yo and through 2 lps) twice (2 lps left on hook), yo hook twice, pull up a lp in next ch-5 sp of rnd below, (yo and through 2 lps) twice, yo and through all 3 lps on hook —* **cluster made;** ch 4, * 1 tr in next 7 tr, ch 4, work a cluster over next 2 ch-5 sps, ch 4; rep from *, end with sl st in top of ch last tr, ch 4. **Rnd 6:** Sl st into 2nd tr, ch 4 work a cluster over next 4 sts, sk last tr, ch 6, 1 sc in ch-4 sp, ch 5, 1 sc in next ch-4 sp, ch 6, * sk first tr, work cluster over next 5 sts, sk last tr, ch 6, 1 sc in ch-4 sp, ch 5, 1 sc in ch-4 sp, ch 6; rep from *, end with sl st in top of first cluster. **Rnd 7:** Sl st in each of next 3 ch sts, ch 4, 7 tr in ch-5 sp, ch 4, 1 sc in ch-6 sp, ch 6, * 1 sc in next ch-6 sp, ch 4, 7 tr in ch-5 sp, ch 4, 1 sc in ch-6 sp, ch 6; rep from *, end with 1 sl st in base of beg ch. **Rnd 8:** 1 sl st in each of next 4 ch, sl st to 2nd tr, ch 4, work cluster over next 4 sts, sk last tr, ch 9, 1 sc in ch-6 sp, ch 6, 1 sc in same

sp, ch 9, * skip first tr, work cluster over next 5 sts, sk last tr, ch 9, 1 sc in ch-6 sp, ch 6, 1 sc in ch-6, ch 9; rep from * end with sl st in top of cluster. **Rnd 9:** Sl st in next 4 ch, ch 10, 5 tr in ch-6 sp, ch 6, 1 tr in 6th ch of ch-9 sp, ch 9, * 1 tr in 4th ch of next sp, ch 6, 5 tr in ch-6 sp, ch 6, 1 tr in 6th ch of ch-9 sp, ch 9; rep from *, end with sl st in 4th ch at beg of rnd. **Rnd 10:** Ch 7, 1 tr in same st, * ch 7; work cluster over next 5 sts, ch 7 (1 tr, ch 3, 1 tr) in next tr, ch 7, (1 tr, ch 3, 1 tr) in next tr; rep from *, end with ch 7 sl st in 4th ch of ch-7 at beg of rnd. **Rnd 11:** Sl st in ch-3 sp, ch 7 and tr in same sp, * ch 3, 1 tr in ch-7 sp, ch 3, (1 tr, ch 3, 1 tr in top of cluster of rnd below), ch 3, 1 tr in ch-7 sp, ch 3 (1 tr, ch 3, 1 tr) in ch-3 sp of rnd below, ch 3, 1 tr in ch-7 sp, ch 3 (1 tr, ch 3, 1 tr) in ch-3 sp; rep from *, end with sl st in 4th ch of ch 7. **Rnd 12:** Sl st in ch-3 sp, ch 4, 6 tr in same ch-3 sp, ch 3, 1 tr in next tr, ch 3, * 7 tr in ch-3 sp, ch 3, 1 tr in tr, ch 3; rep from *, end with sl st in top of beg ch. **Rnd 13:** Ch 4, 6 tr in next 6 sts, ch 4, 1 tr in next tr, ch 4, * tr in next 7 tr, ch 4, 1 tr in next tr, ch 4; rep from *, end with sl st in top of beg ch. **Rnd 14:** Ch 3, 6 dc in next 6 tr, 4 dc in ch-4 sp, 1

dc in tr, 4 dc in ch-4 sp, * dc in next 7 tr, 4 dc in ch-4 sp, 1 dc in tr, 4 dc in ch-4 sp; rep from *, end with sl st in top of beg ch-3. **Rnd 15:** * Ch 4, sk 1 dc, 1 sc in next dc; rep from * to last sp, ch 2, dc in base of ch 4 at beg — 192 sps. **Rnd 16:** * Ch 4, 1 sc in next ch sp; rep from *, end ch 2, 1 dc in ch sp of rnd below. **Rnd 17:** * Ch 5, 1 sc in next ch sp; rep from *, end ch 2, 1 dc in ch sp of rnd below. **Rnd 18:** Same as Rnd 17. **Rnd 19:** * Ch 6, 1 sc in next ch sp; rep from *, end ch 3, 1 tr in first ch sp of rnd below. **Rnd 20:** Same as Rnd 19. **Rnd 21:** * Ch 7, 1 sc in next ch sp; rep from *, end as rnd before. **Rnd 22:** Same as Rnd 21. **Rnd 23:** Same as Rnd 21. **Rnd 24:** *Work 5 tr in same st as ending tr of previous rnd, 1 sc in 4th ch of next sp — 1 shell made;* * ch 9, 1 sc in next sp; rep from * 3 times. ** Ch 9, 1 sc in 4th ch of next sp, 5 tr in next sc, 1 sc in 4th ch of next sp, (ch 9, 1 sc in next sp) 4 times; rep from **, ending with ch 4, 1 tr in first tr — 32 shells with 5 ch-sps between. **Rnd 25:** Work 5 tr in same st as ending tr of previous rnd, 1 sc in middle tr, 5 tr in next sc, 1 sc in 5th ch of next ch-sp, (ch 9, 1 sc in next ch-sp) 3 times, ch 9, 1 sc in 5th ch of next sp, *5 tr in next sc, 1

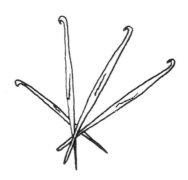

sc in middle tr of rnd below, 5 tr in next sc, 1 sc in 5th ch of next sp, (ch 9, 1 sc in next sp) 3 times, ch 9, 1 sc in 5th ch of next sp; rep from * around, ending with ch 9, 1 sl st in first tr of rnd. Fasten off.

BLOCKING: Pin the crocheted doily Pillow Top to diameter given on a padded surface; cover with a damp cloth and steam lightly (**do not** place iron directly on pillow top); allow it to dry.

PILLOW: Cut two pieces each 16″ dia. for the pillow front and back, allowing ½″ seam. With right sides together, sew the back to the front, leaving 10″ open; turn. Stuff very firmly. Turn the seam allowance at the open edges to the inside and slip stitch the opening closed.

ASSEMBLING: Sew the doily Pillow Top to the top of the pillow on Rnd 14 allowing the remaining edge to hang free.

"PINWHEEL" DOILY PILLOW TOP

(Pillow is 15″ in diameter; doily pillow top is 16½″ in diamter)

TECHNIQUE: Crochet.

AVERAGE: For those with some experience in crochet.

MATERIALS: DMC "Cebelia" crochet cotton size 10, 2 (282 yd.) balls of White; steel crochet hook, Size I; ¾ yd. of velveteen fabric for pillow; polyester fiberfill.

DIRECTIONS:

PILLOW TOP: Starting at center, ch 10. Join with a sl st to form a ring. **Rnd 1:** Ch 4, * 1 dc in ring, ch 1; rep from * 11 times, join with sl st in 3rd ch of ch 4 at beg. **Rnd 2:** Ch 3, 1 dc in same st, * ch 1, 2 dc in next dc;

rep from * 11 times, ch 1, join with sl st in top of ch 3 at beg of rnd. **Rnd 3:** Ch 3, 1 dc in sp after first dc, 1 dc in 2nd dc, * ch 2, 1 dc in first of next 2 dc, 1 dc in sp between the 2 dc, 1 dc in 2nd dc; rep from * 11 times, ch 2, join. **Rnd 4:** Ch 3, 2 dc in next dc, 1 dc in next dc — **last dc before first ch sp,** * ch 3, 1 dc in first of next 3 dc, 2 dc in 2nd dc, 1 dc in last dc; rep from * 11 times, 3 dc, join. **Rnd 5:** Ch 3, 1 dc in same st, 1 dc in each of next 2 dc, 2 dc in next dc — **last dc before first ch-sp,** * ch 3, 2 dc in first of next 4 dc, 1 dc in each of next 2 dc, 2 dc in last dc; rep from * 11 times, ch 3, join. **Rnd 6:** Ch 3, 1 dc in same st, 1 dc in each of next 4 dc, 2 dc in next dc — **last dc before first ch-sp,** *ch 3, 2 dc in first of next 6 dc, 1 dc in each of next 4 dc, 2 dc in last dc; rep from * 11 times, ch 3, join. **Rnd 7:** Ch 3, 1 dc in each of next 7 dc, * ch 4, 1 dc in each of next 8 dc; rep from * 11 times, ch 4, join. **Rnd 8:** Same as Rnd 7. **Rnd 9:** Sl st in next dc, ch 3. 1 dc in each of next 5 dc, * ch 6, sk first dc of next group of 8 dc, 1 dc in each of next 6 dc; rep from * 11 times, ch 6, join. **Rnd 10:** Sl st in next dc, ch 3, 1 dc in each of next 3 dc, * ch 6, 1 dc in ch-sp, ch 6, sk first dc of next group of 6 dc, 1 dc in each of next 4 dc; rpt from * 11 times, ch 6, join. **Rnd 11:** Sl st in next dc, ch 3, 1 dc in next dc, * ch 3, 4 dc in ch-sp before dc, ch 3, 4 dc in next ch-sp, ch 3, sk first dc of next group of 4 dc, 1 dc in each of next 2 dc; rep from * 11 times, (ch 3, 4 dc in next ch-sp) 2 times, ch 3, join. **Rnd 12:** Sl st in sp between ch 3 and first dc (ch 4, 5 tr, ch 1, 6 tr) in same sp before first dc, sk ch-3 and group of 4 dc, (6 tr, ch 1, 6 tr) in next ch-sp, * sk group

of 4-dc and next ch-3, (6 tr, ch 1, 6 tr) in sp between next 2 dc, sk next ch-3 and 4 dc, (6 tr, ch 1, 6 tr) in next ch sp; rep from * 11 times, join. Fasten off.

BORDER: The border is worked in one piece and is joined to doily at ch-sp in center of tr group of the 12th rnd. First form the inner arch; each arch is worked in 2 rows, the 2nd row — the row joining the inner arch to doily — is a right side row and should be joined to the right side of the doily. Ch 8, join with a sl st to form ring for the Inner Arch, ch 3, 12 dc in ring, ch 3, turn, * 1 dc in first dc, (ch 1, 1 dc in next dc) 5 times, ch 1, 1 dc in next dc — 6th of the 12 sts, 1 sc in sp of tr group from 12th rnd of doily, 1 dc in 7th dc, (ch 1, dc in next dc) 5 times. **Outer Arch:** Ch 8, 1 sl st in 8th ch from hook, forming new ring, point this ring away from the center, working toward Inner Arch just completed, ch 3, 12 dc in ring, 1 sl st between 2 rows of inner arch, ch 2, 1 sc in starting ring of inner arch, turn. Work 2nd row of outer arch; 1 dc in first dc, * ch 3, 1 *sl st in 3rd ch from hook — **a picot made,*** 1 dc in next dc; rep from * 11 times. **Ch 8 for inner ring of next inner arch, join with sl st in 8th ch from hook, pointing ring towards center, work towards outer arch just completed, ch 3, 12 dc in ring, 1 sl st between 2 rows of outer arch, ch 2, 1 sc in starting ring of outer arch, turn ***, rep from * to *** 22 times more, work from * to ** once, joining first and 2nd rows of outer arch to inner arch. Fasten off.

BLOCKING: Pin the crocheted doily Pillow Top to diameter given on a padded surface; cover with a damp cloth and steam lightly (*do not* place iron directly on pillow top); allow it to dry.

PILLOW: Cut two pieces each 15″ dia. for the pillow-front and back allowing ½″ seam. With right sides together, sew the back to front, leaving 10″ open; turn. Stuff very firmly. Turn the seam allowance at the open edges to the inside and slip stitch the opening closed.

ASSEMBLING: Sew the doily Pillow Top to the top of the pillow on Rnd 12 allowing the remaining edge to hang free.

"PINECONE" DOILY PILLOW TOP

. . . .

(Pillow is 16½″ in diameter; doily pillow top is 18″ in diameter)

TECHNIQUE: Crochet.

AVERAGE: For those with some experience in crochet.

MATERIALS: DMC "Brilliant" crochet cotton 2 (218 yd.) balls of White; steel crochet hook, Size 6; 1 yd. of velveteen fabric for pillow; polyester fiberfill.

. . . .

DIRECTIONS:

PILLOW TOP: Make a firm chain to measure 14 ins, join with sl st to form ring. **Rnd 1:** Ch 5, dc in ring, ch 2, *dc in ring, ch 2. Rep from * 46 times, join with sl st to 3rd ch of ch 5; 48 dcs made. **Rnd 2:** *Ch 9, sc in next dc. Rep from * around, join with sl st to base of beg ch 9; 48 lps made. **Rnd 3:** Sl st to 3rd st of first lp, ch 3, 2 dc in same lp, *3 dc in next lp. Rep from * around, join with sl st to top of beg ch 3. **Rnd 4:** *Ch 5, sc between next 2 groups of dc. Rep from * around, join. **Rnd 5:** Sl st in first lp, ch 3, 3 dc in same lp, *4 dc in next lp. Rep from * around, join. **Rnd 6:** *Ch 6, sc between next 2 groups of 3 dc. Rep from * around, join. **Rnd 7:** Sl st in first lp, ch 3, 4 dc in same lp, *5 dc in next lp. Rep from * around, join. **Rnd 8:** *Ch 8, sc between next 2 groups of 5 dc. Rep from * around, join. **Rnd 9:** Sl st into first lp, ch 3-1 dc-ch 2-2 dc in same lp, *2 dc-ch 2-2 dc in next lp — a shell made. Rep from * around, join with sl st to top of first ch. **Rnd 10:** Sl st to ch-2 sp in center of first shell, *shell in ch-2 sp, ch 5, sk ch-2 sp, 2 dc-ch 4-2 dc in next ch-2 sp, ch 5, sk ch-2 sp. Rep from * around, join with sl st to first dc of rnd. **Rnd 11:** Sl st to ch-2 sp in center of first shell, *shell in ch-2 sp, ch 5, 9 tr in ch-4 sp, ch 5. Rep from * around, join with sl st to first dc of rnd. **Rnd 12:** Sl st to ch-2 sp in center of first shell, *shell, ch 5, tr in first tr, (ch 1, tr in next tr) 8 times, ch 5. Rep from * around, join with sl st to first dc of rnd. **Rnd 13:** Sl st to ch-2 sp in center of first shell, *2 dc-ch 2-2 dc-ch 2-2 dc in ch-2 sp, ch 5, sc in first ch-1 sp, (ch 4, sc in next ch-1 sp) 7 times, ch 5. Rep from * around, join. **Rnd 14:** Sl st to ch-2 sp in center of first shell, *shell, shell in next ch-2 sp, ch 5, sc in first ch-4 lp, (ch 4, sc in next lp) 6 times, ch 5. Rep from * around, join. **Rnd 15:** Sl st to ch-2 in center of first shell, *shell, ch 3, shell in next ch-2 sp, ch 5, sc in first ch-4 lp, (ch 4, sc in next lp) 5 times, ch 5. Rep from * around, join. **Rnd 16:** Sl st to ch-2 sp in center of first shell, *shell, ch 5, shell in next ch-2 sp, ch 5, sc in first ch-4 lp, (ch 4, sc in next lp) 4 times, ch 5. Rep from * around, join. **Rnd 17:** Sl st to ch-2 sp in center of first shell, *shell, ch 2, (dc, ch 1) 6 times, dc in ch-5 sp, ch 2, shell in next shell, ch 5, sc in first lp, (ch 4, sc in next lp) 3 times, ch 5. Rep from * around, join. **Rnd 18:** Sl st to ch-2 sp in center of first shell, *shell, (3 dc in next ch-1 sp) 6 times, shell in next shell, ch 5, sc in first lp, (ch 4, sc in next lp) twice, ch 5. Rep from * around, join. **Rnd 19:** Sl st to ch-2 sp in center of first

shell, *shell, ch 4, (sc between next 2 groups of 3 dcs, ch 4) 5 times, shell in next shell, ch 5, sc in next lp, ch 4, sc in next lp, ch 5. Rep from * around, join. **Rnd 20:** Sl st to ch-2 sp in center of first shell, *shell, (3 dc in next ch-4 lp) 6 times, shell in next shell, ch 5, sc in ch-4 lp, ch 5. Rep from * around, join. **Rnd 21:** Sl st to ch-2 sp in center of first shell, *shell, ch 4, (sc between next 2 groups of 3 dc, ch 4) 5 times, shell in next shell. Rep from * around, join. **Rnd 22:** Make shell between first and last shells of previous rnd, ch 3, (3 dc in next ch-4 lp) 6 times, ch 3. *Shell between 2 joined shells, ch 3, (3 dc in next ch-4 lp) 6 times, ch 3. Rep from * around, join. **Rnd 23:** Sl st to ch-2 sp in center of first shell, * ch 5, sc in ch-3 sp, (ch 5, sc between next 2 groups of 3 dc) 5 times, ch 5, sc in ch-3 sp, ch 5, sc in ch-2 sp of shell. Rep from * around, ending with sl st in center of shell. **Rnd 24:** Sl st to ch-5 lp, ch 3, 3 dc in ch-5 lp, *4 dc in next ch-5 lp. Rep from * around, join with sl st to 2nd ch of beg ch 3. **Rnd 25:** *Ch 5, sc between next 2 groups of 4 dc. Rep from * around, join with sl st to base of beg ch 5. **Rnd 26:** Ch 1, *2 sc in next ch-5 lp, (ch 3, sl st in last sc) 3 times — **a triple picot made,** 3 sc in same ch-5 lp. Rep from * around. Fasten off.

BLOCKING: Pin the crocheted doily Pillow Top to diameter given on a padded surface; cover with a damp cloth and steam lightly (**do not** place iron directly on pillow-top); allow it to dry.

PILLOW: Cut two pieces each 16½" dia. for the pillow-front and back allowing ½" seam. With right sides together, sew the back to front, leaving 10" open; turn. Stuff very firmly. Turn the seam allowance at the open edges to the inside and slip stitch the opening closed.

ASSEMBLING: Sew the doily Pillow Top to the top of the pillow on Rnd 23 allowing the remaining edge to hang free.

FIVE "BOBBLE" PILLOWS

GENERAL DIRECTIONS FOR FIVE "BOBBLE" PILLOWS

TECHNIQUE: Knitting.

ALL ARE CHALLENGING: For those with more experience in knitting.

PATTERN STITCHES:

LARGE BOBBLE STITCH (LB ST): In next st, k 1, p 1, k 1, p 1, k 1 (5 sts worked in one st), slip st off left-hand needle, turn work, p all 5 sts, turn, k all 5 sts, turn, p all 5 sts, turn, k all 5 sts, turn, p all 5 sts, turn. Slip one st, k 2 tog, psso the k 2 tog, k 2 tog, psso the k 2 tog — one st remains.

SMALL BOBBLE STITCH (SB ST): In next st k 1, p 1, k 1 (3 sts worked in one st), slip st off left-hand needle, turn work, p all 3 sts, turn, k all 3 sts, turn, p all 3 sts, turn. Slip one st, k 2 tog, psso the k 2 tog — one st remains.

BLOCKING: Pin each piece to measurements on a padded, flat surface; steam lightly, but **do not** place the iron directly on the work. Let dry thoroughly before removing.

ASSEMBLING: Work in all loose ends. With right sides of the Pillow Front and Pillow Back together, sew around three sides and four corners; turn right side out. Insert the pillow form. Slip stitch the 4th side closed.

"LARGE DIAMOND" PILLOW

. . . .

(14" square)

MATERIALS: Anny Blatt "Super Kid" (1¾ oz./50 gr. ball): 1 ball each of Peach (A), Medium Turquoise (B), Pale Turquoise (C) and White (D); Anny Blatt "Soft Anny" (1¾ oz./50 gr. ball): 1 ball of Salmon (E); knitting needles, one pair No. 8, OR ANY SIZE NEEDLES TO OBTAIN GAUGE BELOW; 14" x 14" knife-edge pillow form.

GAUGE: In st st using one strand of "Kid Anny" — 4 sts = 1"; 5 rows = 1". TO SAVE TIME, TAKE TIME TO CHECK GAUGE.

PATTERN STITCHES: See General Directions on page 61 for Bobble Stitch.

Note: Large E colored Bobble sts are worked with 2 strands of E held together.

. . . .

DIRECTIONS:

PILLOW FRONT: Starting at lower edge with A, cast on 55 sts. **Rows 1-8:** Work in st st (k 1 row, p 1 row). **Row 9 (First Bobble Row,** *see* FIG. 11): With A k 27, drop A, attach 2 strands of E and in next st work a LB st, cut E, pick up A and k 27. **Rows 10-12** *(not shown in* FIG. 11): With A only, work in st st. **Row 13 (Second Bobble Row):** With A k 25, drop A, attach E and work a LB st, cut E, pick up A and k 3, drop A, attach E and work a LB st, cut E, pick up A and k 25. **Rows 14-16:** With A **only** work in st st. **Row 17 (Third Bobble Row):** With A k 23, drop A, attach E and work a LB st, cut E, pick up A and k 3, drop A, attach B and work a SB st, cut B, pick up A and k 3, attach E and

work a LB st, cut E, pick up A and k 23. Follow FIG. 3 for placement of other Bobble Sts, continuing to work 3 stockinette st rows with A **only,** in between the Bobble st rows (*not shown in* FIG. 3), until the Diamond pattern is complete. Then work 8 stockinette st rows with A only. Bind off loosely.

PILLOW BACK: Starting at lower edge with D, cast on 55 sts. With D **only,** work in st st for 14". Bind off loosely.

BLOCKING AND ASSEMBLING: See General Directions on page 61.

"ROSE" PILLOW

. . . .

(14" x 16")

MATERIALS: Anny Blatt "Soft Anny" (1¾ oz./50 gr. ball): 2 balls of Rose (A), 1 ball each of White (B), Blue (C), Cranberry (D); knitting needles, one pair No. 5, OR ANY SIZE NEEDLES TO OBTAIN GAUGE BELOW; 14" x 16" knife-edge pillow form.

GAUGE: In st st — 4½ sts = 1"; 6 rows = 1". TO SAVE TIME, TAKE TIME TO CHECK GAUGE.

PATTERN STITCHES: See General Directions on page 61 for Bobble Stitch.

Note: When changing color, pick up new color to be used from under old color to prevent holes.

. . . .

DIRECTIONS:

PILLOW FRONT: Starting at lower edge with A, cast on 72 sts. **Rows 1-8:** With A, work in st st (k 1 row, p 1 row). **Row 9 (First Bobble Row):** With A k 3, drop A, attach D and * in next st using D, work a SB st, drop D but do not cut yarn, pick up A and k 3; rep from * across — 16 Small Bobble sts made. Fasten off D. **Rows 10-14:** With A only, work in st st. **Row 15 (Second Bobble Row):** With A k 3, drop A, *attach B and in next st work a LB st, cut B, pick up A and k 5, drop A, attach C and work a LB st, cut C, pick up A and k 5; rep from * 4 times more, ending with attach B and work a LB st, cut B,

FIG. 11 LARGE DIAMOND PILLOW

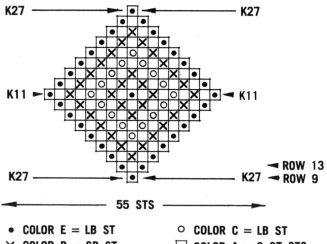

• COLOR E = LB ST   ○ COLOR C = LB ST
✕ COLOR B = SB ST   ☐ COLOR A = 3 ST STS

pick up A and k 3 — 11 Large Bobble sts made. **Rows 16-18:** With A **only,** work in st st. **Row 19 (Third Bobble Row):** With A k 6, drop A, attach D and * in next st using D work a LB st, drop D, pick up A and k 5; rep from * across, ending last rep with k 6 instead of k 5 — 10 Large Bobble sts made. **Rows 20-22:** With A only work in st st. **Row 23 (Fourth Bobble Row):** Rep Second Bobble Row. **Rows 24-28:** With A only, work in st st. **Row 29 (Fifth Bobble Row):** Rep First Bobble Row. **Rows 30-34:** With A only, work in st st. **Row 35 (Sixth Bobble Row):** With A k 1, drop A, attach B and * in next st, using B work a SB st, drop B, pick up A and k 3; rep from * across, ending last rep with k 1 instead of k 3 — 17 Small Bobble Sts made. **Rows 36-38:** With A only, work in st st. **Row 39 (Center Bobble Row):** With A k 3, drop A, attach C and * in next st, using C work a SB st, drop C, pick up A and k 3; rep from * across — 16 Small Bobble Sts made. Complete Pillow Front working rows in reverse order repeating Rows 35-1. Bind off loosely.

Pillow Back: Starting at lower edge with A cast on 72 sts. With A only, work in st st for 14". Bind off loosely.

Blocking and Assembling: See General Directions on page 61.

"ZIGZAG" PILLOW

. . . .

(14" x 18")

MATERIALS: Anny Blatt "Soft Anny" (1¾ oz./50 gr. ball): 2 balls of Light Blue (A), 1 ball each of Dark Blue (B), Medium Blue (C) and Salmon (D); knitting needles, one pair No. 5, or any size needles to obtain gauge below; 14" x 18" knife-edge pillow form.

GAUGE: In st st — 4½ sts = 1"; 6 rows = 1". to save time, take time to check gauge.

PATTERN STITCHES: See General Directions on page 61 for Bobble Stitch.

Note: When changing color, pick up new color to be used from under old color to prevent holes.

. . . .

DIRECTIONS:

Pillow Front: Starting at lower edge with A, cast on 79 sts. **Rows 1-8:** With A **only,** work in st st (k 1 row, p 1 row). Fasten off A. **Row 9-11:** Attach C and work in garter st (k every row). Fasten off C. **Rows 12-14:** Attach A and work in garter st.

Fasten off A. **Row 15:** Attach C and purl across row. **Rows 16 and 17:** With C, work in st st. **Row 18 (Lower Bobble St Row):** With C k 3, drop C, attach D and * in next st, using D, work a SB st, drop D, pick up C and k 3; rep from * across — 19 Small Bobble sts made. Fasten off D. **Rows 19-21:** With C, work in st st. Fasten off C. **Rows 22-24:** Attach A and work in garter st. Fasten off A. **Row 25:** Attach C and purl across. **Rows 26 and 27:** With C, work in st st. Fasten off C. **Rows 28-33:** Attach A and work in st st. Fasten off A. **Rows 34-36:** Attach D and work in garter st. Fasten off D. **Rows 37-39:** Attach A and work in st st. Fasten off A. **Row 40 (First Bobble Row,** see Fig. 12): With A, k 3, drop A, attach B and work a SB st, cut B, pick up A and k 3, drop A, * attach C and work a SB st, cut C and pick up A and k 3, drop A, attach D and work a SB st, cut D, pick up A and k 3, drop A, attach B and work a SB st, cut B, pick up A and k 3, drop A, attach D and work a SB st, cut D, pick up A and k 3, drop A, attach C and work a SB st, cut C, pick up A and k 3, drop A, attach B and work a SB st, cut B, pick up A and k 3; rep from * across 2 times more. **Rows 41-**

FIG. 12 ZIG ZAG PILLOW

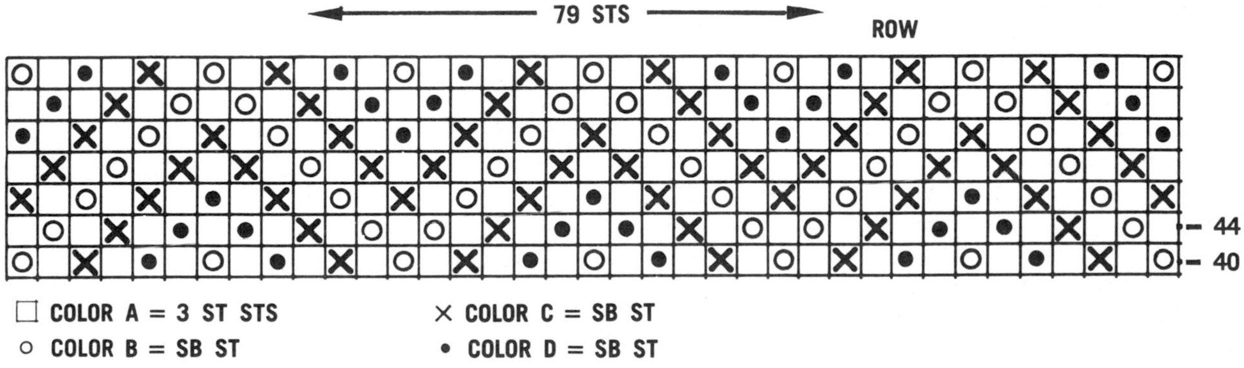

- □ COLOR A = 3 ST STS
- ○ COLOR B = SB ST
- ✕ COLOR C = SB ST
- • COLOR D = SB ST

TIP

From Pillow . . . To Afghan!

For a textural treat, knit and join a mix of all of our bobble pillow patterns to make a splendid afghan.

43: (*not shown in* FIG. 4): With A **only,** work in st st. **Row 44 (Second Bobble Row):** With A, k 5, drop A, * attach B and work a SB st, cut B, pick up A and k 3, drop A, attach C and work a SB st, cut C, pick up A and k 3, drop A, attach D and work a SB st, cut D, pick p A and k 3, drop A, attach D and work a SB st, cut D, pick up A and k 3, attach C and work a SB st, cut C, pick up A and k 3, drop A, attach B and work a SB st, cut B, pick up A and k 3; rep from * across 2 times more, ending last rep with k 5 instead of k 3.

Follow FIG. 11 to complete center panel of small bobble sts, working 3 stockinette st rows with A only in between the Bobble st rows (*not shown in* FIG. 4).

TO COMPLETE PILLOW FRONT: Work rows in reverse order, repeating Rows 39-1. Bind off loosely.

PILLOW BACK: Starting at lower edge with A, cast on 79 sts. With A *only,* work in st st for 14". Bind off loosely.

BLOCKING AND ASSEMBLING: See General Directions on page 61.

"FOUR DIAMOND" PILLOW

(*14" x 18"*)

MATERIALS: Anny Blatt "Soft Anny" (1¾ oz./50 gr. ball): 2 balls of Off-White (A), 1 ball each of Cranberry (B), Turquoise (C); Anny Blatt "Super Kid" (1¾ oz./50 gr. ball): 1 ball of Pink (D); knitting needles, one pair No. 5, **OR ANY SIZE NEEDLES TO OBTAIN GAUGE BELOW;** 14" x 18" knife-edge pillow form.

GAUGE: In st st using Soft Anny — 4½ sts = 1"; 6 rows = 1". **TO SAVE TIME, TAKE TIME TO CHECK GAUGE.**

PATTERN STITCHES: See General Directions on page 61 for Bobble Stitch.

Note: When changing color, pick up new color to be used from under old color to prevent holes.

DIRECTIONS:

PILLOW FRONT: Starting at lower edge with A, cast on 79 sts. **Rows 1-6:** With A only, work in st st (k 1 row, p 1 row). Fasten off A. **Rows 7-9 (ridge row):** Attach D and work in garter st (k every row). Fasten off D. **Rows 10-12:** Attach A and work in st st. **Row 13 (Bobble Row):** With A k 3, drop A, attach C and * in next st with C work a SB st, drop C, pick up A and k 3; rep from * across — 19 Small Bobble sts made. Fasten off C. **Rows 14-16:** With A **only,** work in st st. Fasten off A. **Rows 17-19** (*ridge row*): Attach D and work in gar-

ter st. Fasten off D. **Rows 20-26:** Attach A and work in st st. Fasten off A. **Rows 27 and 28 (ridge row):** Attach C and work in garter st. Fasten off C. **Rows 29 and 30:** Attach A and work in st st. **Row 31 (Bobble Row):** With A k 15, drop A, * attach D and work a SB st, cut D, pick up A and k 15; rep from * across. **Rows 32-34:** With A only, work in st st. **Row 35 (Bobble Row):** With A k 13, drop A, * attach D and work a SB st, cut D, pick up A and k 3, drop A, attach D and work a SB st, cut D, pick up A and k 11; rep from * across, ending last rep with k 13 instead of k 11. **Rows 36-38:** With A **only,** work in st st. **Row 39 (Bobble Row):** With A k 11, * attach D and work a SB st, cut D, pick up A and k 3, drop A, attach B and work a SB st, cut B, pick up A and k 3, drop A, attach D and work a SB st, cut D, pick up A and k 7; rep from * across, ending last rep with k 11 instead of k 7. **Rows 40-42:** With A **only,** work in st st. **Row 43 (Center Bobble Row):** With A k 9, * attach D and work a SB st, cut D, pick up A and k 3, drop A, attach B and work a SB st, cut B, pick up A and k 3, drop A, attach B and work a SB st, cut B, pick up A and k 3, drop A, attach D and work a SB st, cut D, pick up A and k 3; rep from * across, ending last rep with k 9 instead of k 3. **Rows 44-46:** With A only work in st st.

Complete the Four Diamond pattern of Pillow Front by working rows in reverse order, repeating Rows 42-31. Then work Rows 30-1 to correspond with first half of Pillow Front. Bind off loosely.

PILLOW BACK: Starting at lower edge with A, cast on 79 sts.

With A only, work in st st for 14". Bind off loosely.

BLOCKING AND ASSEMBLING: See General Directions on page 61.

"CRANBERRY PINK" PILLOW
. . . .
(14" x 14")

MATERIALS: Anny Blatt "Super Kid" (1¾ oz./50 gr. ball): 1 ball each of Pale Pink (A), Med. Pink (B), Cranberry (C) and White (D); knitting needles, one pair No. 8, OR ANY SIZE NEEDLES TO OBTAIN GAUGE BELOW: 14" x 14" knife-edge pillow form.

GAUGE: In st st — 4 sts = 1";

5 rows = 1". TO SAVE TIME, TAKE TIME TO CHECK GAUGE

PATTERN STITCHES: See General Directions on page 61 for Bobble Stitch.

Note: When changing color, pick up new color to be used from under old color to prevent holes.
. . . .
DIRECTIONS:

PILLOW FRONT: Starting at lower edge with A, cast on 56 sts. **Rows 1-4:** With A **only,** work in st st (k 1 row, p 1 row). **Row 5 (First Bobble Row):** With A k 3, drop A, attach B and * in next st, using B work a LB st, drop B but **do not** cut yarn, pick up A and k 5; rep from * 8 times more,

ending last rep with k 4 instead of k 5. Fasten off B. **Rows 6-10:** With A **only,** work in st st. **Row 11 (Second Bobble Row):** With A k 6, drop A, attach C and * in next st, using C work a LB st, drop B but **do not** cut yarn, pick up A and k 5; rep from * 7 times more, ending last rep with k 7 instead of k 5. Repeat Rows 1-11 until total length is 14" from beg. Bind off loosely.

PILLOW BACK: Starting at lower edge with A, cast on 56 sts. With A **only,** work in st st for 14". Bind off loosely.

BLOCKING AND ASSEMBLING: See General Directions for Blocking on page 61.

"VIOLETS AND LACE" PILLOWS

(14″ square)

TECHNIQUE: Knitting and embroidery.

CHALLENGING: For those with more experience in knitting and embroidery.
Directions are given for a 14″-square velvet pillow back with knitted pillow top.

MATERIALS: Lion Brand "Co-Co" 100% acrylic yarn (40 gr./1.4 oz. ball): 2 balls of white; knitting needles, one pair No. 3, OR ANY SIZE NEEDLES TO OBTAIN GAUGE BELOW; DMC 6-strand floss: 3 skeins each of dark purple and medium purple and 2 skeins of orange; ½ yd. velveteen fabric; No. 20 tapestry needle.

GAUGE: 6 sts = 1″. TO SAVE TIME, TAKE TIME TO CHECK GAUGE.

STITCHES:
Ssk: Slip the first and second stitches knitwise, one at a time, then place the lefthand needle into the front of these two stitches and knit them together.

K1-b: Knit through the back loop of the stitch.

Note: The pattern does not maintain the same number of stitches on every row. After completing Row 16, you will have the original number of stitches you started with.

DIRECTIONS:
   PILLOW TOP: Starting at lower edge, cast on 74 sts. **Row 1 (right side):** K 1, p 3; * k 2, p 6;

rep from * to last 6 sts and k 2, p 3, k 1. **Row 2:** K 4, p 2, * k 6, p 2; rep from * to last 4 sts and k 4. **Row 3:** Rep Row 1. **Row 4:** Rep Row 2. **Row 5:** K 1, p 2, * k 2 tog, yo, ssk, p 4; rep from * to last 3 sts and p 3 instead of p 4. **Row 6:** K 3, * p 1, k into front and back of next st, p 1, k 4; rep from * to last 3 sts and k 3 instead of k 4. **Row 7:** K 1, p 1, * k 2 tog, yo, k 2, yo, ssk, p 2; rep from * to end. **Row 8:** K 2, * p 6, k 2; rep from * to end. **Row 9:** K 1, * (k 2 tog, yo) twice, ssk, yo, ssk; rep from * to last st and k 1. **Row 10:** K 1, p 3, * k into front and back of next st, p 6; rep from * to last 4 sts and p 4 instead of p 6. **Row 11:** K 1, * (yo, ssk) twice, k 2 tog, yo, k 2 tog; rep from * across, ending with yo, k 1. **Row 12:** K 1, k1-b, p 6, * k into front and back of next st, p 6; rep from * across to last 2 sts and k1-b, k 1. **Row 13:** K 1, p 1, * yo, sl 1, k 2 tog, psso, yo, k 3 tog, yo, p 2; rep from * across. **Row 14:** K 2, * k1-b, p 1, k into front and back of next st, p 1, k1-b, k 2; rep from * across. **Row 15:** K 1, p 2, * yo, ssk, k 2 tog, yo, p 4; rep from * across to last 3 sts and p 2, k 1 instead of p 4. **Row 16:** K 3, * k1-b, p 2, k1-b, k 4; rep from * across to last 3 sts and k 3 instead of k 4. Repeat Rows 3-16 to form pattern working until length is 14″ from beg (10 openwork patterns completed). Bind off loosely.

BLOCKING: Pin pillow top to measure 14″ x 14″ on a padded, flat surface; cover with a damp cloth and allow to dry; do not press. (When blocking, you will be stretching the pillow top to open lace work.)

EMBROIDERY: In each solid motif, you will Embroider one Lazy Daisy stitch flower (*see Stitch Guide on pages 298-299*). Use 12 strands of floss and begin at bottom right-hand corner motif with dark purple. Alternate dark or medium purple floss to make each flower. When all flowers are completed, work on orange French Knot (*see Stitch Guide*) in the center of each flower.

ASSEMBLING: Cut two 15″ squares from velveteen; pin-blocked embroidered knitted lace top to right side of one piece and slip stitch in place, leaving 1″ seam allowance on velvet extending all around. With right sides facing and raw edges even, pin front to back all around. Hand sew (1″) seams with back stitch. (If you ever need to remove the knitted top to wash it, it is safer to snip hand stitches than it would be to cut tight machine stitches.) Sew all around, leaving 10″ open on one side; turn. Insert pillow form; slip stitch opening closed.

·3·

SWEATERS

Who can ever have enough sweaters? Knits have been in the fashion foreground for years, and it looks like they're going to stay there. Nothing else captures the relaxed proportions and endless colors of all the best new styles. And with the impressive array of yarns in different weights and fiber contents, the possibilities are endless for terrific pullovers, cardigans, halters, jackets and vests. Our collection of sweaters, for knitters and crocheters alike, spans the four seasons. Whatever you love — classic looks, trendy designs, gorgeous motifs — you'll find them in this chapter.

NAVAJO PULLOVER

(Sweater is shown on the previous page.)

TECHNIQUE: Crochet.

CHALLENGING: For those with more experience in crochet. Directions are for Size Small (8-10). Changes for Size Medium (12-14) are in parentheses.

MATERIALS: Brunswick Pom-fret 100% wool (1¾ oz./50gr. pull skein): 8(9) Sea Oats Heather #5281 (MC), 1 each of Christmas Red #5241 (A), Turquoise #50082 (B), Brew Brown Heather #586 (C), and Black #560 (D); steel crochet hook, Size O, OR ANY SIZE HOOK TO OBTAIN GAUGE BELOW; bobbins.

GAUGE: Dc: 5 sts = 1″; 5 rows = 2″. TO SAVE TIME, TAKE TIME TO CHECK GAUGE.

FINISHED MEASUREMENTS:

Sizes:	Small	Medium
Bust:	39″	41″
Back width at underarm:		
	19½″	20½″
Sleeve width (first row at armhole):		
	20″	21″

DC PAT: Ch necessary length.
Row 1: Dc in 4th ch from hook, dc in each ch. Ch 3, turn.
Row 2: Ch 3 on turn is always counted as first dc, dc in each st. Ch 3, turn. Rep Row 2 for Dc pat.
Note 1: Carry a separate bobbin for each section.
Note 2: When changing color, work off last 2 lps of last st worked in color you are dropping with the new color you are picking up.
Note 3: If you have to carry a color across for just a few sts, work over the color you are carrying along, or carry it loosely across back of work, maintaining gauge.
Note 4: Always work B stripes on the body from the wrong side so they are prominent.
Note 5: Lower bands and cuffs are worked on when the pieces are completed.

DIRECTIONS:

BACK: With MC, ch 103 (109) loosely. **Row 1** (*wrong side*): Dc in 4th ch from hook, dc in each ch — 101 (107) dc, counting turning ch. Ch 3, turn. Follow chart for Back at indicated size. Work even until entire chart is completed.

SHOULDER SHAPING FOR SMALL: With MC, starting at seam edge, work 9 sc, 9 hdc, 10 dc — 28 sts. Fasten off. Leave center 45 sts for back neck, work other shoulder to correspond.

SHOULDER SHAPING FOR MEDIUM: Work 2 rows in Dc Pat with MC after completion of chart. At seam edge with MC, work 10 sc, 10 hdc, 10 dc — 30 sts. Fasten off. Leave center 47 sts for back neck, work other shoulder to correspond.

FRONT: Work same as Back to row on chart indicating neck.

SHAPE NECK: Keeping to pat, work 32 (34) sts. Work on one side only. Keeping to pat, dec 1 st at neck edge every row 4 times (to dec — yo, draw up a loop in next st, draw up a loop in next st, yo, draw through all loops on hook) — 28 (30) sts. Work to shoulder as for Back. Shape shoulder as for one side of Back. Leave out center 37 (39) sts for front neck, work other side to correspond, keeping to pat and reversing shaping.

SLEEVES: Weave shoulder seams. With C, right side facing, starting at armhole row indicated on chart, work 101 (107) dc evenly spaced across to other armhole (Row 1 of chart). Work pat and decreases following chart — 61 (67) sts. Complete chart.

CUFF: Row 1: Working from wrong side with MC, work in dc, decreasing evenly across row to 45 (47) sts. Ch 3, turn. **Row 2:** Ch 3 on turn counts as first dc, * Back Post dc around next dc (yo, insert hook in space before next dc, bring hook across back of dc and out in space after dc and draw up a lp, work off as a dc), dc in next st; rep from *. Ch 3, turn. **Row 3:** Ch 3 on turn counts as first dc, * Front Post dc around next st (yo, insert hook in space before next st from back to front, across front of st and out in space after st, from front to back, draw up a loop and work off as a dc), dc in next st; rep from * across. Ch 3, turn. Rep Rows 2 and 3 for cuff until there are 8 rows in all, or desired cuff length. Fasten off.

LOWER BACK BORDER: Row 1: Working from wrong side with MC, work in dc, decreasing evenly across row to 89 (95) sts. Ch 3, turn. Work as for cuff for 6 rows, or desired length. Fasten off.

LOWER FRONT BORDER: Work as for Back.

NECKBAND: Worked back and forth, starting and ending at center back of neck. **Row 1:** With

BACK

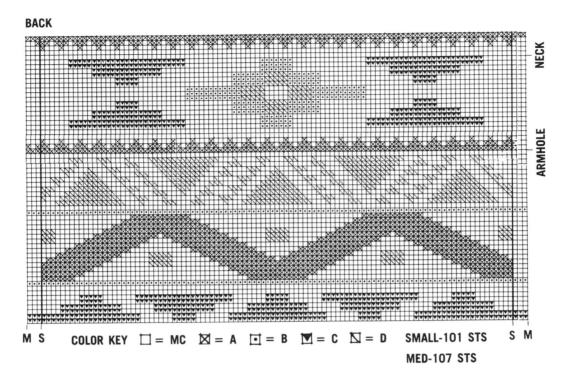

M S   **COLOR KEY** ☐ = MC ☒ = A ⊡ = B ⩒ = C ⧄ = D   **SMALL-101 STS**   S M

MED-107 STS

SLEEVES SMALL-101 STS MED.-107 STS   **ROW**

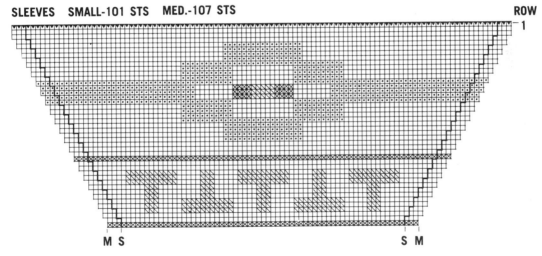

M S   S M

MC, right side facing, work 95 (99) dc evenly spaced around neck. Work as for cuff of sleeve, starting on wrong side with Row 3. Work 4 rows. Fasten off. Weave neckband seam.

FINISHING: Sew the under-sleeve and side seams.

FAIR ISLE SAMPLER
PULLOVER

TECHNIQUE: Knitting.

CHALLENGING: For those with more experience in knitting. Directions are given for size Petite (6). Changes for sizes Small (8-10), Medium (12-14) and Large (16-18) are in parentheses.

MATERIALS: Tahki "Soho Bulky Tweed" (100-gr skein): 2 skeins Oatmeal #322 (A); and 1 skein each of: Red #316 (B), Gray #389 (C), Purple #327 (D), Fuchsia #320 (E), Turquoise #330 (F), Camel #393 (G), Dark Blue #391 (H), Pink #329 (I), Black #332 (J), and 1 ball gold metallic thread (K); knitting needles Size 9 and 10½, OR ANY SIZE NEEDLES TO OBTAIN GAUGE BELOW; 4 buttons.

GAUGE: On Size 10½ needles in stockinette stitch: 13 sts = 4"; 9 rows = 2". TO SAVE TIME, TAKE TIME TO CHECK GAUGE.

FINISHED MEASUREMENTS:

Sizes:	Petite	Small	Medium	Large
Bust:	32"	34"	38"	42"
Back width at underarm:	16"	17"	19"	21"
Sleeve around upper arm:	16"	17"	18"	19"

Notes: When changing colors, pick up new color from under dropped color to prevent holes. Carry color not in use loosely across wrong side of work. Cut and join new colors as needed. Color K is sometimes used together with another color and is stated as A/K etc.

- -

DIRECTIONS:

BACK: With smaller needles and A, cast on 45 (49, 55, 61) sts. **Twisted Ribbing: Row 1** *(right side)*: K 1 through back lp (tbl), * p 1, k 1 tbl, rep from * across. **Row 2:** P 1, * k 1 tbl, p 1, rep from * across. Rep these 2 rows for 3", inc 8 sts evenly spaced across last row and end on wrong side — 53 (57, 63, 69) sts. Change to larger needles. **Row 1** *(right side)*: With A, k across. **Row 2:** With A/K, k across. **Row 3:** With B/K, k across. **Row 4:** With B, k across. Chart: Working in St st (k 1 row, p 1 row), beg chart on row 5 where indicated for size being made and work to row 15 and complete. **Row 16** *(wrong side)*: With B/K, k across. **Row 17:** With D/K, k across. **Row 18:** With D, k across. Beg chart again on row 19 and work to row 27 and complete. **Row 28** *(wrong*

⟋TIP *POINTERS FOR BUYING YARN*

1. CHECK yarn labels for the dye lot number and purchase all yarns of each color from the same dye lot.

2. CHECK the yarn label for washability and other care information. If none is given, you should wash and block your gauge swatch to see how the yarn responds.

3. IF a yarn label gives gauge information, the needle size mentioned is the one recommended for that particular yarn. It is wise to stay within two sizes of the recommendation.

4. IF you choose to substitute another yarn for the one recommended, select yarn as close as possible to the original in weight and type. Buy a single skein first and knit a swatch to see how the gauge and appearance compare with those of the pattern.

5. TO convert ounces to grams or vice versa, use this formula: 100 grams = 3.52 ounces. For example, if 16 ounces of yarn are called for, and you are substituting a yarn weighed in grams, divide 16 by 3.52 and multiply times 100. The quantity is 454 grams.

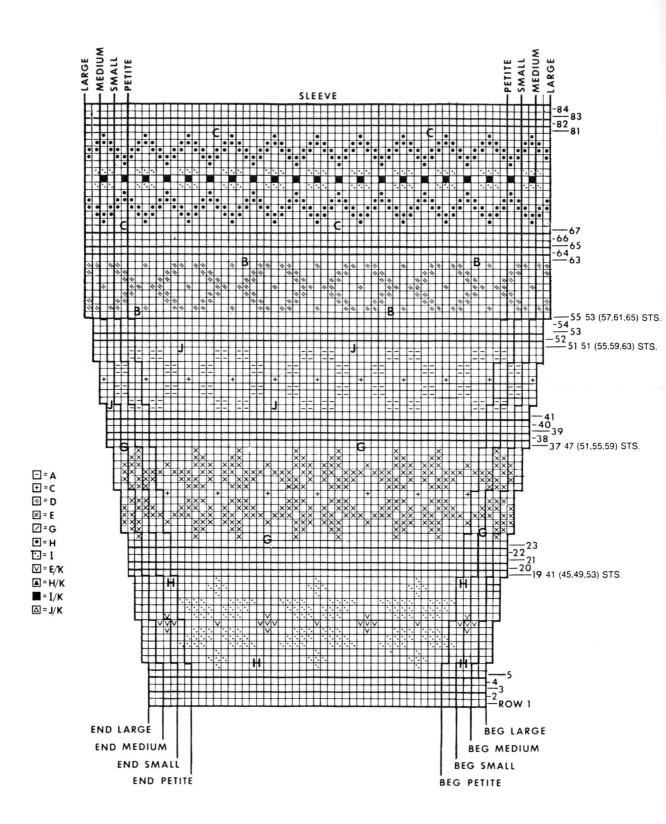

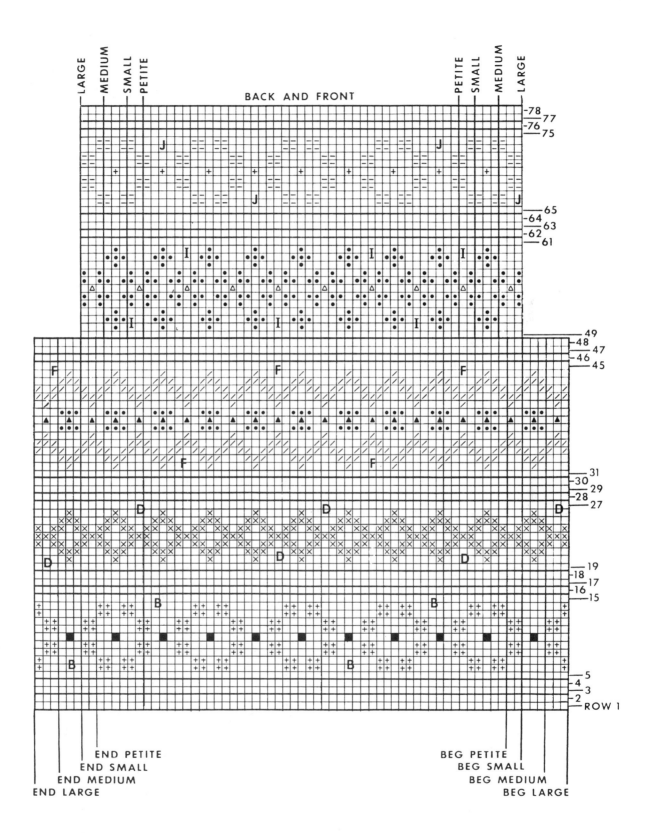

BACK AND FRONT

side): With D/K, k across. **Row 29:** With F/K, k across. **Row 30:** With F, k across. Beg chart again on row 31 and work to row 45 and complete. **Row 46** (*wrong side*): With F/K, k across. **Row 47:** With I/K, k across. **Row 48:** With I, k across. Mark last row. **Armhole Shaping:** Keeping to charted pat (and beg again on row 49), bind off 6 sts beg next 2 rows — 41 (45, 51, 57) sts. Work until row 61 is completed. **Row 62** (*wrong side*): With I/K, k across. **Row 63:** With J/K, k across. **Row 64:** With J, k across. Beg chart again on row 65 and work to row 75 and complete. **Row 76** (*wrong side*): With J/K, k across. **Row 77:** With A/K, k across. **Row 78:** With A, k across. Change to smaller needles and with A only, work in twisted ribbing until armholes measure 8½ (9, 9½, 10)″ above marked row. Bind off loosely in ribbing. Mark the position of 2 buttons on each shoulder, with the first 1″ from armhole edge and the last 3½″ from armhole edge.

FRONT: Work same as for back until ribbing at neck measures 4 rows less than for back; end on wrong side. **Buttonhole Row** (*right side*): * Work in ribbing to marker, bind off next 2 sts; rep from * across. **Following row:** Work across in ribbing, casting on 2 sts over bound-off sts. Continue to work same as for back.

SLEEVES: With smaller needles and A, cast on 25 (27, 29, 31) sts. Work in ribbing same as for back for 2 (2½, 3, 3)″ inc 10 (12, 14, 16) sts evenly spaced across last row and end on wrong side — 35 (39, 43, 47) sts. Change to larger needles. **Row 1** (*right side*): With C, k across. **Row 2:** With C/K, k across. **Row 3:** With H/K, k across. **Row 4:** With H, k across. **Chart:** Beg with row 5 and follow chart, inc 1 st each side where indicated for size being made and work to row 19 and complete. **Row 20** (*wrong side*): With H/K, k across. **Row 21:** With G/K, k across. **Row 22:** With G, k across. Beg chart again on row 23 and work to row 37 and com-

plete. **Row 38** (*wrong side*): With G/K, k across. **Row 39:** With J/K, k across. **Row 40:** With J, k across. Beg chart again on row 41 and work to row 51 and complete. **Row 52** (*wrong side*): With J/K, k across. **Row 53:** With B/K, k across. **Row 54:** With B, k across. Beg chart again on row 55 and work to row 63 and complete — 53 (57, 61, 65) sts. **Row 64** (*wrong side*): With B/K, k across. **Row 65:** With C/K, k across. **Row 66:** With C, k across. Beg chart again on row 67 and work to row 81 and complete. **Row 82** (*wrong side*): With C/K, k across. **Row 83:** With E/K, k across. **Row 84:** With E/K, k across. Bind off all sts loosely.

FINISHING: Overlap front shoulders over back shoulders for 1″ and sew along armhole edge. Weave top of sleeve to straight edge of armhole. Sew side edges of sleeve to each armhole bind-off. Sew side and sleeve seams. Sew on buttons to correspond to buttonholes.

MELON-SLEEVED JACKET & HAT

TECHNIQUE: Crochet.

AVERAGE: For those with some experience in crochet. Directions are for Size Small (8-10). Changes for Sizes Medium (12-14) and Large (16) are in parentheses.

MATERIALS: Thick boucle-type yarn: 35 (35, 39) ounces of Ecru; crochet hooks, Sizes J for jacket and K for hat, OR ANY SIZE HOOKS TO OBTAIN GAUGES BELOW.

GAUGE: Jacket: 8 dc = 3"; 4 rows = 3". Hat: 2 sc = 1". TO SAVE TIME, TAKE TIME TO CHECK GAUGE.

MEASUREMENTS:

Sizes:	Small	Medium	Large
Bust, not wrapped:			
	35½"	37½"	39"
Back width at underarm:			
	17¼"	18"	18¾"
Each Front at underarm:			
	9"	9½"	10"
Sleeve around upper arm:			
	18"	18¾"	19½"
Hat circumference:			
	21"	21"	21"

DIRECTIONS:

BACK: Starting at waist, ch 38 (40, 42). **Row 1** *(right side)*: Dc in 3rd ch from hook and each ch across — 36 (38, 40) dc. **Row 2:** Ch 2, turn, 2 dc in first dc (*inc*), dc to last dc, 2 dc in last dc; *do not* work in ch-2 — 38 (40, 42) dc. **Row 3:** Rep Row 2 — 40 (42, 44) dc. **Row 4:** Ch 2, turn, dc in each dc. **Rows 5-9:** Rep Rows 2 and 4 twice, then rep Row 2 — 46 (48, 50) dc.

ARMHOLE SHAPING: Row 10: Ch 1, turn, sl st in first 3 sts, sc in next st, hdc in next st, dc to last 5 sts, hdc in next st, sc in next st; *do not* work in rem sts. **Row 11:** Ch 1, turn, sl st in first 2 sts, ch 2, dc to last 2 sts — 36 (38, 40) dc. **Rows 12-21:** Work even as for Row 4.

SHOULDER SHAPING: Rows 22 and 23: Rep Row 10 — 20 (22, 24) dc. Fasten off.

PEPLUM: Starting at waistline, ch 52 (54, 56). Rep Row 1 of Back — 50 (52, 54) dc. **Rows 2-5:** Inc 1 dc each end — 58 (60, 62) dc. **Row 6:** Work even. Fasten off.

RIGHT FRONT: Ch 22 (23, 24). **Row 1** *(right side)*: Rep Row 1 of Back — 20 (21, 22) dc. **Row 2:** Rep Row 4 of Back. **Row 3:** Ch 2, turn, dc to last dc, 2 dc in last dc *(side edge)* — 21 (22, 23) dc. **Rows 4-9:** Rep Rows 2 and 3, 3 times — 24 (25, 26) dc.

ARMHOLE SHAPING: Row 10: Ch 1, turn, sl st in first 3 sts, sc in next st, hdc in next st, dc to end. **Row 11:** Ch 2, turn, dc in 17 (18, 19) dc, dec over next 2 sts — 18 (19, 20) dc. **Row 12:** Dec 1 dc at arm edge, dc across — 17 (18, 19) dc. **Rows 13 and 14:** Work even. **Row 15:** Inc 1 dc at arm edge — 18 (19, 20) dc.

NECK SHAPING: Rows 16-20: At front edge dec 1 dc every row — 13 (14, 15) dc.

SHOULDER SHAPING: Row 21: Dec 1 dc at neck edge, work to last 5 sts, hdc in next st, sc in next st; *do not* work in rem sts. **Row 22:** Ch 1, turn, sl st in first 3 sts, sc in next st, hdc in next st, dc to end. Fasten off. *Note: Front is 1 row shorter than Back.*

PEPLUM: Starting at waistline, ch 27 (29, 31). **Row 1** *(right side)*: Rep Row 1 of Back — 25 (27, 29) dc. **Row 2:** Inc 1 dc at end of row *(side edge)*. **Row 3:** Inc 1 dc at beg of row — 27 (29, 31) dc. **Rows 4 and 5:** Rep Rows 2 and 3 — 29 (31, 33) dc. **Row 6:** Work even. Fasten off.

LEFT FRONT: Work to correspond to Right Front and Peplum, reversing all shaping.

SLEEVES: Starting at lower edge, ch 24 (26, 28). **Row 1** *(right side)*: Rep Row 1 of Back — 22 (24, 25) dc. **Row 2:** Ch 2, turn, dc in first 10 (11, 12) dc, (2 dc in next dc) twice, place a safety pin between the two previous inc's to mark center of row, dc to end — 24 (26, 28) dc. Move marker up as needed. **Row 3:** Work even. **Row 4:** Inc in each of 2 center sts — 26 (28, 30) dc. **Rows 5 and 6:** Work even. **Rows 7-9:** Rep Rows 4-6. **Row 10:** Rep Row 4 — 30 (32, 34) dc. **Row 11:** Work even. **Row 12:** Inc 1 dc each end. **Row 13:** Work even. **Rows 14-19:** Rep Row 12, 6 times. **Rows 20-23:** Rep Rows 12 and 13, twice — 48 (50, 52) dc.

CAP SHAPING: Row 24: Rep

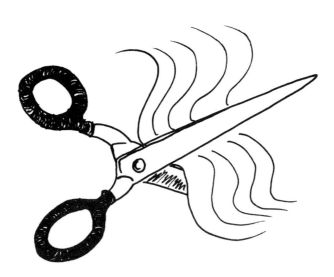

Row 10 of Back. **Row 25:** Ch 2, turn, dec 1 dc over first 2 sts, work to 2 sts before center, (dec over next 2 sts) twice (*2 sts dec at center*), dc to last 2 sts, dec 1 dc — 38 (40, 42) dc. **Row 26:** Ch 2, turn, dec 1 dc, dc to 2 sts before center, dec 2 dc, dc to last 2 sts, dec 1 dc — 34 (36, 38) dc. **Rows 27-29:** Rep Row 26 — 22 (24, 26) dc. **Row 30: Size Small:** Dec 1 dc each end — 20 dc; **Sizes Medium and Large:** Rep Row 26 — (20, 22) dc. **Row 31:** Ch 1, turn, sl st in first st, sc in next st, hdc in next st, dc in next 5 (5, 6) sts, dec 2 dc as before, dc to last 3 sts, end hdc, sc, sl st. Fasten off.

FINISHING: Sew the shoulder, side and sleeve seams. Sew the sleeves in place, easing to fit and forming a puff at the shoulder. Sew the sides of the peplums together. Sew the waistline of the peplum to the lower edge of the jacket, easing evenly to fit, seams matching.

EDGING: From right side, beg at a side seam on lower edge, keeping edge flat, sc around outer edge of jacket, inc as necessary at lower corners; sl st in first sc. Fasten off.

HAT: With K hook, ch 3; join to form ring. **Rnd 1:** Ch 1, 2 sc in each ch — 6 sc. Mark beg of rnds; do not join rnds. **Rnd 2:** 2 sc in each sc — 12 sc. **Rnd 3:** (2 sc in next sc (*inc*), sc in next sc) 6 times — 18 sc. **Rnd 4:** (Inc in next sc, sc in next 2 sc) — 24 sc. **Rnd 5:** (Inc, sc in 3 sc) 6 times — 30 sc. **Rnd 6:** (Inc, sc in 4 sc) 6 times — 36 sc. **Rnd 7:** (Inc, sc in 5 sc) 6 times — 42 sc. **Rnd 8:** Sc in each sc. Work even until 8″ from top, or desired length to beg of cuff. Cut yarn into several 2-yd. lengths and knot ends tog about 1″ from end. Continue in sc for 5 rnds, having knots fall to wrong side; end sl st in first st on last rnd. Fasten off. Turn up cuff.

TURTLENECK HALTER TOP

TECHNIQUE: Knitting.

EASY: Achievable by anyone. Directions are for Petite (6). Changes for Small (8-10) and for Medium (12-14) are in parentheses.

MATERIALS: Tahki Cotton Dot (3½ oz. skein) 4 (4, 5) skeins of No. 505 Sea Foam Green; knitting needles, No. 5 and No. 6, OR ANY SIZE NEEDLES TO OBTAIN GAUGE BELOW; 2 stitch holders.

GAUGE: With larger needles (unstretched) 12 sts = 2"; 6 rows = 1". TO SAVE TIME, TAKE TIME TO CHECK GAUGE.

FINISHED BUST: (unstretched): 25 (27, 29)".

DIRECTIONS

BACK: With larger needles, cast on 81 (87, 93) sts. **Row 1** (*wrong side*): P 1, * k 1, p 1; rep from * across. **Row 2:** K 1, * p 1, k 1; rep from * across. Rep Rows 1 and 2 for Rib pat until total length is 11 (11, 12)" from beg, ending with Row 1.

ARMHOLE SHAPING: Row 1: K 1, p 1, sl 1, k 1, psso, rib to last 4 sts, k 2 tog, p 1, k 1. **Row 2:** K the k sts and p the p sts. Rep last 2 rows 21 (23, 25) times more, then rep Row 1 every 4th row twice. Work 1 row more.

SHOULDER SHAPING: Bind off 3 sts, rib next 27 (29, 31) sts, sl these sts onto a st holder, bind off last 3 sts.

FRONT: Work same as Back until there are 45 (47, 49) sts on needle after beg armhole shaping, ending with a right-side row.

NECK SHAPING: Keep to pat, work 16 sts, sl rem sts to st holder. **Row 1:** Dec one st (neck edge), work in pat to last 4 sts, k 2 tog (armhole edge), p 1, k 1. **Row 2 and All Even Rows:** K the k sts, and p the p sts. **Rows 3 and 5:** Rep Row 1 — 10 sts. **Rows 7 and 11:** Dec one st (neck edge) complete row. **Rows 9 and 13:** Rep Row 1 — 4 sts. **Row 15:** K 2 tog, p 1, k 1. **Row 16:** P 1, k 1, p 1. Bind off. Leave center 13 (15, 17) sts on st holder. Sl rem sts onto larger needle and work as for other side, reversing shaping.

FINISHING: Sew left shoulder seam.

TURTLENECK: With smaller needles and right side facing you, rib sts from back st holder, pick up 17 sts along left neck edge, rib sts from front st holder, pick up 17 sts along right neck edge — 74 (78, 82) sts. Work in rib for 3½". Bind off loosely. Sew right shoulder and neck seams. Sew side seams.

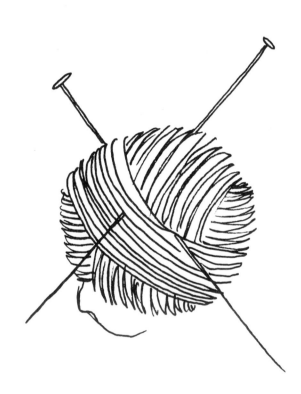

PAISLEY PULLOVER

TECHNIQUE: Knitting.

CHALLENGING: For those with more experience in knitting.

Note: This is an oversized sweater. Directions are for Size Small (8-10). Changes for Sizes Medium (12-14) and Large (16) are in parentheses.

MATERIALS: Tahki "Windsor Tweed" (3.5 oz. skein): 4 (5, 5) skeins of Burgundy #941 (MC), and Tahki "Superkid Mohair" (1.4 oz. ball): 1 each of Blue #1032 (A), White #1010 (B), Grey #1022 (C) and Gold #1026 (D); knitting needles, one pair each No. 6 and No. 8, OR ANY SIZE NEEDLES TO OBTAIN GAUGE BELOW; double pointed needles, one pair No. 6; 9 bobbins.

GAUGE: Stockinette stitch on larger needles: 9 sts = 2"; 5 rows = 1". TO SAVE TIME, TAKE TIME TO CHECK GAUGE.

FINISHED MEASUREMENTS:

Sizes:	Small	Medium	Large
Bust:	38"	41"	43½"
Back width at underarm:			
	19"	20½"	21¾"
Sleeve width at upper arm:			
	18½"	19¼"	20"

Note 1: Wind 3 bobbins of A, 2 bobbins each of B, C and D, 1 bobbin of MC. Use separate balls of MC for each color section. Always twist yarns when changing colors to prevent holes. When working Charts I, III and IV carry the colors not in use loosely at the back of the work.

Note 2: The body is worked in one piece beginning at the lower Front and ending at the lower Back.

....

DIRECTIONS:

FRONT: With smaller needles and MC cast on 86 (92, 100) sts. **Row 1:** * K 1, p 1, rep from * across. Rep Row 1 for rib pat to 1", inc 0 (1, 0) at center of last row — 86 (93, 100) sts. Change to larger needles and stockinette stitch (k 1 row, p 1 row). Work Chart I as indicated. Work until Row 16 is completed. Work in stockinette stitch with MC only inc 2 (1, 0) sts across first row — 88 (94, 100) sts. Beg with Row 2 work entire Chart II — 3 motifs as shown. Work until Row 92 is completed.

NECK SHAPING: Keeping to pat work 37 (39, 41) sts, join another ball MC, bind off center 14 (16, 18) sts, work 37 (39, 41) sts. Working both sides at once, dec 1 st at each neck edge every row 4 times, every other row twice — 31 (33, 35) sts each side of neck. Work even until Row 104 is completed.

BACK-JOINING ROW: Keeping to pat work 31 (33, 35) sts, with MC cast on 26 (28, 30) sts for back neck edge, complete row — 88 (94, 100) sts. Work even in pat until Row 130 is completed. Work with MC only. Work until Back measures same as Front to beg of lower pat, dec 2 (1, 0) sts

across last row. Work Chart III dec 1 st at center of last row. Change to smaller needles. Work in k 1, p 1 rib for 1". Bind off in ribbing.

LEFT SLEEVE: With smaller needles and MC cast on 34 (38, 42) sts. Work in ribbing as on lower Back for 1" inc 1 st at center of last row — 35 (39, 43) sts. Change to larger needles and st st. Work Chart IV at sizes as indicated. *At same time* inc 1 st each end every 4th row 21 times. After Row 16 is completed work with MC only for 14 rows — 49 (53, 57) sts at this point of sleeve. Beg pat. **Row 30:** With MC, k 10 (12-14) work Chart II A over next 29 sts, with MC k 10 (12, 14). Being sure to continue side incs work until Row 50 is completed. Work with MC only for rest of sleeve — 77 (81, 85) sts. Inc 1 st each end every other row 4 times — 85 (89, 93). Work 1 row. Bind off all sts.

RIGHT SLEEVE: Work same as left sleeve using Chart II B.

FINISHING TURTLENECK: From right side with double point needles, starting at center back neck edge, pick up and k 72 (76, 80) sts around neck edge. Mark for beg of rounds. Work in k 1, p 1 ribbing for 8", bind off loosely in ribbing. Match the center top of the sleeves to the shoulder joining Row. Sew in the sleeves. Sew the side and sleeve seams. Block lightly to measurements.

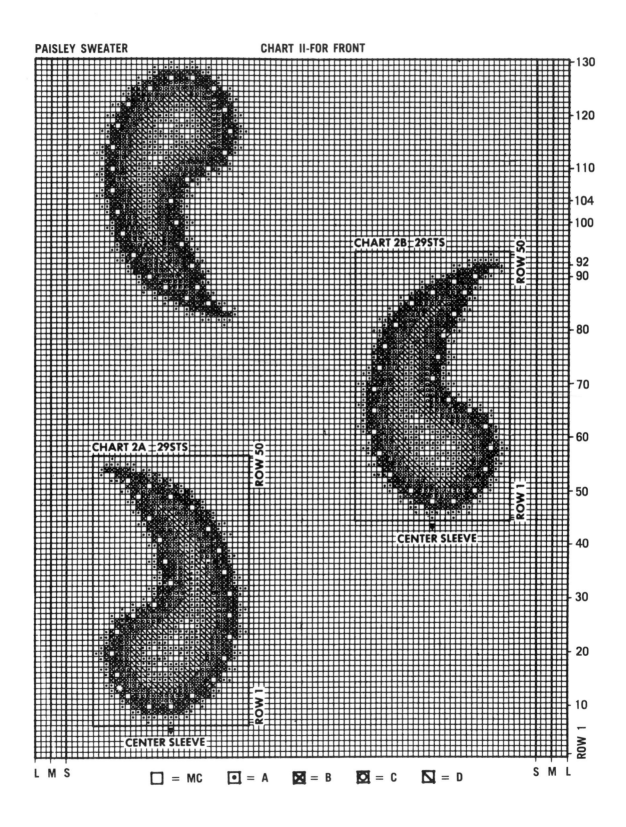

PAISLEY SWEATER   CHART II-FOR FRONT

CHART 2B 29STS

CHART 2A 29STS

CENTER SLEEVE

CENTER SLEEVE

□ = MC   ⊡ = A   ⊠ = B   ⧆ = C   ◩ = D

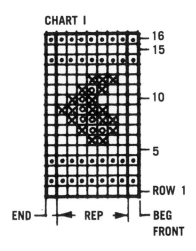

CHART I

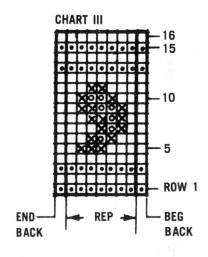

CHART III

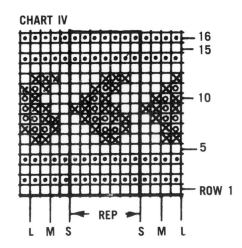

CHART IV

"STRIPES AND CABLE" SLEEVELESS TOP

TECHNIQUE: Knitting.

CHALLENGING: For those with more experience in knitting.
Directions are given for Size Petite (6). Changes for Sizes Small (8-10), Medium (12-14) and Large (16-18) are in parentheses.

MATERIALS: Joseph Galler's Parisian Cotton (1 oz. ball): 4 (4, 5, 5) balls of No. 6196 Light Green (A) and 2 balls each of No. 4095 Mauve (B), No. 4108 Lavender (C), No. 3066 Blue (D), and No. 5272 Pink (E); knitting needles, one pair No. 7, OR ANY SIZE NEEDLES TO OBTAIN GAUGE BELOW; one stitch holder.

Note: The top is worked with two strands of thread held together throughout.

GAUGE: In stockinette stitch (st st) using two strands of thread (without stretching) — 11 sts = 2"; 7 rows = 1". TO SAVE TIME, TAKE TIME TO CHECK GAUGE.

Note: The top is designed to be made smaller than actual body measurements in order to fit snugly.

MEASUREMENTS:
Sizes

Petite	Small	Medium	Large
(6)	(8-10)	(12-14)	(16-18)

Body Bust:

30½″	32½″	36″	40″

Finished
Bust (without stretching):

28½″	30½″	34″	38″

Width across Back or Front at underarms (without stretching):

14¼	15¼″	17″	19″

. . . .

DIRECTIONS:

BACK: Starting at lower edge with two strands of A, cast on 70 (74, 82, 94) sts. Work in k 1, p 1 ribbing for 1¾″, ending with a wrong-side row. Cut thread and attach B. **Row 1** (*right side*): K across row, increasing 10 sts evenly spaced — 80 (84, 92, 104) sts. **Row 2:** P across. **Rows 3-6:** Continue in stockinette stitch (k 1 row, p 1 row) with B. Cut B; attach C. Continue to work in stockinette stitch and stripe pat as follows: 6 rows C, 6 rows D, 6 rows E. Now continue in st st and striped pat as established until there are a total of 10 (10, 11, 12) color stripes or total length is approximately 10¼ (10¼, 11, 11¾)″ from beg or desired length to underarm. End with the 6th row of a color stripe.

ARMHOLE SHAPING: **Rows 1 and 2:** Keeping continuity of stripe pat as established, bind off 6 (6, 7, 8) sts at beg of each of next 2 rows. **Rows 3-6:** Bind off 3 sts at beg of each of the next 4 rows for all sizes. Dec one st at each end every other row 2 (2, 2, 3) times — 52 (56, 62, 70) sts. Continue to work even in stripe pat until length from first row of armhole shaping is 6½ (7, 7½, 8)″, ending with a wrong-side row.

NECK AND SHOULDER SHAPING: Bind off 11 (12, 13, 15) sts at beg of each of next 2 rows for shoulders. Place rem 30 (32, 36, 40) sts on a st holder for neck.

FRONT: Starting at lower edge with two strands of A, cast on 74 (78, 86, 98) sts. Work in k 1, p 1 ribbing for 1¾″, ending with a wrong-side row. Cut thread and attach B. **Row 1** (*right side*): K across first 31 (33, 37, 43) sts, increasing 5 sts evenly spaced; attach two strands of A (for cable) and k 12; attach two strands of B and k across last 31 (33, 37, 43) sts increasing 5 sts evenly spaced — 84 (88, 96, 108) sts. **Row 2:** With B p 36 (38, 42, 48) sts; with A p 12 for cable; with B p 36 (38, 42, 48) sts. **Rows 3 and 4:** Continue in st st and stripe pat as established, working center 12 A sts for cable. **Row 5** (*cable twist row*): With B k 36 (38, 42, 48) sts; with A *sl next 3 sts to a st holder and hold at front of work, k next 3 sts, k 3 sts from st holder, sl next 3 sts to a st holder and hold at back of work, k next 3 sts, k 3 sts from st holder* — **cable twist made;** with B k 36 (38, 42, 48) sts. Now proceed in stripe pat same as for Back, working center 12 A sts for cable. Work a cable twist row (Row 5) every 8th row. Continue to work Front same as for Back until length from first row of armhole shaping is 4½ (4½, 5, 5½)″, ending with a wrong-side row.

NECK SHAPING: **Row 1** (*right side*): K 18 (20, 22, 25) sts, place rem 38 (40, 44, 49) sts on a st holder to be worked later. Turn. **Row 2:** Bind off 4 (5, 5, 6) sts at beg of row for neck shaping, p next 14 (15, 17, 19) sts. **Rows 3 and 5:** K across. **Row 4:** Bind off 2 (2, 3, 3) sts at beg of row, p next 12 (13, 14, 16) sts. **Row 6:** Dec one st at beg of row, p next 11 (12, 13, 15) sts. Work even

until armhole is same length as Back. Bind off rem 11 (12, 13, 15) sts for shoulder. Leave center 20 (20, 22, 24) sts on st holder for neck. Slip the rem 18 (20, 22, 25) sts onto needle, attach thread at neck edge and work to correspond with opposite side, reversing shaping.

FINISHING: Pin each section to measurements on a padded surface, cover with a damp cloth and allow to dry; *do not press.*

NECKBAND: Sew the right shoulder seam. With the right side facing and two strands of A pick up and k 18 sts along right side edge of front of neck, k 20 (20, 22, 24) sts from front st holder, pick up and k 18 sts along other side edge of front of neck; k 30 (32, 36, 40) sts from back st holder — 86 (88, 94, 100) sts. Work in k 1, p 1 ribbing for 5 rows. Bind off loosely in ribbing. Sew the left shoulder seam.

ARMHOLE BANDS: Starting at underarm from right side with A, pick up and k 80 (86, 90, 96) sts along entire armhole edge. Work in k 1, p 1 ribbing for 5 rows. Bind off loosely in ribbing. Sew the side seams.

V-NECK
COWL
PULLOVER

TECHNIQUE: Crochet.

AVERAGE: For those with some experience in crochet. Directions are given for Size Petite (6-8). Changes for Sizes Small (10-12), Medium (14) and Large (16-18) are in parentheses.

MATERIALS: Berroco Dji Dji 77% wool, 23% viscose (50 gr. ball): 9 (10, 12, 13) balls of No. 8521 Sand Mist; crochet hook, Size J, OR ANY SIZE HOOK TO OBTAIN GAUGE BELOW.

GAUGE: In dc pattern — 5 sts = 2″; 4 rows = 3″. TO SAVE TIME, TAKE TIME TO CHECK GAUGE.

Note: The garment is designed to fit loosely.

Sizes:

Petite	Small	Medium	Large
(6-8)	(10-12)	(14)	(16-18)

Body Bust:

31½″	34″	36″	40″

FINISHED MEASUREMENTS:

Bust:

36″	39″	42″	45″

Width across Back at underarms:

18″	19½″	21″	22½″

Width across sleeves at upper arm:

15″	16″	16¾″	17¼″

STITCHES:

FRONT POST DC (FPDC): Yo, insert hook from front to back and again to front around stem of dc one row below, pull through a lp, (yo, pull through 2 lps) twice.

BACK POST DC (BPDC): Yo, insert hook from back to front and again to back around stem of dc one row below. Complete as for FPdc.

Note: After the first row, work the post sts around the posts of the row below.

DIRECTIONS:

BACK: Ch 46 (50, 54, 58) loosely. **Foundation Row:** Dc in 3rd ch from hook, dc in each ch to end — 45 (49, 53, 57) dc (counting turning ch). Ch 2, turn. **Row 1:** Skip first st, FPdc around stem of next st, * BPdc around stem of next st, FPdc around stem of next st; rep from *, end hdc in top of turning ch. Ch 2, turn. **Row 2:** Skip one st, BPdc around post of next st, * FPdc around post of next st, BPdc around post of next st; rep from *, end hdc in top of turning ch. Ch 2, turn. Rep Rows 1 and 2 twice more for Post Rib Pat. **Next Row:** Skip one st, dc in next st and each st to turning ch, dc in top of turning ch. Ch 2, turn. Rep the last row for dc pat. Work 32 (33, 34, 35) dc rows above Post Rib Band. Fasten off and turn. **Next Row:** Skip first 15 (16, 18, 19) sts, join yarn in next dc, ch 2, dc in next 14 (16, 16, 18) dc — 15 (17, 17, 19), (counting turning ch). Ch 2, turn. **Last Row:** Skip one st, dc in each st to turning ch, dc in turning ch. Fasten off.

FRONT: Work as for Back until 22 (23, 24, 25) rows above Post Rib Band.

V-NECK SHAPING: Row 1: Keeping to dc pat, work 20 (22, 24, 26) sts, dec one dc over next 2 sts (to dec: (yo, pull up a lp in next st, yo, draw through 2 lps) twice, yo and draw through remaining lps on hook) — 21 (23,

25, 27) sts. Working over these sts *only*, dec one st at neck edge every row 6 (7, 7, 8) times more — 15 (16, 18, 19) sts. Work until 32 (33, 34, 35) rows above Post Rib Band. Fasten off. On last full row, skip center st, join yarn in next st, ch 2, dec one st over next 2 sts, work to end — 21 (23, 25, 27) sts. Work to correspond to other side, reversing shaping.

SLEEVES: Ch 22 (24, 26, 28) sts. Beg with Foundation Row and work as for lower back on 21 (23, 25, 27) sts. Work until Post Rib Band has been completed. Change to dc pat and inc 11 sts evenly spaced across first row (to inc: work 2 dc in one dc) — 32 (34, 36, 38) sts. Work even for 4 dc rows. Inc one st each end of next row, then every 5th row twice more — 38 (40, 42, 44) sts. Work even until 16″ from beg, or 3″ less than desired length, inc one st at *end* of last row — 39 (41, 43, 45) sts. Change to Post Rib Pat. Work 6 rows even. Fasten off. Turn.

SADDLE-SHOULDER SHAPING: Skip first 16 (17, 18, 19) sts, join yarn in next st, ch 2. Keeping to

Post Rib Pat, work 5 sts more, hdc in next st. Ch 2, turn — 7 sts (counting turning ch). Work in pat over these sts *only* until saddle-side edge measures same as shoulder edge. Fasten off.

FINISHING: Sew or weave the side edges of the saddles to the front and back shoulders. Sew the back half of the top edge of the saddles to the sides of the center back piece. Sew the topside edges of the sleeves to the Front and Back. Sew or weave the side seams, beg 8″ above lower edge. Sew the sleeve seams.

COLLAR: Beg at lower right-front edge, ch 20. Beg with Foundation Row and work Post Rib Pat on 19 sts until side edge of collar is long enough to go around entire neck edge, beginning and ending at front point of V. Sew one side edge to the neck edge. Sew the Foundation Row edge to the left neck edge at the front of the work. Sew the other side to the right neck edge underneath the collar as shown. Work 1 row of sc along the side slits of the Front and Back and along the lower edges, working 3 sc in the corners, keeping the work flat.

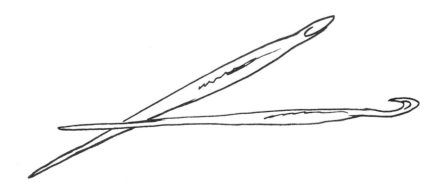

BUFFALO
PLAID
VEST

TECHNIQUE: Knitting.

CHALLENGING: For those with more experience in knitting.
Directions are for Size Small (8-10-12). Changes for Size Medium (14-16) are in parentheses.
Note: This is a loose fitting garment.

MATERIALS: Unger Fluffy 100% acrylic (1¾ oz. 50 gr. ball): 5 Black #461 (A) and 3 (4) Red #481 (B); knitting needles, one pair each No. 7 (8) and No. 9 (10), OR ANY SIZE NEEDLES TO OBTAIN GAUGE BELOW; 17 bobbins; 4 stitch holders; 6 buttons.

GAUGE: Stockinette stitch on Size 9 needles: 7 sts = 2″; 5 rows = 1″. Stockinette stitch on Size 10 needles: 10 Sts = 3″; 9 rows = 2″. TO SAVE TIME, TAKE TIME TO CHECK GAUGE.

FINISHED MEASUREMENTS:

Sizes:	Small	Medium
Bust:	38″	40¼″
Back width at underarm:		
	18½″	19¾″

Note: Wind 5 bobbins with 2 strands of A (called AA), wind 6 bobbins with 2 strands of B (called BB), wind 6 bobbins with 1 strand of A and 1 strand of B (called AB). Always twist yarns on the wrong side when changing color, to prevent holes. The entire vest is worked holding 2 strands of yarn together.

DIRECTIONS:

BACK: With smaller — 7 (8) needles and AA, cast on 65 sts. **Row 1** *(wrong side)*: P 1, * k 1, p 1; rep from * across. **Row 2:** K 1,

* p 1, k 1; rep from * across. Rep these 2 rows for rib pat for 2", end with Row 2. Change to larger needles — 9 (10) and stockinette stitch (st st). P 1 row, inc 1 st at center of work — 66 sts. **Beg Pat: Row 1:** With B bobbin k 6, (with AB bobbin k 6, with BB bobbin k 6) 5 times. **Row 2:** Keeping to colors as established, p across. Rep these 2 rows 3 times more — 8 rows to a Plaid Square. **Row 9:** With AB bobbin k 6, (with AA bobbin k 6, with AB bobbin k 6) 5 times. **Row 10:** Rep Row 2. Rep these 2 rows 3 times more. Rep these 16 rows for Check Pat. Work until 16" from beg, or desired length to underarm, end with a p row.

ARMHOLE SHAPING: Keeping to pat, bind off 6 sts beg next 2 rows — 54 sts. Work even until armholes measure 9 (10)", end with a p row.

SHOULDER SHAPING: Bind off 9 sts beg next 2 rows — 36 sts. Bind off rem sts for back of neck.

POCKET LININGS: Make 2. With larger needles and AA, cast on 16 sts. Beg with a p row and work in stockinette stitch (k 1 row, p 1 row). Work 21 rows. Sl sts to a holder.

LEFT FRONT: With smaller needles and AA, cast on 35 sts. Beg with Row 1 and work in rib as for lower back, end with Row

2. Change to larger needles and st st. P 1 row, inc 1 st at center of work — 36 sts. **Beg Pat: Row 1:** (With AB bobbin k 6, with BB bobbin k 6) 3 times. **Row 2:** Keeping to colors as established, p across. Rep these 2 rows 3 times more. **Row 9:** (With AA bobbin k 6, with AB bobbin k 6) 3 times. **Row 10:** Rep Row 2. Rep these 2 rows 3 times more. Rep these 16 rows for pat. Work until 2nd Row 6 is completed.

POCKET OPENING: Keeping to pat, work 10 sts, sl next 16 sts to a holder, behind holder k 16 sts from pocket lining holder, complete row. Work lining sts into pat and work even to underarm as Back, end at side edge.

ARMHOLE AND V-NECK SHAPING: Keeping to pat, bind off 6 sts for armhole, work to last 2 sts, k 2 tog (neck dec) — 29 sts. Keeping to pat, dec 1 st at neck edge every other row 20 times more — 9 sts. Work until armhole measures same as Back to shoulder, end at armhole edge. Bind off.

RIGHT FRONT: Work to correspond to Left Front, reversing shaping.

FINISHING: Sew the shoulder seams.

POCKET RIB BANDS: Sl 16 sts from holder to smaller needle. Inc 1 st at center of first row and

with AA work in k 1, p 1 rib for 1". Bind off these 17 sts in rib. Tack the pocket rib in place. Sew the pocket linings in place.

LEFT FRONT AND NECKBAND: Beg at center back neck edge, with smaller needles, AA and right side facing, pick up and k 131 sts to lower edge of Left Front. Work in k 1, p 1 rib for 5 rows. Bind off in rib. Make sure band lies flat. Mark for 6 buttons along straight edge of Left Front, placing lower button ½" from lower edge and last button 1" below start of V-neck, spacing others evenly between.

RIGHT FRONT AND NECKBAND: Work same as for Left Front for 2 rows. **Row 3:** Keeping to rib pat (work to opposite a button marker, bind off 2 sts) 6 times, complete row. **Row 4:** Keeping to pat, cast on 2 sts above bound off sts of previous row. Complete as for Left Front.

ARMHOLE BANDS: With smaller needles, AA, right side facing, beg at one underarm edge, pick up and k 109 sts around armhole to other edge. Work in k 1, p 1 rib for 5 rows. Bind off in rib. Sew side seams, matching pats. *Do not press.* Wet block. (Wet with cold water. Roll in a towel to remove excess water. Lay on a dry towel to measurements. Dry away from heat.)

· 4 ·

BAZAAR BEST-SELLERS

Have visions of a wonderful bazaar with profits soaring and good causes benefitting? It can come true when you sell those appealing little items that, once spotted, no one can live without. We have an array of easy, inexpensive crafts that guarantees to draw a crowd. There are irresistible stuffed animals, sachets, picnic baskets, potholders, refrigerator magnets — the list goes on and on! Oh, and don't forget our big bazaar raffle prize: a gorgeous granny square afghan!

BLUE/WHITE
POPCORN AFGHAN

(Afghan, shown on the previous page, is about 52" x 75", including border)

TECHNIQUE: Crochet.

AVERAGE: For those with some experience in crochet.

MATERIALS: Coats & Clark "Red Heart" 4-ply Hand Knitting Yarn (100% Virgin Orlon Acrylic Fiber, 3½ oz. skein): 7 skeins #1 White (A), 9 skeins #818 Blue Jewel (B), 6 skeins #848 Skipper Blue; (C); crochet hook, Size G, OR ANY SIZE HOOK WHICH WILL OBTAIN SQUARE MEASUREMENTS BELOW.

GAUGE: Center 6 rnds (A section) = 6" square. Each complete square = 12" square.
TO SAVE TIME, TAKE TIME TO CHECK GAUGE.

DIRECTIONS:

SQUARE *(Make 24):* Starting at center with A, ch 5. Join with sl st to form ring. **Rnd 1:** Ch 1, 8 sc in ring. Join with sl st to first sc. **Rnd 2:** Ch 3 (to count as 1 dc), * 4 dc in next sc, drop lp from hook, insert hook from front to back in top of first dc of 4-dc group just made and draw dropped lp through ch 1 tightly — **popcorn st made;** in next sc make dc, ch 3 for corner and dc; rep from * 2 more times; make popcorn st in next sc, dc in same st as joining of last rnd, ch 1. Join with hdc in top of ch-3 at beg of rnd to form last corner lp. **Rnd 3:** Ch 3, dc in corner lp just formed, make popcorn st in same st as joining hdc, * dc in top of next popcorn, popcorn st in next dc, in next corner ch-3 lp make 2 dc, ch 3 for corner and 2 dc; popcorn st in next dc; rep from * 2 more times; dc in next popcorn, popcorn st in next dc, 2 dc in same corner space where first dc was made, ch 1. Join with hdc in top of ch-3 to form corner lp. **Rnd 4:** Ch 3, dc in lp just formed, dc in same st as joining hdc, * (popcorn st in next dc, dc in top of popcorn st) 2 times; popcorn st in next dc, dc in next dc, in corner lp make 2 dc, ch 3, 2 dc, dc in next dc; rep from * 2 more times; ending with (popcorn st in next dc, dc in top of popcorn st) 2 times; popcorn st in next dc, dc in next dc, 2 dc in next corner lp, ch 1. Join with hdc to top of ch-3 to form corner lp — 12 popcorns. **Rnd 5:** Ch 3, dc in lp just formed, dc in same st as joining hdc, dc in each of next 2 dc, * dc in next popcorn, (popcorn in next dc, dc in next popcorn) 2 times; dc in each of next 3 dc, in next corner lp make 2 dc, ch 3 and 2 dc; dc in each of next 3 dc; rep from * 2 more times; dc in next popcorn, (popcorn in next dc, dc in next popcorn) 2 times; dc in each of next 3 dc, 2 dc in next corner lp, ch 1. Join with hdc in top of ch-3. **Rnd 6:** Ch 3, dc in lp just formed, dc in same st as joining hdc, dc in each of next 5 dc, * dc in next popcorn, popcorn in next dc, dc in next popcorn, dc in each of next 6 dc, in corner lp make 2 dc, ch 3, 2 dc; dc in next 6 dc; rep from * 2 more times; dc in next popcorn, popcorn in next dc, dc in next popcorn, dc in each of next 6 dc, 2 dc in next corner lp, ch 3. Join with sl st to top of ch-3. Cut yarn and fasten. **Rnd 7:** Attach B to center of any corner lp, ch 3, dc in same lp, * (ch 1, sk next dc, dc in next dc) 4 times; ch 1, sk next dc, dc in next popcorn (ch 1, sk next dc, dc in next dc) 4 times; ch 1, sk next dc, in corner lp make 2 dc, ch 3 and 2 dc; rep from * around, ending last rep with ch 1, sk next dc, 2 dc in corner lp, ch 1. Join with hdc to top of ch-3 to form last corner lp. **Rnd 8:** Ch 3, dc in lp just formed, dc in same st as joining hdc, * dc in each dc and in each ch-1 sp across to within next corner lp, in corner lp make 2 dc, ch 3 and 2 dc; rep from * around, ending last rep with 2 dc in next corner lp, ch 1. Join with hdc to top of ch-3 — 108 dc. **Rnd 9:** Ch 3, dc in lp just formed, ch 1, sk joining of last rnd, popcorn st in next dc, (ch 1, sk next dc, popcorn st in next dc) 12 times; * ch 1, sk next dc, in corner lp make 2 dc, ch 3 and 2 dc; (ch 1, sk next dc, popcorn in next dc) 13 times; rep from * 2 more times; ch 1, sk next dc, 2 dc in next corner lp, ch 1. Join with hdc to top of ch-3. **Rnd 10:**

Ch 3, dc in lp just formed, dc in same st as joining hdc, dc in next dc, * (dc in next ch-1 sp, dc in next popcorn) 13 times; dc in next sp, dc in each of next 2 dc, in corner lp make 2 dc, ch 3 and 2 dc; dc in each of next 2 dc; rep from * around, ending last rep with 2 dc in next corner lp, ch 3. Join with sl st to top of ch-3. Cut yarn and fasten. **Rnd 11:** Attach C to last lp made, ch 3, dc in same lp, ch 1, sk joining, dc in next dc, (ch 1, sk next dc, dc in next dc) 16 times; * ch 1, sk next dc, in corner lp make 2 dc, ch 3 and 2 dc; (ch 1, sk next dc, dc in next dc) 17 times; rep from * around, ending with ch 1, sk next dc, 2 dc in next corner lp, ch 1. Join with hdc to top of ch-3. **Rnd 12:** With C, work same as for Rnd 8 — 172 dc. Cut yarn and fasten.

FINISHING: Pin each square to measurements on a padded surface; cover with a damp cloth and allow to dry; do not press. With a darning needle and C, from right side, working through back lp only of each st, sew squares together from center of corner lp to center of next corner lp, matching sts. Join in 4 rows of 6 squares in each row.

BORDER — **Rnd 1:** With right side facing, attach C to any corner lp of Afghan, ch 3, dc in

same lp, * dc in each of next 43 dc to next lp before joining of squares, 2 sc in next (joined) lp on same square, sk joining of squares, make 2 dc in next lp on next square, dc in each dc on same square to within lp before next joining of square; continue to work 2 dc in each lp before and after each joining of squares and dc in each dc across to within next corner lp of Afghan; in corner lp of Afghan make 2 dc, ch 3 and 2 dc; rep from * 2 more times; work dc in each dc and 2 dc in each lp before and after joining of square across rem edge, ending with 2 dc in next corner lp, ch 1. Join with hdc to top of ch-3. **Rnd 2:** Ch 1, 2 sc in lp just formed, sc in each dc to within next corner lp of Afghan, * in corner lp make 2 sc, ch 3 and 2 sc; sc in each dc to within next corner lp; rep from * 2 more

times; 2 sc in next corner lp, ch 3. Join with sl st to first sc. Cut yarn and fasten. **Rnd 3:** Attach A to any corner lp of Afghan, ch 4, sk next sc, dc in next sc, * ch 1, work dc and ch 1 in every other sc across to within next corner lp, in corner lp make dc, ch 3 and dc; rep from * around, ending last rep with dc in same lp where yarn was attached, ch 1. Join with hdc in 3rd ch of ch-4. **Rnd 4:** Sl st in lp just formed, 4 dc in same st as joining hdc, sl st in next dc, * 4 *dc in next dc, sl st in next dc* — **shell made;** continue to work shells (of 4 dc in next dc, sl st in next dc) across to within 1 dc before next corner lp, 4 dc in next dc, sl st in center ch of corner lp, 4 dc in next dc, sl st in next dc; rep from * around ending last rep with 4 dc in last dc, sl st in first sl st of rnd. Cut yarn and fasten.

TIP / *Raffle Off An Afghan!*
....
Special raffles bring in big money, and you're sure to sell lots of $1 chances on an heirloom-quality afghan or bedspread. Assemble a group of your crafty friends to work square-by-square or strip-by-strip on a knit or crochet item. See our chapter on Afghans to find other perfect raffle prizes to star at your bazaar.

10 TIPS FOR
A SUCCESSFUL BAZAAR

1. Assign a leader for each booth you'll have. Appeal to everyone with a specialty and anyone who can devote time if not expertise.

2. Sell items that are inexpensive to make but usually overpriced in stores (like sachets or potholders—or even infantwear!)

3. Price all of your items at least 30%-50% less than they would cost in stores.

4. Work in groups at weekly workshops — it's more fun and you'll accomplish more.

5. Encourage donations of fabrics, yarns and trims from local businesses in exchange for publicity.

6. Concentrate on traditional best-sellers, such as ornaments, aprons, children's sweaters, cuddly toys.

7. Think of seasonal items — stockings, ornaments and toys for Christmas; jams, dried flower wreaths and arrangements for harvest bazaars.

8. Put someone in charge of publicity — get notices in the local paper; put up signs in advance of the sale.

9. The day of the bazaar, make sure every booth has a supply of change to start with. Provide a central spot where volunteers can go for help, supplies, money, etc.

10. If your bazaar runs longer than one day, have a strategy meeting after the first day to see how you're doing. Consolidate booths so none look empty; mark down items that aren't selling.

LACY CLOSET SACHET

TECHNIQUE: Sewing.

EASY: Achievable by anyone.

MATERIALS: Two squares of lace larger than hoop; lace ruffling; lace ribbon; satin ribbon; embroidery hoop (we used one 5″ in diameter); potpourri.

DIRECTIONS:

1. **CUT** lace ¼″ larger all around than the inner hoop, then cut a second piece ¾″ larger.

2. **LAP** the lace ruffling ¼″ over the edge of the smaller circle, open ends at center top. Stitch. Gather edge of the large circle to fit, pin it over the edges of lace ruffle.

3. **EDGESTITCH** the bottom half; insert the inner hoop; fill with potpourri. Using a zipper foot, stitch the top half, catching in a 1½″ ribbon loop at center top. Tighten the outer hoop over the lace. Pull the lace and satin ribbons through the screw opening and tie a bow.

FABRIC COVERED
PICNIC BASKETS

TECHNIQUE: Sewing.

EASY: Achievable by anyone.

MATERIALS: One mushroom basket or plastic container; fabric; package ⅜″-wide elastic; four Velcro® dots; carpet thread; glue.

DIRECTIONS:

HANDLE: Twist flexible twigs of vines (about 41″ long) together and tie 2″ from ends. Punch a pair of holes (about an inch apart and an inch below top edge) through the basket at each end. Thread carpet thread through the holes, wrap it around the twig ends (which lap about 2″ over outside of basket) and tie securely.

CUTLERY BASKET: 1. Cut a straight strip of fabric the measurement around the top edge of basket, plus ½″ x the height, plus

Love Those Freebies!

. . . .

Raid your local supermarket or vegetable stand to find the "freebies" that can be the makings of some lovely and useful items. Case in point: Those long, light wood mushroom baskets. They're the foundation of our pretty picnic baskets. (The easy-to-make scrap fabric covers are removable for washing.) And berry baskets make the perfect little cache pots for a gift plant; they can be prettied up with fabric leftovers as well.

4″. Seam the ends. **2.** Trace the bottom edge of the basket onto the fabric and cut, adding ¼″ for the seam. **3.** Pin the sides of the strip to the bottom piece, gathering in material at each end. Stitch. **4.** Slip the liner into the

basket and fold it over the top raw edge 2″, then down over top of basket *(see photo)*.
FOOD BASKET OUTER COVER: 1. Cut a strip twice the circumference of the basket x the height, plus 6″. Turn under top

edge ¼″ then 1½″. Stitch the hem, leaving an opening; then stitch again, ½″ away, for the casing. **2.** At bottom edge, turn under ¼″ then ½″ and stitch the hem (casing). **3.** Insert elastic in both casings to fit the basket. **4.** Make lining *(see Step 2)*. **5.** Center and glue Velcro dots to ends and sides of liner near the rim and inside the cover to match. Place on basket, insert the stuffing under the cover for a puffy look.

VIOLET BASKET: Use a 4″ square berry basket *(see Steps 1-3 above)* using the appropriate measurements and eliminating the lining, if you wish.

NAPKINS: Cut an 18″ square of fabric and pull threads around the edges for fringe.

POTPOURRI MINI-HEARTS

TECHNIQUE: Sewing.

EASY: Achievable by anyone.

MATERIALS: 6″ x 12″ fabric for each pillow; synthetic stuffing and (optional) potpourri; buttons with words on them.

DIRECTIONS:

(¼″ seams allowed):

1. **CUT** two No. 6 hearts (*see* FIG. 1) for pillow front and pillow back. See page 294 to enlarge pattern.

2. **STITCH** hearts, right sides together, leaving about 1½″ open. Turn; stuff and slip stitch closed. OR, cut the hearts with pinking shears and topstitch them wrong sides together, leaving an opening. Stuff. Topstitch the opening.

3. **TIE** ¼ yd. of ⅜″-wide ribbon into a bow. Stitch it to top of stuffed heart. Sew on buttons.

TIP

The Right "Stuff"

We've stuffed our mini-hearts with potpourri to make lovely sachets for drawers and closets. But you can also stuff them with batting or other fabric and sell them as handy pincushions.

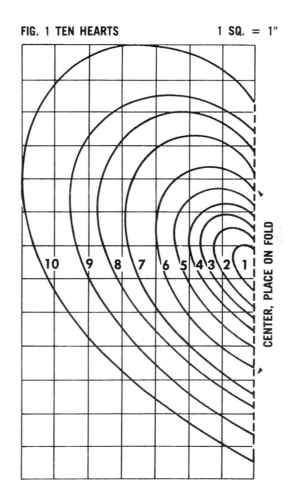

FIG. 1 TEN HEARTS   1 SQ. = 1″

10 9 8 7 6 5 4 3 2 1

CENTER, PLACE ON FOLD

HAND TRIMMED
BANDANNA NAPKINS

TECHNIQUE: Sewing and crocheting.

EASY: Achievable by anyone. Materials and directions are given for one napkin of each design. If you want to make more, multiply accordingly.

MATERIALS: A — One 18″ square of lavender gingham; floral print scraps to coordinate with the gingham; B — One 18″ square of linen-like fabric in natural or ecru; 2⅓ yds. 2″-wide lace trim in natural or ecru; C — One 23″ x 24″ blue neckerchief; J & P Coats—"Knit-Cro-Sheen," 1 (175-yd.) ball of #1; steel crochet hook size 7.

DIRECTIONS:

A — 1. Cut the floral print into 1¼″-wide strip and piece together to make a 40″ length for binding. Press under ¼″ along one long edge. **2.** Pin the flat edge to the right side of the gingham edges, right sides facing and raw edges matching. Turn under the overlapping end of the binding. Stitch a ¼″ seam all around. **3.** Fold the binding over the edge of the gingham to make the binding the same width on both sides. **4.** Pin and slip stitch down.

B — 1. Cut the lace trim into four 21″ lengths. **2.** Sew each to one edge of the linen by matching the right side of the finished edge of the lace to the right side of the fabric — allow 1¾″ of lace to extend at both ends. **3.** When all 4 pieces are sewn on, miter the corners. **4.** Press.

C — Using the "Knit-Cro-Sheen" and size 7 steel crochet hook, work the edging for the neckerchief. **Rnd 1:** Attach thread to any corner of the neckerchief, sc in same corner, * ch 4, work next sc ½″ away from last sc made; rep from * around. Join with sl st to first sc. **Rnd 2:** Sl st into first ch-4 lp, ch 5 (counts as 1 tr and ch 1), working in same ch-4 lp (tr, ch 1) 4 times — **first 5-tr shell made;** * sc in next ch-4 lp, *in next ch-4 lp (tr, ch 1) 5 times* — **5-tr shell made;** rep from * around. Join with sl st to 4th ch of beg ch-5. **Rnd 3:** * (Ch 3, sc in next ch-1 sp) 5 times; sc in next sc between shells; rep from * around. Join with sl st to first sc. Fasten.

POTHOLDERS

TECHNIQUE: Patchwork.

EASY: Achievable by anyone.

MATERIALS: Scraps of 12 different calico prints, half with white backgrounds, the other half with dark backgrounds — all of them as coordinated as possible; 1 small bag of quilt batting; 1 package cording in a coordinating color; a 10″ square of muslin for each potholder.

. . . .

DIRECTIONS:

SQUARE PATCHWORK POT-HOLDER: 1. Cut twelve 2″ squares, 1 of each of 12 prints. **2.** Arrange 4 strips of 4 squares alternating the light and dark —

2 beginning with light, 2 with dark. **3.** Stitch the squares together making ¼″ seams. **4.** Press. **5.** Stitch the strips together alternating the light and dark beginnings, making ¼″ seams. **6.** Press. **7.** Pin the cording to the right side along all edges with the raw edge of the cording matching the wrong edge of the potholder. **8.** Cut a piece of batting to match the potholder. **9.** Place the muslin on the right side of the potholder, then the batting. Pin together along the edges. **10.** Stitch all around following the stitching for the cording and leaving 4″ open. **11.** Trim the edges, turn, press, slip stitch opening closed. **12.** Hand quilt along the square seams.

STRIPED POTHOLDER: 1. Cut five 7″ x 1¾″ strips from calicos — 2 light and 3 dark. **2.** Stitch them together lengthwise, making ¼″ seams and alternating the dark and light, starting with the dark. **3.** Press. **4.** Cut four 1″ x 7¾″ strips of a 3rd light calico and sew 1 to each of the sides, centered, making ¼″ seams and mitering the corners. **5.** Press. **6.** Cut four 1″ x 8½″ strips of a 4th dark calico and repeat the previous step. **7.** Press. **8.** Finish with batting and muslin as for the previous potholder. **9.** Hand quilt along the strip seams to attach to the batting.

STUFFED CALICO CATS

TECHNIQUE: Sewing.

EASY: Achievable by anyone.

MATERIALS: Two 6″ x 8″ (small) or 14″ x 18″ (large) pieces of fabric*; ½ yd. (sm.) or ¾ yd. (lg.) piece of ribbon; synthetic stuffing.

*Note: To make your own patchwork fabric, seam strips (1″-2″ wide) of fabric side by side.

1. **To** enlarge pattern (FIG. 2) see instructions on page 294.

2. **For** large or small cat pattern in FIG. 2: Over the two fabric pieces (right sides together) pin the pattern and cut on the solid lines. Stitch ¼″ inside the cut lines leaving it open between the dots. Clip at the curves and corners.

3. **Turn** right side out and stuff.

4. **After** stuffing, turn in the open edges and slip stitch closed.

FIG. 2 STUFFED CALICO CATS   **1 SQ. = 1″.**

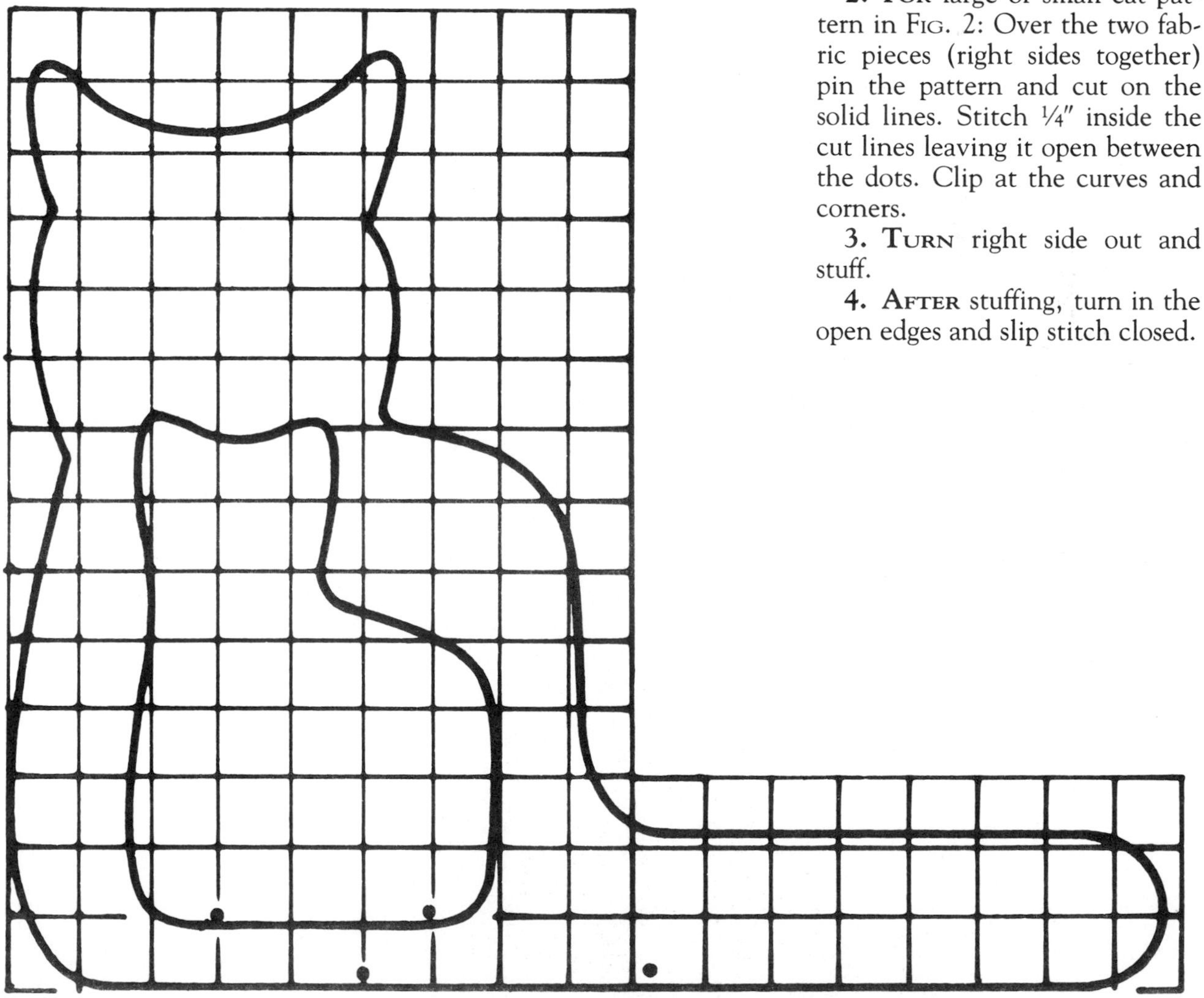

FRIDGE MAGNETS

TECHNIQUE: Needlepoint and embroidery.

EASY: Achievable by anyone.

MATERIALS: 10-mesh plastic canvas (10½" x 13½" sheet makes 9); scraps of tapestry or 3-strand Persian yarn; for baskets, 1 skein (24 yds.) each of off-white, copper and dark brown raffia; tapestry needle; ¼" self-stick magnet squares or magnet tape.

. . . .

DIRECTIONS:

Note: Do not cut canvas until all the embroidery is completed. Leave a few empty meshes between the baskets. Use 2 strands of Persian yarn in your needle.

1. BASKET OF FRUIT (FIG. 3): Work the fruit in the Continental Stitch (*see Stitch Guide on pages 298-299*). With off-white raffia, take a single, long straight

FIG. 3

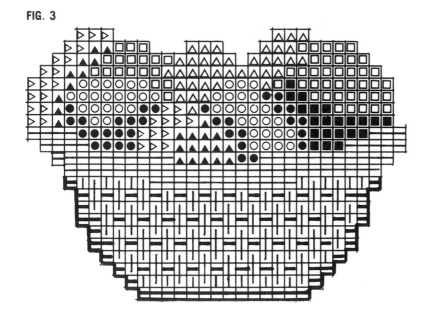

■ = DARK GREEN

□ = LIGHT GREEN

△ = YELLOW

◉ = DARK RED

◎ = RED

▷ = LIGHT ORANGE

▲ = ORANGE

━ = BROWN

──────── = WHITE

FIG. 4

stitch over each vertical row of the basket, then across the horizontal rows at the top edge of basket (*see* FIG. 3). With copper raffia, weave 4 or 5 rows horizontally through the off-white rows (*see photo*).

2. BASKET OF GRAPES (FIG. 4): Work the green and yellow Continental stitches. Fill the 3 empty spaces (*see* FIG. 4) with French Knots of light and dark purple. Add white Lazy Daisies. With copper raffia, make the short vertical stitches at top edge of basket and the rows of diagonal stitches below.

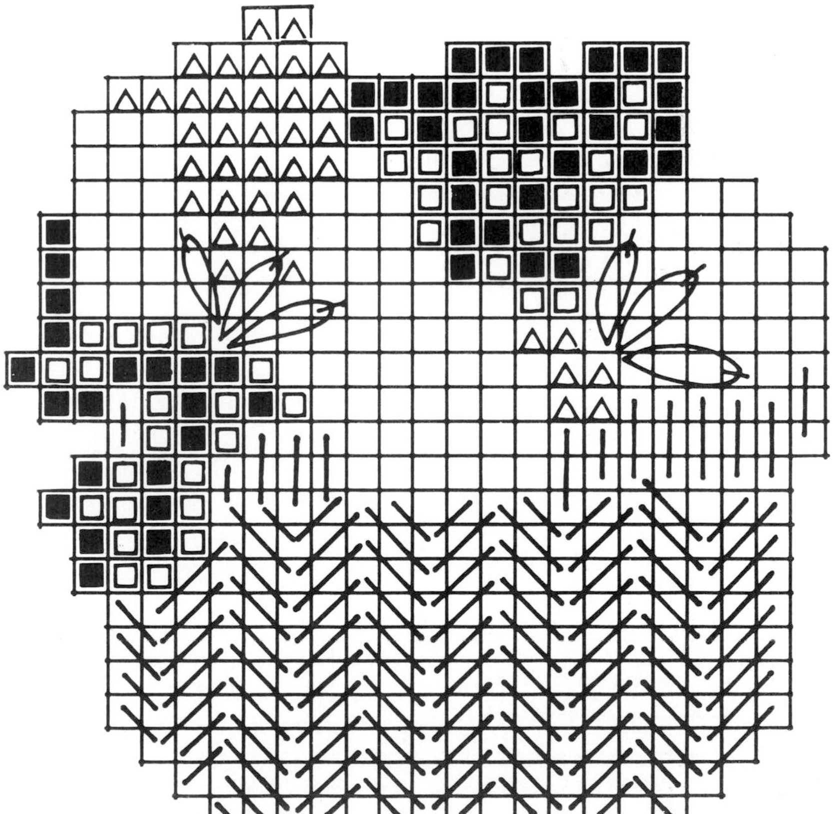

■ = DARK GREEN

□ = LIGHT GREEN

△ = YELLOW

⬭ = WHITE LAZY DAISY

□ = PURPLE FRENCH KNOTS

\/ = GOLD BROWN HERRINGBONE ST.

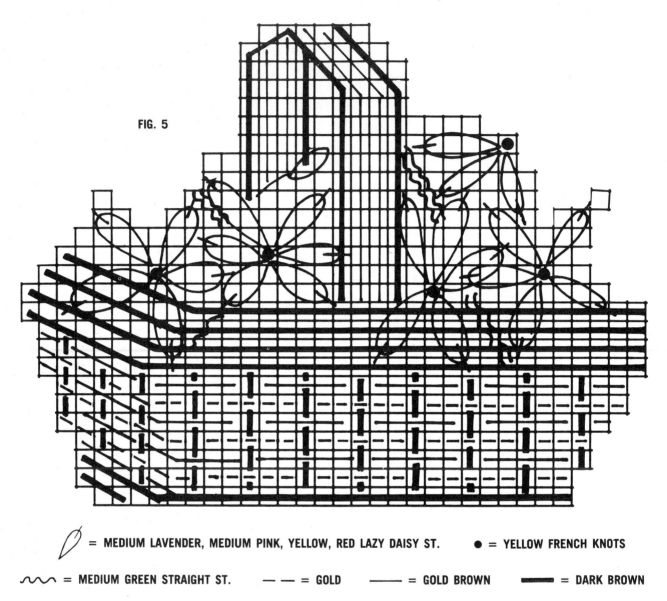

FIG. 5

✐ = MEDIUM LAVENDER, MEDIUM PINK, YELLOW, RED LAZY DAISY ST. ● = YELLOW FRENCH KNOTS

〰 = MEDIUM GREEN STRAIGHT ST. — — = GOLD ——— = GOLD BROWN ▬▬ = DARK BROWN

3. **BASKET OF FLOWERS (FIG. 5):** *Handle* — With the dark brown raffia, take long straight stitches to outline the handles; fill in with the copper. *Basket* — Make a long straight stitch over each vertical line (*see* FIG. 5), then across the long lines at base and brim. Alternating copper with off-white raffia, weave horizontal rows through the brown verticals (*see photo*). Work Lazy Daisy flowers (overlapping the brim) in assorted colors, yellow French Knot centers and scattered green straight-stitch leaves.

4. **FINISHING:** When all the embroideries are finished, cut out each item, leaving a smooth edge of one plastic thread outside each stitch. With yarn that matches the adjacent stitches, overcast these outer plastic threads, all around the design. Press the magnets on the wrong side.

SWITCHPLATE COVER

TECHNIQUE: Needlepoint.

EASY: Achievable by anyone.

MATERIALS: 7-mesh plastic canvas about 8″ square and other materials listed in needlepoint Fridge Magnets on page 108; double-face tape.

DIRECTIONS:
With 3 strands in your needle, work the flowers in Continental Stitch (*see* FIG. 6 *and Stitch Guide on pages 298-299*). Work the basket in raffia (*see photo and Step 3, Needlepoint Fridge Magnets, page 110*); fill in the empty canvas above the basket with long horizontal stitches of white raffia. For Finishing, see Step 4, *Fridge Magnets.* Affix to a switchplate with double-face tape.

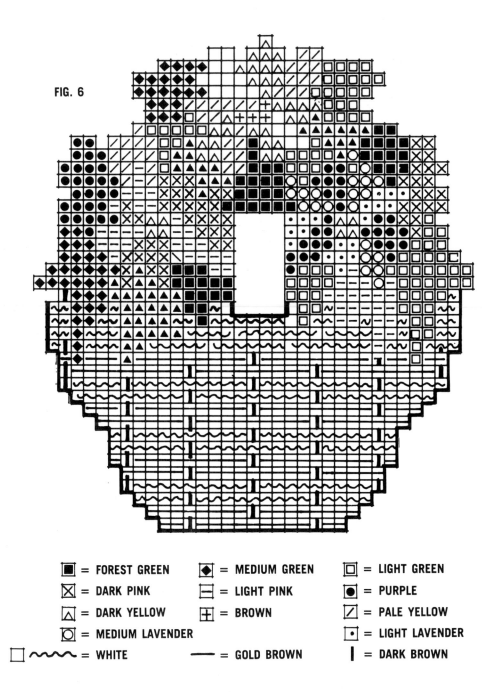

FIG. 6

■ = FOREST GREEN ◆ = MEDIUM GREEN ⊡ = LIGHT GREEN

⊠ = DARK PINK ⊟ = LIGHT PINK ⦿ = PURPLE

△ = DARK YELLOW ⊞ = BROWN ⧄ = PALE YELLOW

⊙ = MEDIUM LAVENDER ⊡ = LIGHT LAVENDER

□ ～～～ = WHITE — = GOLD BROWN | = DARK BROWN

SCENTED TEA COZY

TECHNIQUE: Sewing.

EASY: Achievable by anyone.

MATERIALS: Scrap fabric; ³⁄₈″-wide elastic; aromatic supermarket or garden-grown herbs, fragrant dried leaves or petals for stuffing.

DIRECTIONS:

Note: The cozy is a self-faced circle with elastic in a casing near the edge. Fabric ties draw the edges together behind the spout.

1. CUTTING: Take a tape measure from the top of the pot down, across the bottom and up to the top at the opposite side.

To this measurement, add 2″ (for seam and stuffing) and cut 2 fabric circles of that diameter.

2. COZY: Pin the circles, right sides together, and stitch ½″ from the edge, leaving about 3″ open. Turn right side out and press.

3. CASING: Make two rows of topstitching ½″ apart and parallel to the edge. (Ours starts ½″ from the edge, but place yours wherever it will work best on your pot, probably just before it swells outward.) Leave a 3″ gap in the casing seams just below the gap in the outside seam.

4. STUFFING: Pour herbal or petal stuffing into the gap, about

1″ deep. With a small safety pin, pull the elastic through the casing and tie the ends temporarily. Stitch the three gaps closed.

5. PULL the cozy over the teapot, letting the stuffing settle at the bottom, beneath the pot. Stitch the ends of elastic together, to fit the pot.

6. TIES: Cut a 1″ x 24″ fabric strip. Fold it in half lengthwise and press. Fold each raw edge in to meet center fold; press and edgestitch. Cut in half to make 2 ties. Lapping a raw end behind the casing, sew the strips to the cozy and tie them behind the spout *(see photo).*

GINGHAM DOG AND CALICO CAT SEWING BASKETS

FIG. 7 DOG/CAT BASKETS

1 SQ. = 1"

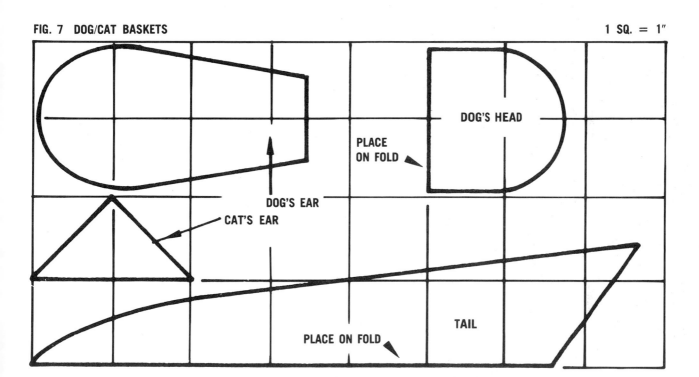

DOG'S HEAD

PLACE ON FOLD

DOG'S EAR

CAT'S EAR

TAIL

PLACE ON FOLD

TECHNIQUE: Sewing.

EASY: Achievable by anyone.

MATERIALS: Small straw baskets with lids; scraps of fabric, felt, ribbon and embroidery floss; synthetic stuffing; button for dog's nose; cardboard.

DIRECTIONS:

1. **TRACE** the lid to cardboard and cut it out, for foundation. Cut fabric 2½" larger all around than cardboard. See page 294 to enlarge patterns (FIG. 7) and cut fabric tails and head, felt ears.

2. **TAILS:** Fold the tail lengthwise, right sides together, and seam the long, raw edges. Stuff it lightly.

3. **SEW** a gathering row around the cut fabric edges. Draw up the gathering around a mound of stuffing. Insert the cardboard foundation and fasten the thread ends. Handsew the "cushion" edges to the lid, tucking in the raw end of tail. Sew the tail to the lid.

4. **HEADS:** Cut a 2½" round cardboard foundation and a 4" round of fabric for the Cat's head. Stuff (see Step 3) and sew it to the cushion. Make the Dog's head the same, but use the pattern (see FIG. 7) for the cardboard and cut the fabric ¾" larger all around.

5. **HEAD:** Sew the Cat's ears to the head, folding over the top corners. Edgestitch two layers of fabric for each Dog's ear and sew them to the head. Embroider the faces (see photo). Sew a button nose and running-stitch paws on the dog. Add bows.

·5·

AFGHANS

Snuggly-warm and oh, so comforting, an afghan offers knitters and crocheters one of the most satisfying projects ever. Many of our cozy throws are ideal take-along projects to be worked in individual squares, hexagons or strips for easy joining later. Some projects are so simple, you'll be able to complete them in practically no time (one secret is a giant Q crochet hook that uses three strands of yarn at a time). Others are so lovely, you may want to use them as wallhangings. Nothing beats an afghan as a very special present, and nothing is a more welcome addition to your home.

IRISH FISHERMAN AFGHAN AND PILLOWS

(Afghan and pillows are shown on the previous page.)

AFGHAN

(about 62″ x 70″, excluding fringe)

TECHNIQUE: Knitting.

AVERAGE: For those with some experience in knitting.

MATERIALS: Lion Brand Sayelle 4-Ply Knitting Worsted Weight Yarn, Art. 410, 16 (3.5 oz.) skeins of No. 99 Eggshell; knitting needles, one pair, No. 7 OR ANY SIZE NEEDLES TO OBTAIN GAUGE BELOW; double pointed needle (dp); darning needle; crochet hook for fringe.

GAUGE: Seed Stitch — 4½ sts = 1″; 6 rows = 1″.
Diamond Cable — 20 sts = 4″; 11 rows = 1″.
Ridge Cable — 44 sts = 9″; 6 rows = 1″. TO SAVE TIME, TAKE TIME TO CHECK GAUGE.

STITCHES: CABLE LEFT (CL) — Sl next 2 sts to dp needle hold to front of work, k next 2 sts, k 2 from dp needle.

CROSS 2 RIGHT (CR2R): Sl next st to dp needle, hold to back of work, k next 2 sts, p st from dp needle.

CROSS 2 LEFT (CR2L): Sl next 2 sts to dp needle, hold to front of work, p next st, k 2 from dp

needle.

Note: Afghan is worked in strips and sewn together afterward.

DIRECTIONS:

SEED STITCH STRIP: 12″ wide x 70″ long *(Make 2)*: Starting at narrow end, cast on 55 sts. **Row 1:** K 1, p 1 across, ending with k 1. Repeat Row 1 for 70″. Bind off loosely in k 1, p 1.

SINGLE DIAMOND CABLE: 4″ wide x 70″ long *(Make 2)*: Starting at narrow end, cast on 20 sts. **Row 1:** P 8, k 4, p 8. **Row 2:** K 8, p 4, k 8. **Row 3:** P 8, CL *(see STITCHES)*; p 8. **Row 4:** K 8, p 4, k 8. **Row 5:** P 7, CR2R, CR2L, p 7. **Row 6:** K 7, p 2, p 1, k 1, p 2, k 7. **Row 7:** P 6, CR2R, k 1, p 1, CR2L, p 6. **Row 8:** K 6, p 2, k 1, p 1, k 1, p 1, p 2, k 6. **Row 9:** P 5, CR2R, p 1, k 1, p 1, k 1, CR2L, p 5. **Row 10:** K 5, p 2, p 1, k 1, p 1, k 1, p 1, k 1, p 2, k 5. **Row 11:** P 4, CR2R, k 1, p 1, k 1, p 1, k 1, p 1, CR2L, p 4. **Row 12:** K 4, p 2, k 1, p 1, k 1, p 1, k 1, p 1, k 1, p 1, p 2, k 4. **Row 13:** P 3, CR2R, p 1, k 1, p 1, k 1, p 1, k 1, p 1, k 1, CR2L, p 3. **Row 14:** K 3, p 2, p 1, k 1, p 1, k 1, p 1, k 1, p 1, k 1, p 1, k 1, p 2, k 3.

Note: Row 14 is the center of the pattern (there will be 10 seed sts in the center). Once Row 14 is com-

pleted, work backwards repeating Rows 13-4 to complete single diamond cable pattern. When working Rows 13, 11, 9, 7, 5 cross the stitches in the opposite direction. For example, work Row 13 as follows: *P 1, CR2L, p 1, k 1, p 1, k 1, p 1, k 1, p 1, k 1, CR2R, p 3. Continue working single diamond cable pat until strip is 70″ long.*

CENTER DIAMOND CABLE STRIP: 12″ wide x 70″ long *(Make one)*: Starting at narrow end, cast on 60 sts and work three patterns of single diamond cable across as follows: **Row 1:** * P 8, k 4, p 8; repeat from * 2 more times. **Row 2:** * K 8, p 4, k 8; rep from * 2 more times. **Row 3:** * P 8, CL, p 8; rep from * 2 more times. Continue working three patterns of single diamond cable across until strip is 70″ long.

RIDGE CABLE STRIP: 9″ wide x 70″ long *(Make 2)*: Starting at narrow end, cast on 44 sts. **Row 1:** P 17, k 2, p 6, k 2, p 17. **Row 2** *(right side)*: K 17, p 2, k 6, p 2, k 17. **Row 3:** P 17, k 2, p 6, k 2, p 17. **Row 4** *(cable twist row)*: K 17, p 2, *sl next 3 sts onto dp needle and hold in back of work, k next 3 sts, k 3 sts from dp needle — cable twist made*; p 2, k 17. **Row 5:** Repeat Row 1. **Rows 6 and 8:** Repeat Row 2. **Row 7:** Repeat Row 3. * Repeat Rows 1-3 and 5-8 as before but work Row 4 for ridge row as follows: P 17 for ridge, p 2, cable twist, p 2, p 17 for ridge*. Repeat from * to * for ridge cable pattern until strip is 70″ long. Bind off on right side.

FINISHING: Pin each strip to measurements on a padded, flat surface; cover with a damp cloth and allow to dry; do not press.

ASSEMBLING: Starting at lower right corner of Afghan from right side, pin strips together as follows: Seed stitch, single diamond cable, ridge cable, center diamond cable, ridge cable, single diamond cable, seed stitch. With yarn and a darning needle from right side of work, sew strips together taking a small running stitch at the edge of one strip, then taking a small stitch at the edge of the corresponding strip.

Repeat working back and forth until entire seam is joined. Join other strips in same way.

FRINGE: Wind yarn 6 times around a 9″ square of cardboard; cut at one end, making 18″ strands. Hold 6 strands tog and fold in half to form a loop. With right side of Afghan facing, working along a narrow edge of Afghan, insert hook from back to front in corner st of seed st strip and draw loop through; draw loose ends through loop and pull tightly to form knot. Tie 6 strands in same way along narrow edge, evenly spacing 5 fringes on each seed st strip, 3 fringes on each single diamond cable strip, 5 fringes on each ridge cable strip and 9 fringes on center diamond cable strip. Repeat fringe directions along opposite edge of Afghan. Trim all fringes evenly.

RIDGE PATTERN PILLOW

. . . .

(14″ x 16″)

TECHNIQUE: Knitting.

EASY: Achievable by anyone.

MATERIALS: Lion Brand Bulky Knit 3-ply yarn, Art. 870, two 3.5 oz. skeins of No. 99 Eggshell; knitting needles, one pair No. 10, OR ANY SIZE NEEDLES TO OBTAIN GAUGE BELOW; 15″ x 17″ fabric for pillow back; synthetic stuffing or 14″ x 16″ pillow form; darning needle; crochet hook for fringe; double-pointed needle (dp).

GAUGE: Stockinette stitch — $3\frac{1}{2}$ sts = 1″; 4 rows = 1″. TO

SAVE TIME, TAKE TIME TO CHECK GAUGE.

. . . .

DIRECTIONS:

PILLOW TOP: Starting at the lower edge of the pillow top, cast on 56 sts and work in ridge pattern as follows: **Row 1:** K across. **Row 2:** P across. **Row 3:** K across. **Row 4:** P across. **Row 5:** P across to form ridge. Rep Rows 1-5 until the piece measures 14" in length. Bind off loosely.

BLOCKING, PILLOW AND FRINGE: See *Seed Stitch Pillow*, below.

SEED STITCH PILLOW

. . . .

(14" x 16")

TECHNIQUE: Knitting.

EASY: Achievable by anyone.

MATERIALS: Lion Brand Bulky Knit 3-ply yarn, Art. 870, two 3.5 oz. skeins of No. 99 Eggshell; knitting needles, one pair No. 10, OR ANY SIZE NEEDLES TO OBTAIN GAUGE BELOW; 15" x 17" fabric for pillow back; synthetic stuffing or 14" x 16" pillow form; darning needle; crochet hook for fringe; double-pointed needle (dp).

GAUGE: Seed Stitch — 3½ sts = 1"; 5 rows = 1". TO SAVE TIME, TAKE TIME TO CHECK GAUGE.

. . . .

DIRECTIONS:

PILLOW TOP: Starting at the lower edge of the pillow top, cast on 57 sts and work in seed st as follows: **Row 1:** K 1, p 1 across, ending with k 1. Repeat Row 1 until the piece measures 14". Bind off loosely in k 1, p 1.

BLOCKING: Pin the knitted pillow top to measurements on a padded surface, cover with a damp cloth and allow to dry; *do not press.*

PILLOW: Pin the pillow top to a 15" x 17" fabric pillow back, right sides together, with knitted edges ½" from fabric edges. Stitch just inside the knitted edges, around three sides and four corners. Turn right side out, fill the case with stuffing and slip stitch the opening closed.

FRINGE: Wind yarn 4 times around a 5" square of cardboard. Cut at one edge, making 10" strands. Continue to cut strands as needed. Hold 4 strands together and fold in half to form a loop. Insert the hook from back to front in the corner st at a side edge of the pillow top and draw the loop through; draw the loose ends through the loop and pull up tightly to form a knot. Tie 4 strands in the same manner every other st along the side edge of the pillow top. Repeat for the opposite side edge. Trim even.

FRINGED BLUE AND WHITE AFGHAN

(about 41" x 55", plus fringe)

TECHNIQUE: Crochet.

AVERAGE: For those with some experience in crochet.

MATERIALS: Lion Brand Sayelle (3.5 oz. skein): 6 skeins each of No. 109 Colonial Blue (A) and No. 99 Eggshell (B); afghan hook, No. 10; crochet hook, Size H, OR ANY SIZE HOOK TO OBTAIN GAUGE BELOW; tapestry needle.

GAUGE: In Afghan St — 8 sts = 2"; 6 pairs of rows (12 rows) = 2"; TO SAVE TIME, TAKE TIME TO CHECK GAUGE.

Note: The afghan is made up of 5 strips of 7 blocks each, which are sewn together afterwards.

. . . .

DIRECTIONS:

STRIP 1: Block 1: With afghan hook and A, ch 31. **Row 1:** Retaining all lps on hook, draw up a lp in 2nd ch from hook and in each ch across (*see* FIG. 1, *Step 1*) — 31 lps. *There are the same number of lps on hook as there were ch sts. Drop A but do not fasten off.* **Row 2:** With B, yo and draw through 1 lp, * yarn over and draw through 2 lps; rep from * across (*see* FIG. 1, *Step 2*). **Row 3:** Retaining all lps on hook, with B, draw up a lp in 2nd vertical bar and in each vertical bar across to within last vertical bar (*see* FIG. 1, *Step 3*): insert hook

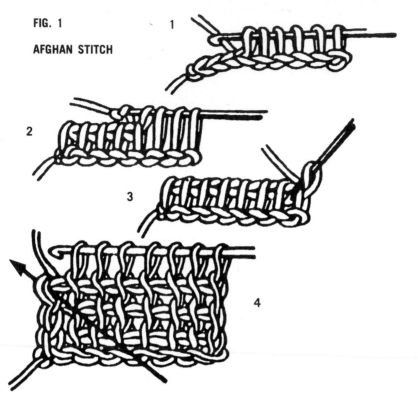

FIG. 1

AFGHAN STITCH

1

2

3

4

Row 1: Retaining all lps on hook, draw up a lp in 2nd ch from hook and in each ch across — 31 lps. Continue working same as Block 2 of Strip 1 using B *only* for a total of 22 pairs of rows (44 rows). **Block 2:** Repeat Rows 2-5 as for Block 1 of Strip 1, starting with A, for a total of 22 pairs of rows (44 rows). Continue to work Blocks 1 and 2 of Strip 2 alternately until a total of 7 blocks has been completed, ending with Block 1. Fasten off.

ASSEMBLING: With the right side facing and A, pin and sew Strips 1-5 together in consecutive order, matching sts along the side edges, with the top and bottom edges even.

OUTER EDGING: With the right side facing, using one strand each of A and B held together and Size H hook, work 1 sc in each st around the edges of the Afghan, making 3 sc in each corner st.

FRINGE: Cut eight 24″ lengths of each color. Hold 16 strands tog (eight of each color) and knot in every 4th st at the bottom edge of the Afghan. Repeat at the top edge of the Afghan. Trim evenly.

through last vertical bar and the st directly behind it (*see arrow on Step* 4) and draw up a lp. *There are the same number of lps as on Row 1.* Drop B *but do not* fasten off. **Row 4:** With A, rep Row 2. **Row 5:** With A, rep Row 3. Repeat Rows 2-5 for a total of 22 pairs of rows (44 rows). Cut B *only.* **Block 2:** With A *only,* rep

Rows 4 and 5 for a total of 22 pairs of rows (44 rows). Continue to work Blocks 1 and 2 alternately until a total of 7 blocks has been completed, ending with Block 1. **Last Row:** Sl st in each vertical bar across. Fasten off.

STRIPS 3 AND 5: Work the same as for Strip 1.

STRIPS 2 AND 4: Block 1: With afghan hook and B, ch 31.

PUFF-STITCH GRANNY SQUARE AFGHAN

(about 57" x 63½")

TECHNIQUE: Crochet.

AVERAGE: For those with some experience in crochet.

MATERIALS: Coats & Clark Red Heart® 4-ply Hand Knitting Yarn (3.5 oz. skein): 10½ ozs. of No. 412 Silver and 7 ozs. each of No. 730 Grenadine, No. 737 Pink, No. 720 Young Pink, No. 755 Pale Rose, No. 739 Ultra Pink, No. 261 Maize, No. 251 Vibrant Orange, No. 230 Yellow, No. 245 Orange, No. 246 Sea Coral, No. 679 Nile Green, No. 516 Bright Turquoise, No. 818 Blue Jewel, No. 810 Yale Blue, No. 814 Robin Blue, No. 603 Light Gold, No. 591 Cassis, No. 575 Orchid, No. 593 Ultra Violet and No. 584 Lavender; crochet hook, Size I, OR ANY SIZE HOOK TO OBTAIN GAUGE BELOW; tapestry needle.

GAUGE: Each Motif = 6½" from point to point. TO SAVE TIME, TAKE TIME TO CHECK GAUGE.

Note: The Afghan is made up of 71 Motifs which are sewn together afterwards.

. . . .

DIRECTIONS:

MOTIF A *(Make 24):* Starting at center of motif with Pale Rose, ch 6. Join with sl st to form ring. **Rnd 1:** Ch 1, 12 sc in ring. Join with sl st to ch-1. **Rnd 2:** *Yo, insert hook in first sc and draw up a lp, (yo, insert hook in same sc and draw up a lp) 2 times, yo and draw through all 7 lps on hook —* **starting puff st made;** *ch 3, sk 1 sc, (yo, insert hook in next st and draw*

·123

up a lp) 3 times, yo and draw through all 7 lps on hook — **puff st made;** rep from * 4 times more — 6 puff sts. Ch 3, insert hook in top of first puff st, yo with Ultra Pink and draw through puff st and lp on hook. Cut Pale Rose. *Hereafter change colors as stated above.* **Rnd 3:** * Puff st in next ch-3 sp, ch 4; rep from * around. Change to Young Pink. **Rnd 4:** * In same ch-4 sp (work puff st, ch 3, puff st), ch 1, dc in top of next puff st, ch 1; rep from * around. Change to Grenadine. **Rnd 5:** * In same ch-3 sp (work puff st, ch 3, puff st), ch 1, dc in ch-1 sp, dc in next dc, dc in next ch-1 sp, ch 1; rep from * around. Change to Pink. **Rnd 6:** * In same ch-3 sp (work puff st, ch 3, puff st), ch 1, dc in next ch-1 sp, dc in each of next 3 dc, dc in next ch-1 sp, ch 1; rep from * around. Change to Silver.

Motif Edging: * In same ch-3 sp (work 2 sc, ch 1, 2 sc), sc in next ch-1 sp, sc in each of next 5 dc. Sc in next ch-1 sp; rep from * around. Join with sl st to first sc. Fasten off.

Motif B *(Make 23):* Work same as for Motif A, using Maize for Rnds 1 and 2, Vibrant Orange for Rnd 3, Yellow for Rnd 4, Orange for Rnd 5 and Sea Coral for Rnd 6.

Motif C *(Make 23):* Work same as for Motif A, using Nile Green for Rnds 1 and 2, Bright Turquoise for Rnd 3, Blue Jewel

Fig. 2 — TOP / BOTTOM

for Rnd 4, Yale Blue for Rnd 5 and Robin Blue for Rnd 6.

Motif D *(Make 24):* Work same as for Motif A, using Light Gold for Rnds 1 and 2, Cassis for Rnd 3, Orchid for Rnd 4, Ultra Violet for Rnd 5 and Lavender for Rnd 6.

Blocking: Pin each motif to measurements on a padded sur-face, cover with a damp cloth and allow to dry; *do not press.*

Assembling *(see* Fig. 2): With right sides facing you and Silver, pin and sew motifs together following Fig. 2, from the center of a corner to the center of the next corner, matching sts and working through the back lps *only.*

QUEEN ANNE'S LACE AFGHAN AND PILLOW

AFGHAN

. . . .

(about 45" x 59")

TECHNIQUE: Crochet and embroidery.

AVERAGE: For those with some experience in crochet and embroidery.

MATERIALS *(for both Afghan and Pillow):*
Caron Wintuk (3½ oz. skein): 12 skeins of No. 3009 Black (A), 1 skein of No. 3065 Christmas Green (C); Caron Sayelle (3½ oz. skein): 2 skeins each of No. 3036 Baby Green (B) and No. 1001 White (D); crochet hook, No. 9, OR ANY SIZE HOOK TO OBTAIN GAUGE BELOW; large

ACTUAL-SIZE PATTERN

embroidery or darning needle; tailor's chalk or cloth marker; 12" knife-edge pillow form. *Note: All yarns used for crocheting and embroidering the Afghan and Pillow are 4-ply orlon yarn.*

GAUGE: 18 sc = 5"; 4 rows = 1". TO SAVE TIME, TAKE TIME TO CHECK GAUGE.

DIRECTIONS:

SQUARE *(Make 12):* Starting at lower edge of Square with A, ch 50. **Row 1** *(right side):* Sc in 2nd ch from hook, sc in each ch across — 49 sc. Ch 1, turn. **Row 2:** Sc in each sc across. Ch 1, turn. Rep Row 2 until total length is 13" from beg. Fasten off.

SQUARE EDGING: **Rnd 1:** With right side facing you, join D to right corner sc and work *(ch 4, dc, ch 2, dc, ch 1, dc) into the same sc* — **first corner made;** * sk next 2 sc, (dc, ch 1, dc) into the next st; rep from * across to within the next corner sc and work *(dc, ch 1, dc, ch 2, dc, ch 1, dc) into the same sc* — **another corner made;** now continuing along side edge of Square ** sk next 2 rows, (dc, ch 1, dc) into the end of next row; rep from ** across to within the next

corner st of this side and work (dc, ch 1, dc, ch 2, dc, ch 1, dc) into this st ***; rep from * to *** around. Join with sl st to 3rd ch of beg ch-4. Fasten off.

EMBROIDERY: Trace the shaded full-size pattern on a 13" square of thin cardboard or brown paper, with centers *(see arrows)* matching. With a craft knife or single-edge razor blade, cut out the leaves, florets and central stems, to make a stencil.

Place the stencil on a crocheted square, edges even. With tailor's chalk or a cloth marker, trace the openings. Remove the stencil and work clusters of white French Knots *(see Stitch Guide, pages 298-299)* in each floret. Fill in the leaves with a green straight stitch. Chalk the rest of the stems *(see photo).* Work the stems in green stem stitch. Work 4 white French Knots at the end of the lowest sprig *(see photo).*

FINISHING: Pin each square to measurements (13" square) on a padded, flat surface, cover with a damp cloth and allow to dry; *do not press.*

ASSEMBLING: Join 4 rows of 3 squares each. With the right side of the squares facing you, sew the

squares together with D, from the center of a corner to the center of the next corner, matching sts and working through the back lps *only.*

AFGHAN EDGING: **Rnd 1:** With the right side facing you, work (dc, ch 1, dc) with D into each ch-sp around. Join. Fasten off.

PILLOW

(13" square)

DIRECTIONS:

MAKE 2 squares as for the Afghan but *do not* edge at this point. Work the embroidered design on *only* the front square for the pillow front.

ASSEMBLING: With the wrong sides of the squares together, sc around 3 sides, working through both thicknesses and *only* the front square of the 4th side (for Pillow opening), making 3 sc in each corner st. Insert the pillow form. With a tapestry needle, slip stitch the 4th side closed.

PILLOW EDGING: **Rnd 1:** Work same as Rnd 1 of edging for each square. **Rnd 2:** Work same as Rnd 1 of edging for Afghan. Fasten off.

STAINED GLASS AFGHAN

(48" x 62")

TECHNIQUE: Crochet.

CHALLENGING: For those with more experience in crochet.

MATERIALS: Reynolds Reynelle (4 oz. skein): 7 skeins Black (A), 2 skeins Clay (B), 1 skein each Raspberry (C), Purple (D), Royal (E), Turquoise #3 (F), Gold (G), Cardinal (H), Kelly (I); afghan hook, Size I, OR ANY SIZE HOOK TO OBTAIN GAUGE BELOW; crochet hook Size H; tapestry needle, Size 14, for embroidery; yarn bobbins as desired.

GAUGE: Afghan St: 4 upright bars = 1"; 3 rows = 1". TO SAVE TIME, TAKE TIME TO CHECK GAUGE.

Note: Wind colors on yarn bobbins, or cut into long working strands, as needed. Keep bobbins on the wrong side of the work. To change colors at the beginning of a row, work off the last 2 lps of the previous row with the next color. To change colors in the middle of a row, draw up lp in the next color in the next upright bar. Twist colors as necessary to prevent holes. Black outlines are embroidered later in chain st.

AFGHAN ST: With afghan hook, ch required number of sts. **Row 1:** Draw up a lp in 2nd ch from hook and each ch across; work off lps as follows: yo, thru 1 lp on hook, * yo, thru 2 lps on hook; rep from * across — 1 lp on hook, counts as first lp on next row. **Row 2:** Sk first upright bar at edge, draw up a lp in next upright bar and each upright bar across; work off lps as for Row 1. Rep Row 2 for afghan st. *Note: The number of lps drawn up on each row will be the same as the number of sts in starting ch. Each upright bar, formed by lp, counts as one st.*

DIRECTIONS:

PANEL *(Make 3)*: Starting at lower edge, with the afghan hook and A, ch 33. Work Row 1 of afghan st, changing to D at end — 33 upright bars. **Row 2:** With D, draw up a lp in next 5 upright bars (6 D lps on hook); join C, with C draw up a lp in next 21 upright bars; join D bobbin, with D, draw up a lp in last 6 upright bars; work off lps in colors as established, twisting colors once when changing, to prevent holes. Follow chart for afghan st panel, Rows 3-43; turn chart upside down and work Rows 44 thru 85. With A, sl st in each upright bar on last row. Fasten off.

EMBROIDERY: With the tapestry needle and A, outline each color section in chain st. Following the chart, work additional rows of chain st as indicated by the broken lines.

PANEL EDGING: Rnd 1: Right side facing, with the crochet hook, join A in a corner of panel, ch 1, 3 sc in corner, work an odd number of sc to opposite corner; rep from * around, working same number of sc on corresponding sides and spacing sts to keep edge flat; join with sl st in first sc. **Rnd 2:** Sl st to center st at corner, ch 6, dc in same st *(first corner)*; ch 1, sk 1 sc, * dc in next sc, ch 1, sk 1 sc; rep from * to next corner st, (dc, ch 3, dc) in corner st, ch 1, sk 1 sc; rep from * around, end ch 1, sk 1 sc, join in 3rd ch of ch-6. **Rnd 3:** Working 5 sc in each corner ch-3 sp, sc in each dc and ch-1 sp around; join. Fasten off.

LONG SIDE EDGING: Row 1: Wrong side facing, join C in first sc after center sc at corner on a long edge; in same sc as joining work sc and dc *(group made)*, * sk 1 sc, sc and dc in next sc; rep from * across long edge, end in sc before corner sc. Fasten off. Turn. **Row 2** *(right side)*: Join A in corner sc before first group, ch 1, sc in same sc, * ch 1, sc between next 2 groups; rep from * across, end ch 1, sc in corner after last group. **Row 3:** Ch 4; turn, sk first ch-1 sp, dc in next sc, * ch 1, sk next ch-1 sp, dc in next sc; rep from * across. **Row 4:** Ch 1, turn, sc in each dc and ch-1 sp across, sc around ch-4, sc in 3rd ch of ch-4. Fasten off. Turn. **Row 5:** With D, sk first sc, join in next sc, work as for Row 1 to sc before last sc. Fasten off. Turn. **Row 6:** Beg in st before first group and ending in st after last group, work as for Row 2. **Rows 7-8:** Rep Rows 3 and 4. **Row 9:** With F, rep Row 5. **Rows 10-12:** Rep Rows 6-8. Fasten off. Work the opposite long edge to correspond.

TOP EDGING: At the upper edge of the panel, work as for long side edging, working Row 1 with color I, Row 5 with E, Row

·129

STAINED GLASS AFGHAN ST PANEL

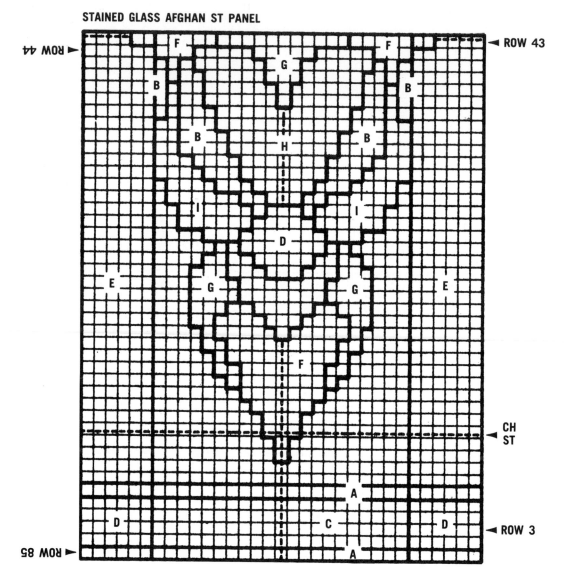

EACH SQ. = 1 UPRIGHT BAR

NOTE: BROKEN LINES ARE CH ST.

EMBROIDERED AFTER PANEL IS COMPLETED

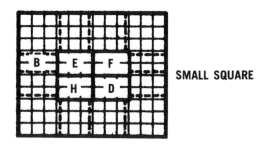

SMALL SQUARE

9 with H. Work the lower edging the same as the top edging.

SMALL SQUARE *(Make 12):* With the afghan hook and B, ch 12. Follow the chart for the small square for 10 rows. Fasten off.

EMBROIDERY: With the tapestry needle and A, outline each color and follow the broken lines in chain st.

SMALL SQUARE EDGING: With A, rep Rnd 1 of the panel edging. **Rnd 2:** Sc in each sc, working 3 sc in center st at each corner; join. Fasten off. With A, sew or sl st squares into corners between the long and short edgings on the panel.

FINISHING: Block the panels, being careful to block the corners at right angles. With A, sew or sl st the long edges of the panels together.

SIDE EDGING: **Row 1:** Right side facing, with the crochet hook, join A in the right corner on one long side of the Afghan, ch 4, sk next st, dc in next st, *ch 1, sk next st, dc in next st; rep from * across. **Row 2:** Rep Row 4 of the long side edging. Rep Rows 5-8 of the long side edging 3 times, working first Row 5 with D, 2nd Row 5 with E, and 3rd Row 5 with H. Fasten off. Work the same edging along the opposite edge of the Afghan; *do not* fasten off after 3rd rep.

OUTER EDING: Work the same as panel edging Rnds 1 thru 3 around the entire Afghan. **Rnd 4:** Sl st in each sc around; join. **Rnd 5:** * Sc in next st, ch 2, sk 3 sts, (dc, ch 3, tr, ch 3, dc) in next st, ch 2, sk 3 sts; rep from * around; join. **Rnd 6:** * 3 sc in next ch-2 sp, 4 sc in next ch-3 sp; ch 3, sl st in 3rd ch from hook for picot, ch 5, sl st in 5th ch from hook, ch 3, sl st in 3rd ch from hook; 4 sc in next ch-3 sp, 3 sc in next ch-2 sp; rep from * around; join. Fasten off. Block the edging.

SCHOOLHOUSE AFGHAN
AND PILLOWS

AFGHAN

(52" x 68", including border)

TECHNIQUE: Crochet and appliqué.

AVERAGE: For those with some experience in crochet and appliqué.

MATERIALS: 4-ply Sayelle yarn (3.5 oz. skein) *For Afghan:* 10 skeins of Off-White (A), 4 skeins of Medium Blue (B) and 1 skein of Light Rose (C); *For Each Pillow:* 2 skeins of Off-White (A), 2 ozs. of Medium Blue (B) and ½ oz. of Light Rose (C); 12" pillow form; *For Embroidery:* Leftover yarns in rust (flowerpots), light green (leaves) and pink and red (flowers); *For Each Appliquéd House* (we used calico in three different color combinations — #1, #2 and #3): 9"-square fabric for house, 3½" x 7" for roof, 1½" x 9" for grass and 14" x 1¼" for trim OR 44/45" fabric, ¼ yd. makes four houses, ⅛ yd. makes 8 roofs or 12 grass or 9 trims; crochet hook, Size I, OR ANY SIZE HOOK TO OBTAIN GAUGE BELOW.

GAUGE: 14 sc = 4"; 4 rows = 1". Each square = 13" x 13" (excluding border). TO SAVE TIME, TAKE TIME TO CHECK GAUGE.

DIRECTIONS:

1. SQUARE *(Make 12 for the Afghan)*: With A, ch 46. **Row 1** *(right side)*: Sc in 2nd ch from hook, sc in each ch across — 45 sc. Ch 1, turn. **Row 2:** Sc in each sc across. Ch 1, turn. Work even in sc until total length is 13" from beg. Fasten off. To complete square, sc along side edges *only*, with right side up as follows: * Sc in first 5 rows, sk next row; rep from * across. Fasten off.

2. BLOCKING: Steam lightly with an iron to 13"-square but *do not* place the iron directly on the work. Let it dry thoroughly.

3. APPLIQUÉS *(Make 12 for the Afghan and one for each Pillow)*: **Pattern:** Draw an 8¼" x 8¾" rectangle (*see* FIG. 3). Cut away a 2" x 3¼" triangle (*see actual size,* FIG. 4) at each upper corner (*see* FIG. 3) to leave a cutting pattern for the House. On it, draw the left and lower edges of the roof and the broken lines only for the three windows (*these broken lines are all ¼" from the solid cutting lines; see* FIG. 3). Trace a separate cutting pattern for the Roof. **Cutting:** For each house appliqué, cut one House, one Roof (*see* FIG. 3), one 1½" x 8¾" Grass, two 1½"-square Chimneys and two 1¼"-wide Trim strips, one 9" and one 5" long. **House:** Pin a Roof to each House, with the top and right

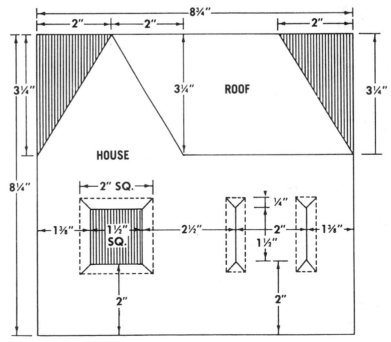

FIG. 3 CUT AWAY SHADED PARTS

edges even; edgestitch. Trace, then topstitch along broken window lines (the turn-under fold). **Trim:** Turn under ¼″ at long edges of Trim strips and press. Sew the shorter strip along the roof edge and the longer one from top to bottom, folding a dart at the turn at the roof bottom edge (*see photo*). Topstitch or slip stitch. **Assembling:** Seam Grass to the lower edge of the house; press the seam open. Turn under ¼″ at all house edges and at the three edges of each Chimney. Press. Lap the house ¼″ over the raw edge of each Chimney and slip stitch. With small scissors, carefully cut window openings on the solid lines in FIG. 3. **Appliqué:** Slip stitch the house to the crocheted square. Turn under the window edges on broken (topstitched) lines; slip stitch to the crocheted square. **Flowers:** Straight-stitch the flowerpot and the stems (*see photo*); French Knot a flower at the end of each stem (*see Stitch Guide, pages 298-299*).

4. SQUARE EDGING: With the right side of the square up, sc in each st around, working (sc, ch 1, sc) in each corner-st, in the following color sequence: 1 rnd B, 1 rnd C, 3 rnds B. Fasten off.

5. JOINING SQUARES: Join 4 squares together in a vertical

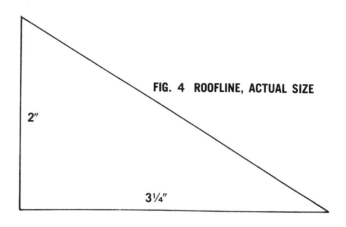

FIG. 4 ROOFLINE, ACTUAL SIZE

2″

3¼″

row, with House #1 appliquéd on them, working as follows: With appliquéd side up, sew the squares together, using B, from the center of a corner to the center of the next corner, matching sts and working through the front loops *only*. Repeat to make two other vertical rows with Houses #2 and #3 appliquéd on them. Join the 3 vertical rows together to complete the Afghan.

6. AFGHAN EDGING: Rnds 1 and 2: Starting at the upper right-hand corner of the Afghan, with the right side facing and B, sc in each st around, working (sc, ch 1, sc) in each corner-st. **Rnd 3** (*picot rnd*): Sc in next 5 sc, ch 4, sc in same sc for picot, * sc in next 4 sc, ch 4, sc in same sc for picot; rep from * around. Join with sl st to first sc. Fasten off.

PILLOWS

(*18″-square including border*)

DIRECTIONS:
(*Make 2 squares for each pillow*):

1. REPEAT Steps 1-4 of Afghan, appliquéing House #1, 2 or 3 onto one square *only* for each pillow.

2. ASSEMBLING: With the wrong sides of the 2 squares together and A, sc around 3 sides working through both thicknesses and *only* the front square of the 4th side (for the Pillow opening), making (sc, ch 1, sc) in each corner-st. Work sc rnds in the following color sequence: 1 rnd B, 1 rnd C, 4 rnds B and 1 picot rnd with B as for the Border around the Afghan. Insert the pillow form. With a tapestry needle, slip stitch the 4th side closed.

GIANT GRANNY SQUARE AFGHAN

(56" square, plus fringe)

TECHNIQUE: Crochet.

EASY: Achievable by anyone.

MATERIALS: Unger's Fluffy (1¾ oz. ball): 2 balls of No. 497 Light Peach (A), 5 balls of No. 538 Light Coral (B) and 6 balls of No. 537 Watermelon (C); crochet hook, Size Q, OR ANY SIZE HOOK TO OBTAIN GAUGE BELOW.

GAUGE: 3 dc = 2"; 2 dc rows = 4". TO SAVE TIME, TAKE TIME TO CHECK GAUGE.

Note: Afghan is made up of one large square, using 3 strands of yarn held together throughout. All rounds are worked from the right side.

DIRECTIONS:

SQUARE: Starting at center of Square with 3 strands of A held together, ch 5. Join with sl st to form ring. **Rnd 1:** With A ch 3, work 2 dc in ring, * ch 3, 3 dc in ring; rep from * 2 times more, ending with ch 3 — 12 dc with four ch-3 sps between (counting beg ch-3 as 1 dc). Join with sl st to top of beg ch-3. **Rnd 2:** Sl st to first ch-3 sp, *ch 3, (2 dc, ch 3, 3 dc) in same space* — **first corner made;** * ch 1, (3 dc, ch 3, 3 dc) in next ch-3 sp — **corner made;** rep from * 2 times more, ch 1 — 4 corners made. Join with sl st to top of ch-3. **Rnd 3:** Sl st to next ch-3 corner sp, ch 3, (2 dc, ch 3, 3 dc) in same sp, * ch 1, 3 dc in next ch-1 sp; ch 1,

•135

(3 dc, ch 3, 3 dc) in next corner-sp; rep from * 2 times more, ending with ch 1, 3 dc in next sp, ch 1. Join with sl st to top of ch-3. **Rnd 4:** Sl st to next corner-sp, break 1 strand A and join 1 strand B (you will have 2 A and one B). Ch 3, (2 dc, ch 3, 3 dc) in same sp, * (ch 1, 3 dc in next ch-1 sp) twice, ch 1, (3 dc, ch 3, 3 dc) in next corner-sp; rep from * around, ending with (ch 1, 3 dc in next ch-1 sp) twice, ch 1. Join with sl st to top of ch-3. **Rnd 5:** Sl st to next corner-sp, ch 3, (2 dc, ch 3, 3 dc) in same sp, * (ch 1, 3 dc in next sp) 3 times, ch 1, (3 dc, ch 3, 3 dc) in corner-sp;

rep from * around, ending with (ch 1, 3 dc in next sp) 3 times, ch 1. Join with sl st to top of ch-3. **Rnd 6:** Sl st to next corner-sp, break 1 A and join 1 strand B (you will have 1 A and 2 B). Ch 3, (2 dc, ch 3, 3 dc) in same sp, * (ch 1, 3 dc in next sp) 4 times, ch 1, (3 dc, ch 3, 3 dc) in corner-sp; rep from * around, ending with (ch 1, 3 dc in next sp) 4 times, ch 1. Join with sl st to top of ch-3. Continue to work as for Rnd 6, adding one more group of 3 dc between corner-sps on each rnd in the following color sequence: **Rnd 7:** 1A, 2B. **Rnds 8 and 9:** 3B. **Rnds 10 and 11:** 2B,

1C. **Rnds 12 and 13:** 1B, 2C. **Rnds 14 and 15:** 3C.

FRINGE: Wind C several times around a 6″ square of cardboard; cut at one end making 12″ strands. Holding 4 strands together, fold in half to form a loop. Insert the hook from back to front in the first sp on one side of the Afghan and draw the loop through. Draw the loose ends through the loop and pull up tightly to form a knot. Tie 4 strands in the same manner to every 2nd st along the same side. Repeat for the opposite side. Trim the fringe evenly.

CROSS-STITCHED HEIRLOOM AFGHAN

(about 45" x 57" plus tassels)

TECHNIQUE: Crochet and embroidery.

AVERAGE: For those with some experience in crochet and embroidery.

MATERIALS: Brunswick Germantown (3½ oz. skein): 3 skeins of No. 438 Kasha Heather (A), 1 skein of No. 422 Garnet (B), 3 skeins of No. 4182 Orien- tal Rose (C), 2 skeins each of No. 4000 Ecru (D) and No. 4233 Hurricane (E), 3 skeins of No. 467 Jade Heather (F); afghan hook, Size H, OR ANY SIZE HOOK TO OBTAIN GAUGE BELOW; tap- estry needle.

GAUGE: 28 sts = 6½"; 8 rows = 2¼". TO SAVE TIME, TAKE TIME TO CHECK GAUGE.

Note 1: The Afghan is made up of 7 panels which are sewn together afterwards.

Note 2: When changing colors, work last st until 2 lps remain on hook, drop working strand, pick up new color, yarn over and draw lp through 2 lps on hook.

....

DIRECTIONS:

CENTER PANEL: Border: Starting at lower edge with A and afghan hook, ch 28 to mea- sure 6½". Work in afghan (*see* FIG. 5) st as follows: **Row 1:** Re- taining all lps on hook, draw up a lp in 2nd ch from hook and in each ch across (see FIG. 5, Step 1) — 28 lps. *There are the same number of lps on hook as there were ch sts.* **Row 2:** Yarn over and draw through 1 lp, * yarn over and draw through 2 lps; rep from * across (see FIG. 5, Step 2.) **Row 3:** Retaining all lps on hook, draw up a lp in 2nd vertical bar and in each vertical bar across to within last vertical bar (see FIG. 5, Step 3); insert hook through last vertical bar and the st directly behind it (see arrow in Step 4) and draw up a lp. *There are the same number of lps as on Row 1.* Rep Rows 2 and 3 for afghan st. With A work in afghan st for 8 rows, changing colors at end of 8th row. Continue in afghan st using colors as follows: 1 row B, 1 row C, 2 rows D, 1 row E, 1 row C, 8 rows E, 1 row B, 1 row C, 2 rows D, 1 row E, 1 row B, 1 row A, 1 row B, 1 row A, 1 row C, 2 rows D, 1 row F, 1 row C, 8 rows F, 1 row A, 1 row B, 1 row C, 2

rows D. Border is completed. **Now** attach A for main color and work in afghan st for 110 rows. Cut A; attach D. **Now** work Border in reversed color sequence, ending with 8 rows of A. **Last row:** Sl st in each vertical bar across. Fasten off. Make 6 more panels working the Borders the same as for the Center Panel in the following colors: 2 panels using F as the main color, 2 panels using B as the main color and 2 panels using C as the main color.

EDGING FOR EACH PANEL: With the right side facing you, attach A to any corner of the panel, ch 1 and work 208 sc along one long edge of the panel. Cut the yarn and fasten off. Repeat along the other long edge of the same panel.

EMBROIDERY: The design is worked in cross st. When making the cross sts, the top strands should point in the same direction. Making cross sts over vertical bars (see FIG. 5A), follow FIG.

5B, charts 1-4. Use D on color F panels and A on color C panels. The remaining panels are not embroidered.

ASSEMBLING: Arrange the panels in the following sequence: F, B, C, A (center), C, B, F. With A, picking up the back lps **only,** sl st in each sc along the two long edges of the adjoining panels.

EDGING FOR AFGHAN: With A, sc evenly around the entire Afghan, making 3 sc in each corner st. Cut the yarn and fasten off.

TASSEL (Make 16): Cut two 10″ lengths of A and set aside. Wind A 28 times around a 4½″ piece of cardboard. Tie one 10″ length under the strands at one end. Cut the loops at the bottom and slip off the cardboard. Wind a 2nd length twice around the tassel, 1″ below the tied end. Trim evenly and sew 8 tassels evenly spaced to the corners of each short edge.

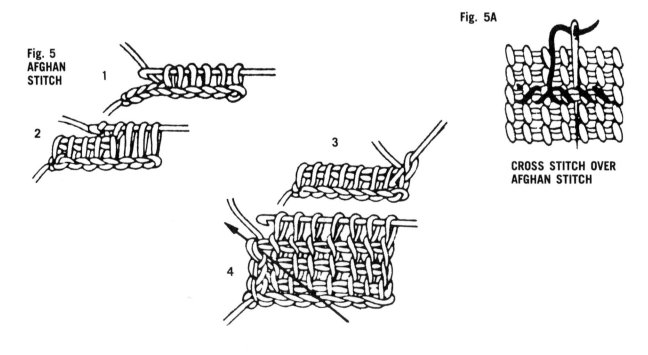

**Fig. 5
AFGHAN
STITCH**

1

2

3

4

Fig. 5A

**CROSS STITCH OVER
AFGHAN STITCH**

CHART 1

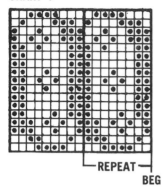

└─REPEAT─┘
BEG

Fig. 5B

⊡ = D   ⊠ = A

CHART 2

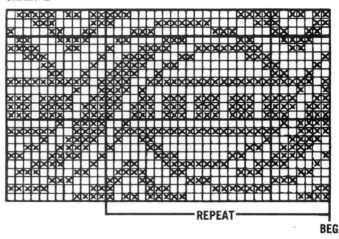

└────REPEAT────┘
BEG

CHART 3

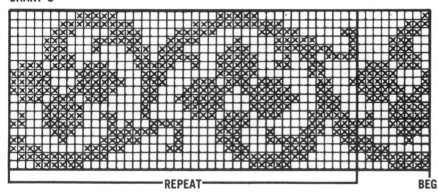

└────REPEAT────┘
BEG

CHART 4

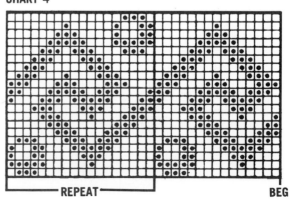

└────REPEAT────┘
BEG

LOG CABIN AFGHAN

(about 55" x 73")

TECHNIQUE: Crochet.

AVERAGE: For those with some experience in crochet.

MATERIALS: Bucilla Spectator (2 oz. skein): 5 skeins of No. 12 Camel (A), 6 skeins of No. 14 Moroccan Brown (B), 6 skeins of No. 46 Terracotta (C), 7 skeins of No. 52 Baby Blue (D), 3 skeins of No. 44 Light Rust (E), 4 skeins of No. 35 Stone Blue (F), 3 skeins of No. 39 Newleaf (G), and 3 skeins of No. 32 Winter White (H); crochet hook, Size G, OR ANY SIZE HOOK TO OBTAIN THE MOTIF MEASUREMENT BELOW; tapestry needle.

GAUGE: Each Motif = 9" square. TO SAVE TIME, TAKE TIME TO CHECK GAUGE.

Note: Each Motif is made up of Sections 1-7, joined together as they are worked. When working each section, refer to FIG. 6 for placement. Crochet over yarn ends, whenever possible, to conceal them.

DIRECTIONS:

MOTIF *(Make 48)*, SECTION 1: **Center Square — Rnd 1** *(right side)*: With A, ch 2, 8 sc in 2nd ch from hook. Join with sl st to first sc. **Rnd 2:** Ch 1, turn. Sc in first sc, * yo, insert hook in next sc, *yo and draw up a lp, yo and through first lp on hook, (yo and through next 2 lps on hook) 2 times* — **long dc made;** keeping long dc at back of work, sc in same sc to form a bobble on reverse side, long dc in same sc, keeping long dc at back of work, sc in next sc to form

second bobble; rep from * 2 more times, work a long dc, sc and long dc all in last sc. Join with sl st to first sc — 8 bobbles made. *Note: To hdc: Yo, draw up a lp in next sc, yo and through 3 lps on hook.* **Rnd 3:** Ch 1, turn. Sc in first long dc, *3 hdc all in next sc —* **corner made;** * sc in each of next 3 sts, 3 hdc all in next sc; rep from * 2 more times, sc in each of next 2 sts. Join with sl st to first sc. Fasten off.

Note: Sections 2-7 are worked in Rows.

SECTION 2: **Row 1:** From right side, attach B in center hdc of any corner as follows: *Make a slipknot on hook, then insert hook in center st, yo and draw up a lp, yo and through 2 lps on hook* — **first sc made;** sc in each of next 5 sts, 3 sc in next st, sc in each of next 6 sts. Fasten off. *Hereafter, attach all new strands in this way.* *Note: Center sc of 3-sc group will be referred to as corner-sc.* **Row 2:** Turn, with C, sc in first sc and in

each st to within corner-sc, 3 sc in corner-sc, sc in each st to end of row. Fasten off. **Row 3:** With B, repeat Row 2. **Row 4:** With C, repeat Row 2. **Row 5:** Turn, attach B to first st as follows: *Make a slipknot on hook, then insert hook in first st, yo and draw up a lp, draw up a lp in next st, yo and through 3 lps on hook* — **dec made;** sc in each st to within corner-sc, 3 sc in corner-sc, sc in each st to within 2 sts of end, draw up a lp in next 2 sts, yo and through all 3 lps on hook* — **dec made.** There are 10 sc to each side of corner-sc. Fasten off. *Note: With right side up, hold work so that last st made is at upper right corner.* **Begin first row of each section at upper right corner and work toward left. Start each section in this manner unless otherwise specified.**

SECTION 3: **Row 1:** With D, sc in end of last row worked, sc in each of next 4 rows, sk corner-st of center square, sc in each of

---

TIP *Log Cabin Facts*

The basic Log Cabin block has a small square in the center. Around this piece four narrow strips are placed in a "swastika" arrangement. Usually, two are dark, two are light. You can arrange blocks so that light and dark areas form concentric diamonds, (such as the "Barn Raising" effect on our afghan shown) or long diagonal zigzags. When light strips are placed opposite one another, instead of at right angles, checkered patterns on the overall quilt emerge. Whichever colors you choose, be certain to keep their positive/negative contrast values in mind.

next 5 sts, 3 sc in corner-st, sc in each of next 5 sts, sk corner-st of center square, sc in each of next 4 rows, sc in end sc of last row — 11 sc to each side of corner-sc. Fasten off. **Row 2:** With E, repeat Row 2 of Section 2. **Row 3:** With D, repeat Row 2 of Section 2. **Row 4:** With E, repeat Row 2 of Section 2. **Row 5:** With D, repeat Row 5 of Section 2 — 14 sc to each side of corner-sc. Fasten off.

SECTION 4: **Row 1:** With F, sc in end of last row worked, sc in each of next 4 rows, sc in each sc of next section to within corner-sc, 3 sc in corner-sc, sc in each remaining sc of same section, sc in each of next 4 rows, sc in end sc of last row — 16 sc to each side of corner-sc. Fasten off. **Row 2:** Turn, with G, sc in each of first 2 sc, * long dc in next sc, sc in next sc *; rep from * to * to within corner-sc, work long dc, sc and long dc all in corner-sc, sc in next sc; rep from * to * to within one st of end, sc in last sc. Fasten off. **Row 3:** With F, repeat Row 2 of Section 2. **Row 4:** Turn, with G, sc in first sc, long dc in next sc, * sc in next sc, long dc in next sc *; rep from * to * to within corner-sc, 3 sc in corner-sc, long dc in next sc; rep

FIG. 7 JOINING DIAGRAM

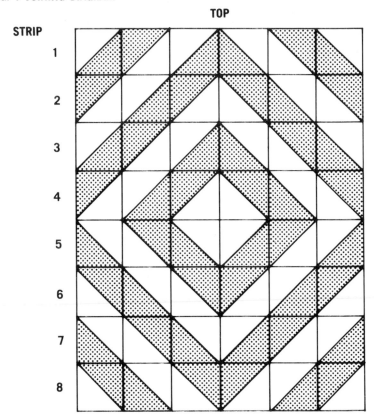

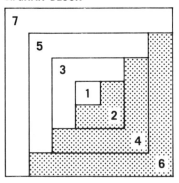

FIG. 6 AFGHAN BLOCK

from * to * to within one st of end, sc in last sc. Fasten off. **Row 5:** With F, repeat Row 5 of Section 2 — 19 sc to each side of corner-sc. Fasten off.

SECTION 5: Repeat Section 4 in following color sequence: Row 1-H, Row 2-A, Row 3-H, Row 4-A, Row 5-H. Mark first st of Row 5 — 23 sc to each side of corner-sc. Fasten off.

SECTION 6: *Note: With wrong side up, hold work so that marked st is at upper right corner. Work first st of next row in end of marked st, remove marker, work toward left.* **Row 1:** From wrong side, with C, repeat Row 1 of Section 4 — 25 sc to each side of corner-sc. *Do not cut yarn.* **Row 2:** Ch 1, turn, continue same as Row 2 of Section 2. **Row 3:** Turn, with F,

sc in first sc, * ch 1, sk next sc, sc in next sc *; rep from * to * to within one st of corner-sc, ch 1, sk next sc, 3 sc in corner-sc; rep from * to * to end. Fasten off. **Row 4:** Turn, with C, sc in first sc, * keeping next ch-1 at back, work 1 dc in sc two rows below, just *under* ch-1, sc in next sc*; rep from * to * to within corner-sc, 3 sc in corner-sc, sc in next sc; rep from * to * to end. *Do not cut yarn.* **Row 5:** Ch 1, turn, dec over first 2 sts, sc in each st to within corner-sc, 3 sc in corner-sc, sc in each st to within 2 sts of end, dec over last 2 sts. Mark last dec — 28 sc to each side of corner-sc. Fasten off.

SECTION 7: Follow "Note" under Section 6 and work Rows 1-4 of Section 6 in following color sequence: Rows 1 and 2-D, Row 3-E, Row 4-D. *Do not cut yarn.* **Row 5:** Ch 1, turn, with D, repeat Row 2 of Section 2 — 33 sc to each side of corner-sc.

MOTIF EDGING: From the right side, with B, 3 sc in corner-sc of Section 7, sc in each sc to within last st, 3 sc in last sc of this section, sc in each of next 4 rows, sc in each sc across next section to within corner-sc, 3 sc in corner-sc, sc in each sc across remainder of same section, sc in each of next 4 rows, 3 sc in end sc, sc in each remaining sc. Join with sl st to first sc — 34 sc to each side of corner-sc. Fasten off.

BLOCKING: With the right side up, pin each motif to measurements on a padded, flat surface, like an ironing board; steam lightly, but *do not* place the iron directly on the motif, until thoroughly moist. While the motif is damp, gently stretch it diagonally to square up the sections. Let it dry thoroughly before removing it.

ASSEMBLING: Follow the joining diagram FIG. 7. **Step 1:** Pin the motifs together to form 8 strips of 6 motifs. Identify each strip with a numbered tag. Mark the top edge of each strip. **Step 2:** With B and a tapestry needle, sew the motifs together from the right side, working through the back lp *only* of each st and keeping the seams as elastic as the crochet fabric. Sew with overcast st from center sc of one corner to center sc of next corner, matching sts. **Step 3:** Pin the strips together in numerical sequence, keeping the top edge of each strip facing in the same direction. Sew the strips together as in Step 2.

AFGHAN EDGING: *Note: Work with slightly tighter tension to help keep edges flat.* **Rnd 1:** From the right side, with B, work 3 sc in center sc of any corner, * sc in each sc to within corner-sc of same motif, hdc in corner-sc, *yo, insert hook in seam, yo and draw up a lp, yo and through 2 lps on hook, yo, insert hook in corner-sc of next motif, yo and draw up a lp, yo and through 2 lps on hook, yo and through all 3 lps on hook* — **dec made;** rep from * across side, end with 3 sc in center sc of next Afghan corner. Continue around rem 3 sides in this manner. Join with sl st to first sc. *Do not cut yarn.* **Rnd 2:** Ch 1, from right side, sc in each sc around all sides, working 3 sc in center sc of each corner. Join with sl st to first sc. Fasten off. Place the Afghan right side down and steam the edging flat (*do not* place the iron down directly).

VIOLETS AFGHAN

(about 49" x 71")

TECHNIQUE: Cross stitch on crochet.

AVERAGE: For those with some experience in crochet and embroidery.

MATERIALS: Brunswick Windrush (3½ oz. skein): 9 skeins of #90100 Ecru (A), 2 skeins of #90721 Light Denim (B), 1 skein each of #9014 Purple (C), #9085 Earth Green (D), #9083 Meadow Green (E), #9031 Maize (F); afghan hook No. 10/J, OR ANY SIZE HOOK TO OBTAIN THE SQUARE MEASUREMENT BELOW; crochet hook Size J *(optional for edging)*; tapestry needle.

GAUGE: Each Square = 12" x 14". TO SAVE TIME, TAKE TIME TO CHECK GAUGE.

. . . .

DIRECTIONS:

AFGHAN STITCH: With the afghan hook, crochet a chain. **Row 1:** Draw up a lp in 2nd ch from hook and each rem ch, leaving all lps on hook. Work off lps as follows: Yo hook, draw through 1 lp, * yo, draw through 2 lps; rep from * across row, leaving 1 lp on hook. **Row 2:** Skip first upright bar, draw up a lp in each following upright bar, leaving all lps on hook; work off lps in same manner as for Row 1. Repeat Row 2 to end.

SQUARE *(Make 20):* With A, ch 29, work in afghan st for 33 rows. **Note:** *Last row may be worked with afghan hook or Size J hook.* **Last Row:** Sl st in each st across; *do not* fasten off.

SQUARE EDGING: Rnd 1: Ch 1, 2 sc in same corner sp, sc in end of each row to next corner, 3 sc in corner, sc in other side of each ch to next corner, 3 sc in corner, sc in end of each row to next corner, 3 sc in corner, sc in each sl st to corner, 1 more sc in first corner, drop A, with B, join with sl st to first sc. **Rnd 2:** With B, ch 3, 1 dc in same corner st, dc in each sc around, working 3 dc in each corner, end with 1 more dc in first corner, fasten off B, with A, join with sl st to 3rd ch of starting ch. **Rnd 3:** With A, ch 3, 3 dc in same corner st, dc in each dc around, working 5 dc in each corner, end with 1 more dc in first corner, join with sl st to 3rd ch of starting ch. Fasten off A.

FINISHING: Pin each square to measurements on a padded surface, cover with a damp cloth and allow to dry; *do not press.* Working in Cross Stitch *(see Stitch Guide, pages 298-299)*, follow the chart for embroidering the violet *(see FIG. 8)*. With A, working through the back lp of each dc, sew the squares together from the center of a corner to the center of the next corner, matching sts. Sew the squares in 5 rows of 4 squares each.

AFGHAN EDGING: Join A in any corner, ch 3, dc in same sp, dc in each dc to next Afghan corner, 3 dc in corner, continue in this manner, end 1 more dc in first corner, join with sl st to 3rd ch of starting ch. Fasten off.

FIG. 8 VIOLET AFGHAN

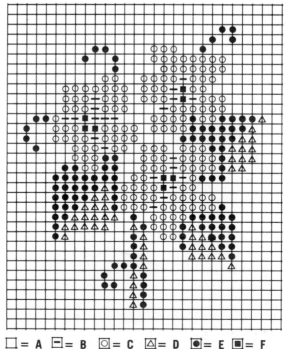

□ = A   ⊟ = B   ⊡ = C   △ = D   ⊙ = E   ■ = F

SNOWFLAKE AFGHAN AND PILLOW

AFGHAN

(52" x 76")

TECHNIQUE: Crochet.

AVERAGE: For those with some experience in crochet.

MATERIALS: Bucilla "Softex" (3½ oz. skein): 7 skeins of #5 Winter White (A) and 10 skeins of #87 Deep Rose (B); crochet hook, Size H, OR ANY SIZE CRO-CHET HOOK TO OBTAIN GAUGE BELOW; tapestry needle. *For Pillow:* One knife-edged pillow form; 14" square; a piece of backing fabric, 15" x 15"; matching sewing thread.

GAUGE: Small Square = 3" x 3". Large Square = 9" x 9". TO SAVE TIME, TAKE TIME TO CHECK GAUGE.

DIRECTIONS:

LARGE SQUARE *(Make 24)*: Starting at center with A, ch 4. Join with sl st to form ring. **Rnd 1:** Ch 4, into ring make (dc and ch 1) 7 times. Join with sl st to 3rd ch of ch-4 — 8 dc, counting chain at beg of rnd as 1 dc. *Do not* turn. Entire square is worked from right side. **Rnd 2:** Ch 2, dc in next dc, * ch 5, yarn over hook, draw up a lp in same st as last dc, yarn over hook, draw through 2 lps on hook, yarn over hook, draw up a lp in next dc, yarn over hook, draw through 2 lps on hook, yarn over, draw through all 3 lps on hook; rep from * 5 more times; ch 5, hold-ing back on hook last lp of each dc, make dc in same st as last dc, dc in same ch as joining of last rnd, yarn over hook, draw through all 3 lps on hook, ch 5. Join with sl st to first dc — 8 ch-5 lps. **Rnd 3:** Sl st in next ch-5 lp, ch 3, * in same ch-5 lp make dc, ch 3 and dc; ch 1, holding back on hook last lp of each dc, make dc in same ch-5 lp and dc in next ch-5 lp, yarn over hook, draw through all 3 lps on hook, ch 1; rep from * around, ending with dc, ch 3 and dc all in same ch-5 lp, ch 1, holding back on hook last lp of dc, make dc in same ch-5 lp, insert hook in 2nd ch of ch-3 at beg of rnd and draw a lp through ch and through the 2 lps on hook. **Rnd 4:** Ch 1, sc in same ch as joining just made, * ch 1, sc in next dc, ch 1, *in next ch-3 lp make dc, ch 2 and dc — point;* ch 1, sc in next dc, ch 1, sk next ch, sc in next st; rep from * around, ending last rep with ch 1. Join with sl st to first sc — 8 points. Break off and fasten. **Rnd 5:** Attach B in ch-2 sp of any point, in same sp make sc, ch 2 and sc; * ch 1, sc in next ch-1 sp, ch 1, draw up a lp in each of next 2 sps, yarn over hook, draw through all 3 lps on hook; ch 1, sc in next sp, ch 1, in next ch-2 sp make sc, ch 2 and sc; rep from * around, ending last rep with ch 1, sc in last ch-1 sp, ch 1. Join with sl st to first sc. **Rnd 6:** Sl st in next ch-2 sp, ch 1, sc in same sp, * ch 1, hdc in next sc, ch 1, (sk next ch, dc in next st) 3 times; ch 1, hdc in next sc, ch 1, sc in next ch-2 sp; rep from * around, ending last rep with ch 1, hdc in same sc as joining of last rnd, ch 1. Join with sl st to first sc. **Rnd 7:** Ch 1, sc in same sc as joining, (ch 1, sk next ch, sc in next st) 2 times; * ch 1, sk next dc, sc in next dc, (ch 1, sk next ch, sc in next st) 2 times; ch 1, dc in next hdc, ch 1, tr in next dc, ch 1, *in next dc make dtr (yarn 3 times around hook for dtr), ch 3 and dtr — **corner;** ch 1, tr in next dc, ch 1, dc in next hdc, (ch 1, sk next ch, sc in next st) 3 times; rep from * around, ending last rep with ch 1, tr in last dc after last corner, ch 1, dc in next hdc, ch 1. Join with sl st to first sc — 4 corners. **Rnd 8:** Sl st in next sp, ch 1, sc in same sp, (ch 1, sc in next sp) 7 times; * ch 1, in next corner sp make sc, ch 3 and sc; (ch 1, sc in next sp) 11 times; rep from * 2 more times; ch 1, in next corner sp make sc, ch 3 and sc; (ch 1, sc in next sp) 3 times; ch 1. Join with sl st to first sc. **Rnd 9:** Ch 4, dc in next sc, * ch 1, work dc and ch 1 in each sc to within next corner sp, in corner sp make dc, ch 3 and dc; rep from * 3 more times; ch 1, dc and ch 1 in each rem sc. Join with sl st to 3rd ch of ch-4. **Rnd 10:** Ch 4, * work dc and ch 1 in each dc to within next corner sp, in corner sp make dc, ch 3 and dc; ch 1; rep from * 3 more times; work dc and ch 1 in each rem dc. Join to 3rd ch of ch-4. **Rnd 11:** Rep Rnd 10. Break off and fasten. **Rnd 12:** Attach A in any corner sp, ch 1, in same sp make sc, ch 3 and sc; * (ch 1, sc in next sp) 18 times; ch 1, in next corner sp make sc, ch 3 and sc; rep from * 2 more times; (ch 1, sc in next sp) 18 times; ch 1. Join with sl st to first sc. Break off and fasten.

SMALL SQUARE (*Make 209*): Starting at center with A, ch 4. Join with sl st to form ring. **Rnd 1:** Ch 4, into ring make (dc and ch 1) 7 times. Join with sl st to 3rd ch of ch-4 — 8 dc, counting chain at beg of rnd as 1 dc. Break off and fasten. **Rnd 2:** Attach B in any ch-1 sp, ch 6, dc in same sp, ch 1, dc in next sp, * ch 1, in next sp make *dc, ch 3 and dc* — **corner;** ch 1, dc in next sp; rep from * 2 more times; ch 1. Join with sl st to 3rd ch of ch-6. **Rnd 3:** Ch 1, sc in same ch as joining, * ch 1, in next corner sp make sc, ch 2 and sc, (ch 1, sc in next dc) 3 times; rep from * around, ending last rep with (ch 1, sc in next dc) 2 times; ch 1. Join with sl st to first sc. Break off and fasten. **Rnd 4:** Attach A in any corner ch-2 sp, ch 1, in same sp make sc, ch 3 and sc; (ch 1, sc in next ch-1 sp) 4 times; * ch 1, in next corner sp make 7 sc, ch 3 and sc; (ch 1, sc in next sp) 4 times; rep from * 2 more times; ch 1. Join with sl st to first sc. Break off and fasten.

FINISHING: Darn in all loose ends. Pin each square to measurements on a padded surface cover with a damp cloth and al-

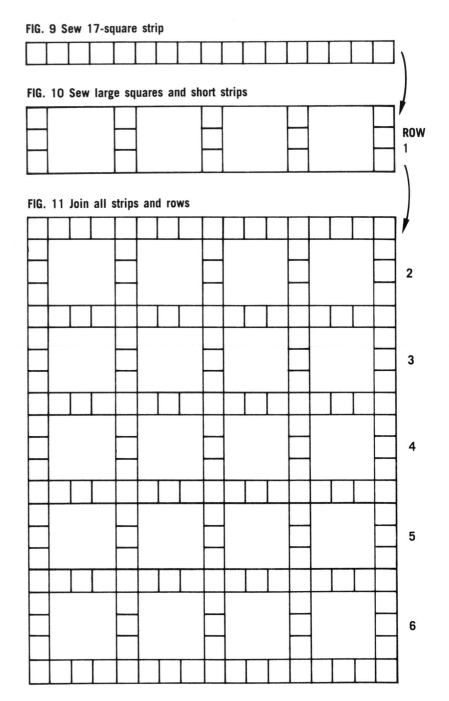

FIG. 9 Sew 17-square strip

FIG. 10 Sew large squares and short strips

ROW 1

FIG. 11 Join all strips and rows

2

3

4

5

6

low to dry; *do not press.*

ASSEMBLING: Arrange the small squares in seven separate strips of 17 squares in each strip, as shown in FIG. 9, and sew the squares together (*see Sewing directions at right*). Sew remaining squares together in short strips of three squares each (*see* FIG. 10).

SEWING: With a tapestry needle and A, from the right side, working through both top lps of each st, sew the squares together, matching sts, starting at the center of one corner and ending at the center of the next corner. Arranging squares as shown in Fig. 10, make 6 rows of 4 large and 15 small squares in each row. Join all the rows together as shown in Fig. 11, being careful to match the small squares.

EDGING: **Rnd 1:** With the right side facing, attach A in any corner sp of Afghan, ch 1, in same sp make sc, ch 1 and sc, * ch 1, work sc and ch 1 in each sp across to within next corner sp of Afghan, in corner ch 1, make sc and ch 1 in each rem sp. Join last ch 1 with sl st to first sc. **Rnd 2:** *Ch 1, sl st in next corner sp, ch 1, make sl st and ch 1 in each sc across to within next corner sp of Afghan; rep from * around, ending with ch 1, sl st in same st as joining of last rnd. Break off and fasten.

PILLOW
. . . .
(14" x 14" plus fringe)

DIRECTIONS:

SMALL SQUARE: Following the directions for the Small Square for the Afghan, make 16 Small Squares for the pillow top.

FINISHING: Darn in all loose ends. Pin each square to measurements on a padded surface,

cover with a damp cloth and allow to dry; *do not press.*

ASSEMBLING: Working the same as for the Afghan, sew the squares into 4 rows of 4 in each row; sew the rows together, matching the corners.

EDGING: **Rnd 1:** Attach A in any corner sp of pillow top, in same sp make sc, ch 2 and sc; * work sc in each sc, in each sp and in each seam across to within next corner sp of pillow top, in next corner sp make sc, ch 2 and sc; rep from * 2 more times; sc in each sc, in each sp and in each seam across rem side. Join with sl st to first sc. Break off and fasten. **Rnd 2:** Attach B in any corner ch-2 sp, in same sp make sc, ch 2 and sc; ch 1, * sk next sc, sc in next sc, ch 1, continue to work sc and ch 1 in every other sc across to within next corner sp, in corner sp make sc, ch 2 and sc; ch 1; rep from * 2 more times; work sc and ch 1 in every other sc across next side edge. Join last ch 1 with sl st to first sc. **Rnd 3:** * In next corner sp make sc, ch 2 and sc; ch 1, work sc and ch 1 in each ch-1 sp across to within next corner sp; rep from * around. Join last ch 1 with sl st to first sc. **Rnds 4-5:** Rep Rnd 3 twice. Break off and fasten.

JOINING FRONT AND BACK:

Pin the backing fabric and the crocheted pillow top together, right sides together and edges matching. Baste along three sides and four corners, ½" in from the outer edges (top of 3rd rnd from edge on crocheted side). From the crocheted side, machine or hand-stitch over the basting stitches. Turn back a ½" seam allowance on the fabric backing along the opening, finger press and baste. Turn back to the wrong side the last two rnds of the crochet seam allowance and baste in place. Diagonally clip the corners of the fabric ⅛" from the stitching. Turn right side out; push out the corners. Insert the pillow form. Slip stitch closed.

FRINGE: Wind B several times around a 3" square of cardboard. Cut at one edge, making 6" strands. Hold four strands evenly together and fold in half to form a loop. With the right side of the Pillow facing, insert the hook from back to front in any sc on the round close to the seam along the outer edge, draw the loop of strands through sc, draw the loose ends through the loop on the hook and pull tightly to form a knot. Tie four strands in each sc along the entire rnd close to the seam, in the same manner. Trim evenly.

•6•

FOR HIM

Make something special for the men in your life! How about a handsome houndstooth sweater, or a rugged fisherman's knit? If you'd like to take on a smaller project, you can knit a tie in a simple seed stitch or crochet a pair of slippers in handsome colors. Of course, we didn't forget about the youngest man in your life — there's a mittens and scarf set especially for him!

MAN'S PATTERNED PULLOVER

(Pullover is shown on the previous page.)

TECHNIQUE: Crochet.

AVERAGE: For those with some experience in crochet. Directions are for Size Small (36-38). Changes for Sizes Medium (40-42) and Large (44) are in parentheses.

MATERIALS: Pingouin "Iceberg" (50-gr. ball): 10 balls Oxford #178 (A); 4 balls Bone #136 (B); 3 balls each Blue #205 (C) and Gray #193 (E); 2 skeins Tan #196 (D); crochet hooks Sizes J and K, OR ANY SIZE HOOK TO OBTAIN GAUGE BELOW.

GAUGE: With larger hook: 11 sts = 6". TO SAVE TIME, TAKE TIME TO CHECK GAUGE.

MEASUREMENTS:

Sizes:	Small	Medium	Large
Finished			
Chest:	40"	42½"	44¾"
Sleeve around upper arm:			
	15¾"	15¾"	15¾"

Note: The sweater is worked in one piece.

DIRECTIONS:

YOKE: Starting at neck edge, with larger hook and A, ch 40 (44, 48). **Rnd 1:** Dc in 4th ch from hook and next 4 (5, 6) ch, *2 dc, ch 1, 2 dc in next ch — corner;* dc in next 5 ch for sleeve, make corner as before in next ch, dc in next 12 (14, 16) ch for Front, corner in next ch, dc in next 5 ch for sleeve, corner in next ch, dc in last 6 (7, 8) ch, sl st in top of ch-3 to join rnd — 50 (54, 58) dc. Make sure rnd fits over man's head; if not, ch more loosely. *Note: Ch-3 at beg of rnds counts as 1 dc.* **Rnd 2:** Ch 3, turn, dc in each dc, working *dc, ch 1, dc in ch-1 sp at corners;* join — 58 (62, 66) dc. Fasten off A, join D. **Rnds 3 and 4:** With D, rep Rnd 2 — 74 (78, 82) dc. Fasten off D, join B. **Rnd 5:** With B, ch 2, turn, puff st in next st as follows: *(yo, draw up lp in st) 5 times, yo, thru all lps on hook, ch 1 —* **puff st made;** *sc in next 2 sts, puff st in next st; rep from * around working dc, ch 1, dc in corner ch-1 sp and adjusting puff st pat as necessary at corners; join in top of ch-2. **Rnds 6 and 7:** With A, ch 2, turn, sc in each st around, working *dc, ch 1, dc* in corners; join in top of ch-2. **Rnd 8:** With B, rep Rnd 5. **Rnd 9:** With C, ch 3, turn, rep Rnd 2 — 114 (118, 122) dc. **Rnd 10:** With C, rep Rnd 6. **Rnd 11:** With D, rep Rnd 2 — 130 (134, 138) sts. **Divide for Body — Next Rnd:** With A, ch 3, turn, work to next corner; work 1 dc around ch-1 sp of this corner and next corner to join underarm, dc to next corner, join underarm as before, dc to beg of rnd; join — 74 (78, 82) dc.

BODY: **Rnd 1:** With A, ch 3, turn, dc in each st around; join. **Rnd 2:** With E, rep Rnd 1. **Rnd 3:** Ch 2, turn, sc in each dc, dec 1 st at each underarm; join — 72 (76, 80) sts. **Rnd 4:** Working over color not in use, with B, ch 3, turn, dc in next 2 (3, 3) sts, *with E, dc in next st; with B, dc in next 3 (3, 4) sts; rep from * around, end pat as established; join. **Rnd 5:** Rep Rnd 4, working B over B, E over E. **Rnds 6-7:** With B, rep Rnd 1. **Rnds 8-9:** With B, and C instead of E, rep Rnds 4 and 5. **Rnds 10-11:** With

C, rep Rnd 1. **Rnd 12:** With D, rep Rnd 1. **Rnd 13:** With D, and C instead of E, rep Rnd 4. **Rnds 14-15:** With C, rep Rnd 1.

RIBBING: Rnd 1: With smaller hook and A, rep Body Rnd 1. **Rnd 2:** Ch 3, turn, Back-Post-dc (BP) around next dc as follows: *yo, insert hook from back in sp before next dc, and out to back in next sp (whole dc is across hook), complete a dc —* **BP made;** * dc in next dc, BP around next dc; rep from * around; join. **Rnd 3:** Ch 3, turn, Front-Post-dc (FP) around BP *(same as BP, but insert hook from front)*; dc in next dc; rep from * around. **Rnd 4:** Rep Rnd 2. Fasten off.

SLEEVES: Rnd 1: Join A at underarm, ch 3, dc in each dc around sleeve sts; join in top of ch-3. **Rnd 2:** Ch 3, turn, dc in each dc; join. Rep Rnd 2 until 18 (18½, 19)″ from beg, or desired length to cuff. **Last Rnd:** Ch 2, turn, (work 2 sc tog) around; join.

RIBBING: With smaller hook, work Rnds 1 and 2 of Body Ribbing. Fasten off.

FINISHING: From the right side with the larger hook and C, sc around the neck edge, drawing in to the desired fit if necessary; join. Fasten off.

MAN'S ICELANDIC YOKE PULLOVER

TECHNIQUE: Knitting.

AVERAGE: For those with some experience in knitting. Directions are for Size Small (34-36). Changes for Sizes Medium (38-40) and Large (42-44) are in parentheses.

MATERIALS: Any Bulky-Weight yarn (4-oz. skein): 4 (5, 6) skeins oatmeal (A), 3 skeins brown (B), 1 skein off-white (C); 29" circular knitting needles, sizes 6 and 10; 4 double-pointed needles (dp) each, sizes 6 and 10, OR ANY SIZE NEEDLES TO OBTAIN GAUGE BELOW; 3 long stitch holders.

GAUGE: On larger needles: 7 sts = 2", 5 rows = 1". TO SAVE TIME, TAKE TIME TO CHECK GAUGE.

MEASUREMENTS:

Sizes:	Small	Medium	Large
Chest:	37"	41"	45¾"
Sleeve around upper arm:			
	16"	17"	17"

(*Note: For color patterns, carry second color loosely along wrong side of work; when changing colors, twist colors once to prevent holes.*)

DIRECTIONS:

BODY: With smaller circular needle and B, cast on 110 (120, 130) sts; with care not to twist sts, join rnd. Mark beg of rnds. Carry marker. Work in k 1, p 1 ribbing for 3". **Next Rnd:** K, inc 18 (24, 30) sts evenly spaced — 128 (144, 160) sts.

Change to larger circular needle. K 1 rnd. **Border Pat:** Follow chart, Rows 1-7, working in st st (k each rnd). Cut B and C. With A, continue in st st until 15 (16, 17)" from beg, or desired length to underarm. K to last 5 (6, 6) sts on last rnd.

DIVIDE FOR FRONT AND BACK: Bind off next 10 (12, 12) sts for underarm, k until there are 54 (60, 68) sts on right needle for Front, sl to holder, bind off next 10 (12, 12) sts, k to end; leave on needle for Back.

SLEEVES: With smaller dp needles and B, cast on 30 (32, 34) sts; divide sts evenly on three needles. Join rnd; mark beg of rnd. Carry marker. Work in k 1, p 1 ribbing for 3". **Next Rnd:** K, inc 10 (16, 14) sts evenly spaced — 40 (48, 48) sts. Change to larger dp needles. K 1 rnd. Work Border Pat as for Body. With A, continue in st st, inc 1 st at beg and end of next rnd, then every 1½" until there

are 56 (60, 60) sts. Work even until 18 (19, 20)" from beg, or desired length to underarm. **Next Rnd:** K to last 10 (12, 12) sts on rnd, bind off next 10 (12, 12) sts for underarm — 46 (48, 48) sts. Sl to holder.

BORDER PAT

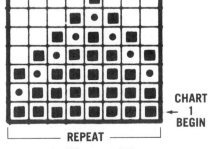

CHART 1 BEGIN ←

⟵ REPEAT ⟶

☐ = A ◼ = B ◘ = C
◆ = DECREASE

YOKE PAT

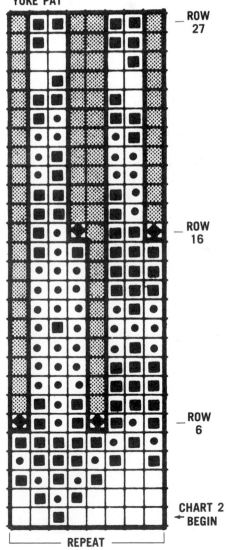

— ROW 27

— ROW 16

— ROW 6

CHART 2 BEGIN ←

⟵ REPEAT ⟶

YOKE: Right sides facing, sl sts of one sleeve, Front and other sleeve to larger circular needle to left of Back — 200 (216, 232) sts. Mark beg of rnds. Join A. K 6 (7, 8) rnds. **Pattern:** Continuing in st st, follow chart for Yoke, Rows 1-27, decreasing as indicated on Row 6 to 150 (162, 174) sts and Row 16 to 100 (108, 116) sts. When chart is completed, cut A and C. **Next Rnd — Size Small:** * K 1, [k 2 tog] twice; rep from * around — 60 sts. **Size Medium:** * K 1, [k 2 tog] 3 times; rep from * , end k 1, k 2 tog — 62 sts. **Size Large:** * [K 2 tog] 3 times, k 1; rep from *, end k 2 tog twice — 66 sts.

NECKBAND: With smaller dp needles and B, work in k 1, p 1 ribbing for 3½". Bind off loosely in ribbing. Fold neckband in half to wrong side; sew loosely in place.

FINISHING: Sew or weave the underarm seams. Steam the sweater lightly; do not press.

MAN'S BANDANNA VEST

TECHNIQUE: Knitting, embroidery.

AVERAGE: For those with some experience in knitting with embroidery accents.
Directions are for Medium (40-42). Changes for Large (44-46) are in parentheses.

MATERIALS: Phildar "Perlé Cotton Akala" (50 gr. ball). 10 (11-12) Red #84 (MC), 1 ball each White #10 (A) and Black #67 (B); sizes 5 and 7 knitting needles, OR SIZE TO OBTAIN GAUGE BELOW; tapestry needle; 6 buttons.

GAUGE: St st on larger needles: 5 sts = 1″; 6 rows = 1″. TO SAVE TIME, TAKE TIME TO CHECK GAUGE.

FINISHED MEASUREMENTS:

Sizes:	Medium	Large
Chest buttoned:	43¼″	46¾″
Back width at underarm:	21¼″	23″

Note: Motifs are duplicate stitched and embroidered on afterwards (see Stitch Guide on pages 298-299).

DIRECTIONS:

BACK: With smaller needles and MC cast on 108 (116) sts. **Row 1:** * K 1, p 1, rep from * across. Rep Row 1 for rib pat to 17 rows. Change to larger needles and st st. Work to 15″ from beg, end with a p row.

ARMHOLE SHAPING: Bind off 6 sts at beg of next 2 rows — 96 (104) sts. Work even until armholes measure 9½″ (10)″.

SHOULDER SHAPING: Bind off 8 (9) sts at beg of next 2 rows, then bind off 9 (10) sts at beg of next 2 rows. Bind off 10 (11) sts at beg of next 2 rows. Bind off remaining 42 (44) sts for back neck edge.

RIGHT FRONT: With smaller needles and MC cast on 62 (66) sts. Beg k 1, p 1, work in ribbing for 17 rows. Change to larger needles. **Row 1:** [k 1, p 1] 5 times (front ribband) k to end. **Row 2:** P to last 10 sts, work in ribbing to end. Rep these 2 rows for pat. Work to 14″ from beg, end at front edge.

ARMHOLE AND V-NECK SHAPING: Rib 10 sts, k 2 tog (neck dec) k to end. Continue to dec 1 st inside ribband as established every other row 4 (5) times, every 4th row 14 times. *At same time* when piece measures 15" from beg, at side edge bind off 6 sts — 37 (40) sts. Work even until armhole measures same as back to top, end at armhole edge.

SHOULDER SHAPING: Bind off 8 (9) sts, complete row. Work 1 row. Bind off 9 (10) sts, complete row. Bind off 10 (11) sts — 10 rib sts left. Work in ribbing on these sts only until band is long enough to reach center back. Bind off. Along straight edge of front band mark places for 6 buttons, having top button approx ½" below start of V, bottom but-

ton approx 1" above lower edge and spacing other buttons evenly between.

LEFT FRONT: As right front, reversing shaping and forming buttonholes opposite markers. **Buttonhole Row 1:** Work to 6 sts before front edge, yo twice, k 2 tog, p 1, k 1, p 1, k 1. **Row 2:** P 1, k 1, p 1, k 1, dropping extra loop k yo, complete row.

FINISHING: Sew shoulder seams. Sew neckband tog at center back. Sew to back neck edge.

ARMHOLE BANDS: With smaller needles and MC cast on 11 sts. Work in k 1, p 1 ribbing until long enough to reach

around entire straight edge of armholes. Sew bands to straight edges of armholes. Sew short ends to bound off sts at underarms. Sew side seams. See diagrams on pages 298-299 for Duplicate stitch and other embroidery stitches. Following Chart, duplicate st pat to lower fronts and back (on fronts only work 2 large motifs as shown), starting 1 row above ribbands, then rep Rows 32 thru 63 to top of pieces. Following chart, embroider Running sts and Lazy Daisy sts with B and French Knots with A. Sew on buttons.

MAN'S BANDANNA VEST

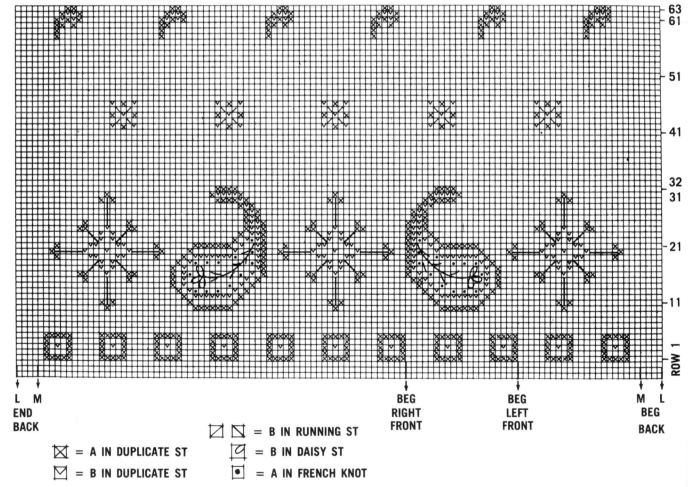

FRENCH FISHERMAN'S STRIPED PULLOVER

TECHNIQUE: Knitting.

AVERAGE: For those with some experience in knitting. Directions are given for Size 38. Changes for Sizes 40, 42, 44 and 46 are in parentheses.

MATERIALS: Paton's "Astra" (50 gr. ball): 8 (8, 8, 9, 9) balls of No. 2849 Navy (A), 3 (3, 3, 3, 3) balls of No. 2783 Aran (B); knitting needles, one pair each No. 3 and No. 5, OR ANY SIZE NEEDLES TO OBTAIN GAUGE BELOW; five ¾"-dia. buttons; 2 stitch holders.

GAUGE: In stockinette stitch (k 1 row, p 1 row) using larger needles — 6 sts = 1"; 8 rows = 1". TO SAVE TIME, TAKE TIME TO CHECK GAUGE.

MEASUREMENTS:

Sizes: (38) (40) (42) (44) (46)
Body
Chest: 38" 40" 42" 44" 46"
Finished Measurements:
Chest: 40" 42" 44" 46" 48"
Width across back or front at under-arms:
      20" 21" 22" 23" 24"
Width across sleeve at upper arm:
    15½" 16" 16" 16½" 16½"

Note 1: Sweater buttons at one shoulder seam.
Note 2: Carry color not in use loosely up side of work.

. . . .

DIRECTIONS:

Back: Starting at lower edge with smaller needles and A, cast on 119 (125, 131, 137, 143) sts. Work in ribbing as follows: **Row 1** *(right side):* K 1, * p 1, k 1; rep from * across. **Row 2:** P 1, * k 1, p 1; rep from * across. Rep Rows 1 and 2 for 1", increasing one st at center of last row, ending with Row 2 — 120 (126, 132, 138, 144) sts. Change to larger needles and work in stockinette stitch (k 1 row, p 1 row) in the following stripe pattern: Work * 2 rows with B, 6 rows with A; rep from * for stripe pattern until

total length is about 15 (15, 16, 16, 17)" from beg, ending with 6 rows of A.

Armhole Shaping: Keeping continuity of stripe pattern, bind off 3 sts at beg of next 2 rows. Dec one st each end of next row, then every right-side row until 90 (96, 102, 108, 114) sts rem. Work even until armhole measures 8¼" above bound-off sts, ending with 1 row of A.

Shoulder Shaping for Buttonband: Bind off 8 (9, 10, 11, 12) sts at beg of next 2 wrong-side rows. Work even for 1 row. Bind off 9 (9, 10, 10, 11) sts at beg of next row.

Shoulder Shaping: Bind off 8 (9, 10, 11, 12) sts at beg of next 2 right-side rows. Work even for 1 row. Bind off 9 (9, 10, 10, 11) sts at beg of next row. Work even for 1 row, ending with a wrong-side row. Place rem 40 (42, 42, 44, 44) sts on a st holder for back neck.

Front: Work same as Back until 6¼" above armhole bound-off sts, ending with 2 rows of B.
Divide for Neck — Left Front: Keeping continuity of stripe pat, work across 31 (33, 36, 38, 41)

sts, **turn** and put rem sts on a st holder. Work even for 1 row. Dec one st at neck edge on next row, then every right-side row at neck edge until 25 (27, 30, 32, 35) sts rem. Work even until 9" above bound-off sts, ending with a wrong-side row.

Shoulder Shaping: Bind off 8 (9, 10, 11, 12) sts at beg of next 2 right-side rows. Work even for 1 row. Bind off rem 9 (9, 10, 10, 11) sts.

Right Front: With right side facing you, leave center 28 (30, 30, 32, 32) sts on st holder, and slip rem 31 (33, 36, 38, 41) sts onto needle. Join yarn and work Right Front to correspond to Left Front, reversing shaping.

Sleeves: Starting at lower edge with smaller needles and A, cast on 49 (53, 53, 57, 57) sts. Work in ribbing same as Back for 3", increasing 7 sts evenly spaced on last row, ending with Row 2 — 56 (60, 60, 64, 64) sts. Work in stripe pattern, increasing one st each end of the 11th row, then every 6th row until there are 92 (96, 96, 100, 100) sts. Work even until total length

is about 18 (18, 19, 19, 19)″ from beg, ending with 6 rows of A.

Cap Shaping: Keeping continuity of pat, bind off 3 sts at beg of next 2 rows. Dec one st each end of next row, then every right-side row until 58 (66, 66, 74, 74) sts rem. Dec one st each end of next row, then every row until 12 sts rem; end with 2 rows of A. Bind off.

Finishing: Collar: Sew right shoulder seam. With right side facing you, using smaller needles and A, pick up 22 sts along left front neck edge, k 28 (30, 30, 32, 32) sts from front st holder, pick up 22 sts along right front neck edge, k 40 (42, 42, 44, 44) sts from back st holder, decreasing one st at center — 111 (115, 115, 119, 119) sts. Work in ribbing as follows: **Row 1** *(right side)*: K 2, * p 1, k 1; rep from * across to last st, k 1. **Row 2:** K 1, * p 1, k 1; rep from * across. Rep Rows 1 and 2 for 4½″, ending with Row 2. Bind off loosely in ribbing using larger needle. Fold collar in half to wrong side and loosely sl st in place.

Button Band: With smaller needles and A, cast on 7 sts. Work in ribbing same as collar until band, slightly stretched, fits along left back shoulder seam to top of collar; sew in place as you go along; end with Row 2. Bind off loosely in ribbing using larger needle.

Buttonhole Band: Mark the position of 3 buttonholes along left front shoulder seam and 2 buttonholes along left collar edge, the first 1″ from armhole edge and the last ½″ below top of collar, evenly spacing 3 button-

holes in between. Work same as Button Band, making buttonholes on right-side of work at markers as follows: **Row 1** *(right side)*: Rib 3, bind off 2 sts, rib to end. **Row 2:** Rib 2, turn, cast on 2 sts, turn, rib to end. Sew on buttons. Overlap buttonhole band over button band at armhole edge and tack lower edges tog. Sew side and sleeve seams. Sew in sleeves.

FATHER/DAUGHTER
SWEATERS

FATHER'S SWEATER

TECHNIQUE: Knitting.

CHALLENGING: For those with more experience in knitting.
Directions are given for Size Small (34-36). Changes for Sizes Medium (38-40) and Large (42) are in parentheses.

MATERIALS: Galler "Cotton Express" (1¾ oz./50 gr. ball): 14 (15, 16) balls of Ciel (MC), 1 ball of Bluet (A); George Picaud Zig (1¾ oz./50 gr. ball): 1 ball each of Dark Blue (B); Green Tweed (C) and Beige Tweed (D); knitting needles, one pair each No. 3 and No. 4, OR ANY SIZE NEEDLES TO OBTAIN GAUGE BELOW; 8 bobbins.

GAUGE: In stockinette stitch (k 1 row, p 1 row) using larger needles — 6 sts = 1"; 8 rows = 1". TO SAVE TIME, TAKE TIME TO CHECK GAUGE.

MEASUREMENTS:

Sizes:	Small (34-36)	Medium (38-40)	Large (42)
Body Chest:	36"	40"	42"
Finished Chest:	40"	44"	46"
Width, Upper Arm:	15½"	16½"	17½"

Note 1: Colors B, C and D are worked with two strands held together throughout. MC and A are worked with one strand.
Note 2: Wind 3 bobbins with MC; 1 bobbin each with A, B and D; 2 bobbins with C.
Note 3: When changing colors, twist the yarn on the wrong side to
prevent holes in the work; **do not** carry the yarn.

DIRECTIONS:

BACK: Starting at lower edge with smaller needles and MC, cast on 97 (107, 115) sts. **Row 1** (*wrong side*): P 1, * k in back lp of next st to twist st — **k1b made;** p 1; rep from * across. **Row 2:** K1b, * p 1, k1b; rep from * across. Rep these 2 rows for twisted rib until length is 3", ending with Row 2. Work Row 1, increasing 25 sts evenly spaced across row — 122 (132, 140) sts. Change to larger needles and stockinette stitch (st st) until total length is 16" from beginning; end with a p row.
ARMHOLE SHAPING: Bind off 5 (6, 7) sts at beg of next 2 rows. Dec one st each end every other row 4 times — 104 (112, 118) sts. Work even until armholes measure 7½ (8, 8½)"; end with a p row.
NECK SHAPING: K 39 (42, 44) sts; join 2nd ball of MC, bind off center 26 (28, 30) sts; k 39 (42, 44) sts. Working both sides at once, dec one st at each neck edge every k row 4 times — 35 (38, 40) sts. P 1 row. Bind off all sts.

FRONT: *Note: When following the chart, work A sections in seed st. Work the same as the Back until the total length is 6" from the beg; end with a p row.* **Now start** chart as follows: **Row 1:** With MC k 26 (31, 35) sts, work Row 1 of chart over next 70 sts; with MC k 26 (31, 35) sts. Keeping to chart over center 70 sts, work same as Back until armholes measure 6 (6½, 7)", ending with a p row — 104 (112, 118) sts. *Note: Work*
with MC only after completion of Row 88 of chart.
NECK SHAPING: K 48 (51, 53) sts; join a 2nd ball of MC, bind off center 8 (10, 12) sts, k 48 (51, 53) sts. Working both sides at once, dec one st at each neck edge **every** row 8 times, then every **other** row 5 times — 35 (38, 40) sts. Work even until same length as Back armholes. Bind off.

SLEEVES: Starting at lower edge with smaller needles and MC, cast on 45 (51, 57) sts. Work in twisted rib, same as Back, until length is 3", ending with Row 2. Work Row 1, increasing 12 sts evenly spaced across row — 57 (63, 69) sts. Change to larger needles and st st, increasing one st each end of row every ¾" 19 times — 95 (101, 107) sts. Work even until total length is 19" from beginning or desired length, ending with a p row.
CAP SHAPING: Bind off 5 (6, 7) sts at beg of next 2 rows, then bind off 3 sts at beg of next 2 rows. Dec one st each end **every** row 4 times, then every **other** row 22 (24, 26) times — 27 sts. Bind off 3 sts at beg of next 6 rows — 9 sts. Bind off rem sts.
FINISHING: Steam lightly, without placing iron directly on the sweater. Sew the left shoulder seam.
NECKBAND: With the right side facing, using the smaller needles and MC, pick up and k 107 (111, 115) sts around the entire neck edge. Work in twisted rib for 1". Bind off. Sew the right shoulder/neckband seams. Sew the side and sleeve seams. Sew in the sleeves.

FATHER AND DAUGHTER SWEATERS

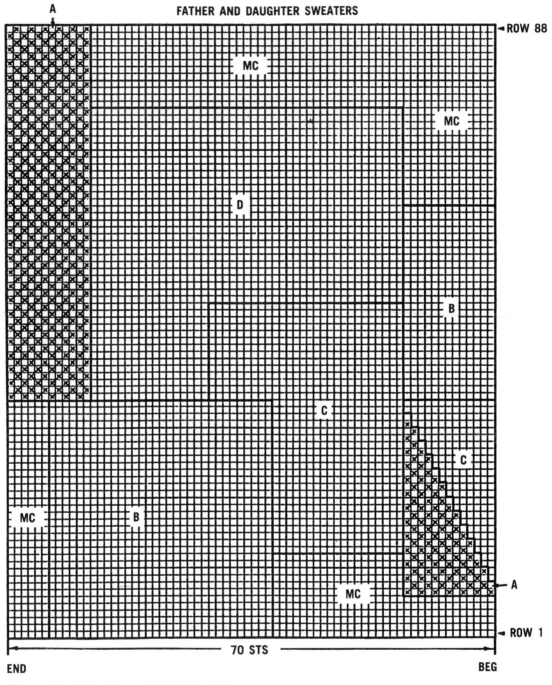

= P ON RIGHT SIDE, K ON WRONG SIDE
= K ON RIGHT SIDE, P ON WRONG SIDE

DAUGHTER'S SWEATER

TECHNIQUE: Knitting.

CHALLENGING: For those with more experience in knitting.

Note: This is an oversized sweater. Directions are for Size Petite (6). Sizes Small (8-10), Medium (12-14) and Large (16) are in parentheses.

MATERIALS: Galler "Cotton Express" (1¾ oz./50 gr. ball): 8 (9, 10, 11) balls of Ciel (MC), 1 ball each of Bluet (A) and Lin Lit Beige (D); George Picaud Zig (1¾ oz./50 gr. ball): 1 ball each of Dark Blue (B) and Green Tweed (C); knitting needles, one pair each of No. 3 and No. 4, OR ANY SIZE NEEDLES TO OBTAIN GAUGE BELOW; 8 bobbins; shoulder pads (optional).

GAUGE: In stockinette stitch (k 1 row, p 1 row) using larger needles — 6 sts = 1"; 8 rows = 1". TO SAVE TIME, TAKE TIME TO CHECK GAUGE.

MEASUREMENTS:

Sizes:

Petite (6)	Small (8-10)	Medium (12-14)	Large (16)
Body Bust:			
30½"	32½"	36"	38"
Finished Bust:			
38"	40"	44"	46"

Note 1: Colors B and C are worked with two strands of yarn held together throughout. MC, A and D are worked with one strand of yarn.

Note 2: Wind 3 bobbins with MC; 1 bobbin each with A, B and D. Wind 2 bobbins with C.

Note 3: See Father's Note No. 3.

DIRECTIONS:

BACK: Starting at lower edge with smaller needles and MC, cast on 89 (97, 107, 115) sts. **Row 1** *(wrong side)*: P 1, * k 1 in back lp of next st to twist st — **klb made**; p 1; rep from * across. **Row 2:** K1b, * p 1, k1b; rep from * across. Rep these 2 rows for twisted rib until length is 2", ending with Row 2. Work Row 1, increasing 13 sts evenly spaced across row — 102 (110, 120, 128) sts. Change to larger needles and stockinette stitch (st st) for 2" more. Increase one st each end of next row, then every 2" five times more — 114 (122, 132, 140) sts. Work even in st st until total length is 18" from beg, ending with a p row. Mark beg and end of next row for start of armholes. *Note: There is no armhole shaping.* Work even to measure 6½ (7, 7½, 8)"; end with a p row.

NECK SHAPING: K 43 (46, 50, 53) sts; join 2nd ball of MC, bind off center 28 (30, 32, 34) sts, k 43 (46, 50, 53) sts. Working both sides at once, dec one st at each neck edge **every** row 4 times — 39 (42, 46, 49) sts. P 1 row. Bind off all sts.

FRONT: *Note: When following chart, work A sections in seed st.* Work same as Back until ½" above 2nd side inc (about 6½"), ending with a p row — 106 (114, 124, 132) sts. **Now start** chart as follows: **Row 1:** With MC k 18 (22, 27, 31) sts, work Row 1 of chart over 70 sts, with MC k 18 (22, 27, 31) sts. Keeping to chart over center 70 sts, work side incs as on Back. Work until armholes measure 4½ (4¾, 5¼, 5¾)"; end with a p row — 114 (122, 132, 140) sts. *Note: Work with MC only after completion of Row 88 of chart.*

NECK SHAPING: K 48 (51, 55, 58) sts; join a 2nd ball of MC, bind off center 18 (20, 22, 24) sts, k 48 (51, 55, 58) sts. Working both sides at once, dec one st at each neck edge **every** row 2 times, then every **other** row 7 times — 39 (42, 46, 49) sts. Work even until armholes measure same as Back armholes. Bind off all sts.

FINISHING: Steam lightly, without placing the iron directly on the sweater. Sew the left shoulder seam.

NECKBAND: With the right side facing, using the smaller needles and MC, beg at the right back neck, pick up and k 119 (123, 127, 131) sts around the neck edge. Work in twisted rib for 1". Bind off. Sew the right shoulder and neckband seams.

ARMBANDS: With the right side facing, using the smaller needles and MC, beg at one armhole marker, pick up and k 87 (91, 95, 99) sts around the armhole to the other marker. Work in twisted rib for 1". Bind off. Sew the side and armband seams. Sew in the shoulder pads (this is optional).

"HONEYCOMB AND CABLES" FISHERMAN PULLOVER

TECHNIQUE: Knitting.

CHALLENGING: For those with more experience in knitting.

Directions are given for Size 38. Changes for Sizes 40, 42 and 44 are in parentheses.

MATERIALS: Bernat "Blarney-Spun" (1¾-oz. skein) of No. 7959 Natural: 17 (18, 19, 20) skeins; knitting needles sizes 4 and 8, OR ANY SIZE NEEDLES TO OBTAIN GAUGE BELOW; cable needle.

GAUGE: On larger needles in Pat #1: 4 sts = 1"; 7 rows = 1". TO SAVE TIME, TAKE TIME TO CHECK GAUGE.

FINISHED MEASUREMENTS:

Sizes:	38	40	42	44
Chest:	40"	42"	44"	46"
Back width at underarm:				
	20"	21"	22"	23"
Sleeve around upper arm:				
	16"	17"	18"	19"

DIRECTIONS:

PATTERN #1: Row 1 (*right side*): * K 1, p 1; rep from * to end. **Row 2:** P. **Row 3:** * P 1, k 1; rep from * to end. **Row 4:** P. Rep Rows 1-4 for Pat #1.

PATTERN #2: Worked on 18 sts. **Row 1** (*right side*): * P 2, k 2; sl next st to cable needle and hold at back of work, sl next st as to p, k st from cable needle (Right Slip — RS); rep from * once more, p 2; k 2nd st on left needle, then k first st (Right Cross — RC): k 2nd st thru back lp, then k first st (Left Cross — LC). **Row 2 And All Even Numbered Rows:** K the k sts and p the purl sts. **Row 3:** * P 2, k 1, RS, k 1; rep from * once more, p 2, k 4. **Row 5:** * P 2, RS, k 2; rep from * once more, p 2, LC, RC. **Row 6:** Rep row 2, Rep Rows 1-6 for Pat #2.

PATTERN #3: Worked on 18 sts. **Row 1** (*right side*): RC, LC, p 2, * k 2nd st on left needle thru back lp, sl first st as to p (Left Slip — LS), k 2, p 2; rep from * once more. **Row 2 And All Even Numbered Rows:** K the knit sts and p the purl sts. **Row 3:** K 4, p 2, * k 1, LS, k 1, p 2; rep from * once more. **Row 5:** LC, RC, p 2, * k 2, LS, p 2; rep from * once more. **Row 6:** Rep Row 2. Rep Rows 1-6 for Pat #3.

PATTERN #4: Worked on 28 sts. **Row 1** (*right side*): * P 4; sl next 2 sts to cable needle, hold at front, k next 2 sts, k 2 from cable needle (Cable Front — CF); rep from * twice more, p 4. **Row 2 And All Even Numbered Rows:** K the knit sts and p the purl sts. **Row 3:** P 2, * sl next 2 sts to cable needle, hold at back, k 2, p 2 sts from cable needle (Right Twist — RT); sl next 2 sts to cable needle, hold at front, p 2, k 2 sts from cable needle (Left Twist — LT); rep from * twice more, p 2. **Row 5:** P 2; k next 2 sts tog then k first st again (Twist 2 — T2); * p 4; sl next 2 sts to cable needle, hold at back, k 2, k 2 sts from cable needle (Cable Back — CB); rep from * once more, p 4, T2, p 2. **Row 7:** P 2, T2, p 2, * RT, LT; rep from * once more, p 2, T2, p 2. **Row 9:** * P 2, T2; rep from * once more, p 4, CF, p 4; *T2, p 2; rep from * once more. **Row 11:** * P 2, T2; rep from * once more, p 4, k 4, p 4 * T2, p 2; rep from * once more. **Row 13:** Rep Row 9. **Row 15:** Rep Row 11. **Row 17:** Rep Row 9. **Row 19:** P 2, T 2, p 2, * LT, RT; rep from * once more, p 2, T 2, p 2. **Row 21:** P 2, T 2, p 4, * CB, p 4; rep from * once more, T 2, p 2. **Row 23:** P 2, * LT, RT; rep from * twice more, p 2. **Row 24:** Rep Row 2. Rep Rows 1-24 for Pat #4.

BACK: With smaller needles, cast on 98 (102, 106, 110) sts. Work in k 1, p 1 ribbing for 2". **Next Row** (*wrong side*): P 17 (19, 21, 23), place marker in work, [k 2, p 4] 3 times, k 4, [p 4, k 4] 3 times, [p 4, k 2] 3 times, place marker, p 17 (19, 21, 23). Change to larger needle. Beg Pats — **Row 1** (*right side*): Work Pat #1 over first 17 (19, 21, 23) sts, sl marker, work Pat #2 over next 18 sts, Pat #4 over next 28 sts, Pat #3 over next 18 sts, sl marker, work Pat #1 over last 17 (19, 21, 23) sts. Continue in pats as established until piece measures 16″ from beg, or desired length to underarm, end with a wrong-side row.

ARMHOLE SHAPING: Bind off 8 sts at beg of next 2 rows. Beg Raglan Shaping — **Row 1** (*right side*): K 4, work pat to last 4 sts, k 4. **Row 2:** K 4, work pat to last 4 sts, k 4. **Row 3:** K 2, sl 1, k 1, psso, work pats to last 4 sts, k 2 tog, k 2. **Row 4:** Rep Row 2. Rep Rows 1-4, 4 (5, 5, 6) times more. Rep Rows 3 and 4 only 21 (21, 23, 23) times. Place rem 30 (32, 32, 34) sts on holder for back of neck.

FRONT: Work same as Back, until there are 46 (48, 48, 50) sts. Continuing armhole decs,

place center 20 (22, 22, 24) sts on a holder for neck, and working each side with separate yarn, dec 1 st at neck edges every 2nd row 5 times.

SLEEVES: With smaller needles, cast on 46 (46, 48, 48) sts. Work in k 1, p 1 ribbing for 3″, inc 10 sts evenly spaced across last row — 56 (56, 58, 58) sts. Change to larger needles. **Beg Pats — Row 1** (*right side*): Work Pat #1 over first 2 (2, 3, 3) sts, place marker, work Pat #2 over next 12 sts (working from * only once), work Pat #4 over next 28 sts, work Pat #3 over next 12 sts (working from * only once), place marker, work Pat #1 over last 2 (2, 3, 3) sts. Continue in pats as established, inc 1 st before first marker and 1 st after 2nd marker every 6th row (working inc sts into Pat #1) 10 (12, 13,

15) times. Work even on 76 (80, 84, 88) sts until piece measures 19″ from beg, or desired length to underarm, end with a wrong-side row.

SLEEVE CAP SHAPING: Bind off 8 sts at beg of next 2 rows. Rep Rows 1-4 of raglan shaping as on Back 3 (4, 4, 5) times. Rep Rows 3 and 4 *only* 25 (25, 27, 27) times. Place rem 4 (6, 6, 8) sts on holder.

NECKBAND: With smaller needles from right side, pick up and k 96 (104, 104, 112) sts around neck, including sts on holders. Work in k 1, p 1 ribbing for 3″. Bind off loosely in ribbing. Fold band in half to wrong side and sew.

FINISHING: Sew the raglan sleeve caps to the raglan armholes. Sew the side and sleeve seams.

MAN'S NECKTIE

(2" x 55")

TECHNIQUE: Knitting and crochet.

EASY: Achievable by anyone.

MATERIALS: Lion Brand "Co-Co" 1 (1.4-oz.) ball of Burgundy No. 144; knitting needles, one pair of No. 2, OR ANY SIZE NEEDLES TO OBTAIN GAUGE BELOW; 12" of ⅞" wide matching color grosgrain ribbon; steel crochet hook No. 1.

GAUGE: In seed st — 7 sts = 1"; 12 rows = 1". TO SAVE TIME, TAKE TIME TO CHECK GAUGE.

DIRECTIONS:

TIE BORDER: Starting at lower edge, cast on 17 sts. **Row 1** *(Right Side)*: K 1, * p 1, k 1; rep from * across. **Row 2:** P 1, * k 1, p 1; rep from * across. Rep Rows 1 and 2 for ½", change to seed st and work as follows: **Row 1** *(Right Side)*: K 1, * p 1, k 1; rep from * across. Rep Row 1 until total length is 17" from beg.

SHAPING TIE: Dec one st at each end on next row, then every 2" 4 times more — 7 sts. Work even on 7 sts until total length is 54½" from beg.

BORDER: Rep Rows 1 and 2 of border for ½" — 55". Bind off loosely in ribbing.

Note: The edging will conceal end decreases made.

CROCHETED EDGING: From right side, attach yarn to right corner of narrow end and work 2 sc in same sp, sc in each st along edge of tie working 2 sc in each corner st. Join with sl st to first sl st. Fasten off.

FINISHING: Pin tie to shape and measurements on a padded, flat surface; cover with a damp cloth; allow to dry. **Do not** press. At 25" from wide end pin 12" length of same color ⅞"-wide grosgrain inside neckline to prevent stretching; sew all around with invisible stitches.

TIP — The Trick To Knitting Ties

Knitting a tie can be tricky — too much thickness will yield a bulky knot. Take your cue from our single-layer tie, made with only two needles. It's worked in seed stitch for strength without bulk.

MAN'S CLASSIC SCUFFS

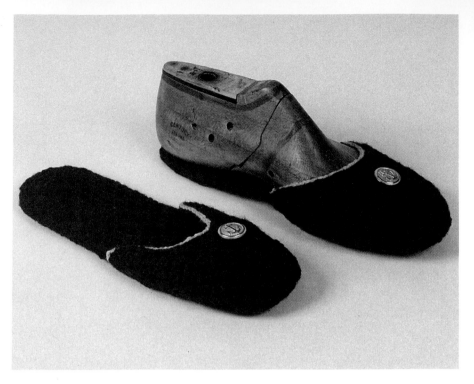

TECHNIQUE: Crochet.

AVERAGE: For those with some experience in crochet. Directions are given for Size Small (6-7), Medium (8-9) and Large (10-11).

MATERIALS: Lion Brand Sayelle 4-Ply Worsted Weight Yarn (3.5-oz. skein): 1 (1, 2) skeins of No. 114 Cardinal; crochet hook, Size G, OR ANY SIZE HOOK TO OBTAIN GAUGE BELOW; 1 pr. of insoles in Size (6-7), (8-9) or (10-11); two ¾"-diameter military buttons; scrap of beige yarn for edging.

GAUGE: 4 sc = 1"; 4 rows = 1". TO SAVE TIME, TAKE TIME TO CHECK GAUGE.

HDC: Yo, draw up a lp; in next st, yo and draw through 3 lps on hook.

DIRECTIONS:

SCUFF — **Sole** (*Make 2*): Measure length of insole and make chain 2½" less. **Rnd 1:** 2 sc in 2nd ch from hook, sc in each st to center ch, hdc (*see above*) in 4 sts, dc to fourth st from end, hdc in 2 sts, 5 sc in end st. Continuing on other side of ch, hdc in first 2 sts, dc in each st opposite dc on other side, hdc in 4 sts, sc to end. **Place marker at beg of rnd. Rnd 2:** 3 sc in first sc, 2 sc in next sc for heel, sc around to toe and 2 sc in next sc, 1 sc in each of next 2 sc, 2 sc in next sc, 1 sc in each of next 2 sc, 2 sc in next sc for toe, continue to sc to beg of rnd. **Rnds 3-5:** (2 sc in next sc, 1 sc in next sc) 2 times, 2 sc in next sc for heel, sc around to toe and (2 sc in next sc, 1 sc in each of next 2 sc) 2 times, 2 sc in next sc, continue to sc around. **Rnd 6:** Sl st in each sc. Fasten off. Repeat for second sole. Sew soles together from right side with insole in center.

UPPER (*Make 2*): Starting at toe, ch 9. **Row 1:** Sc in 2nd ch from hook, sc in each sc across — 8 sc. Ch 1, turn. **Rows 2 and 3:** 2 sc in first sc — **inc made;** sc in each sc across to within last sc, 2 sc in last sc — 12 sc, Ch 1, turn. **Row 4:** Sc in each sc across to within last sc, 2 sc in last sc — 13 sc. Ch 1, turn. Work even on the 13 sc until 11 rows have been completed. **Do not** fasten off.

SIDES: **Next Row:** Sc in each of first 5 sc; **do not** work rem sts. Ch 1, turn. **Next Row:** Working on the 5 sc, sc in each st across. Ch 1, turn. **Next Row:** Dec one st at end of next row. Repeat dec at same edge every 3rd row twice more. Work even for 1 (2, 3) more rows (depending on size scuff). Fasten off. Leaving 3 sc free at center on last long row, join yarn in next sc, 1 sc in next st and in each sc to end. Ch 1, turn. Finish same as other side reversing shaping. Sl st all around entire piece to round out. Fasten off. With right side facing you, sew Upper to Sole.

EDGING: With beige yarn, sl st along inner edge of Upper. Fasten off. Sew on button.

BOY'S MITTENS AND SCARF SET

MITTENS

(One size fits all)

TECHNIQUE (for set): Knitting and crochet.

AVERAGE: For those with some experience in knitting.

MATERIALS: Green Mountain "Spinnery" 2-ply (4-oz. skein*). For Mittens:* 1 skein each of Garnet (A) and Natural Grey (B). *For Scarf:* 1 skein each of the same colors (A and B); knitting needles, one pair each No. 6 and No. 7, OR ANY SIZE NEEDLES TO OBTAIN GAUGE BELOW; 2 stitch holders; tapestry needle; crochet hook, size G.

GAUGE: In stockinette stitch (st st) with larger needles — 9 sts = 2"; 6 rows = 1". TO SAVE TIME, TAKE TIME TO CHECK GAUGE.

DIRECTIONS:

MITTENS *(Make 2)* — **CUFF EDGING:** Starting at lower edge of cuff with larger needles and A, cast on 45 sts (leaving a long end to make crocheted loop), with A, k 6 rows. Cut A; attach B. With B, k 1 row.

CUFF RIBBING: Continuing with B, unless otherwise stated, work as follows: **Row 1** *(wrong side)*: K 1, * p 1, k 2; rep from * across, ending last rep with k 1 instead of k 2. **Row 2:** P 1, * k 1, p 2; rep from * across, ending last rep with p 1 instead of p 2. Rep Rows 1 and 2 until total length is 3" from beg, ending with a wrong-side row. *Note: Cuff is tightened at the wrist by changing to smaller needles and decreasing the number of stitches across the next row.* **Next Row** *(right side)*: Change to smaller needles and work as follows: P 1, k 1, * p 2

```
TIP
```
A Perfect Kid-Fit

There's a secret to knitting these mittens in boys' sizes. We used smaller needles for the wrist area to make them snug and larger needles for the cuff so they can be easily pulled over bulky sleeves.

tog, k 1; rep from * across ending with p 1 — 31 sts. **Next Row:** * K 1, p 1; rep from * across, ending with k 1. **Next Row:** * P 1, k 1; rep from * across, ending with p 1. Rep last 2 rows until total length is 4½″ from beg, ending with a wrong-side row. **Next Row** (*right side*): Change to larger needles and continue working with B as follows: * P 1, k 1, p 1, increase in next st by knitting in the st below, then knit the st on the needle; rep from * across — 38 sts. **Next Row:** P across. **Next 2 Rows:** With B, k 1 row, p 1 row. *Note: Drop B but do not cut B, and attach A.*

Thumb: Continuing in stockinette stitch (k 1 row, p 1 row) begin thumb as follows: **Row 1:** With A k 18, inc as before in the next 2 sts, work to end. **Row 2:** P across. **Row 3:** K 18, inc in next st, k 2, inc in next st, work to end. **Row 4:** P across. **Row 5:** Drop A, pick up B and with B k 18, inc in next st, k 4, inc in next st, work to end. **Row 6:** P across. Continue to increase every other row, having 2 more stitches between increases, and change color every 4th row for

stripe pattern, until there are 50 sts on needle, ending with a p row. **Next Row:** With B k 19 and place on a st holder, k 12 for thumb sts; place rem 19 sts on another st holder. **Next 13 Rows:** Work even in st st with B on the 12 thumb sts *only*. **Next Row:** * K 2, k 2 tog; rep from * across — 9 sts. **Next Row:** * P 1, p 2 tog; rep from * across — 6 sts.

With Tapestry Needle: Draw yarn through rem sts and fasten off. Sew thumb seam.

Body of Mitten: Place sts from st holders onto needle and attach B yarn, work even in st st, following stripe pattern until 4″ from base of thumb, ending with a P row and A. Cut A. **Shape Tip** — With B only, work as follows: **Row 1:** * K 2, k 2 tog; rep from * across — 29 sts. **Row 2:** P across. **Row 3:** * K 2, k 2 tog; rep from * across, ending with k 1 — 22 sts. **Row 4:** P across. **Row 5:** * K 2, k 2 tog; rep from * across ending with k 2 — 17 sts. With tapestry needle draw yarn through rem sts and fasten off, sew side seam.

Crocheted Loop for Hanging Mittens: With cro-

chet hook and long end at cast-on edge, ch 12. Fasten off. Pull through end at Cuff edge and secure to form loop.

SCARF

(10″ x 53″)

DIRECTIONS:
*Note: Carry colors in stripe pattern up the side of work; **do not** break yarn.*

Starting at narrow end with A and larger needles, cast on 46 sts. **Next 6 Rows:** With A, k across. Drop A, attach B. **Row 7:** With B, k across. **Row 8:** With B, k 2, p to last 2 sts, k 2. **Row 9:** Rep Row 7. **Row 10:** Rep Row 8. Drop B, pick up A. **Rows 11-14:** With A rep Rows 7-9. Rep Rows 7-14 for stripe pattern until total length is 52″, ending with a B stripe. **Last 6 Rows:** With A, k across, bind off.

Finishing: Steam press lightly (**do not** place iron directly on scarf).

Edging: With crochet hook and A, work a row of sc along the sides of scarf, having 2 sc's to each stripe.

MAN'S HOUNDSTOOTH
CARDIGAN

TECHNIQUE: Knitting.

AVERAGE: For those with some experience in knitting. Directions are for Small (38-40). Changes for Medium (42-44) and Large (46) are in parentheses.

MATERIALS: Neveda "Mondial" (100 gr. ball): 6 (6, 7)

Gray #7138 (MC), 2 (2, 3) Ecru #7117 (A); knitting needles, one pair each No. 6 and No. 8, OR ANY SIZE NEEDLES TO OBTAIN GAUGE BELOW; 29" circular needle, Size 6; 6 buttons.

GAUGE: Stockinette stitch on larger needles: 9 sts = 2"; 6 rows

= 1". TO SAVE TIME, TAKE TIME TO CHECK GAUGE.

MEASUREMENTS:

Sizes:	Small	Medium	Large
Finished			
Chest:	41"	44"	48"
Back width at underarm:			
	20½"	22"	24"
Sleeve width at upper arm:			
	15"	16½"	18"

Note: Always twist yarns when changing colors to prevent holes. Carry color not in use loosely at the back of the work, being careful to maintain the gauge.

· ·

DIRECTIONS:

BACK: With smaller needles and MC cast on 93 (101, 109) sts. **Row 1** *(wrong side)*: P 1, * k 1, p 1, rep from * across. **Row 2:** K 1, * p 1, k 1, rep from * across. Rep these 2 rows for rib pat to 2", end with Row 1. Change to larger needles and stockinette stitch (st st). Work to 15" from beg, end with a p row.

ARMHOLE SHAPING: Bind off 4 (5, 6) sts at beg of next 2 rows. **Row 3:** K 2, sl 1, k 1, psso, k to last 4 sts, k 2 tog, k 2. **Row 4:** P. Rep Rows 3 and 4 for 4 times more — 75 (81, 87) sts. Work even until armholes measure 9 (9½, 10)", end with a p row.

NECK SHAPING: Row 1: K 20 (22, 24) sts, k 2 tog, k 2, join 2nd ball of MC, bind off center 27 (29, 31) sts, k 2, sl 1, k 1, psso, k to end — 23(25, 27) sts each side of neck. Working both sides at once, p 1 row. **Row 3:** K to 4 sts from neck edge, k 2 tog, k 2, with 2nd ball k 2, sl 1, k 1,

psso, k to end — 22(24, 26) sts. P 1 row.

SHOULDER SHAPING: Bind off 11 (12, 13) sts at each arm edge every other row, twice. Fasten off yarns.

LEFT FRONT: With smaller needles and MC cast on 45 (49, 53) sts. Work in ribbing as on lower Back to 2". Change to larger needles and st st. Work 2 rows. Beg pat. **Row 1:** With MC, k 3, follow chart over next 40 (44, 48) sts, with MC, k 2. Keeping front and side edge sts in MC, work in pat over remaining sts. Rep Rows 1 thru 4 for pat. Work same length as Back to armholes.

ARMHOLE AND V-NECK SHAPING: Row 1: Keeping to pat at arm edge, bind off 4 (5, 6) sts, work to 4 sts from front edge, k 2 tog (neck dec), k 2. Work 1 row even. **Row 3:** K 2, sl 1, k 1, psso, complete row. Continue to dec 1 st at armhole edge every other row 4 times more and at neck edge every 4th row 13 (14, 15) times more — 22 (24, 26) sts. Work even in pat until armhole measures same as Back to shoulder, end at armhole edge.

SHOULDER SHAPING: Keeping to pat, bind off 11 (12, 13) sts

every other row twice.

RIGHT FRONT: Work same as left Front, reversing shaping. Be sure to work 2 MC sts at front edge and 3 MC sts at side edge.

SLEEVES: With smaller needles and MC, cast on 45 (49, 53) sts. Work in ribbing as on lower Back to 2". Change to larger needles and st st, inc 4 (6, 8) sts evenly across first row — 49 (55, 61) sts. Work 8 rows. Inc 1 st each end of next row, then every 8th row 9 times more — 69 (75, 81) sts. Work until sleeve measures 19" from beg or desired length, end with a p row.

CAP SHAPING: Bind off 4 (5, 6) sts at beg of next 2 rows — 61 (65, 69) sts. **Rows 3 and 4:** Rep Rows 3 and 4 of Back armhole shaping. Rep Rows 3 and 4 for 4 (5, 6) times more, then rep Row 3 every 4th row 5 times. Bind off 5 sts at beg of next 4 rows. Bind off remaining sts.

FINISHING: Sew the shoulder, side and sleeve seams. Sew in the sleeves.

FRONT AND NECKBAND: From right side with the circular needle and MC, beg at the lower right Front pick up 80 sts to beg of V-neck, pick up 42 (45, 48)

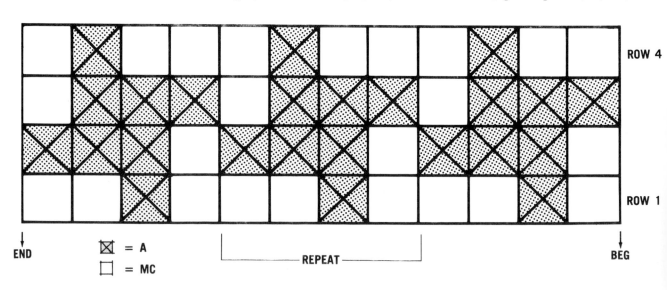

END   ⊠ = A   □ = MC   REPEAT   BEG

ROW 4

ROW 1

sts to right shoulder, pick up 37 (39, 41) sts around Back neck edge to shoulder, pick up 42 (45, 48) sts down left Front to beg of V-neck, pick up 80 sts to lower left Front edge — 281 (289, 297) sts. Beg p 1, k 1, work in ribbing. Work 1 row. Along straight edge of right front, mark places for 6 buttons, having the top button approx 4″ below the start of the V-neck, the bottom button approx 1″ above the lower edge and spacing the others evenly between.

Buttonholes: Row 1: (In ribbing work to opposite marker, bind off 2 sts) 6 times, complete row. **Row 2:** (Work to bound off sts, cast on 2 sts) 6 times, complete row. Work 2 rows more. Bind off in ribbing. Block lightly to measurements. Sew on the buttons.

·7·

ACCENTS & BRIGHT IDEAS

I t doesn't take lots of money to transform the ordinary into the extraordinary — but it does take a little ingenuity! We offer some easy-to-achieve flourishes that will perk up your wardrobe, as well as lift your spirits. You can transform an ordinary sweatshirt into a dazzling top for you, or create an "instant argyle" look for your man. There are also sensational totes and hats, plus a gorgeous heirloom-look lace collar — in short, an array of accessories you'll love!

VICTORIAN COLLAR

(Collar is shown on the previous page.)

TECHNIQUE: Crochet.

CHALLENGING: For those with more experience in crochet.

MATERIALS: J. & P. Coats "Knit-Cro-Sheen": 1 (350 yd.) ball of No. 61 Ecru; steel crochet hook, No. 7, OR ANY SIZE HOOK TO OBTAIN GAUGE BELOW; three ⅜″-dia. buttons.

GAUGE: Each Large Motif = 2″ in diameter. TO SAVE TIME, TAKE TIME TO CHECK GAUGE.

DIRECTIONS:

LARGE MOTIF *(Make 16):* Starting at center of motif, ch 6. Join with sl st to form a ring. **Rnd 1:** Ch 3 for first dc, work 4 dc in ring, draw up a long lp in last dc and drop lp from hook, insert hook in top of ch-3 starting ch, pick up dropped lp, draw through and tighten (starting popcorn made), * ch 5, work 5 dc in ring, draw up a long lp in last dc and drop lp from hook, insert hook in first dc of 5-dc group, pick up dropped lp, draw through and tighten (popcorn made); rep from * 4 times more, ch 5. Join with sl st to tip of first popcorn — 6 popcorns with 6 ch-5 lps completed. **Rnd 2:** Sc in tip of pop-

corn, * ch 5, sc in next ch-5 lp, ch 5, sc in tip of next popcorn; rep from * around, ending last rep with sl st in first sc — 12 lps. **Rnd 3:** Sl st in next 3 ch, sc in same lp, * ch 5, sc in next lp; rep from * around, ending with sl st in first sc — 12 lps. Fasten off, leaving a 5″ end. Following FIG. 1 and using 5″ end, sew 16 Large Motifs tog into one long strip. Take care to note that there must be 5 free lps between joinings.

MEDIUM MOTIF *(Make 16):* **Rnds 1 and 2:** Work same as Large Motif, Rnds 1 and 2. Fasten off, leaving a 5″ end. Following FIG. 1 and using 5″ end, sew 16 Medium Motifs tog into one long strip. Take care to note that there must be 5 lps between joinings. Next, sew Medium Motif Strip to Large Motif Strip. Note on FIG. 1 that when the strips are joined, there must be 2 free center lps on each motif between joinings.

SMALL MOTIF *(Make 25):* **Rnd 1:** Work same as Large Motif, Rnd 1. Fasten off, leaving a 5″

end. Following FIG. 1 for placement, and using 5″ end, sew 15 Small Motifs in open center area as indicated. For remaining 10 Small Motifs *(not shown in FIG. 1)*, arrange these pieces in a straight line with popcorns touching. Sew pieces tog at the popcorns and note that there will be 2 free popcorns between joinings. Set this piece aside.

BORDER: **Row 1:** With right side facing you, join thread with sc at lp indicated by **A** and, working up center back edge, work 2 more sc in same lp, (ch 2, 3 sc in next lp) 3 times, ch 2, sc in last lp of motif, skip joining, sc in first free lp of next motif (another joining worked in 2 motifs), (ch 2, 3 sc in next lp) 3 times (mark this corner for top of center back edge of collar), * (ch 5, sc in next lp) to one lp before next joining, sc in last free lp of motif, skip joining, sc in first free lp of next motif (another joining worked in 2 motifs); rep from * across top edge (neck) to corresponding corner on opposite side of top, mark this corner, and work remaining center back edge as before. Ch 1, turn. **Row 2:** Sc in each sc, 3 sc in each ch-sp to marker, (ch 5, sc in next lp) to next marker, sc in each sc, 3 sc in each ch-sp along remaining center back edge. **Row 3:** Sc in each sc along center back edge, * ch 4, sc in next lp; rep from * along neck edge; ending with sc in each sc along remaining center back edge. Fasten off. **Row 4** (*Buttonloop Row*): Mark for 3 buttonloops, each 4-sc long on right center back edge, the first beginning 3 sc up from bottom, the last 2 sc down from top, the remaining evenly spaced between. With right side facing you, attach thread and sc in each sc on left center back edge, working across neck with ch 4, sc in next lp pattern as established. On right center back edge of collar, sc in each of next 2 sc, * ch 4, skip 4 sc, sc in each sc to next marker; rep from * across, ending with sc in each of last 3 sc. Fasten off.

SMALL MOTIF BORDER: Work around 10-motif strip as follows: At one edge, join thread with sc

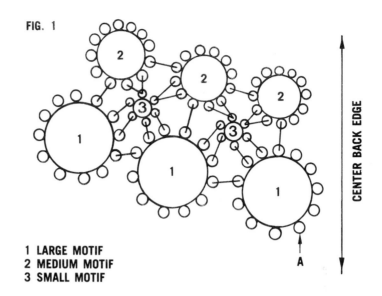

FIG. 1

1 LARGE MOTIF
2 MEDIUM MOTIF
3 SMALL MOTIF

CENTER BACK EDGE

in popcorn, * (ch 5, sc in next lp, ch 5, sc in next popcorn) to one lp before joining, sc in last free lp of motif, skip joining at popcorns, sc in first free lp of next motif; repeat from * around as established. Join to first sc.

Fasten off. Pin and sew Small Motif unit to neck edge of collar, easing as necessary to fit.

FINISHING: Sew buttons in place opposite buttonloops. Starch lightly, if desired.

SUNDRESS APPLIQUÉS

TECHNIQUE: Crochet.

EASY: Achievable by anyone.

MATERIALS: Sundress similar to one in photo; *For Crocheted Squares* — J. & P. Coats "Knit-Cro-Sheen" (175 yd. ball): 1 ball each of Light Pink, Dark Pink, Green, Purple, Gold, White, Blue and Cranberry; crochet hook, No. 7, OR ANY SIZE HOOK TO OBTAIN GAUGE BELOW.

GAUGE: Each Square = 1½″ square. TO SAVE TIME, TAKE TIME TO CHECK GAUGE.

. . . .

DIRECTIONS:

SQUARE: Starting at lower edge of square, ch 16. **Row 1:** Dc in 6th ch from hook (counts as 1 dc and ch-1 sp), * ch 1, sk 1 ch, 1 dc in next ch; rep from * across — 6 ch-1 spaces made. **Row 2:** Ch 4 (counts as 1 dc and ch-1 sp), turn 1 dc in next dc, * ch 1, 1 dc in next dc; rep from * across, ending with 1 dc in turning ch — 6 ch-1 spaces made. **Rows 3-5:** Rep Row 2. Fasten off. For Size 10, make 44 white squares and 88 colored squares. Add or delete squares for other sizes, as needed, to fit dress.

ASSEMBLY *(see photo):* Pin 3 squares together with one white square in center and one colored square at each end. With darning needle and matching thread, from right side, sew the squares together from the center of a corner to the center of the next corner along side edges, matching sts and working through back lps **only.**

Note: Adapt the number of appliqués for your dress following placement on bodice and skirt in photo.

FRONT AND BACK YOKE BORDER: Make 14 rows of 3 squares each. Pin and sew rows together in a diagonal pattern so that a colored end square is over a white square. With white square centered at CF, tack Border to top edge of Front and Back Yoke *(see photo).* Remove any square which falls over the zipper; add a colored square if needed for symmetry and tack the loose edges to the dress.

BOTTOM BORDER: Pin, sew and join 30 rows of 3 squares, the same as above. Tack the border around the skirt, 7″ above the hem edge.

TIP — ## Crochet Some Color!

. . . .

We've added pizzazz to summertime dressing with these cheery crocheted appliqués. You can do the same by prettying up a lightweight sweater, shorts, skirt — anything you love to wear in warm weather. The tiny squares are portable and a breeze to crochet. Sew them together in groups of three and appliqué them in diamond pattern borders.

RED
SWEATSHIRT
JACKET

TECHNIQUE: Sewing.

EASY: Achievable by anyone.

MATERIALS: Red sweatshirt; 5½ yds. of 1⅞″-wide black bias rayon hem-facing.

DIRECTIONS:

1. CUT off ribbing at the neck, wrist and bottom edges. Mark the center front from top to bottom edges and cut along the mark.

2. BINDING: Bind the wrist edges with hem facing. Also bind the neck, front and bottom edges, mitering at corners.

3. BOWS: Fold the 50″ length of hem facing in half, right sides together. Seam the long edges together to make a ⅞″ wide tube. Center the seam at the back of the tube and press. Cut off 8″; lap ends at the center back to make a 3¾″ flat loop. Cut off 2½″ of

tube and wrap it around the center of the loop (*see photo*); lap ends at the center back, turn under the raw end and slip stitch it to complete a bow.

4. FASTENING: Pin a bow to the top front of the jacket, with the center of the bow at the right edge. Pin 3 more bows below, generally spaced about 5″ apart. Sew a hook behind each bow; sew eyes on the left edge.

"INSTANT ARGYLE" SWEATSHIRT

TECHNIQUE: Sewing.

EASY: Achievable by anyone.

MATERIALS: Sweatshirt; 3 (4¾") squares of cotton knit fabric; contrasting embroidery floss.

DIRECTIONS: Pin squares of cotton knit fabric to the front of the sweatshirt (*see photo*). Sew along the edges with narrow zigzag machine stitching and matching thread. Using 3 strands of contrasting embroidery floss in your needle, embroider 4¾" "squares" in long back stitches across the jersey squares and shirt to simulate an "argyle" design of diamond scoring over solid diamond-angled squares.

TIP

Is It Really Argyle?

Know why we call this sweater "instant" argyle? Because you start with a plain sweatshirt, and sew on squares of cotton knit fabric. Then you score the diamond-angled squares with easy stitching that mimics an authentic Argyle pattern!

HAT
COVER
AND
TOTE BAG

HAT COVER
. . . .
(23″ wide at crown x 5″ deep)
TECHNIQUE: Crochet.

EASY: Achievable by anyone.

MATERIALS: Coats and Clark "Speed-Cro-Sheen" — 2 (100 yd.) skeins of No. 61-D Nu-Ecru; steel crochet hook, No. 1, OR ANY SIZE HOOK TO OBTAIN GAUGE BELOW; darning needle; purchased straw hat.

GAUGE: 5 dc = 1″; 2 rnds = 1″. TO SAVE TIME, TAKE TIME TO CHECK GAUGE.

Note: The Hat Cover is made separately and sewn to the crown of a hat afterward. All rnds are worked from the right side.

DIRECTIONS:

HAT COVER: Starting at center of crown, ch 6. Join with sl st to form ring. **Rnd 1:** Work 10 sc in ring. Join with sl st to first sc. **Rnd 2:** Ch 4 (counts as 1 dc and ch-1), in next sc work (dc, ch 1, dc), ch 1, * dc in next sc, ch 1, in next sc work (dc, ch 1, dc), ch 1; rep from * around — 15 dc. Join with sl st to 3rd ch of ch-4. **Hereafter ch-4 counts as 1 dc and ch-1, unless otherwise stated. Rnd 3:** Ch 4, dc in next dc, ch 1, in next dc work (dc, ch 1, dc), ch 1, * (dc in next dc, ch 1) 2 times, in next dc work (dc, ch 1, dc), ch 1; rep from * around — 20 dc. Join with sl st to 3rd ch of ch-4. **Rnd 4:** Rep Rnd 3 to within last 2 sts and work dc in next dc, ch 1, in last dc work (dc, ch 1, dc) ch 1 — 27 dc. Join as before. **Rnd 5:** Rep Rnd 3 — 36 dc. **Rnd 6:** Ch 4, (dc in next dc, ch 1) 2 times, in next dc work (dc, ch 1, dc), ch 1, * (dc in next dc, ch 1) 3 times, in next dc work (dc, ch 1, dc), ch 1, rep from * around — 45 dc. Join as before. **Rnd 7:** Ch 4, (dc in next dc, ch 1) 3 times, in next dc work (dc, ch 1, dc), ch 1, * (dc in next dc, ch 1) 4 times, in next dc work (dc, ch 1, dc), ch 1; rep from * around — 54 dc. Join as before. **Rnd 8:** Ch 4 (dc in next dc, ch 1) 3 times, in next dc work (dc, ch 1, dc), ch 1, * (dc in next dc, ch 1) 8 times, in next dc work (dc, ch 1, dc) ch 1; rep from * around, ending with (dc in next dc, ch 1) 4 times — 60 dc. Join as before. **Rnd 9:** * Ch 5, sk 2 dc, sl st in next dc, ch 5, sk 1 dc, sl st in next dc; rep from * around, ending with ch 5. Join with sl st to first sl st — 24 ch-5 lps. **Rnd 10:** Ch 3, 4 dc in same ch-5 sp, * ch 3, sl st in next ch-5 lp, ch 3, work 5 dc in next ch-5 lp; rep from * around, ending with ch 3. Join with sl st to top of ch-3. **Rnd 11:** Ch 3, 1 dc in each of next 4 dc, * ch 5, 1 dc in each of next 5 dc; rep from * around, ending with ch 5. Join with sl st to top of ch-3. **Rnd 12:** Sl st in each st to center dc of first 5-dc group, ch 3, * 5 dc in next ch-5 lp, ch 3, sl st in center dc of next 5-dc group, ch 3; rep from * around, ending with ch 3. Join with sl st to sl st of center dc. **Rnd 13:** Sl st in each of next 3 ch and first dc, ch 3, 1 dc in each of next 4 dc, * ch 5, 1 dc in each of next 5 dc; rep from * around, ending with ch 5. Join with sl st to top of ch-3. Rep Rnds 12 and 13 three times more. Fasten off.

TO ASSEMBLE: Fit the Hat Cover over the crown of the hat. With darning needle and sewing thread, tack the last rnd of the Hat Cover to the hat.

TOTE BAG

(12" wide x 13" deep)

TECHNIQUE: Knitting.

AVERAGE: For those with some experience in knitting.

MATERIALS: Coats & Clark Red Heart 100% Cotton "Knit & Crochet Yarn" 5 (2.5 oz.) skeins of No. 6 Off-White; knitting needles, one pair No. 6, OR ANY SIZE NEEDLES TO OBTAIN GAUGE BELOW; two 1"-wide x 12"-long wooden bars; 1½ yds. of link chain; tapestry needle.

Note: Tote is worked with two strands of yarn held together throughout.

GAUGE: In garter st (k every row) using two strands of yarn — 4 sts = 1"; 8 rows (4 ridges) = 1". TO SAVE TIME, TAKE TIME TO CHECK GAUGE.

DIRECTIONS:

BAG — First Side: Starting at lower edge of Bag with two strands of yarn held together throughout, cast on 49 sts. K 5 rows for garter st. Work Pat 1 as follows: **Row 1:** * P 3 tog, (k 1, p 1, k 1) in next st; rep from * across, ending with p 1. **Rows 2 and 4** (*right side*): P across. **Row 3:** * (K 1, p 1, k 1) in next st, p 3 tog; rep from * across, ending with p 1. Rep Rows 1-3 once, ending with a wrong-side row. K 4 rows for garter st. Work Pat II as follows: **Row 1** (*right side*): * K 1, p 1; rep from * across, ending with k 1. **Row 2:** Rep Row 1. Rep Rows 1 and 2 four times more. K 4 rows for garter st, decreasing one st on last row — 48 sts. Work Pat III as follows: **Row 1** (*right side*): * K 3, p 3; rep from * across. **Rows 2 and 3:** Rep Row 1. **Row 4:** * P 3, k 3; rep from * across. **Rows 5 and 6:** Rep Row 4. Rep Rows 1-6 once, then rep Row 1 four times more. K 4 rows for garter st, decreasing one st on last row — 47 sts. Work Pat IV as follows: **Row 1** (*right side*): P 3,

* (k 1, yo, k 1) in next st, p 3; rep from * across — 69 sts. **Row 2:** K 3, * p 3, k 3; rep from * across. **Row 3:** P 3, * k 3, p 3; rep from * across. **Row 4:** K 3, * p 3 tog, k 3; rep from * across — 47 sts. **Row 5:** P across. **Row 6:** K across. **Row 7:** P 1, * (k 1, yo, k 1) in next st, p 3; rep from * across, ending last rep with p 1 — 71 sts. **Row 8:** K 1, * p 3, k 3; rep from * across, ending last rep with k 1. **Row 9:** P 1, * k 3, p 3; rep from * across, ending last rep with p 1. **Row 10:** K 1, * p 3 tog, k 3; rep from * across, ending last rep with k 1 — 47 sts.

Row 11: P across. K 4 rows for garter st, increasing 2 sts evenly spaced across last row — 49 sts. Work Pat V as follows: **Row 1** (*wrong side*): P across. **Row 2:** K 1, * yo, k 3, *then slip the 3rd st on right-hand needle over the last 2 sts worked* — **horizontal st made;** rep from * across. **Row 3:** P across. **Row 4:** * Yo, horizontal st; rep from * across, ending with k 1. **Row 5:** P across. **Row 6:** K 2, * yo, horizontal st; rep from * across, ending with yo, k 2 tog. Work Pat VI as follows: **Rows 1 and 2:** P 1 row, k 1 row. **Rows 3 and 4:** K 2 rows for garter st. **Rows 5-8:** Rep Rows 1-4. **Rows**

9-13: Work in stockinette st (k 1 row, p 1 row). Bind off.

SECOND SIDE: With two strands of yarn held together throughout, pick up and k 49 sts along cast-on edge of First Side. K 5 rows for garter st. Work Patterns I-VI as for First Side. Bind off.

FINISHING: Sew the side seams. Fold the top edge of First Side over one wooden bar and sew on the wrong side. Repeat for the Second Side. Attach chain to each side of the tote, drawing the chain through spaces of Pat V (*see photo*).

SWEAT-SHIRT SAVVY: SHINY SEW-ONS

TECHNIQUE: Sewing.

EASY: Achievable by anyone.

MATERIALS (For one sweatshirt): Shoulder pads; large glittery appliqué (sequinned or beaded) or nine 4½" satiny bows in assorted colors; thread to match sweatshirt color.

DIRECTIONS:
1. **SEW** shoulder pads in place.
2. **PLACE** appliqué on sweatshirt; decide specific positioning. Or, place satiny bows where desired (*see photo as guide*).
3. **SLIP STITCH** appliqué or bows to sweatshirt.

CHECKERBOARD STOLE

(20½" x 65", without fringe)

TECHNIQUE: Knitting.

AVERAGE: For those with some experience in knitting.

MATERIALS: Welcomme and Pernelle "Les Saisons" 12 (1¾ oz.) balls of No. 21 Souris (A), and "Super Mohair" (1½ oz. ball); 2 balls of No. 129 Feu (B) and 1 ball of No. 150 Noir (C); knitting needles, one pair No. 9, OR ANY SIZE NEEDLES TO OBTAIN GAUGE BELOW.

GAUGE: In stockinette stitch (st st) — 4 sts = 1"; 6 rows = 1". TO SAVE TIME, TAKE TIME TO CHECK GAUGE.

Note: Stole is worked with double strand of A held tog throughout. Duplicate sts are embroidered after Stole is completed.

....

DIRECTIONS:

BORDER SECTION I: Starting at narrow end with A, cast on 75 sts. Work in garter st (k every row) for 12 rows. Change to st st (k 1 row, p 1 row) and work for 17 rows more.
*Note: K row is right side of work. Continue to work border as follows: * 3 rows garter st, 9 rows st st; rep from * 4 times more.*

CENTER SECTION: Now work in garter st until total length is 33" from beg, ending on wrong side.
BORDER SECTION II: Rep same as for opposite side, working rows in reverse order.
BORDER SECTION I — CHECKERBOARD DESIGN: *(see photo):* **Note:** *Checkerboard design is worked in duplicate sts (see FIG. 2) over st st only with double strand of B or C yarn. Fasten off each time you change color.*
FIRST st st group: First Half: Starting at lower right-hand corner, with double strand of B, insert needle in first st st and * work in duplicate st (*see* FIG. 2) as follows: 5 sts for 4 rows with B, 5 sts for 4 rows with C; rep from * across 6 times more, ending with 5 sts for 4 rows with B.

FIG. 2
DUPLICATE STITCH

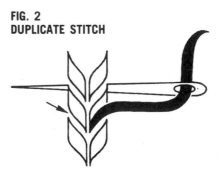

SECOND HALF: Rep as above starting with C color and alternating with B across.
SECOND st st GROUP: Work in duplicate st * with double strand of B **only** over first 5 sts for 4 rows, skip next 5 st st; rep from * across 6 times more, ending with 5 sts for 4 rows with B.
THIRD st st GROUP: * Skip first 5 st st and work in duplicate st with double strand of C **only** over next 5 sts for 4 rows; rep from * across 6 times more, leaving last 5 st st unworked.
FOURTH-SIXTH st st GROUP: Work in duplicate st as for Second and Third st st groups alternating colors B and C.
BORDER SECTION II: Work Checkerboard Design as for Border Section 1.
FRINGE: Wind yarn four times around a 9" square of cardboard; cut at one end making 18" strands. Hold four strands tog and fold in half to form a loop. Insert hook from back to front in first st on one narrow end of Stole and draw lp through. Draw loose ends through loop and pull tightly to form a knot. Tie four strands in the same manner for each fringe and attach to every other st along narrow end. Rep for opposite end.

CLOCHE
WITH FLOWER

TECHNIQUE: Crochet.

AVERAGE: For those with some experience in crochet. Directions are given for one size only.

MATERIALS: Phildar "Leader" (100-gram, 3½-oz ball): 1 ball Flannel (A) and Phildar Alpa Phil (50-gr ball): 1 ball Light Gray (B); crochet hook Sizes E and G, OR ANY SIZE HOOK TO OBTAIN GAUGE BELOW.

GAUGE: On larger hook: 5 sc = 1″; 4 sc rows = 1″. TO SAVE TIME, TAKE TIME TO CHECK GAUGE.

DIRECTIONS:

LINING: Beg at top, with larger hook and A, ch 4. Join with sl st to first ch to form ring. **Rnd 1:** 2 sc in each ch (8 sc). *Note:*

Work thru back lp of each st for entire hat. **Rnds 2 & 3:** 2 sc in each sc (32 sc). **Rnds 4, 6, 8, 10 and 12:** Sc in each sc. **Rnd 5:** * Sc in next sc, 2 sc in next sc; rep from * around (48 sc). **Rnd 7:** Rep Rnd 5 (72 sc). **Rnd 9:** * Sc in next 5 sc, 2 sc in next sc; rep from * around (84 sc). **Rnd 11:** Rep Rnd 9 (98 sc). **Rnd 13:** Sc in each of next 2 sc, * sc in next 7 sc, 2 sc in next sc; rep from * around (110 sc). **Rnds 14 thru 30:** Sc in each sc. **Rnd 31:** * Sc in next sc, 2 sc in next sc; rep from * around (165 sc). **Rnds 32 thru 39:** Sc in each sc. Fasten off. **Exterior:** Beg at top, with larger hook and B, work sc in outside ridge of each sc on lining. Continue around all rnds in this way to end of hat. Fasten off.

FLOWER BASE: Beg at center, with larger hook and A, ch 4. Join with sl st to first st to form ring. **Rnd 1:** Work 2 sc in each ch (8 sc). **Rnd 2:** Working thru both lps, work sc in each sc (16 sc). *Note: Work thru back lp of each st for rem of flower.* **Rnd 3:** * Dc in next st, 2 dc in next st; rep from * around (24 dc). **Rnd 4:** Rep Rnd 3 (36 dc). **Rnd 5:** * Sc in next st, 2 sc in next st; rep from * around (54 sc). Fasten off.

FLOWER PETALS: With smaller hook and B, sk last row of sc on base and working in outside ridge of each st on flower base, work rnds as follows: **Rnds 1 thru 3:** * Work 4 sc in next st, sc in each of next 2 sts; rep from * around. Fasten off.

FINISHING: Sew the edge of the flower base to the side of the hat.

· 8 ·

COUNTRY CRAFTS

Warm hearted. Down to earth. Simply beautiful. Beloved Americana folk themes recur like an old refrain through all craftwork: quilting, rug making, crochet, embroidery. Our potpourri of projects range from homey patchwork tablecoverings and quilts to accents like lace-look "chicken scratch" pillows and a trapunto print framed in a wreath of rustic vines. The charm of country crafts is timeless, and country-inspired designs complement virtually any interior. If you're already a fan of country, we don't have to convince you. And if you're not — just take a look. You may be in for a pleasant surprise.

TABLE RUNNER AND
SCREEN "SLIP COVER"

(Both are shown on the previous page).

TABLE RUNNER

(about 22" x 64")

TECHNIQUE: Patchwork.

EASY: Achievable by anyone.

MATERIALS: Scraps of print and solid fabrics; 4 yds. each of blanket binding and braid.

DIRECTIONS:
(¼" seams allowed):

1. Draw the pattern (*see* Fig. 1) on firm cardboard and cut out 240 triangles from mixed fabrics.

2. Seam two triangles (of contrasting fabric), right sides together, along the longest edge; open to form a square and press the seam in one direction. Repeat, to make 120 squares.

3. Seam the squares into 20 horizontal rows of six squares each. Seam one row below another to make the runner (6 x 20 squares).

4. Cut a runner back (or piece it from large scraps) 2" larger all around than the patchwork top. With wrong sides together, pin the patchwork, centered, over the runner back. Topstitch ¼" from the patchwork edges, through both layers.

5. Enclose the short ends of the runner in blanket binding, lapping the binding edge to the topstitching. Edgestitch and cut the ends flush with the patchwork. Repeat at the long edges, turning in raw ends.

6. Stitch braid along the inside edge of the binding.

SCREEN "SLIPCOVER"

TECHNIQUE: Patchwork.

CHALLENGING: For those with more experience in patchwork.

MATERIALS: 3½ yds. 44/45"-wide fabric for main color patches; scraps of various fabrics to make 96 patches, each 6½" square; 6 yds. (or pieced remnants) of fabric for screen back; four 24" x 66" foamcore panels.

DIRECTIONS:
(¼" seams allowed):

1. From the main color fabric, cut 117 patches, 6½" square. From the other colors, cut 96 patches 6½" square. Seam them into 19 horizontal rows graduating from 3 to 17 patches long (*see* Fig. 2). Seam the rows together vertically, adding one patch at the top and bottom to complete the piece.

2. Draw a straight line connecting the inside corners (at raw edges) across each of the four sides of the piece. Cut on the drawn lines, leaving a rectangle a little over 68" x 102". Cut a back rectangle the same size.

3. Seam (½") the front and back pieces around both short ends and one long (top) edge. Turn right side out and press. Measure and mark three "hinges" at 25½" intervals (*see* Fig 2). Pin, then stitch through both layers along the marked lines.

4. Slide the panels into the four "pockets". Turn in open edges at the bottom and slip stitch.

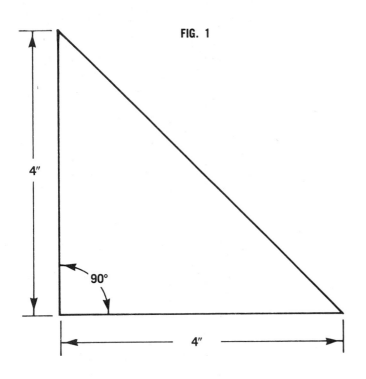

FIG. 1

4"

90°

4"

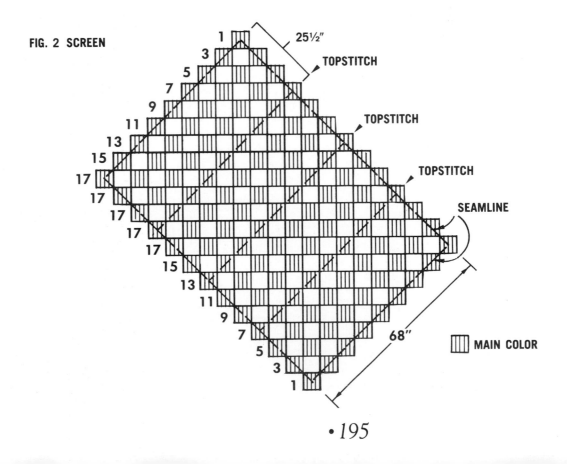

FIG. 2 SCREEN

1
3
5
7
9
11
13
15
17
17
17
17
17
15
13
11
9
7
5
3
1

25½"

TOPSTITCH

TOPSTITCH

TOPSTITCH

SEAMLINE

68"

▦ MAIN COLOR

GRANNY SQUARE RUG

(about 42" x 51", including border)

TECHNIQUE: Crochet.

EASY: Achievable by anyone.

MATERIALS: Caron "Aunt Lydia's" Heavy Rug Yarn (60 yd. skein): 4 skeins each of No. 405 Beige, No. 323 Copper, No. 105 Medium Pink, No. 310 Coral and 3 skeins each of No. 559 Gold, No. 905 Natural, No. 550 Sunset, No. 320 Burnt Orange, No. 505 Light Yellow, No. 565 Antique Gold, No. 560 Bronze Gold; crochet hook, Size J, OR ANY SIZE HOOK TO OBTAIN GAUGE BELOW; tapestry needle.

GAUGE: 3 hdc = 1"; 2 rows = 1". Each Center Square = 8½" square. TO SAVE TIME, TAKE TIME TO CHECK GAUGE.

DIRECTIONS:

Note 1: The rug is made up of 12 Center Squares which are sewn together afterward.

Note 2: The border is crocheted with different lengths of yarns, using the same colors as Center Squares.

Note 3: To hdc: Yo, draw up a lp in next st, yo and through 3 lps on hook.

CENTER SQUARE (Make 12): Starting at center of Square with any color, ch 4. Join with sl st to form ring. **Rnd 1:** Ch 2 (counts as 1 hdc), 11 hdc in ring — 12 hdc. Join with sl st to top of ch-2. Fasten off. **Rnd 2:** Join another color between any 2 hdc, ch 2 (counts as 1 hdc), 5 hdc in same place, * skip 3 hdc, 6 *hdc between next 2 hdc* — **corner made;** rep from * 2 times more — 4 corners made. Fasten

off. **Rnd 3:** Join another color in corner between 2 groups of 3 hdc for corner-sp, ch 2, 5 hdc in same place, * 3 hdc in sp bet next 2 corners, 6 hdc in next corner-sp; rep from * around. Join. Fasten off. **Rnd 4:** Join another color in corner-sp, ch 2, 5 hdc in same sp, * 3 hdc in each sp bet next 2 corners, 6 hdc in corner-sp; rep from * around. Join. Fasten off. **Rnds 5 to 8:** Rep Rnd 4, working with a new color in each rnd, having 1 more 3 hdc between corners than in previous rnd.

BLOCKING: Pin each square to measurements on a padded surface, cover with a damp cloth and allow to dry; *do not press.*

ASSEMBLING: Join 4 rows of 3 squares each to form a rectangle. With right sides facing you, sew squares tog from the center of a corner to the center of the next corner, matching sts and working through **both** lps of each square.

BORDER — Preparation and Method: From the remaining yarn, cut different lengths of yarn, using the same colors as the Center Squares. Join colors randomly (middle of row, every row or every 2 or 3 rows), drawing the new color through the last 2 lps of the previous st. Work over ends. **Row 1:** With the right side facing you, join any color at the upper-right edge of the rectangle, ch 2, hdc in same st, hdc in each st along one edge of the rectangle. Turn. **Row 2:** Ch 2, hdc in first hdc, hdc in each hdc across. Rep Row 2, 14 times more, using colors randomly. Work the same border on the other 3 edges of the rectangle.

CORNER SQUARES: Make 4 each of Copper, Medium Pink, Coral and Beige. Work Rnds 1 to 4 as for the Center Square without changing any of the colors.

ASSEMBLING: Sew 4 different color squares together to form a large square, working through **back lps only** of each square. Sew a large square to a corner of the Rug. Rep for the other 3 corners.

TIP

Great Grannies!

Do you love granny squares? We do too — so why not experiment with the yarn colors you have on hand? Granny squares originated as a frugal way to crochet: square by square, yarn leftovers were used in whichever colors were found in the scrap basket. Today, you can do the same with your scrap yarn. When the scraps are joined together, they create dazzling yarn palettes in everything from cozy afghans to wonderful rugs. Granny herself would approve!

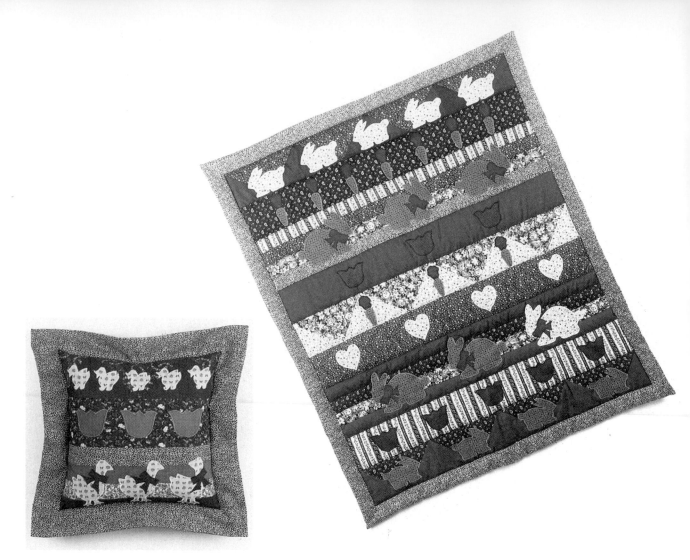

CHILD'S BUNNY QUILT AND
DUCK PILLOW

QUILT

. . . .

(38″ x 46″)

TECHNIQUE: Patchwork and appliqué quilting.

CHALLENGING: For those with more experience in quilting.

MATERIALS: Assorted cotton calicos (see below); pillow form

14″ x 14″; 12″ blue zipper; Poly-fil® Extra Loft Crib Batting 45″ x 60″; template material; gluestick; matching threads; zig-zag sewing machine; optional — rotary cutter, mat and plexiglass measuring bar for cutting strips; fabrics in the following amounts:

Color 1: white and rust calico — ¼ yard

Color 2: rust calico — ¼ yard

Color 3: solid dark green — ¼ yard

Color 4: solid dark blue — ¼ yard

Color 5: blue and white stripe — ¼ yard plus 1⅓ yards for backing

Color 6: dark green calico — ⅓ yard

Color 7: large blue floral print —

¼ yard

Color 8: dark blue calico — ¼ yard

Color 9: green and white stripe — ⅛ yard

Color 10: light blue calico — ⅓ yard (includes border).

Note: All machine appliqué in pictured quilt was done without fusibles or stabilizers. You may wish to purchase these products if desired.

. . . .

DIRECTIONS:

CUTTING: Enlarge patterns (*see page 294*). When enlarged, glue patterns onto template material. Trace and cut out the appliqué pattern pieces in the following amounts:

5 small bunnies facing right — Color 1

1 large bunny facing right — Color 1

4 hearts — Color 1

4 small bunnies facing left — Color 2

3 large bunnies facing left; 2 large bunnies facing right — Color 2

10 carrots — Color 2

10 carrot tops — Color 3

8 tulips — Color 3

3 bows facing right; 3 bows facing left — Color 4

Set cut pieces aside.

Note: Use ¼″ seam allowance for all patchwork sewing and always press sewn seams to one side.

PATCHWORK: Cut 8 triangles each from pairs of Colors 3 and 6, 4 and 8, and 1 and 7. Sew the triangles together, right sides facing, along the long sides in color pairs. Repeat for the other two sets of colors. Sew each pair of triangles (now square) to the next square to form zig-zag patchwork for each set of colors. You now will have three zig-zag patchwork rows. Cut out strips, selvage to selvage, in the follow-

ing measurements and colors:

Color 3: 2″ x 44″

Color 4: 4½″ x 44″; 2″ x 44″

Color 5: 4½″ x 44″

Color 6: 4½″ x 44″; 2″ x 44″

Color 7: two 2″ x 44″

Color 8: 4½″ x 44″; 2″ x 44″

Color 9: 2″ x 44″

Color 10: five 2″ x 44″ (includes 4 border strips)

Sew all the patchwork rows and cut strips together in the following order: **Row 1:** Colors 3 and 6 zig-zag patchwork (calico on top side). **Row 2:** 4½″ strip Color 8. **Row 3:** Color 9. **Row 4:** 2″ strip Color 6. **Row 5:** Color 7. **Row 6:** Color 10. **Row 7:** 4½″ strip Color 4. **Row 8:** Colors 1 and 7 zig-zag patchwork (floral on top side). **Row 9:** 4½″ strip Color 6. **Row 10:** Color 3. **Row 11:** 2″

BUNNY QUILT   1 SQ. = 1″

strip Color 8. **Row 12:** Color 7. **Row 13:** Color 4. **Row 14:** Color 5. **Row 15:** Colors 4 and 8 zigzag patchwork (calico on top side). Trim off all excess strips beyond the patchwork zig-zag strips.

APPLIQUÉ: Pin all the appliqué pieces onto the patchwork as pictured in the photograph, centering and evenly spacing the appliqué pieces as you go. **Row 1:** 5 small white calico bunnies. **Row 2:** 7 carrots and tops. **Rows 3-6:** 3 large rust bunnies facing left plus bows. **Row 7:** 3 tulips. **Row 8:** 3 carrots and tops on light calico "V"s. **Row 9:** 4 hearts. **Rows 10-13:** Remaining large bunnies plus bows. **Row 14:** 5 tulips. **Row 15:** 4 small rust calico bunnies. Use matching threads and a straight stitch around all the outside raw edges very close to the raw edges. Change the sewing machine stitch to a close zig-zag stitch and, using matching threads, zig-zag all the appliqué pieces in place. Press the quilt top on the wrong side. Sew the 2 side borders (Color 10) onto the quilt top sides; cut off excess fabric from the strip ends. Repeat for the top and bottom borders.

ASSEMBLING QUILT: Layer the batting, quilt back right side up and quilt top right side down together. Pin around the entire quilt, leaving a 8"-10" opening at the bottom center. Trim off excess batting and backing to match the quilt top. Use a loose (6-8 stitches per inch) straight stitch and sew all the layers together. Turn the quilt through to the right side through the center bottom opening. Slip stitch the opening closed.

MACHINE QUILTING: Stitch "in the ditch" around the inside border seam and across all the

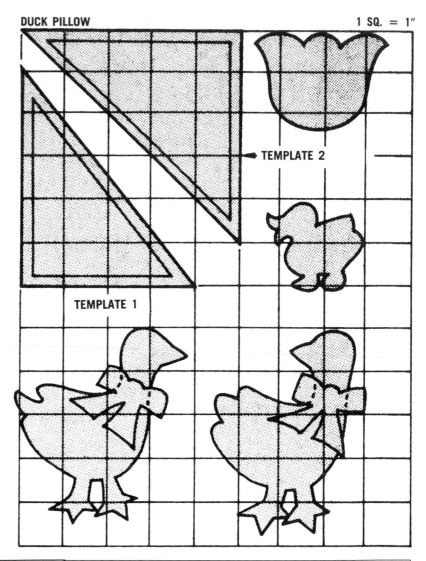

DUCK PILLOW   1 SQ. = 1"

TEMPLATE 2

TEMPLATE 1

TIP

When you're planning a quilt project:

• Choose fabric with prints in proportion to the size of your patchwork and appliqué pieces. See-through templates help; you can move them over printed yardage to get an instant idea of the final effect.

• Buy extra fabric! This gives you leeway for mistakes if you change your mind about colors as the work progresses. Store extra material in a scrap bag; "file" cut shapes by threading them in stacks or securing them in orderly groups with clothespins.

rows of the quilt. Do not stitch through the appliqués.

PILLOW

(14" square plus 2" borders)

Fabrics and matching threads in the following amounts and colors:

Color 1: navy solid — ¼ yard

Color 2: dark green calico print — ⅛ yard

Color 3: dark green solid — ⅛ yard

Color 4: green calico print — ⅛ yard

Color 5: blue calico — ⅔ yard (includes back of pillow)

Color 6: medium blue calico — ⅓ yard (includes border)

Color 7: yellow calico — ⅛ yard

Note: Appliqué patterns are for machine appliqué; add ¼" seam allowance for hand appliqué.

Enlarge patterns *(see page 294).* When enlarged, glue patterns onto template material.

DIRECTIONS:

CUTTING: See Quilt directions for preparing appliqué. Trace and cut out: 5 ducklings facing left — Color 7; 3 tulips — Color 3; 2 ducks, 1 duck looking backward — Color 7; 3 bows — Color 1. Set aside.

PATCHWORK: Cut 2 each of right and wrong sides of Colors 1 and 6 of Template 1. From the same colors, cut 2 each of Template 2. Sew the two colors together, along the long side of the triangles, right sides facing. Sew together the patchwork to form a zig-zag in the following order: Template 1, Template 2, Template 2; and Template 1. Cut strips as follows:

Color 1 — 2" x 15"

Color 2 — 2" x 15"

Color 3 — 2" x 15"

Color 4 — 2" x 15"

Color 5 — 4½" x 15"

Sew all the cut strips together in the same order. Add zig-zag patchwork to the bottom row, the calico zig-zag on the top edge. Trim off strips to match the width of the zig-zag strip.

APPLIQUÉ: Pin and center 5 ducklings along Rows 1-4, 3 tulips on Row 5 and 3 ducks on the zig-zag patchwork. The far right duck is looking backward. Pin the bows onto the necks. See the quilt directions for appliqué sewing.

BORDER: Cut 2 strips 3" x 44" of Color 6. Sew each strip to each side of the patchwork. Cut off excess strips. Sew the remaining strips onto the top and bottom of the patchwork. For the back cut 2 rectangles of Color 5, 22" x 14" and 22" x 8". Set the zipper in the center of two 22" lengths. Trim the pillow back to match the pillow front. Open the zipper. Pin the back to the front, right sides together. Sew entirely around the outside edge. Turn to the right side and press the edges. Pin the pillow together around the inside border seam. Stitch "in the ditch" around the seam to finish the pillow.

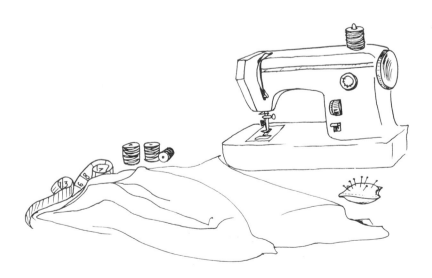

"CHICKEN SCRATCH"
PILLOWS

(about 15½" square)

TECHNIQUE: Embroidery.

EASY: Achievable by anyone.

MATERIALS *(For each pillow):* ½ yd. ¼" checked fabric; 4 yds. of 2¼"-wide white eyelet edging; synthetic stuffing; for **Pillow 1** — two and a half skeins of white and two skeins of green perle cotton, **Pillow 2** — two skeins each of white and blue, **Pillow 3** — two skeins each of white and red; embroidery needle and hoop.

DIRECTIONS *(½" seams allowed):*

1. FROM the checked fabric, cut two 18" squares for the pillow front and back. On the pillow front, pin-mark the center white square. *Note: Choose a pattern (see FIGS. 3, 4, 5 on pages 204-205), then follow the Stitch Details (see FIGS. 6 and 7) and directions below to work the design. For FIG. 1, begin the embroidery at the light green square to the right of the center pin-marked square (working spokes around the dark green center below). For FIGS. 2 and 3, begin the embroidery at the pin-marked center white square, working spokes across the light blue (or red) squares around the white center. Embroider one quarter of the design, working the woven stitches vertically from top to bottom, row-by-row. (Fill in the plus-stitch rows after-*ward.) The heavy dark lines in the patterns denote colored thread, the thin lines white thread. White spokes and woven circles are embroidered around the white squares, colored spokes and woven circles around solid dark squares.

2. STRAIGHT STITCH: Place the fabric in the hoop. With one strand of perle cotton in the needle, bring the needle up from the back of the fabric at START *(see FIG. 6)*, then down at the opposite side of the square to complete one spoke. Work three more spokes around the central square at A, B and C.

3. WOVEN CIRCLE: Bring the needle up from the back of the fabric and under the spoke at C *(see FIG. 6)*. Weave the thread under each spoke, then insert the needle down to the back of the fabric at C. Pull the thread gently to create a circle around the square. Move down to the next empty square and start at A again *(see FIG. 6A)* to make three spokes. Weave as before and continue in this manner to the end of the row. Begin at START again at the top of the next row, embroidering the spokes necessary to complete the pattern down the row *(see FIGS. 3, 4 or 5)*. When one quarter of the pattern is embroidered, work the other three quarters the same way.

4. PLUS-STITCH: Make a horizontal straight stitch across the center of one square *(see FIG. 7)*, then work a vertical straight stitch over it. Repeat to complete the design *(see FIGS. 3, 4 or 5)*.

5. TRIM the pillow ½" outside the seamline *(see FIGS. 3-5)*. Trim the pillow back to match.

6. RUFFLE: With wrong sides together, seam (¼") ends of the eyelet edging to make a loop. Turn right side out and stitch ¼"

TIP | *Just What Is Chicken-Scratch?*

It may *look* like appliqué lace on checks — but it's really a time-honored embroidery technique. These 'chicken-scratch' pillows require just two basic stitches worked on even-weave checked fabric. We recommend gingham checks because they provide a graph-like guide for the stitches.

again, encasing raw edges, to make a French seam. Stitch two gathering rows ⅛″ and ¼″ from the cut edge of the eyelet. Fold the loop into quarters and pin-mark. With right sides together, and a pin-mark at each corner, pin the eyelet to the pillow top along the seamline (*see* Figs. 3-5). Pull up gathers to fit, easing in extra fullness at the corners. Pin, then stitch.

7. Assembly: With right sides together, edges even, pin the pillow front over the back. Stitch over previous stitching around three sides and four corners. Turn right side out; stuff; stitch the opening closed.

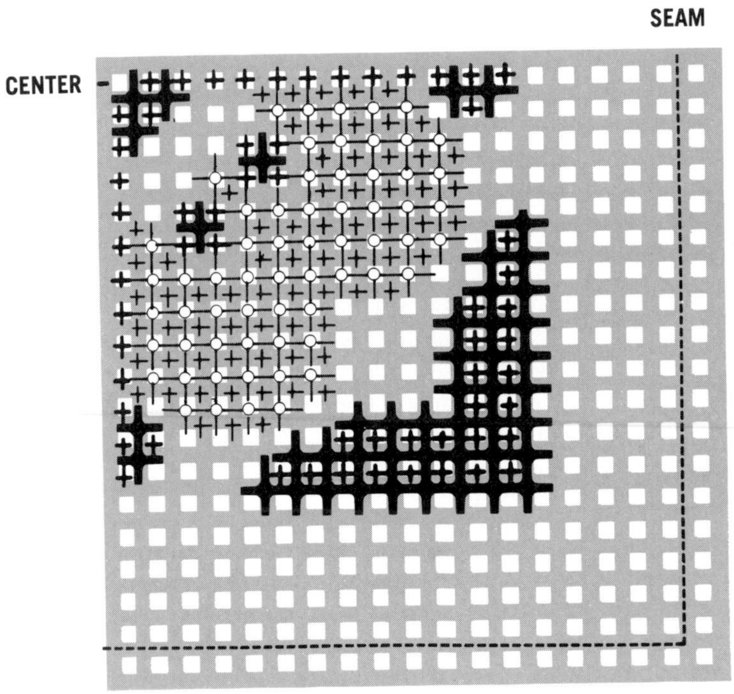

SEAM

FIG. 3   QUARTER PATTERN

——— WHITE THREAD

━━━ COLORED THREAD

FIG. 4   QUARTER PATTERN

SEAM

CENTER

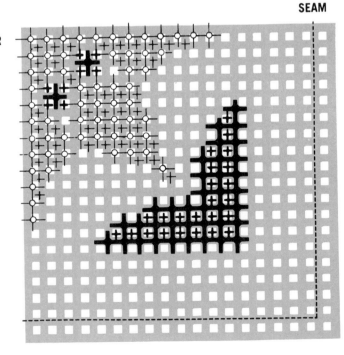

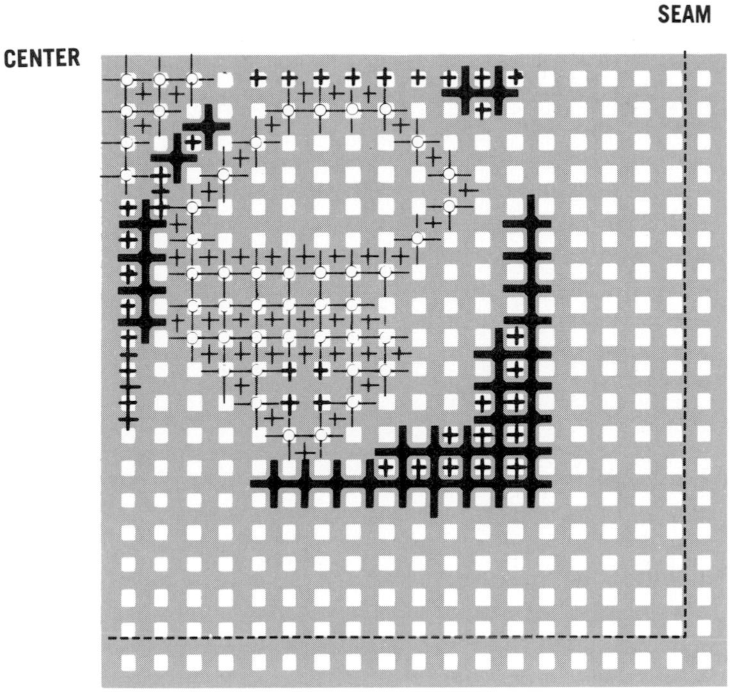

SEAM

CENTER

FIG. 5   QUARTER PATTERN

FIG. 6 WOVEN STITCHES

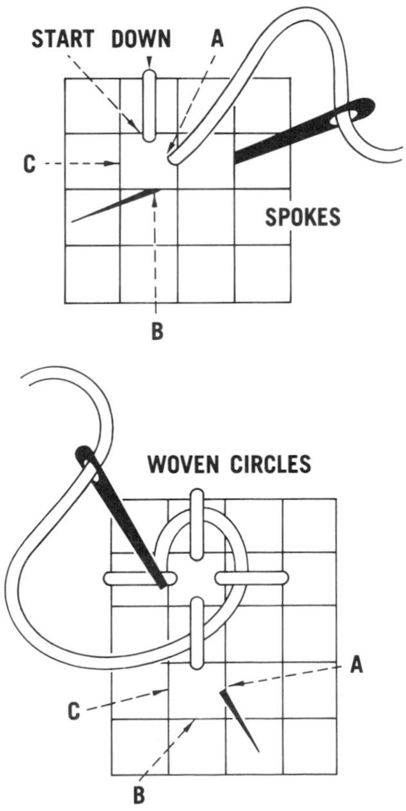

START DOWN   A

C

B

SPOKES

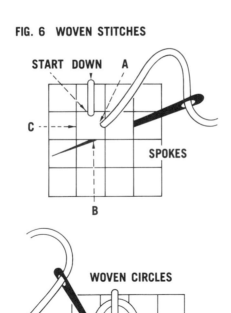

WOVEN CIRCLES

A

C

B

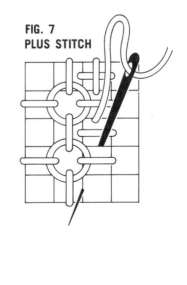

**FIG. 7
PLUS STITCH**

RAG PILLOW FOOTSTOOL AND
STRIPED COUNTRY PILLOW

FOOTSTOOL

(18″ square, plus 6″ fringe)

TECHNIQUE: Crochet.

AVERAGE: For those with some experience in crochet.

MATERIALS *(For Pillow Top):* Odd pieces (about 3 yds. each) of assorted fabrics (such as cotton, calico, print, gauze, in prints or solids, lightweight stripes); wooden crochet hook, Size 11, OR ANY SIZE HOOK TO OBTAIN GAUGE BELOW; 18″-square knife-edged purchased pillow; tapestry needle.

GAUGE: 4 hdc = 2″; 5 rows = 2″. TO SAVE TIME, TAKE TIME TO CHECK GAUGE.

Note: Pillow is crocheted from ½″ strips of different prints or solid fabrics. Use as many different fabrics as desired and work in a random pattern.

PREPARATION: 1. Cut the fabric back and forth, making one long ½″ strip; start at selvage, stop about ½″ before opposite selvage (*see* FIG. 8, A1 to A2). **2.** Move ½″ over and cut from the opposite edge (*see* FIG. 8, B1 to B2); continue in this manner until you have the desired amount of this color. **3.** Roll the strip into a ball as you continue to cut, to avoid knotting. **4.** Cut strips of all other fabrics in the same manner.

DIRECTIONS:

PILLOW TOP: Starting at the lower edge of the Pillow Top with Color 1 (any color of your choice), ch 38. **Note: To hdc,** *yo, draw up a lp in next st, yo and draw through all 3 lps on hook.* **Row 1** *(right side):* Hdc in 3rd ch from hook, hdc in each ch across — 36 hdc; *do not* count beg-ch as one st. Ch 2, turn. **Row 2:** Hdc in each hdc across — 36 hdc. Ch 2, turn. Rep Row 2 for pattern, changing colors as desired. **To change color:** Work last st of row until there are 2 lps on hook, drop old color, yo with new color, and draw through last 2 lps on hook. With new color ch 2, turn. Fasten off old color, leaving a 6″ end for fringe on side edges. Continue working until piece measures about 18″ from beg. Fasten off.

FINISHING: Pin the Pillow Top to measurements on a padded, flat surface, cover it with a damp cloth and allow it to dry; *do not* press.

**FIG. 8
TO CUT
A CONTINUOUS
FABRIC STRIP
FOR CROCHETING**

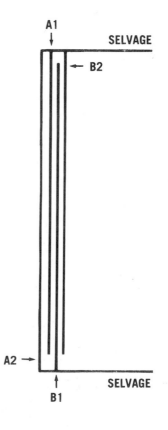

·207

ASSEMBLING: Pin the Pillow Top onto the pillow. Stitch it to the seam edge of the pillow.

PILLOW

....

(13″ square)

TECHNIQUE: Crochet.

AVERAGE: For those with some experience in crochet.

MATERIALS *(For Pillow Top):* Conshohocken Cotton Co. "Softball Wool" — 1 ball (3½ oz.) each of No. 510 Blue Violet (A), No. 525 Ivory (B) and No. 565 Turquoise (C); 5½ yds. each of No. 530 Lipstick Red (D), No. 670 Crocus Yellow (E) and No. 630 Frosty Magenta (F); 8½ yds. of No. 515 Electric Blue (G); crochet hook, Size H, OR ANY SIZE HOOK TO OBTAIN GAUGE BELOW; 13″-square knife-edged purchased pillow; tapestry needle.

GAUGE: 7 hdc = 2″; 3 rows = 1″. TO SAVE TIME, TAKE TIME TO CHECK GAUGE.

DIRECTIONS:

FIRST HALF OF PILLOW TOP — Hdc Pattern: Starting at the lower edge of the Pillow Top with A, ch 47. *Note: To hdc,* yo, *draw up a lp in next st, yo and draw through all 3 loops on hook.* **Row 1** *(right side):* Hdc in 3rd ch from hook, hdc in each ch across — 45 hdc; *do not* count beg-ch as one st. Ch 2, (counts as first hdc of next row), turn. **Row 2:** Hdc in each hdc across — 45 hdc. Ch 2, turn. ** With A, rep Row 2 for a total of 5 rows. At end of last row, change to D as follows: Work last st of row until there are 2 lps on hook, drop A, yo with D and draw through last 2 lps on hook. Ch 2, turn. Fasten off A. **Hereafter change colors in this way.** Rep Row 2 for Hdc pattern, working 1 row each of D and B. On next row, work in Hdc pattern as follows: * With B, hdc in each of the next 2 hdc, drop B, change to E and, with E, hdc in each of the next 2 hdc; rep from * across. Fasten off E. With B

only, work in Hdc pattern for 1 row. Change to C and ch 2, turn. Fasten off B. With C, work in Cross St pattern as follows: **Row 1:** Hdc in 2nd st, * *sk one st, hdc in next st, hdc in skipped st* — **Cross St made;** rep from * across, ending with hdc in turning-ch — 21 Cross Sts. Ch 2, turn. Rep Row 1 of Cross St pattern three times more. Change to B and work in Hdc pattern for 2 rows. Change to G and work in Cross St pattern for 1 row. Working in Hdc pattern, work 1 row each of A* and F.

SECOND HALF OF PILLOW TOP: Now work in reverse order, starting from * to ** to complete the Pillow Top. Fasten off.

FINISHING: Pin the Pillow Top to measurements on a padded, flat surface, cover it with a damp cloth and allow it to dry; *do not* press.

ASSEMBLING: Pin the Pillow Top onto the pillow. Stitch it to the seam edge of the pillow.

FRUIT
PILLOWS

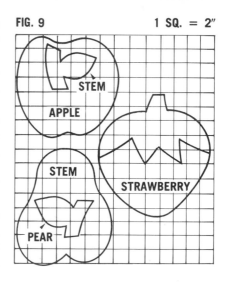

TECHNIQUE: Topstitch patchwork.

EASY: Achievable by anyone.

MATERIALS: Scraps of red, green, yellow and natural muslin fabric; stuffing.

DIRECTIONS:

1. **PILLOW FRONT:** Enlarge (*see page 294*) patterns (*see* FIG. 9) and cut one of each, from muslin. Cover the muslin with scraps of fabric. Topstitch ⅛" from the overlapping edges. Trim excess fabric near the topstitching. Set your sewing machine for wide zig-zag and stitch over raw edges. Trim outside edges even

with the muslin. Cut a green stem section for the strawberry and sew it over the berry.

2. **CUT** a pillow back to match the pillow front. Seam (¼") them right sides together, leaving 2 or 3 inches open at the top edge. Clip the seam allowance at curves and corners. Turn right side out and stuff.

3. **STEMS:** Cut a pair of pear and apple stems. Seam each pair, right sides together, except at the lower edge of the stem. Turn and stuff. Slide the stem into the top opening of the pillow. Slip stitch the open edges closed, over the stem.

FIG. 9 **1 SQ. = 2"**

STEM

APPLE

STEM

STRAWBERRY

PEAR

STAR APPLIQUÉS AND "TRIANGLES" PILLOW

STAR APPLIQUÉS

TECHNIQUE: Patchwork.

AVERAGE: For those with some experience in patchwork.

MATERIALS: Scraps of muslin, batting and thin backing fabric.

DIRECTIONS:

1. CUTTING: Enlarge (*see page 294*) and draw patterns (*see* FIG. 10), using the numbers in parentheses for the smaller (chair seat) star. Trace the pattern to muslin and cut it out *¼" outside the drawn lines.* Cut 8 diamonds for each star.

2. PATCHWORK: Pin two stars together and stitch at one edge along the drawn lines (*Do not stitch beyond the drawn lines*). Repeat four times. Stitch two pairs together to make half a star. Repeat, then stitch two halves together. With a hard pencil, draw quilting lines parallel to the edges and equally spaced.

3. QUILTING (*Optional*): Pin the star over a layer of batting and a thin backing. Baste through both layers, from the center outward to each point and along each seam. Stitch (by hand or machine) along the drawn lines. Trim the edges of the batting and backing back to the seamline.

4. PIN the appliqué to the center of the cloth. Turn under the muslin edge along the seamline, and slip stitch or edgestitch it to the cloth.

5. CHAIR SEATS: Using the smaller pattern, make a muslin star and slip stitch it to the center of a chair seat. It will be easier to work if you open the cushion seam far enough to get your hand in underneath the fabric.

> ### TIP *All About Patchwork*
>
> Patchwork isn't just pretty — it's also a clever way to conceal a stained or worn cloth! Other patchwork ideas:
> • Dress up 'plain Jane' tablecloths or napkins with striking appliqués. • Give a country touch to store-bought chair cushions. *Hint:* If you machine-stitch, your projects will be speedy, too!

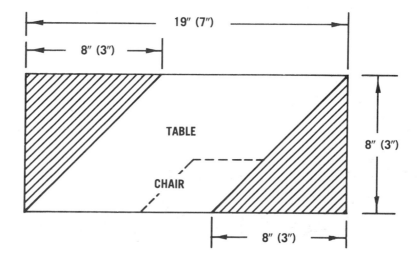

FIG. 10 STAR PATCH

19" (7")

8" (3")

TABLE

CHAIR

8" (3")

8" (3")

"TRIANGLES" PILLOW

(12" square)

TECHNIQUE: Patchwork.

EASY: Achievable by anyone.

MATERIALS: Scraps of light and dark fabrics; stuffing.

DIRECTIONS:
(¼" seams allowed):

1. **USING** the triangle pattern for the runner (*see* FIG. 11), cut sixteen light and sixteen dark patches. Seam (¼") each light patch to a dark one, along the long edge, to make a square.

2. **PILLOW TOP:** Seam the squares into four horizontal rows of four squares each, with light patches abutting light, and dark patches abutting dark (*see photo*). Seam one row below the other, to complete the pillow top. Cut the pillow back the same size.

3. **RUFFLE:** Cut a 3½" x 96" strip (pieced as needed) and seam the short ends together to make a loop. Stitch a ¼" hem at one long edge. Fold the loop in half twice and mark the four folds at the raw edge. Sew a gathering row ¼" from the raw edge, starting and stopping at each fold mark. Pin the ruffle to the pillow top, right sides together, with a fold mark at each corner. Pull up the gathering to fit. Stitch along the gathering line.

4. **SEAM** the pillow back to the pillow top around three sides and four corners. Turn right side out and stuff. Turn in the open edges and slip stitch.

FIG. 11

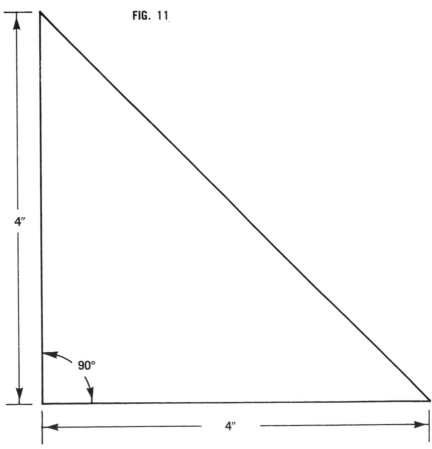

4"

90°

4"

TRAPUNTO PRINT IN VINE WREATH

TECHNIQUE: Trapunto.

EASY: Achievable by anyone.

MATERIALS: Vine wreath with a 12″-dia. opening; 12″-dia. embroidery hoop; printed fabric about 14″-dia. and same-size piece of muslin; synthetic stuffing; dried flowers; silicone glue.

DIRECTIONS:

1. **BASTE** the muslin to the back of the fabric. Choose a motif that you'd like to stuff (in our case, the duck) and machine-stitch along its outline, through both layers.

2. **PLACE** the fabric in the hoop. With the fabric taut, tighten the outer hoop.

3. **CUT** a short slash *in the muslin only* within the stitch-outlined motif; push in the stuffing, using a blunt-pointed tool, such as a wooden knitting needle. Stuff up to the outlines, but do not overstuff which will distort the fabric — check the right side of the fabric as you work. Close the muslin slash with long stitches.

4. **GLUE** the hoop to the inside of the wreath with silicone glue. Let it dry at least an hour.

5. **GLUE** or tie dried flowers to the wreath.

TIP *Trapunto Materials*

For your trapunto vine wreath, choose fabric printed with a design or a floral motif. Vine frames can be spray-painted in soft pastels and laced with ribbons and silk flowers. Or for a romantic floral print, skip the vine and use a lace-ruffled border on an embroidery hoop to give your print a Victorian heirloom look.

·9·

THE YOUNGER SET

There's nothing more adorable than fashions for kids and tiny tots — but sometimes, there's nothing more expensive! How to be budget-wise? With your knitting needle, crochet hook or needle and thread. On the following pages you'll find sensational sweaters in cheery brights, darling infantwear, great-looking playwear. There's even an exquisite christening gown with slip and bonnet to show off your handstitchery talents.

BABY'S KNITTED "ARGYLE" PULLOVER

(Pullover is shown on the previous page).

TECHNIQUE: Knitting.

CHALLENGING: For those with more experience in knitting.

Directions are given for Size 6 Months. Changes for Sizes 1 and 2 are in parentheses.

Note 1: The sweater buttons at the shoulders.

Note 2: Diagonal C (white) lines are embroidered in duplicate stitch when the pullover is finished.

MATERIALS: Unger "Britania" (46 gr. skein) 2 (2, 3) skeins of No. 541 Blue (A), 1 skein each of No. 561 Green (B) and No. 3 Off-White (C); knitting needles, one pair each No. 4 and No. 6, OR ANY SIZE NEEDLES TO OBTAIN GAUGE BELOW; 3 stitch holders; four ½"-dia. buttons; crochet hook, Size F; 3 bobbins.

GAUGE: With larger needles in stockinette stitch (st st) — 11 sts = 2"; 7 rows = 1". TO SAVE TIME, TAKE TIME TO CHECK GAUGE.

MEASUREMENTS:

Sizes:	6 mos.	1 yr.	2 yrs.
Body chest:	19"	20"	21"
Finished chest:	20"	21"	22"
Width across back or front at underarms:	10"	10½"	11"
Width across sleeve at upper arm:	7½"	8"	9"

DIRECTIONS:

BACK: Starting at lower edge with smaller needles and A, cast on 56 (58, 60) sts. Work in k 1, p 1 ribbing for 2", increase one st at end of last row — 57 (59, 61) sts. Change to larger needles and purl 1 row. Work in stockinette stitch (k 1 row, p 1 row) for 28 (32, 36) rows more, ending with a p row.

ARMHOLE SHAPING: Bind off 2 sts at beg of next 2 rows — 53 (55, 57) sts. Work even in st st for 21 (23, 25) rows more, decreasing one st at end of last row — 52 (54, 56) sts. Change to smaller needles and work in k 1, p 1 ribbing for 6 rows. Bind off loosely in ribbing.

Note: Wind 3 bobbins with B color yarn and join as needed. When changing colors, always twist color not in use around the other once, to prevent making holes in work. Carry A color yarn loosely along wrong side.

FRONT: Starting at lower edge with smaller needles and A, cast on 56 (58, 60) sts. Work in k 1, p 1 ribbing for 2", increasing one st at end of last row — 57 (59, 61) sts. Change to larger needles and purl 1 row. Now start Row 2 of Diamond Pattern (*see* FIG. 1), working in st st as follows: **Row 2:** With A k 2 (3, 4), place marker on needle, with A k 8, with B k 1, with A k 17, with B k 1, with A k 17, with B k 1, with A k 8, place marker, with A k 2 (3, 4). Slip marker on every row, working sts outside marker with A. Follow chart back and forth for size indicated, working 6 Month Size from a to b; Size 1 from c to d and Size 2 from e to f. Work until Row 19 is completed (first group of Diamonds), then repeat Rows 2-11 (2-15, 2-19) once, ending with a p row.

ARMHOLE SHAPING — For 6 Month and Size 1 only: Bind off 2 sts at beg of next 2 rows and continue to follow chart for Diamond pat until Row 19 is completed, then repeat Rows 2-7 (2-13) once (3rd group of Diamonds). **For Size 2 only:** Bind off 2 sts at beg of next 2 rows and continue to follow chart (Rows 2-19) once until 3rd group of Diamonds is completed.

TIP *Just Like Daddy's*

Knit this pint-size pullover in "grown-up" colors, and your tot can have the same dashing look as his father! The diamond pattern is knitted in; the white scoring lines are duplicate-stitched over the diamonds.

FIG. 1 'ARGYLE' PULLOVER

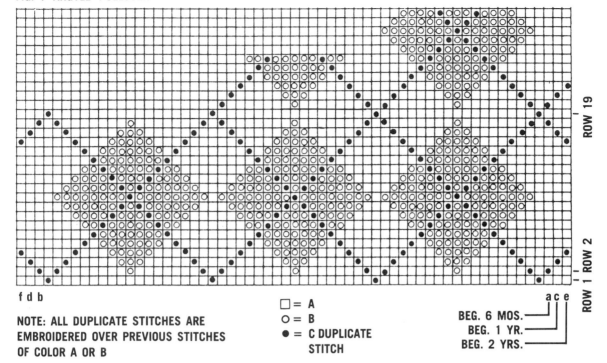

ROW 19

ROW 1 ROW 2

f d b

**NOTE: ALL DUPLICATE STITCHES ARE
EMBROIDERED OVER PREVIOUS STITCHES
OF COLOR A OR B**

□ = A
○ = B
● = C DUPLICATE
STITCH

a c e

BEG. 6 MOS.
BEG. 1 YR.
BEG. 2 YRS.

NECK SHAPING: *Next Row:* Continue in Diamond pat, k 19 (20, 21), slip next 15 sts onto a st holder for front neck, join 2nd ball of yarn and k 19 (20, 21). Working each side with a separate ball, dec one st at neck edge on next row, then every other row 4 times — slip rem 14 (15, 16) sts on each side, onto st holders for shoulders.

FRONT NECK RIBBING: With smaller needles and A, from right side, pick up 8 sts along left neck edge, k 15 sts from st holder, pick up 9 sts along right neck edge — 32 sts. Work in k 1, p 1 ribbing for 6 rows. Bind off loosely in ribbing.

FRONT SHOULDER RIBBING: With smaller needles and A, k 14 (15, 16) sts from left shoulder st holder, pick up 4 (5, 4) sts along side of neck ribbing. Work in

k 1, p 1 ribbing for 6 rows. Bind off in ribbing. Work right shoulder ribbing to correspond with left shoulder ribbing. From right side of work, sew shoulders tog ¾" in from shoulder edge.
Note: Remainder of shoulder is left open.

SLEEVES: With larger needles and A, from right side of work, pick up 42 (45, 48) sts along armhole edge. Work in st st for 6½ (7, 7½)", ending with a p row. *Next Row:* * K 1, k 2 tog; rep from * across — 28 (30, 32) sts. Change to smaller needles and work in k 1, p 1 ribbing for 2". Bind off loosely in ribbing.

DUPLICATE STITCH (*see* FIGS. 1 and 1A): With C, work duplicate stitch diagonally across Front of Pullover.

FINISHING: Pin Pullover to measurements on a padded sur-

face, cover with a damp cloth and allow to dry; *do not press.* Sew side seams. Sew sleeve seams, starting at ribbing and sewing last ¼" to bound-off sts at underarm. Sew 2 buttons onto each Front shoulder ribbing, with first at neck edge and second at center of shoulder ribbing.

BUTTON LOOPS: With right side facing and crochet hook, sl st across Back neck ribbing, working a ch-6 for each button loop opposite buttons.

**FIG. 1A
DUPLICATE STITCH**

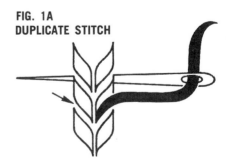

CHILD'S "WASHLINE"

PULLOVER

TECHNIQUE: Knitting.

AVERAGE: For those with some experience in knitting. Directions are for size 6 mos. Changes for sizes 1 yr., 2 yrs., and 3 yrs. are in parentheses.

MATERIALS: Coats & Clark Red Heart "Super Sport" yarn 3-ply (3 oz. skein): 2 (2, 2, 2) skeins of No. 819 Blue Jewel; knitting needles, one pair each No. 4 and No. 6, OR ANY SIZE NEEDLES TO OBTAIN GAUGE BELOW; *For "Wash"*: 2 yds. of beige yarn and small amounts of brown embroidery floss for clothespins; crochet hook, Size E; scraps of denim, floral print, red and white felt, orange and yellow rickrack, tapestry needle; *For Tiny Washline Sweater*: small amounts of white and red cotton thread; No. 1 knitting needles.

GAUGE: In stockinette stitch (k 1 row, p 1 row) using larger needles — 11 sts = 2"; 7 rows = 1". TO SAVE TIME, TAKE TIME TO CHECK GAUGE.

MEASUREMENTS:

Sizes:	6 mos.	1 yr.	2 yrs.	3 yrs.
Body chest:	19"	20"	21"	22"
Finished chest:	21"	22"	23"	24"
Width across back or front at underarms:	10½"	11"	11½"	12"
Width across sleeve at upper arm:	7½"	8"	9"	9½"

DIRECTIONS:

BACK: Starting at lower edge with smaller needles and MC, cast on 56 (60, 64, 68) sts. Work in k 1, p 1 ribbing for 1½". Change to larger needles and stockinette stitch (st st) until total length is 6 (7, 8, 9)" from beg or for desired length, ending with a p row.

ARMHOLE SHAPING: Bind off 5 (6, 6, 6) sts at beg of next 2 rows — 46 (48, 52, 56) sts. Work even in st st for 12 (14, 16, 18) rows more, ending with a k row.

NECK SHAPING: P 15 (16, 17, 18) sts, slip next 16 (16, 18, 20) sts onto a st holder for center neck; join new ball of yarn and p rem sts. Working both sides at the same time, dec one st at each neck edge on next row, then every other row until there are 4 sts on needle. Bind off.

FRONT: Work same as Back.

SLEEVES: Starting at lower edge with smaller needles and MC, cast on 34 (38, 42, 46) sts. Work in k 1, p 1 ribbing for 1½", increasing 6 sts evenly spaced across last row — 40 (44, 48, 52) sts. Change to larger needles and work in st st until total length is 7 (7½, 8½, 9½)" from beg or for desired length. Bind off all sts.

FRONT NECKBAND: With right side facing, using smaller needles and MC, pick up and k 24 (25, 26, 27) sts along left-

FIG. 2   **1 SQ. = ½"**

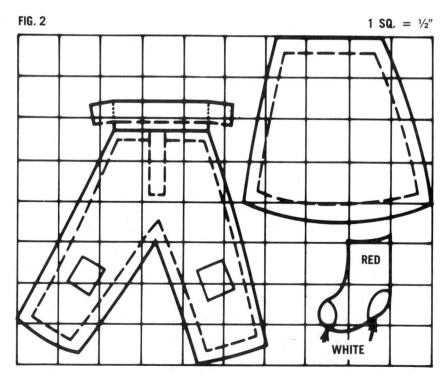

RED

WHITE

neck edge, k 16 (16, 18, 20) sts from st holder, then pick up and k 24 (25, 26, 27) sts along right neck edge — 64 (66, 70, 74) sts. Work in k 1, p 1 ribbing for 5 rows. Bind off loosely in ribbing.

BACK NECKBAND: Work same as Front Neckband.

FINISHING — To Assemble: Pin each piece to measurements on a padded flat surface, cover with a damp cloth and allow to dry; *do not press.* Overlap shoulders, placing Back over Front so that shoulder seam is 3 rows below neckline. Insert sleeves, and pin to armhole edge. Sew in sleeves, taking care to stitch through double thickness at shoulders. Sew side and sleeve seams.

FINISHING — TINY SWEATER: With red thread and No. 1 needles, cast on 13 sts. Work in k 1, p 1 ribbing for 3 rows. Change to st st; work in the following striped pattern: * 2 rows with white, 2 rows with red; rep from * until total length is 2″ from beg, ending with a p row. **Neck Shaping:** K first 4 sts; join a new ball of thread and bind off center 5 sts, k rem 4 sts. Working both sides at the same time, work even for 2 rows more. Bind off. **Sleeves:** Mark each side edge 1″ from top for armholes. With the right side facing you and red, pick up 7 sts along armhole edge. Work in striped pat for 16 rows. Change to red and work in k 1, p 1 ribbing, decreasing one st each end of next row. Work even in ribbing for 2 rows more. Bind off.

FINISHING CLOTHES: Following enlarging instructions (*page 294*) and diagram (*page 219*), cut, then sew clothing pieces (*see photo*) on the machine. Using beige yarn and an E hook, work a chain about 11″ long. Sew the line, Tiny Sweater and clothes onto Front of sweater (*see photo*). Using brown embroidery floss, work two long stitches for clothespins.

BABY'S BUTTON SHOULDER PULLOVER

TECHNIQUE: Crochet.

AVERAGE: For those with some experience in crochet. Directions are given for Size 6 Months. Changes for Sizes 1 and 2 are in parentheses.

Note 1: The sweater buttons at the shoulders.

Note 2: Body of sweater is made in one piece to armholes.

MATERIALS: Talon American Wintuk Baby Yarn (1 oz. skein): 1 (1, 2) skeins of White (A), 1 skein each of Blue (B), Pink (C), Lilac (D), Yellow (E) and Green (F); steel crochet hook, Size O or any size hook to obtain gauge below; four ½"-dia. buttons.

GAUGE: (1 cluster, 1 dc and 1 cluster) = 1"; 5 cluster rows = 2". TO SAVE TIME, TAKE TIME TO CHECK GAUGE.

MEASUREMENTS:

Sizes:	6 mos.	1 yr.	2 yrs.
Body chest:	19″	20″	21″
Finished chest:	20″	21″	22″
Width across sleeve at upper arm:			
	7½″	8″	8½″

. . . .

DIRECTIONS:

SWEATER: Ribbing: Starting at narrow edge with A, ch 9. **Row 1:** 1 hdc in 2nd ch from hook and in each ch across — 8 hdc. Ch 2, turn. **Row 2:** 1 hdc in back lp of each hdc across — 8 hdc. Ch 2, turn. Rep Row 2 until 58 (60, 64) rows have been completed. Fasten off A, leaving a 5″ end, and sew narrow edges together.

BODY: Rnd 1 *(right side):* Working across long edge of ribbing with A, make 2 sc in each hdc around — 116 (120, 128) sc. Join with sl st to first sc. Place a marker at beg of rnd to indicate side edge. Ch 1, turn. **For 6 Month Size — Rnd 2:** Sc in each sc around. Join with sl st. Fasten off A. Turn. **For Size 1 — Rnds 2 and 3:** Sc in each sc around. Join with sl st. Ch 1, turn. On last sc rnd, fasten off A and turn. **For Size 2 — Rnds 2-5:** Sc in each sc around. Join with sl st. Ch 1, turn. On last sc rnd, fasten off A and turn. Now start Pattern as follows — **Rnd 1** *(Beg of cluster stripe):* Attach B with sl st to first sc of this rnd, ch 4 (counts as 1 dc and ch 1), sk next st, * *holding back the last lp of each dc, work 3 dc in next st, yo and through 4 lps on hook* — cluster made; ch 1, sk next st, dc in next st, ch 1, sk next st; rep from * around, ending with cluster in next st, ch 1, sk next st. Join with sl st to 3rd ch of beg ch-4. Fasten off B and turn. **Rnd 2:** Attach C with sl st to first dc of this rnd, *ch 3, holding back the last lp of each dc, work 2 dc in first dc, yo and through 3 lps on hook —* beg cluster made; ch 1, * dc in next cluster, ch 1, cluster in next dc, ch 1; rep from * around, ending with dc in next cluster, ch 1. Join with sl st to top of beg cluster. Fasten off C, turn. **Rnd 3:** Attach D with sl st to first cluster of this rnd, ch 4 (counts as 1 dc and ch 1), * cluster in next dc, ch 1, dc in next cluster, ch 1; rep from * around, ending with cluster in next dc, ch 1. Join with sl st to 3rd ch of beg ch-4. Fasten off D, turn. **Rnd 4:** Attach E with sl st to first dc of this rnd and rep Rnd 2. Fasten off E and turn. **Rnd 5:** Attach F with sl st to first cluster of this rnd and rep Rnd 3. Fasten off F and turn. **Rnd 6** *(Beg of A stripe):* Attach A with sl st to first dc of this rnd, ch 1, work 1 sc in each cluster, dc and ch-1 sp around. Join with sl st to first sc. *Do not* fasten off A, ch 1, turn. **For 6 Month Size — Rnd 7:** Sc in each sc around. Join with sl st. Fasten off A, turn. **For Size 1 — Rnds 7 and 8:** Sc in each sc around. Join with sl st. Ch 1, turn. On last sc rnd, fasten off A and turn. **For Size 2 —**

Rnds 7-10: Sc in each sc around. Join with sl st. Ch 1, turn. On last sc rnd, fasten off A and turn. Rnds 1-7 (1-8, 1-10) form pattern. Now rep Rnds 1-7 (1-8, 1-10) once more for size being made — *2 patterns completed.* Fasten off A, turn. *Note: Hereafter work back and forth in rows.*

BACK ARMHOLE SHAPING: Continuing in pattern, attach B to the 3rd (3rd, 4th) sc from marker (right armhole edge) and work across next 53 (55, 57) sts. Work even in pattern until Rnd 3 of the fourth pattern is completed, counting from beg. Complete Back by working Rnds 6-7 (6-8, 6-10) for size being made. Fasten off A.

FRONT ARMHOLE SHAPING: Skip next 5 (5, 7) sc on last rnd worked (left armhole edge); attach B to next sc and work in pattern across next 53 (55, 57) sts. Work even in pattern until the 3rd pattern is completed.

NECK SHAPING — Next Row: From wrong side, attach B and work in pattern across first 19 (20, 21) sts, skip center 15 sts for front neck, join 2nd ball of B yarn and work last 19 (20, 21) sts. Turn. *Note: Ch-1 is considered a stitch.* Working each side with a separate ball, dec 2 sts at each neck edge every row until Rnd 3 of the fourth pattern is completed — 13 (14, 15) sts. Fasten off.

FRONT NECK EDGING: Left Half — Row 1: Starting at left

shoulder, from right side, with A sc in each st of left shoulder, working 3 sc in each corner-sp of left neck edge, sl st in next st of last A stripe made. Fasten off A. **Right Half:** Work right half to correspond with left half. **Row 2** *(button loop row):* Starting at right shoulder, from wrong side, with A sc in next 4 (5, 6) sc, *ch 3, sk next 3 sc, sc in each of next 3 sc, ch 3, sk 3 sc* — 2 button loops made; sc in each sc along right neck edge, last A stripe and along left neck edge, then work 2 button loops on left shoulder and complete as before. *Do not* fasten off. Ch 1, turn. **Row 3** *(picot st row):* Sc in next 4 (5, 6) sc, 4 sc in ch-3 button loop, sc in each of next 3 sc, 4 sc in ch-3 button loop, * *in next sc work (sc, ch 3, sc)* — picot st made; sc in next sc; rep from * along left neck edge, A stripe and right neck edge to button loop and complete to correspond with other half. Fasten off A.

BACK EDGING: Working across middle 25 sts of Back, work picot sts as for Front. Fasten off A. Sew shoulders 4 (5, 6) sts in from shoulder edge.

SLEEVES — Rnd 1: Attach A from right side, to center sc of armhole and work a rnd of sc along armhole edge, making 5 (5, 7) sc at underarm, 2 sc in each dc and cluster st, 1 sc in each sc of A stripe and 3 sc in top of shoulder — 44 (46, 52) sts. Ch 1, turn. **For 6 Month Size only:** Work 1 more sc rnd. Fasten off A, turn. **For Size 1 only:** Work 2 more sc rnds. Fasten off A, turn. **For Size 2 only:** Work 4 more sc rnds. Fasten off A, turn. Now start pattern as for Back, decreasing 3 (3, 4) sts evenly spaced on each A stripe until 3 patterns are completed — 35 (37, 40) sts. Fasten off A. **Sleeve Ribbing:** Work as for Sweater Ribbing until 18 (19, 20) rows have been completed. Fasten off A, leaving a 5″ end and sew edges together. Sew Ribbing to bottom of sleeve. Sew 2 buttons on each back shoulder, opposite button loops.

CHILD'S "AZTEC" PULLOVER

TECHNIQUE: Crochet.

CHALLENGING: For those with more experience in crochet. Directions are for child's size 4. Changes for sizes 6, 8 and 10 are in parentheses.

MATERIALS: Brunswick "Pomfret" (1¾ oz. skein): 1 (2, 2, 2) skeins Rust (A), 1 (2, 2, 2) skeins Green (B), 1 (1, 2, 2) skeins Blue (C), 2 (2, 3, 3) skeins Beige (D); 1 steel crochet hook Size 0 OR ANY SIZE HOOK TO OBTAIN GAUGE BELOW.

GAUGE: 5 sts = 1″; 11 dc rows = 4″. TO SAVE TIME, TAKE TIME TO CHECK GAUGE.

MEASUREMENTS:

Sizes:	C-4	C-6	C-8	C-10
Chest:	23½″	26″	28½″	30″
Sleeve around upper arm:				
	9¼″	9¼″	12¼″	12¼″

Note: When changing to a new color, work dc over the ends of the previous color.

DIRECTIONS:

BACK: With A, ch 61 (67, 73, 77). **Row 1** (*right side*): Dc in 4th ch from hook and in each ch to end — 59 (65, 71, 75) dc. Ch 3, turn on this and all following rows. *Note: Ch 3 at beg of rows counts as 1 dc.* **Row 2:** Dc in each dc. Ch 3, turn. Rep Row 2 for dc pat and beg following Row 3 of appropriate chart by working to center st, then repeating chart after center st from left to right. Follow chart thru Row 33 (33, 47, 47). **Next Row:** Dc in first 18 (21, 23, 25) sts, cut yarn; leave center 23 (23, 25, 25) sts unworked (neck); join A and dc in last 18 (21, 23, 25) sts.

FRONT: Work same as Back following appropriate chart.

•224

With color C, work 1 row sc along entire top edge of Front and Back (neck & shoulders). Sew tog 10 (13, 15, 17) sts each side for shoulders.

LEFT SLEEVE: From right side, join color C at front underarm as indicated on chart and work 46 (46, 62, 62) sc evenly to back underarm. Working in dc, work 1 row D. **For Size 8 and 10 only:**

Work 4 rows C, 1 row D. **For all Sizes:** Work 1 row D dec 0 (0, 1, 1) sts each end of row, work 4 rows C, then work 1 row C dec 1 st each end of row. Rep dec every 5th (5th, 3rd, 3rd) row 2 (2, 6, 6) times more, continuing pat following chart for left sleeve. Fasten off.

RIGHT SLEEVE: Join color C and work sc same as left sleeve. **For Sizes 8 and 10 only:** Working in dc, work 3 rows B, 2 rows

D. **For all Sizes:** Continue pat following chart for right sleeve. Fasten off.

FINISHING: Sew side and sleeve seams. With C, work 1 rnd sc around lower edge of body and sleeves.

BRAIDS — **Make 4:** Using 4-10″ strands of 3 colors for each braid, braid yarn and knot one at each neck edge.

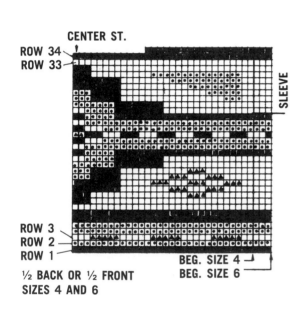

½ BACK OR ½ FRONT
SIZES 4 AND 6

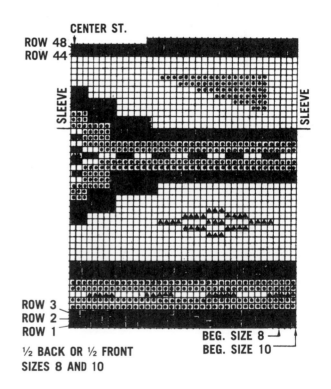

½ BACK OR ½ FRONT
SIZES 8 AND 10

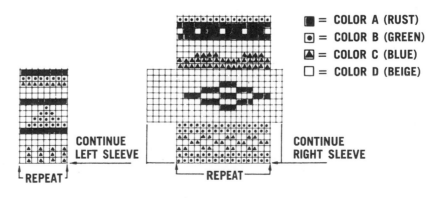

■ = COLOR A (RUST)
◉ = COLOR B (GREEN)
▲ = COLOR C (BLUE)
□ = COLOR D (BEIGE)

BABY'S "BISCUIT"
COMFORTER, ROBE & PILLOWS

COMFORTER

TECHNIQUE: Patchwork.

AVERAGE: For those with some experience in patchwork.

MATERIALS: (44/45″-wide fabric) ⅝ yd. each of rose and white for patches, ¾ yd. of muslin, ⅜ yd. of blue, and 1⅝ yds. of rose for quiltback; batting for borders and stuffing for "biscuits". Select poly-cotton prints to approximate photo quilt.

DIRECTIONS:
(½″ seams allowed):

1. CUTTING: Cut 18 rose and 17 white patches 6″ square, and 35 muslin patches 5″ square. Cut four 5½″-wide blue borders, two 21″ and two 39″ long. Cut a pink quiltback 46″ x 38″. Cut four 7″-wide strips of batting, two 42″ and two 34″ long.

2. BISCUITS: Pin each 6″ patch to a muslin 5″ patch, right sides out and corners matching; fold the extra fabric into a tuck at the center of each edge. Top stitch around 4 sides, ½″ from the cut edge, through all layers.

3. QUILT TOP: Seam 7 horizontal rows of 5 patches each, alternating the colors and starting four rows with rose. Seam one row beneath the other, alternating colors. To each short end of the patchwork, seam a shorter blue border; to the longer sides, seam the longer borders.

4. BISCUITS: Into the muslin *back only* of each patch cut a short (less than an inch) slash. Stuff each square through the slash to "raise the biscuit". Close the slash with a couple of stitches or a scrap of iron-on fabric.

5. PLACE the quilt top in the center of the quilt back, wrong sides together. At each side 4″

TIP

What's A "Biscuit" Comforter?

"Biscuits" are a form of dimensional quilting; an area is raised with soft padding inserted through the back of the work between the layers. For this baby comforter, the areas to be padded are relatively small, uniform in size and biscuit-shaped. Hence the term, "raising the biscuit."

will extend for binding. Pin, then top stitch along the inside border seams through both layers.

6. **PLACE** the batting strips under the borders (batting will extend 2″ beyond the border). Pin the outside border edges to the quilt back (through the batting) and topstitch ½″ from the blue cut edge.

7. **BINDING:** Turn under ½″ at the short edges of the quilt-back. Fold it over to the right side and pin the turned-under edge to the previous topstitching; edgestitch. Repeat at the other two edges.

ROBE

TECHNIQUE: Patchwork.

AVERAGE: For those with some experience in patchwork.

MATERIALS: Scraps of cotton flannel; 5 yds. bias tape; 36″ square each of batting and cotton flannel for lining; 7 yds. narrow ribbon *(optional)*.

DIRECTIONS:
(¼″ seams allowed):

1. **FROM** flannel scraps, cut eight 4″ x 4½″ rectangular and forty 4″ square patches.

2. **SEAM** the patches together (a row of longer patches in the middle) as shown in FIG. 6, to make half the robe. Seam the other half the same way, but have the sleeve extending from the opposite side. Seam the two parts together from the lower back edge to the shoulder line (*see* FIG. 6).

3. **SPREAD** the batting over the lining fabric. On top, spread the patchwork. Baste the three layers together from the center outward; finally, baste along the outside edges. Cut the batting and lining flush with the patchwork. *Optional:* topstitch the ribbon over the seamlines.

4. **DRAW** neck edge (*see* FIG. 6 Detail) in the two central patches. Pin along the drawn lines; then top stitch, removing pins. Cut out neck opening close to the topstitching.

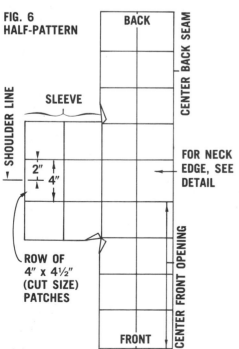

FIG. 6 HALF-PATTERN

BACK — CENTER BACK SEAM — SHOULDER LINE — SLEEVE — FOR NECK EDGE, SEE DETAIL — 2″ — 4″ — ROW OF 4″ x 4½″ (CUT SIZE) PATCHES — CENTER FRONT OPENING — FRONT

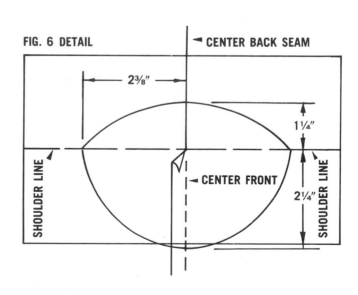

FIG. 6 DETAIL

CENTER BACK SEAM — 2⅜″ — 1¼″ — SHOULDER LINE — CENTER FRONT — SHOULDER LINE — 2¼″

5. FOLD the robe in half, right sides together, along the shoulder line. Seam the side and sleeve edges.

6. WITH bias tape, bind raw edges. Cut six 12″ lengths of tape for ties. Turn under one end and sew it under the front edge at the neck. Sew two more 3″ apart, then sew three at the opposite edge to match. Edgestitch long open edges together to finish ties.

"MOCK PATCH" ANIMAL PILLOWS

. . . .

TECHNIQUE: Sewing, optional quilting.

EASY: Achievable by anyone.

MATERIALS: ⅜ yd. 45″-wide muslin for each; scraps of printed pastel fabric; stuffing; fusible web; scrap of black iron-on fabric (for eye); batting (*optional*).

. . . .

DIRECTIONS:

1. ENLARGE (*see page 294*) pattern (*see* FIG. 3). Fold muslin in half (bringing selvages together). Trace the pattern to muslin and, ¼″ *outside the traced lines,* cut through both layers. Cut 2″ squares of assorted prints and fusible web.

2. LIGHTLY mark the grainline (a gridline up and down the body) on one animal body (pillow front). Pin the colored squares (over fusible web) to the muslin along the grainline, alternately to the left and right of it. Following the same line-up, pin the rest of the squares in place; iron to fuse. For the hen, iron the yellow beak to muslin. Edgestitch or zigzag stitch the raw edges of the patches and the beak to secure them.

FIG. 3 PILLOWS   1 SQ. = 2″.

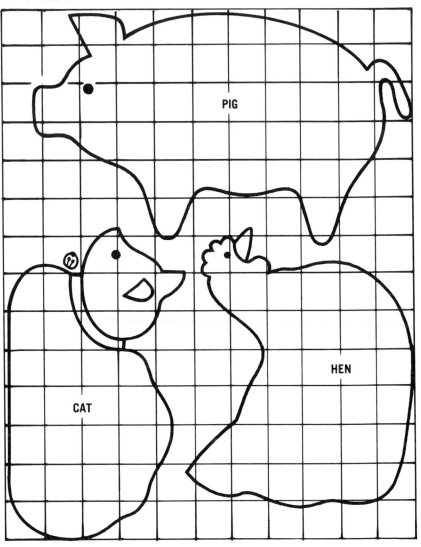

3. OPTIONAL QUILTING: Draw diagonal lines, connecting opposite corners of the patches. Repeat in the opposite direction, to make squares. Topstitch along the drawn lines (first basting the batting to the wrong side, if you wish).

4. WITH right sides together, seam (¼″) the pillow front to the pillow back, leaving about 3″ open at the bottom edge. Turn right side out; stuff and slip stitch the opening closed.

5. WITH a paper punch, cut an "eye" from iron-on fabric; fuse to the pillow. For the cat, cut an ear and fuse it to the pillow. Slip stitch the edges of the eye and ear to secure them.

"NINE-PATCH" CORNER PILLOW

. . . .

(24″ square)

TECHNIQUE: Patchwork, optional quilting.

EASY: Achievable by anyone.

MATERIALS: ½ yd. blue and ¾ yd. muslin 44/45″-wide fabric; stuffing; batting *(optional)*.

. . . .

DIRECTIONS:

(¼″ seams allowed):

1. **FROM** the blue, cut one 12½″ square, twenty 2½″ squares and four 2½″ x 12½″ strips. From the muslin, cut eight 2½″ x 12″ strips, sixteen 2½″ squares and a 24½″ square pillowback.

2. **NINE-PATCH BLOCK:** Seam one muslin square between two blue squares. Repeat. Seam one blue square between two muslin squares. Seam the three rows, one below the other with a blue square in the middle. Make three more blocks the same, one for each corner.

3. **ROW ASSEMBLY:** Seam a blue strip between two muslin

strips. Repeat three times.

4. **SEAM** a row assembly to two opposite sides of the large blue block.

5. **SEAM** a 9-patch block at each end of the two remaining row assemblies and seam them to the central assembly, to complete the pillowtop *(see photo)*.

6. **OPTIONAL QUILTING:** Baste batting to the back of the pillowtop. Lightly draw (with a compass and hard pencil) overlapping 5″ circles in the center square, then rule diagonals across the borders *(see photo)*. Sew running stitches along the drawn lines to quilt.

7. **PIN** the pillowtop to the pillow back, right sides together. Seam (¼″) around three sides and four corners. Turn right side out, stuff; turn in open edges and slip stitch.

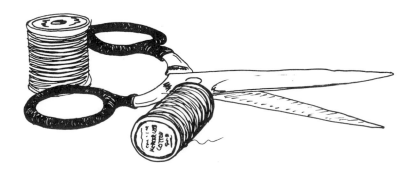

CHILD'S RAINBOW DRESS

TECHNIQUE: Knitting.

AVERAGE: For those with some experience in knitting. Directions are given for Size 3. Changes for Sizes 5 and 6 are in parentheses.

MATERIALS: Lion Brand "Bianca" (1.4 oz. ball): 4 (8, 12) balls of No. 304 Sherbet; knitting needles, one pair each of No. 8 and No. 10, OR ANY SIZE NEEDLES TO OBTAIN GAUGE BELOW; ¾ yd. of ribbon.

GAUGE: In stockinette stitch (k 1 row, p 1 row) with larger needles — 5 sts = 1"; 6 rows = 1". TO SAVE TIME, TAKE TIME TO CHECK GAUGE.

MEASUREMENTS:

Sizes:	3	5	6
Body chest:	22"	24"	25"
Finished chest:	22"	24"	26"
Width across back or front at underarms:			
	11"	12"	13"
Width across sleeve at upper arm:			
	10½"	11"	11½"
Length of Skirt:			
	6"	8"	11"

DIRECTIONS:

BACK: Starting at the lower edge of the skirt with larger needles, cast on 124 (134, 147) sts. Work in garter stitch (k every row) for 4 rows. Change to stockinette stitch (st st) and work until total length is 4¾ (6, 8½)" from beg, ending with a p row. **Next Row** (*Dec row*): K 4 (2, 3), * sl 2, k 1, psso, k 3; rep from * across — 84 (90, 99) sts. Continue in st st until total length is 6 (8, 11)" from beg, ending with a p row. **Next Row** (*Dec row*): * Sl 2, k 1, psso; rep from * across — 28 (30, 33) sts. Change to smaller needles and work in k 1, p 1 ribbing for 12 rows. **Next Row** (*Inc row*): Change to larger needles and work in st st, increasing one st in every st across — 56 (60, 66) sts. Continuing in st st work 5 (6, 7½)" above ribbing, ending with a p row.

ARMHOLE SHAPING: Continuing in st st, bind off 4 sts at beg of next 2 rows. Dec one st each end of next row — 46 (50, 56) sts. Change to smaller needles and work in k 1, p 1 ribbing for 3¾ (4¾, 5¼)" ending on p-side of work.

SHOULDER SHAPING: Continuing in k 1, p 1 ribbing, bind off 10 (11, 12) sts at beg of next 2 rows. Place rem 26 (28, 32) sts on a st holder for back neck.

FRONT: Work same as Back, placing rem 26 (28, 32) sts on a st holder for front neck.

SLEEVES: Starting at lower edge of sleeve with smaller needles, cast on 28 (30, 32) sts. Work in k 1, p 1 ribbing for 4 rows. Change to larger needles and work in st st, increasing across row to 54 (58, 60) sts. Work in st st for 8 (12, 12) rows more.

CAP SHAPING: Continuing in st st, bind off 4 sts at beg of next 2 rows. Dec one st at each end every 4th row 3 (4, 4) times, then every other row 4 (5, 6) times — 32. **Next 2 Rows:** K 3 tog across row. **Last Row:** K 1, pull remaining sts through first st tightly and secure.

FINISHING: Pin each piece to measurements on a padded, flat surface, cover with a damp cloth and allow to dry; *do not press.* Sew the left shoulder seam only. *Note: Work back and forth in rows.*

NECKBAND: Starting at open right shoulder seam, from right side of work, using smaller needles, slip sts from back and front st holders onto needle — 52 (56, 64) sts and work as follows: **Row 1** (*eyelet row*): * K 2 tog, yo; rep from * across, turn. **Rows 2-5:** Work in k 1, p 1 ribbing. Turn. Bind off loosely in ribbing. Sew right shoulder seam, leaving right edge of neckband open. Sew side and sleeve seams. Sew in sleeves, gathering fullness at shoulder. Weave ribbon through the eyelet opening on Row 1 of the neckband.

PATCHWORK PULLOVER

TECHNIQUE: Knitting.

AVERAGE: For those with some experience in knitting. Directions are given for Size 4. Changes for Sizes 6, 8 and 10 are in parentheses.

MATERIALS: Lion Brand Knitting Worsted 4-ply (3.5 oz. skeins): 1 (1, 1, 2) skeins of #114 Cardinal (A), 1 skein each of #113 Scarlet (B), #133 Tile (C), #141 Dusty Rose (D), #183 Lilac (E), #130 Emerald (F), #148 Turquoise (G); knitting needles, 1 pair No. 8 OR ANY SIZE NEEDLES TO OBTAIN GAUGE BELOW; crochet hook, Size G.

GAUGE: 9 sts = 2"; 8 rows (4 ridges) = 1". TO SAVE TIME, TAKE TIME TO CHECK GAUGE.

MEASUREMENTS:

Sizes:	4	6	8	10
Chest:	24"	25"	27½"	29"

Width across back or front at underarms:

	12"	12½"	13¾"	14½"

Width across sleeve at upper arm:

	9½"	10"	10½"	11"

DIRECTIONS:

Note: The stripe patches for Back and Front are made in 3 strips, then strips are joined together. Work in garter st (k each row) throughout.

BACK: FIRST STRIP: Starting at lower edge with B, cast on 18 (19, 21, 22) sts. **Rows 1 through 4:** With B, k 4 rows. Mark Row 1 for right side. Drop B; pick up A. **Rows 5 through 8:** With A, k 4 rows. Drop A; pick up B. Repeat last 8 rows (rows 1 through 8) 3 (3, 4, 4) more times. Cut A and B; attach E and F. **Next 8 Rows:** Work 4 rows F and 4 rows E. Repeat last 8 rows 3 (3, 4, 4) more times. Cut E and F; attach C and D. **Following 8 Rows:** Work 4 rows D and 4 rows C. Repeat last 8 rows 3 (3, 4, 4) more times. Bind off. Cut D and C. Cut and attach colors as needed.

SECOND STRIP: Starting at lower edge with E, cast on 18 (19, 21, 22) sts. **Rows 1 through 8:** Work 4 rows E and 4 rows G. Mark Row 1 for right side. Repeat last 8 rows 3 (3, 4, 4) more times. **Next 8 Rows:** Work 4 rows C and 4 rows A. Repeat last 8 rows 3 (3, 4, 4) more times. **Following 8 Rows:** Work 4 rows F and 4 rows G. Repeat last 8 rows 3 (3, 4, 4) more times. Bind off. Cut F and G.

THIRD STRIP: Starting at lower edge with D, cast on 18 (19, 21, 23) sts. **Rows 1 through 8:** Work 4 rows D and 4 rows A. Repeat last 8 rows 3 (3, 4, 4) more times. **Next 8 Rows:** Work 4 rows E and 4 rows F. Repeat last 8 rows 3 (3, 4, 4) more times. **Following 8 Rows:** Work 4 rows A and 4 rows B. Repeat last 8 rows 3 (3, 4, 4) more times. Bind off. Cut A and B. Darn in all loose ends on wrong side. Using a darning needle, sew strips together, matching rows.

RIBBING: With right side facing, working along lower edge of joined stips, with A, pick up and k 54 (56, 62, 66) sts evenly along lower edge. Work in k 1, p 1 ribbing for 3 (3½, 3½, 4)". Bind off loosely in ribbing.

FRONT: Work same as Back.

RIGHT SLEEVE: Starting at lower edge with A, cast on 40 (42, 44, 46) sts. Work in k 1, p 1 ribbing for 2½ (2½, 3, 3)", inc 2 (2, 4, 4) sts evenly spaced in last row — 42 (44, 48, 50) sts. **Rows 1 through 8:** Working in garter st, make 4 rows A and 4 rows C. Repeat last 8 rows for stripe pat until the total length is 11½ (12½, 14, 16)" ending with a complete stripe. Bind off all sts.

LEFT SLEEVE: Work same as right sleeve until ribbing has been completed — 42 (44, 48, 50) sts. Drop A; attach D. **Rows 1 through 8:** Working in garter st, make 4 rows D and 4 rows A. Repeat last 8 rows until same length as right sleeve. Bind off all sts.

FINISHING: Pin each piece to measurements on a padded surface, cover with a damp cloth and allow to dry; *do not press.* Starting at side edges, sew approximately 1½ (2, 2½, 3)" shoulder seams across top edge, leaving center section open for neck. With center of top edges of sleeves at shoulder seams, sew top edges of sleeves along 4¾ (5, 5¼, 5½)" of back and front side edges. Sew sleeve and side seams, matching stripes. With crochet hook, holding yarn on wrong side, from right side work 1 row of sl sts evenly over each seam, being careful to keep work flat.

CHRISTENING GOWN, BONNET AND SLIP

CHRISTENING GOWN

TECHNIQUE: Sewing and embroidery.

CHALLENGING: For those with more experience in embroidery.

MATERIALS (*for all three*)**:** 4¼ yds. 45"-wide white batiste; 2½ yds. ⅝"-wide scalloped lace edging; 2 yds. ⅞"-wide lace panel for skirt front; 1¾ yds. of 1¾"-wide crocheted lace for hem; 6-strand embroidery floss; embroidery hoop.

DIRECTIONS:
(*½" seams allowed*):

1. CUTTING: Enlarge (*see page 294*) pattern (*see* FIG. 8). From batiste, cut 1 each of Bodice Front and Skirt Front, 1 pair each of Bodice Back, Sleeve, Bonnet Mid-section, Skirt Sides and Skirt Backs, 2 pairs of Bonnet Sides. Also cut two 2" x 9¼" Sleeve Bands, a 2½" x 21" Bonnet Ruffle and a 2" x 14" bias strip for neck binding. *For Slip,* cut 1 Bodice Front and a pair of Bodice Back pieces; also a Skirt Front and Skirt Back, each piece measuring 22" long x 30" wide.

2. FRONT BODICE: Matching CF's trace the design (*see* FIG. 8A) to the Bodice. Place the Bodice in an embroidery hoop and, using 6-strand floss, work stems in Stem Stitch, blossoms in Satin Stitch and baby's breath in French Knots. Outline the bow in Stem Stitch. Work the enclosing circle in pairs of small Lazy Daisy "petals" (*see Stitch Details on pages 298-299*). Gather a 24" strip of narrow lace and stitch it to the Bodice with its straight edge inside, along the broken line.

3. BODICE: Seam the Bodice Front to the Bodice Back at the shoulders and at side edges; press seams open.

4. SLEEVES: Sew a gathering row at the cap edge between the circles and another row along the bottom edge. At one long edge of the Sleeve Band, turn ½" to the wrong side and press. Fold the band in half, right side together, and seam the short ends. Seam the underarm edges of the Sleeve together. With right sides together, pin the raw edge of the band to the lower edge of the Sleeve, underarm seams matching; pull up gathers to fit; stitch. Turn the folded edge of the band to the wrong side and slip stitch it along the seam line.

5. ARMHOLE: With right sides together, pin the Sleeve to the armhole; match the circle to the Bodice Front, match the notch to the Bodice Back, match underarm seams to each other; pull up gathers to fit; stitch.

6. SKIRT FRONT: Measuring from the top edge, draw five horizontal lines across the Skirt Front at the following intervals: 7", 5", 5", 5" and 3". Fold the piece in half lengthwise and press, to make a center front crease. Open the Skirt again and plan the embroidery as you like. It is all based on FIG. 8B. Trace the actual-size motif on transparent paper. The large (broken line) leaf can be substituted for the double leaf; the leaf to the right can be omitted; the middle spray can be shortened by 2 bells. Trace your design (centered between the horizontal lines). Trace from CF toward the left, ending no closer than ¾" from a side edge. Trace the same design reversed (pattern wrong side up) to the right of the center. Work embroidery like the Bodice motif. Outline leaves in Stem Stitch and fill in their lower section with Herringbone Stitch (*see Stitch Details on pages 298-299*).

7. LACE INSETS: Pin 5 lace bands across the Skirt Front, centered over the 5 horizontal lines; edgestitch. From the wrong side, *carefully* cut the fabric across the

---

Did You Know

That our christening gown is based on a 19th-century original! Our version is made of poly/cotton batiste embroidered with lily of the valley sprays and lavished with lace trims. Embroider as much, or as little, of the floral pattern as you like for an equally lovely effect.

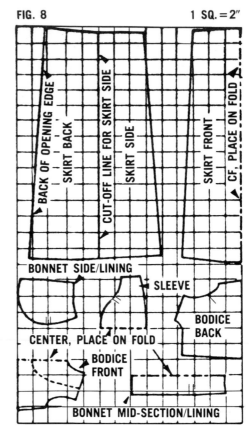

FIG. 8   1 SQ. = 2"

BACK OF OPENING EDGE

SKIRT BACK

CUT-OFF LINE FOR SKIRT SIDE

SKIRT SIDE

SKIRT FRONT

CF, PLACE ON FOLD

BONNET SIDE/LINING

SLEEVE

BODICE BACK

CENTER, PLACE ON FOLD

BODICE FRONT

BONNET MID-SECTION/LINING

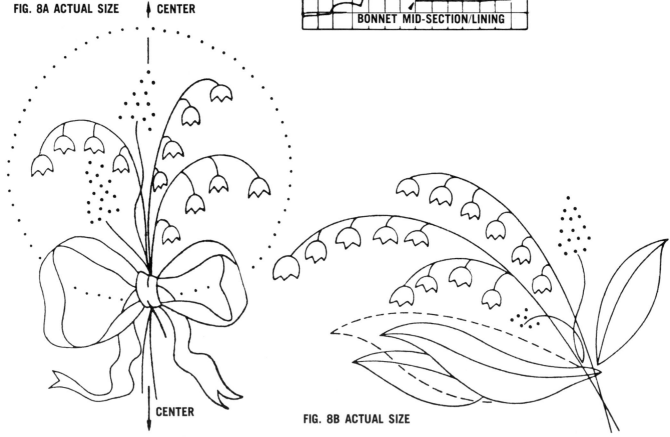

FIG. 8A ACTUAL SIZE   ↑ CENTER

CENTER

FIG. 8B ACTUAL SIZE

lines and fold it up (or down) against the fabric, so the lace will be transparent; stitch along the fold; trim excess to about ¼″.

8. SKIRT: Seam the Skirt Front between two Skirt Side Panels; press seams toward the panels. Topstitch ⅝″ lace along each seam, scallops facing away from the center. Seam the slanted edge of a Skirt Back to each Side Panel; press seams open.

9. WAIST SEAM: Sew 2 rows of gathering stitches ½″ from the top edge of the Skirt. With right sides together, pin the Skirt to the Bodice at waist edges, matching the front seams to notches in the Bodice, and the side seams to each other, back edges flush. Pull up gathers to fit; adjust fullness evenly and stitch. Press seam allowance upward.

10. BACK CLOSING: At back edges, turn ¼″ to the wrong side and stitch; then turn under 1¼″ and press. With a 2″ x 14″ bias strip, bind the neck edge. Turning under each end, stitch the straight edge of the lace along the seamline, scalloped edge upward. Sew three snaps (one at the waist, one at the neck and one between) to back edges. Hem the lower edge. Turning under each end, lap the wide lace over the hem edge and topstitch.

BONNET

1. SEAM a Bonnet Midsection between the Bonnet sides, notches matching; press the seams open, clipping as needed. Repeat for the lining.

2. TOPSTITCH a lace band ½″ from the front edge of the Bonnet. Fold a 2½″ x 15″ strip of muslin in half, right side together. Stitch ½″ from each end and turn right side out. Every ¾″, make a ¼″ tuck; press and pin them. With right sides together and raw edges even, pin the tucked strip to the front edge of the Bonnet, starting and stopping ½″ from the lower edge of the Bonnet; adjust tucks, if needed, to fit; stitch ½″ from the raw edge.

3. PLACE bonnet lining on Bonnet, right sides together and stitch ½″ from all raw edges, leaving 3″ open at back, for turning. Turn right side out; turn in open edges and slip stitch. Sew one end of an 18″ ribbon to the inside of the cap at the lower edges against the front seam.

SLIP

1. FOLD a skirt piece in half vertically (22″ x 15″). At one (top) end, mark 11″ from the fold. Along a yardstick, draw a tapered side edge from this mark to the end of the bottom edge. Cut on the line through both layers. Repeat on the other skirt piece.

2. SLASH one skirt (back) piece down the center fold. Follow Steps 3, 9 and 10, for Christening Gown, omitting lace. Bind the armhole edges like the neck edge.

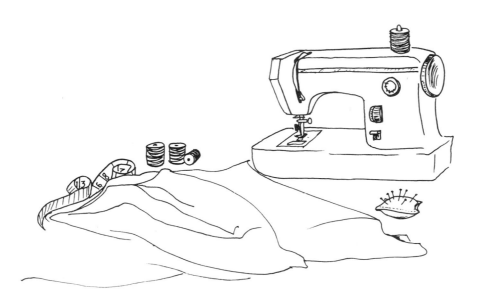

·10·

FOR THE HOME

It seems you can never get enough of things to make for the home — they're wonderful hostess or housewarming gifts, great Christmas presents, not to mention something special for you! In this chapter, there's an elegant trapunto tea cozy, a crocheted tablecloth with the look of Irish lace, a handsome needlepoint inspired by an early 19th century heirloom. And if you're a fan of cross-stitch samplers, our full-size motifs will delight you. Take a look — you'll find projects here for novices and seasoned needleworkers alike!

CHINTZ COLLAGE
APPLIQUÉS

(Collage appliqués are shown on the previous page).

FLORAL APPLIQUÉ COMFORTER COVER

TECHNIQUE: Sewing.

EASY: Achievable by anyone.

MATERIALS: Sharp scissors; colorfast thread to match the fabric colors; fiberfill stuffing; buttons or snaps for cover closure. With a 1″ seam allowance, enough muslin to make the back and front of the comforter; the same fabric amounts for the collage-appliquéd comforter cover with an extra 1″ added to all sides for an easy fit.

DIRECTIONS:

1. PIECE the muslin to meet the dimensions for both sides. Pin right sides together and stitch all around, leaving 10 inches open. Turn right side out and stuff with fiberfill to the desired fullness. Pin the opening together and machine-stitch close to the edge.

2. PIECE the front and back of the comforter cover together in the same manner as for the comforter. Complete the collage as explained. Assemble the cover by seaming one end and both sides together, making ½″ seams. Turn under the raw edges and topstitch them down. Use buttons with button holes or snaps spaced 10 inches apart for cover closure. Slip the comforter into the cover and fasten.

Tips On Appliqué Technique

Chintz is recommended for appliqué work because it tends not to fray when cut. In choosing chintz patterns, look for designs with well-delineated shapes.

1. Start with something simple — a few flowers from a bouquet or butterflies snipped from a multitude.

2. Cut out the motifs and arrange them on the background fabric (linen or muslin is suggested). Allow the chintz pattern to inspire your design arrangement. To give a 3-dimensional effect to your collage, overlap the cutouts slightly.

3. On a comforter or quilt, confine the design to the outer dimensions. If you work in the center, the fabric may bunch up as you machine stitch the collages.

4. Pin your cutout motifs in place and baste lightly.

5. Using the machine zig-zag stitch on the appliqué setting, stitch around each cutout doing outline stitches of each color thread at the same time; change thread color to match the color of the cutout fabric edges. Use larger stitches for bigger cutouts; vary the machine setting from a #1 to a #3½.

6. With a hot iron and spray starch, press each collage piece after basting, then press again after each successive color group has been machine-stitched down. Try reversing some of the cutouts and stitching them down inside out — lovely on a floral design to capture the subtle shadings of nature.

7. You can appliqué on solid color either both sides or one side of your comforter, or use a complementary print for the reverse.

PILLOW

MATERIALS: Muslin or linen (see Comforter Materials): ½″ seam allowance; ruffle fabric; fiberfill stuffing.

DIRECTIONS: Measure and cut the fabric and complete the collage. (*See* Tips On Appliqué Technique *on page 240*).

1. FOR the ruffle, choose a fabric to pick up or contrast with a color from the collage.

2. FOR the length of the ruffle, double the measurement around the entire pillow (triple for a very full ruffle). The width can be 2″ to 4″, but cut out twice the width plus a 1″ seam allowance in order to fold in half.

3. ESTIMATE the total width and length, then cut and piece the ruffle together.

4. SEAM the ends together. Fold in half and gather the raw edges to fit.

5. PIN the ruffle to the edges of the collage, matching the raw edges so that the ruffle faces the center of the collage. Sew the ruffle down along what will be the ½″ seam.

6. PIN the front and back sides together. For the pillow, stitch the seam around, leaving six inches open for the stuffing. Turn right side out and stuff as firmly as desired, then close with a slip stitch. For the cover, stitch along three sides. Turn and slip over the pillow then slip stitch closed.

FRAMED PICTURE

FOLLOW the techniques described above to create a fabric collage the size you want for framing.

PRE-QUILTED OVAL PLACE MAT AND NAPKINS

PLACE MAT

(about 14"x19")

TECHNIQUE: Embroidery, sewing.

EASY: Achievable by anyone.

MAT MATERIALS: Pre-quilted white fabric; printed fabric; DMC six-strand embroidery floss: blueberry, yellow-orange, green, dark blue, light blue, lilac; embroidery needle.

DIRECTIONS:
(½" seams allowed):

1. **FOLLOWING** the instructions on page 294, enlarge the cutting pattern (see FIG. 1) on folded brown paper.

2. **CUTTING:** From the quilted fabric, cut out one oval. From the print fabric, cut 2"-wide bias strips and seam them (on the straight grain) to make a binding strip about 55" long.

3. **ASSEMBLING:** With right sides together and edges matching, stitch the binding strip around the oval (turning over the beginning end, lapping the final end). Press. Turn the binding to the wrong side, turn under its edge ½" and slip stitch the fold to the stitch line.

4. **EMBROIDERING:** Use 3 strands in needle (see Stitch Guide, pages 298-299). Work a chain stitch along each side of the quilting stitches already in the material (see photo). In the spaces

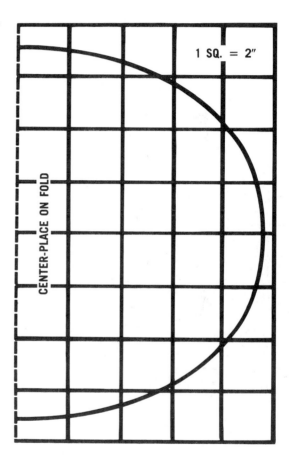

FIG. 1 PLACE MAT

1 SQ. = 2"

CENTER-PLACE ON FOLD

•243

within the chain stitching, embroider flower sprays alternating with a cluster of French Knots. (With a marking pencil, you can first draw the flower stems if you wish.) Work the stems in Stem Stitch and at the top of each add a Lazy Daisy.

NAPKIN

. . . .

(12" square)

EASY: Achievable by anyone.

MATERIALS: White linen; printed fabric; six-strand embroidery floss *(see Place Mat for colors)*; embroidery hoop and needle.

. . . .

DIRECTIONS:

Cut a 12" linen square and 2"-wide printed bias strips (pieced as necessary to make a binding strip about 50" long). With the wrong side in, fold the strip in half lengthwise. Turn in each long

FIG. 2 BOUND EDGES

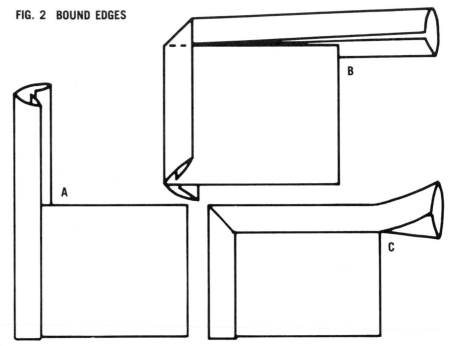

edge to meet the center fold and press the binding. Pin the binding over the edges of the napkin, mitering the corners *(see* FIG. 2), then slip stitch or machine stitch. Embroider (see *Place Mat*) three flower sprays and a French Knot cluster in one corner of the napkin *(see photo)*.

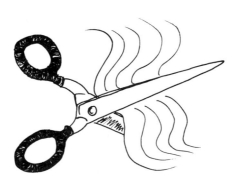

BRAIDED CANDLE RINGS,
HOT MATS
AND BREAD BASKET

TECHNIQUE: Sewing.

EASY: Achievable by anyone.

MATERIALS (*for all pieces shown*): ¾ yds. each of three co-ordinated fabrics; 35 yds. of soft filler cording about 2″ circumference; 1 yd. of 1½″-wide grosgrain ribbon; white glue.

DIRECTIONS:
(¼″ *seams allowed*):

1. Cut the fabric crosswise into 2½″-wide strips and seam the ends to make one long strip for each color. From the three colors, cut the following lengths: 3¾ yds. for the basket; 3 yds. for the oval mat; 2 yds. for the 9″ round mat; and ½ yd. for each candle ring.

2. With right sides together, seam the long edges of each strip and turn right side out. Wrap one end of the cording with masking tape to make it hard. Push it through the fabric tube, leaving about an inch empty at each end.

3. Oval Mat: Catching in the cord, sew three fabric strips together at one end and braid flatly. Sew the ends together. Starting with a straight 8″ center, coil the braid around it to make a flat oval. Tuck the ends under and sew the coils together by hand on the underside.

4. Round Mat: Make · the same as the oval, omitting the 8″ center.

5. Basket (*11″ dia. x 4″ deep*): Braid (as above) three rounds, the same as the round mat, for the bottom. For the sides, turn the braid on edge and flare it out as you coil upward.

6. Candle Ring: Braid (*see Step 3*). Lap the ends to fit the candle and stitch. Glue ribbon and a flat bow over the seam.

FLORAL TEA COZY WITH APPLIQUÉD NAPKINS

TEA COZY

TECHNIQUE: Trapunto quilting.

AVERAGE: For those with some experience in quilting.

MATERIALS: Remnants of floral fabric and contrasting fabric; 1½ yds. of ¼" cording; polyester batting; sewing or embroidery thread to match flower outline.

DIRECTIONS:

1. MEASURE your teapot from spout to handle over the curve of the body, then, from the top of the cover (or the highest spot) to the bottom edge. Add 1" all around.

2. USING these measurements, cut one piece each of floral fabric (with a large motif in the center) for the front, contrasting fabric for the back, and two pieces each of muslin and quilt batting.

3. QUILTING THE FRONT: Cut a piece of muslin 1" larger all around than the flower motif and baste it over the back of the motif. Working from the front and using the backstitch, outline the outside edges of the flower, and several center petals (*see photo*). Cut a small slit in the muslin behind each petal section and stuff with batting to the desired puffiness. Sew the openings closed.

4. LAYER the muslin, batting and fabric "sandwich" for the tea cozy front.

5. QUILTING THE BACK: Layer the muslin, batting and fabric, right side up, in that order. Pin the edges. Slightly loosen your sewing machine presser foot tension and lengthen the stitch to 8 per inch. Starting at the center, stitch a line from the top to the bottom edges. Repeat on both sides, spacing the stitch lines 1¼" apart.

6. WITH edges matching, pin the front and back layered pieces together and trim the top corners into curves to round them (*see photo*).

7. SEE page 247 for "How to Make Bias-Covered Welting" and make enough to go around the top edge of the cozy, cutting the bias strip 1⅝" wide.

8. STITCH the welting around

the sides and top of the front piece. Right sides together, stitch the front piece to the back piece over the previous stitching. Trim the seam to ¼″ and stitch the layers of the seam allowance together, close to the edges.

9. AT the bottom edge, trim the batting ¼″. Turn under ¼″ twice and edgestitch.

NAPKINS
. . . .
DIRECTIONS:

WITH machine zigzag or satin stitch, appliqué to the corners of purchased solid-color napkins (*see photo*) floral motifs cut from the same fabric as the tea cozy.

HOW TO MAKE BIAS COVERED WELTING

Note: ½ yd. of fabric will yield 12 yds. of 1⅝″-wide bias strips for ¼″ welting cord, and about 9 yds. of 2½″ bias strips for jumbo (⅜″) welting cord.

1. To make sure the fabric edges are straight, place an open newspaper over the fabric to be used, matching one paper edge to the selvage (or an edge cut parallel to the selvage). Trim the crosswise edge of the fabric even with the other edge of the paper.

2. MARKING AND **C**UTTING: From one corner, mark off equal distances along the lengthwise and crosswise of the fabric and draw a diagonal line, using a yardstick and chalk, connecting the two points (*see* FIG. 3). From this line continue marking the desired width of bias strips needed, across the fabric. Cut along the marked lines.

3. JOINING THE **S**TRIPS: With right sides together and straight edges matching (with points extending), lap and pin two ends together (*see* FIG. 3A); stitch. Continue this procedure until you have the desired length. Press the seams open and trim off the extending points.

4. COVERING THE **C**ORD: Fold the wrong side of the bias strip over the cord, matching the edges. With the corded side to the left of the zipper foot, stitch close to the cord.

5. SEWING **W**ELTING TO **F**AB-RIC: With cut edges matching, stitch the welting to the right side of the fabric close to the cord. Clip at the corners. Right sides together, pin the welted piece to the back piece, and stitch over the previous stitching.

6. To avoid thickness where the welting overlaps, trim away the ends of the *cord only* (from inside the bias strip).

FIG. 3 CUTTING AND JOINING BIAS STRIPS

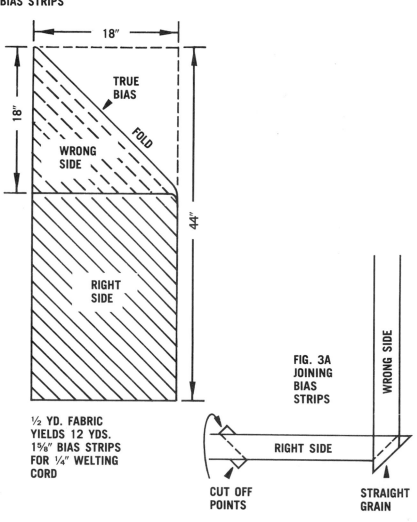

18″

TRUE BIAS

FOLD

18″

WRONG SIDE

44″

RIGHT SIDE

½ YD. FABRIC YIELDS 12 YDS. 1⅝″ BIAS STRIPS FOR ¼″ WELTING CORD

FIG. 3A JOINING BIAS STRIPS

WRONG SIDE

RIGHT SIDE

CUT OFF POINTS

STRAIGHT GRAIN

TECHNIQUE: Cross-stitch embroidery.

EASY: Achievable by anyone.

MATERIALS: 16 x 20″ Pearl Aida cloth, 11 blocks (stitches)-to-the-inch; 6-strand embroidery cotton in the following colors — red, dark red, royal blue, dark blue, light blue, dark green, light green, brown, dark tan, light tan, black, dark grey, light grey, yellow, gold, pink, white; 14″ x 18″ (at inside) frame; embroidery hoop; size 24 tapestry needle; cardboard backing.

DIRECTIONS:

1. **BORDER:** On the grain and centered on the fabric, pin-mark the outside border so that it will enclose a space of 147 x 190 blocks. Work a cross-stitch (*see Step 4*) in each block of the marked border until you come to a corner, then follow the *photo on page 248*. Baste a vertical center line halfway between the side borders.

2. **HORIZONTAL PLACEMENT:** On pages 248-250, measuring between the side edges of the outside borders of the picture of your choice, draw the vertical center line right on the page. It will fall either midway between a pair of motifs or halfway through one motif. It will also show you the center of each line of letters.

3. **VERTICAL PLACEMENT:** Over the basted center line, pin-mark the top of the center motif in each row, counting downwards from the first empty block under the top border, as follows (B stands for empty block; the number of cross-stitch rows for each center motif is in parentheses; the number given for word rows includes empty rows between):

A Friend: 14B, brown border (1); 10B, 3 rows of words (49); 10B, brown border (1); 8B, squirrels (18); 3B, cherries (18); 3B, bunnies (22); 3B, birds (23); 7B, bottom border.

My Heart: 7B, hearts (15); 3B, birds (23); 3B, flowers (19); 3B, red border (1); 6B, 4 rows of words (69); 4B, border (1); 11B, cherries (18); 7B, bottom border.

May Peace: 7B, bouquet (25); 8B, 2 rows of words (29); 11B, flag (28); 10B, flowers (19); 9B, bottom border.

Happy Is: 5B, house (24); 5B, red row (1); 3B, flowers (19); brown row (1); 7B, hearts (15); 3B, red row (1); 5B, 4 rows of words (69); 7B, squirrels (18); 7B, bottom border.

I Hear: 6B, hearts (15); 3B, blue row (1); 3B, house (24); 4B,

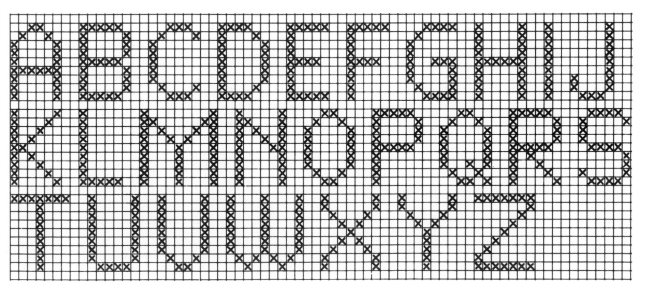

blue row (1); 8B, words (9); 10B, eagle (27); 7B, trees (23); 6B, bottom border. *Note: White part of eagle's head is outlined in light tan straight stitches.*

In God: 16B, blue row (1); 4B, flag (28); 8B, words (9); 8B, flower (19); 7B, trees (23); 7B, blue row (1); 16B, bottom border.

4. EMBROIDERING: With three strands in the needle and the colors shown on the full-size photographs *(on page 248)*, work the cross-stitches. (One completed cross-stitch covers one block.) First embroider the letters (starting from the basted centerline), following the alphabet chart. Leave two squares empty between each letter, seven squares empty between each word, and 11 blocks empty between each row. Then work the inside borders and horizontal lines. (Those which appear dotted have a cross-stitch only in every other square.) Finally, work the pictorial motifs, reversing some of them (rabbits, squirrels and birds) and spacing them so that the left and right sides of the center line are symmetrical *(see photos).*

5. FINISHING: Lightly press the finished embroidery, face down on a towel. Center it over the cardboard backing. Fold fabric edges to the wrong side and tape them down. Insert "picture" into the frame.

CROSS STITCH

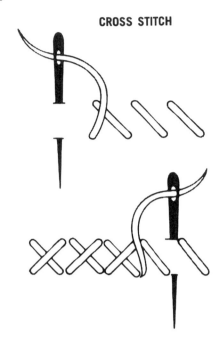

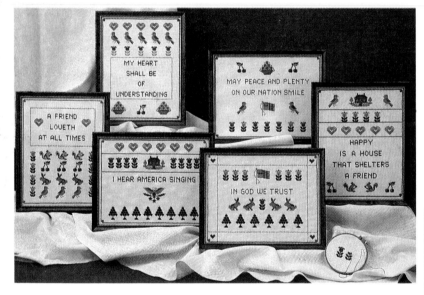

IRISH HEIRLOOM TABLECLOTH

(about 56″ round)

TECHNIQUE: Crochet.

AVERAGE: For those with some experience in crochet.

MATERIALS: Bucilla Tempo Acrylic Yarn, 11 (2 oz.) skeins; crochet hook, Size E, OR ANY SIZE HOOK TO OBTAIN THE MOTIF MEASUREMENT BELOW.

GAUGE: Each Motif = about 12″ in diameter. TO SAVE TIME, TAKE TIME TO CHECK GAUGE.

Note: All rounds are worked from the right side.

DIRECTIONS:

MOTIF *(Make 19)*: Ch 6, join with sl st to form a ring. **Rnd 1** *(right side)*: Ch 9, * work 1 tr in ring, ch 4; rep from * 6 times. Join with sl st to fifth ch of ch-9 — 8 sps made. **Rnd 2**: Ch 1, sc in same st as joining st, * 5 sc in

next sp, sc in top of next tr; rep from * around, ending with 5 sc in last sp. Join with sl st to first sc. Work should measure 1¾″ in diameter. **Rnd 3** *(Picot Petal Rnd)*: * Ch 6, *(yo twice, draw up a loop in next sc, yo and through 2 loops twice, keeping remaining loops on hook) 5 times, yo and through*

You *can* take it with you!

The 12″ motifs of our Irish heirloom tablecloth are portable for easy crocheting. Put them all together for a 56″ round of elegance with the look of Irish heirloom lace.

remaining 6 loops, ch 1 (ch 1 forms the eye of petal), ch 3, sl st in eye, ch 6, sl st in next sc — **picot petal made;** rep from * around, end with ch 6. Join with sl st to joining st of previous rnd — 8 picot petals made. **Rnd 4:** Sl st in each st across to picot of first picot petal, ch 1, sc in same place as last sl st, * ch 10, sc in picot of next picot petal; rep from * around, end with ch 10. Join with sl st to first sc. **Rnd 5:** Ch 1, sc in joining st, * 11 sc in next sp, sc in next sc; rep from * around, ending with 11 sc in last sp. Join with sl st to first sc. **Rnd 6:** Repeat Rnd 3 — 16 picot petals made. **Rnd 7:** Ch 1, sc in last sl st, * ch 10, sc in picot of next picot petal, ch 16, sc in picot of next picot petal; rep from * around, end with ch 16. Join with sl st to first sc. **Rnd 8:** Ch 1, * work 12 sc in next sp, 19 sc in next sp; rep from * around. Join with sl st to first sc. **Rnd 9:** Ch 1, * sc in each of next 4 sc; **work a 7-picot loop as follows:** *Ch 6, sl st in 4th ch from hook to make a picot, ch 5, work a 2nd picot, ch 5, work 3rd picot, ch 4, work 4th picot, ch 5, work 5th picot, work sl st in free st between 3rd and 2nd picots, ch 4, work 6th picot, sl st in free st between 2nd and 1st picot, ch 4, work 7th picot, ch 2, work sl st in same place as last sc worked* — **7-picot loop made;** sc in each of next 2 sc, work a 7-picot loop, sc in each of next 4 sc, skip 2 sts, sc in each of next 8 sc, 3 sc in next st (center sc of group), sc in each of next 8 sc, skip next 2 sts; rep from * 7 times. Join with sl st to first sc. Cut thread and fasten off. **Rnd 10:** From right side, make a loop on hook and work 1 sc in center st of any group of 3-sc, * ch 11, sc in 4th picot of next 7-picot loop, ch 11, sc in 4th picot of next 7-picot loop, ch 11, sc in center st of next group of 3-sc; rep from * around, ending with ch 11. Join with sl st to first sc. **Rnd 11:** Ch 1, * in next sp work 7 sc, *ch 3, sl st in 3rd ch from hook* — **ch-3 picot made** and 6 sc; in next sp work 4 sc, ch-3 picot, 3 sc, ch-3 picot, 3 sc, ch-3 picot, 3 sc; in next sp work 7 sc, ch-3 picot, and 6 sc; rep from * around. Join with sl st to first sc.

FIG. 4 TABLECLOTH

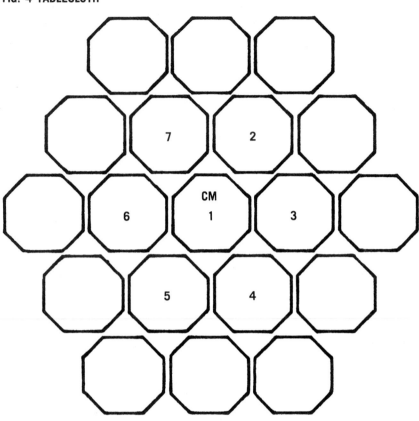

CM = CENTER MOTIF

Cut the thread and fasten off.

FINISHING: Pin each motif to measurements on a padded surface, cover with a damp cloth and allow to dry; *do not press.*

ASSEMBLING: Following the arrangement chart (FIG. 4), pin motifs together as follows: **Rnd 1:** Having one motif as the center, arrange a ring of 6 motifs around the center motif, matching the corresponding picots, and tack together with a small stitch at the picots. **Rnd 2:** Attach a ring of 12 motifs the same way as the first round.

ANTIQUE CORNUCOPIA

TECHNIQUE: Needlepoint.

AVERAGE: For those with some experience in needlepoint.

MATERIALS: 18″ sq. of 10-mesh needlepoint canvas; tapestry or Persian yarn in light beige background and colors in FIG. 6; tapestry needle.

DIRECTIONS:

1. WORK the design in Continental Stitch (*see Stitch Guide, pages 298-299*), following the chart (*see* FIG. 5). Block, mount and frame. See pages 296-297 for tips on blocking needlepoint.

Did You Know

Richly overflowing cornucopia patterns have figured importantly in needlework design for centuries? Our is a faithful reproduction of an authentic 19th century English masterpiece. Hint: Be sure to see our tips on blocking your needlework, page 296-297.

FIG. 5

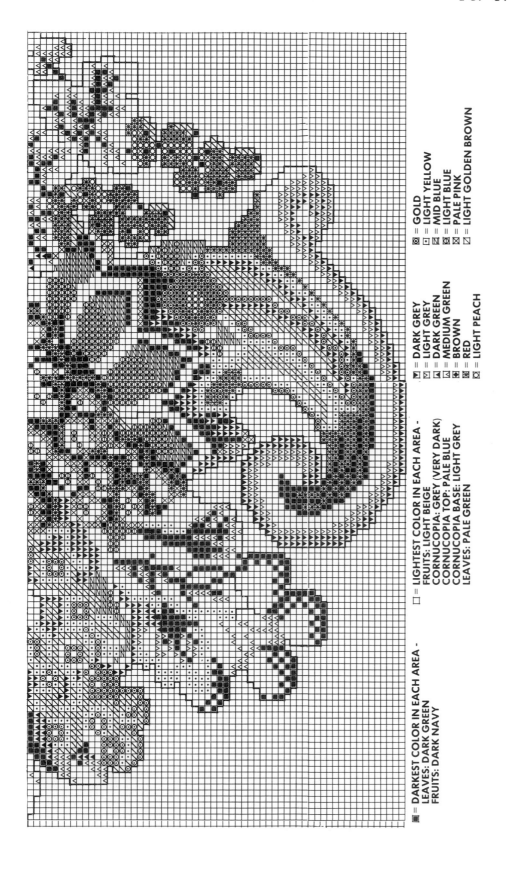

■ = DARKEST COLOR IN EACH AREA -
LEAVES: DARK GREEN
FRUITS: DARK NAVY

□ = LIGHTEST COLOR IN EACH AREA -
FRUITS: LIGHT BEIGE
CORNUCOPIA: GREY (VERY DARK)
CORNUCOPIA TOP: PALE BLUE
CORNUCOPIA BASE: LIGHT GREY
LEAVES: PALE GREEN

◙ = GOLD
⊡ = LIGHT YELLOW
▨ = MID BLUE
⊠ = LIGHT BLUE
⊠ = PALE PINK
⊠ = LIGHT GOLDEN BROWN

▼ = DARK GREY
⊠ = LIGHT GREY
◀ = DARK GREEN
◪ = MEDIUM GREEN
⊞ = BROWN
⊠ = RED
⊡ = LIGHT PEACH

PANSY PATTERN BENCH COVER

(15" square as shown; or extend background as desired).

TECHNIQUE: Embroidery.

AVERAGE: For those with some experience in embroidery

MATERIALS: 15" square of 14-mesh-to-the-inch Aida cloth; small amount of crewel yarn in peach, orange, pale pink, pink, rose, dark rose, pale green, green, dark green, pale blue and yellow; tan crewel yarn for herringbone background; 6-strand white cotton floss for border.

DIRECTIONS:

1. **OVAL CENTER:** Enlarge *(see page 294)* the pattern *(see* Fig. 6) and trace it to center of a 15" square of Aida cloth. With the full 6-strands of white cotton floss in a needle, couch *(see Stitch Guide on pages 298-299)* over 2 lengths (12 strands) of the same floss which has been laid on the cloth along the traced scallops. With 2 strands in the needle, work 8-10 rays from the dot toward the outline of each scallop *(see photo)*. With 1 strand of

crewel yarn, work the rest of the design in vertical satin stitches *(see Stitch Guide)*. Work the four horizontal stitches at one pansy center in dark rose. Over each pansy center, with 2 strands in the needle, work a pair of bullion stitches in yellow or white.

2. HERRINGBONE BACK-GROUND: Work repeated rows, like those in FIG. 6A, using one thread of crewel yarn or 3 of cotton floss in the color of your choice.

FIG. 6A　　　　**1 SQ. = 1 MESH**

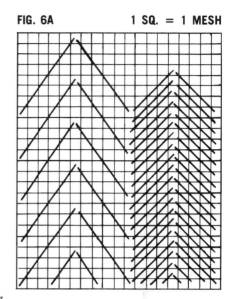

FIG. 6 PANSY BENCH COVER　　　　**1 SQ. = 1"**

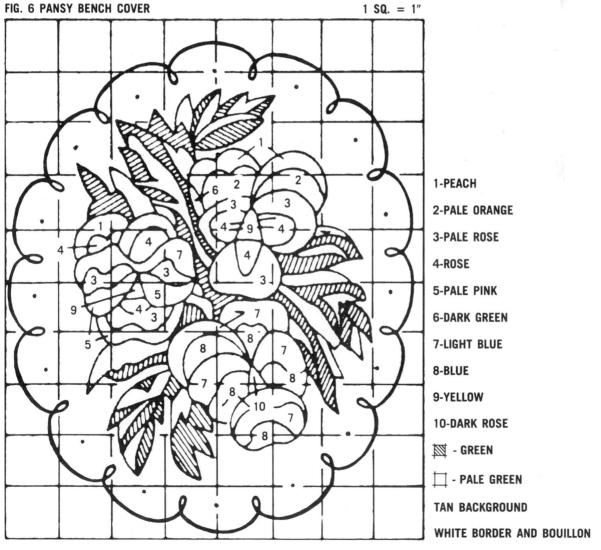

1-PEACH

2-PALE ORANGE

3-PALE ROSE

4-ROSE

5-PALE PINK

6-DARK GREEN

7-LIGHT BLUE

8-BLUE

9-YELLOW

10-DARK ROSE

▧ - GREEN

▢ - PALE GREEN

TAN BACKGROUND

WHITE BORDER AND BOUILLON

SCALLOPED
BED LINENS

FIG. 7   ACTUAL SIZE

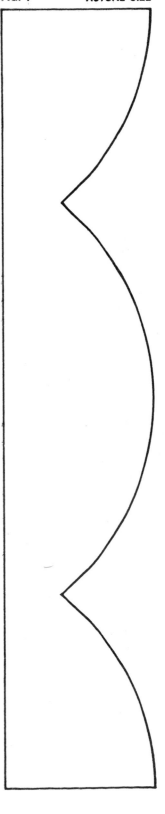

TECHNIQUE: Sewing.

EASY: Achievable by anyone.

MATERIALS: Purchased bed pillows, shams and sheets.

DIRECTIONS:

1. Cut the actual-size scallop guide (*see* Fig. 7 *at right*).

2. With centers matching, trace the scallops to the edge of a purchased pillow case. Move the pattern to the left (overlapping ½ scallop) and trace. Continue to the left edge of the case. If the final scallop is too short, extend the last scallop to the edge. Draw scallops to the right of center the same way.

3. Machine zigzag, using a wide satin stitch, over the drawn lines. After completing the zigzag stitches, cut away the excess fabric outside the stitching.

4. Scallop the edges of sheets in the same manner.

TIP

Sewing $mart$

Do you love the look of elegant bed linens but not the price? Take to your sewing machine to glamorize any sheet or pillow case you'll find at a White Sale. Simply cut scallops (see our actual-size cutting pattern at right) on solid or print linens; machine satin stitch the edges to discourage fraying. See the specifics above.

·11·

RUGS

They define space, muffle sound, and are a treat for the eyes as well as the feet! Rugs have come a long way since the first nomadic tribes tried to warm the earth in their tents with primitive animal-hair weavings. Today, you can make a rug in any number of needlework techniques, and the combinations of color, texture and design are limitless. Try your hand at a needlepoint rug that captures the look of an antique hooked rug. Or use your knitting or crocheting skills in rug making. Even if you're a newcomer to needlecrafts, you can whip up our no-sew coiled rug — its sturdy practicality is perfect for a "country kitchen" look.

NEEDLEPOINT "RAG"
RUGS

(Rugs are shown on the previous page.)

GENERAL DIRECTIONS FOR NEEDLEPOINT "RAG" RUGS

TECHNIQUE: Needlepoint.

ALL ARE EASY: Achievable by anyone.

MATERIALS: 24" x 28" piece of 3.3 mesh (openings) per inch rug canvas; cotton or cotton-blend fabric (broadcloth weight) in solids or small prints *(see individual listings for yardages, and Figs. 1 to 6 for the color charts)*; masking tape; tapestry needle; liquid latex for backing *(optional)*.

CANVAS: Tape the edges with masking tape. Baste across each center (vertical and horizontal) row of meshes. These will match the arrow-marked rows in the charts *(see Figs. 1 to 6)*.

FABRIC: Wash the fabric. When it's dry, tear it into 1"-wide strips while wearing a particle mask. Roll each color into a separate ball.

NEEDLEPOINT: Thread a tapestry needle with a fabric strip and start to work the center of the design at the center of the canvas. Each square on the chart represents one Continental Stitch or 1 thread. Stitch rather loosely, so the fabric fills the mesh. Turn the canvas upside down at the end of a color row to start the next row.

EDGES: When you've worked up to 4 or 5 meshes from an edge of the chart, fold the canvas to the back at the last row of the chart; trim the hem to 1" wide and finish working the needlepoint through both layers. Finish each edge the same, mitering (and trimming off the excess) at the corners. Overcast the folded edges with fabric to match the outside color.

BLOCKING: With thumbtacks or push pins, fasten the finished piece, face down, on a blocking board or old table covered with clean muslin. Make sure the rug's edges are straight and its corners squared. Over a damp cloth, iron until the backs of the stitches are moist, pulling the canvas into a true rectangle. Let it dry thoroughly, then unfasten it.

OPTIONAL: On its wrong (back) side, spread the piece with liquid latex.

CONTINENTAL STITCH

PEACEABLE LAMB RUG

(about 17½" x 24")

MATERIALS *(also see General Directions)*: 45"-wide fabric (small prints) — 1 yd. turquoise, ⅞ yd. white, ⅝ yd. light green, ⅓ yd. peach, ½ yd. light blue, ⅛ yd. dark rose, ⅜ yd. solid ecru and ¼ yd. black.

DIRECTIONS:

See General Directions and Fig. 1. Cut the following into 1"-wide strips: 45 yds. of turquoise, 40 yds. of white, 27 yds. of light green, 23 yds. of light blue, 19 yds. of ecru, 15 yds. of peach, 12 yds. of black, 5 yds. of dark rose.

TURKEY STITCH

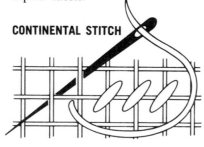

LEAVE LOOP

SITTING DUCK

(about 17½" x 23")

MATERIALS *(also see General Directions)*: 45"-wide fabric (small prints) — 1¼ yds. black, 1 yd. each dark green and ecru, ½ yd. each rust, dark brown and light brown, ¼ yd. each tan and gold.

DIRECTIONS:

SEE General Directions and FIG. 2. Cut the following 1"-wide strips: 56 yds. of black, 45 yds. each of dark green and ecru, 23 yds. each of rust, dark brown and light brown, 12 yds. each of tan and gold.

RUNNING HORSE

(about 19" x 24")

MATERIALS *(also see General Directions)*: 45"-wide fabric (small prints) — 1⅞ yds. cranberry, 1⅛ yds. ecru, ⅔ yd. blue, ⅓ yd. black, ¼ yd. gray.

DIRECTIONS:

SEE General Directions and FIG. 3. Cut the following 1"-wide strips: 85 yds. of cranberry, 50 yds. of ecru, 30 yds. of blue, 15 yds. of black, 12 yds. of gray.

FOLK-ART BASKET

(about 17¼" x 23¼")

MATERIALS *(also see General Directions)*: 45"-wide fabric (small prints) — 2 yds. ecru, 1 yd. medium blue, ⅔ yd. light blue, ⅙ yd. rose and ⅓ yd. each of light green and pink.

I used ½ strips of fleece.

DIRECTIONS:

SEE General Directions and FIG. 4. Cut the following 1"-wide strips: 90 yds. of ecru, 45 yds. of medium blue, 30 yds. of light blue, 15 yds. each of light green and pink, 8 yds. of rose.

LOG CABIN SQUARES

(about 18" x 23½")

MATERIALS *(also see General Directions)*: 45"-wide solid-color fabric — ⅜ yd. dark green, ½ yd. black, ⅓ yd. each of dark blue, medium blue, light green, medium green and dark purple, ¼ yd. each light blue and medium purple, ⅙ yd. light purple.

DIRECTIONS:

SEE General Directions and FIG. 5. Cut the following 1"-wide strips: 23 yds. of black, 19 yds. of dark green, 15 yds. each of medium blue, dark blue, light green, medium green and dark purple, 12 yds. each of light blue and medium purple, 8 yds. of light purple.

SLEEPING CAT

(about 17½" x 23½")

MATERIALS *(also see General Directions)*: 45"-wide fabric — 2 yds. black, ⅜ yd. pink, ⅔ yd. aqua and ½ yd. each light blue, ecru and white.

DIRECTIONS:

1. CUT the following 1"-wide strips: 90 yds. of black, 30 yds. of aqua, 23 yds. each of light blue, ecru and white, 19 yds. of pink.

2. OPTIONS: You can work the whole design in Continental Stitch *(see General Directions and FIG. 6)*. Or you can use the stitches shown *(see photo)*. For the cat, we cut the black and white strips ½" wide and worked rows of Turkey Stitches, leaving a loop about ½" long between stitches; then we cut the loops to make fringe. The outside and the inside (interrupted) border are Continental Stitch. The rest of the canvas is worked in long, straight stitches over several threads to fill in the design outline for each color. Break up the larger areas, such as the white background, into horizontal rows of stitches about 5 threads long.

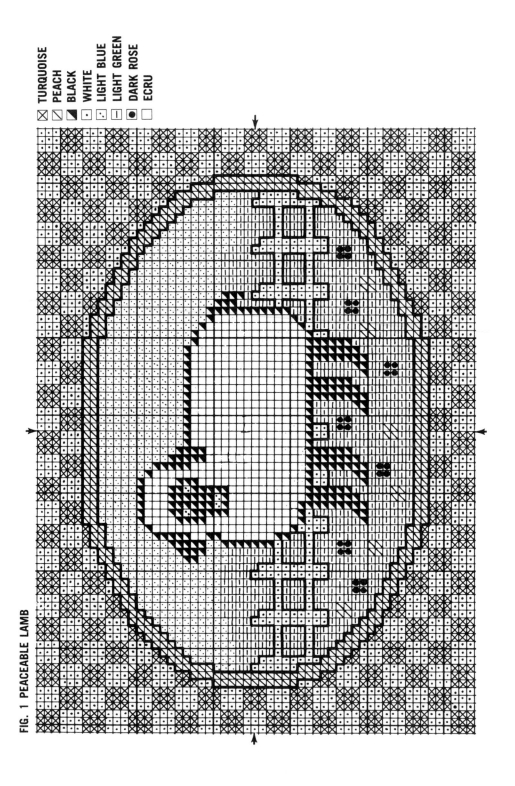

FIG. 1 PEACEABLE LAMB

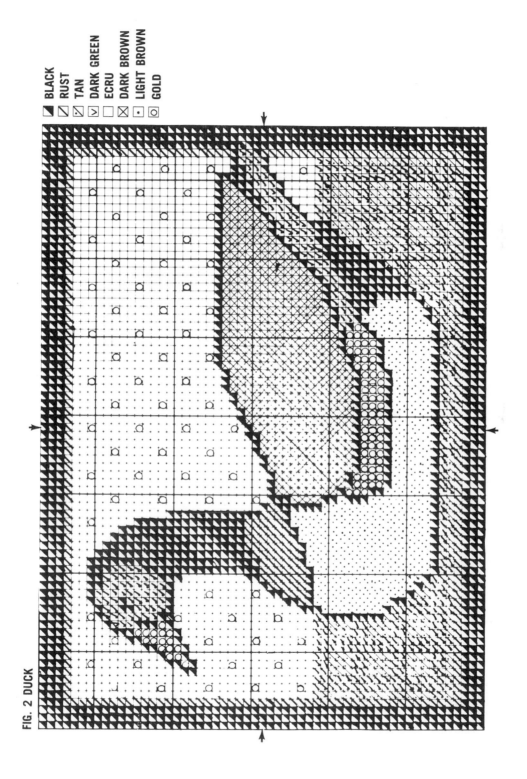

FIG. 2 DUCK

BLACK
RUST
TAN
DARK GREEN
ECRU
DARK BROWN
LIGHT BROWN
GOLD

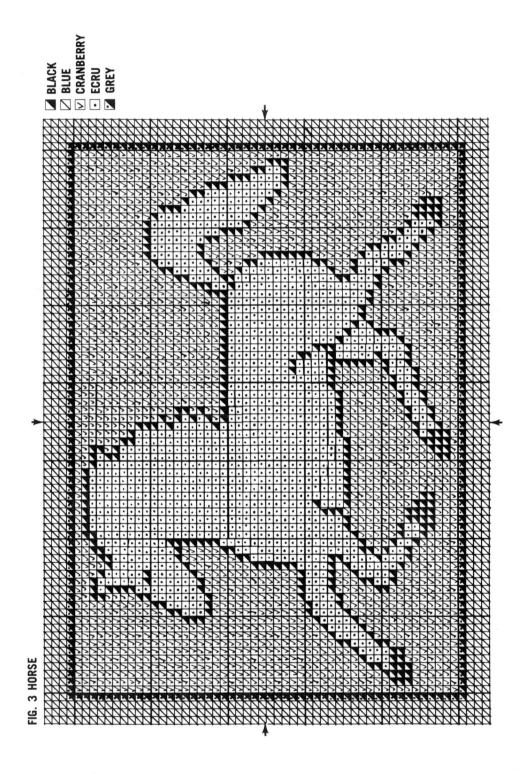

BLACK
BLUE
CRANBERRY
ECRU
GREY

FIG. 3 HORSE

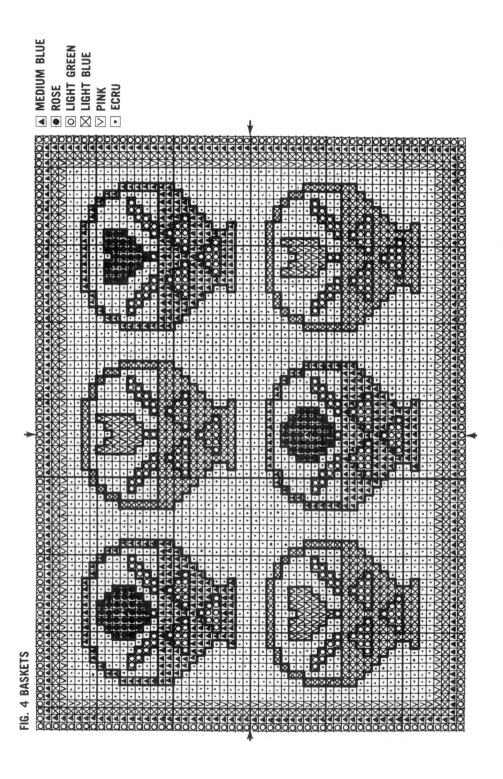

FIG. 4 BASKETS

MEDIUM BLUE ◀
ROSE ●
LIGHT GREEN ○
LIGHT BLUE ☒
PINK ▽
ECRU ·

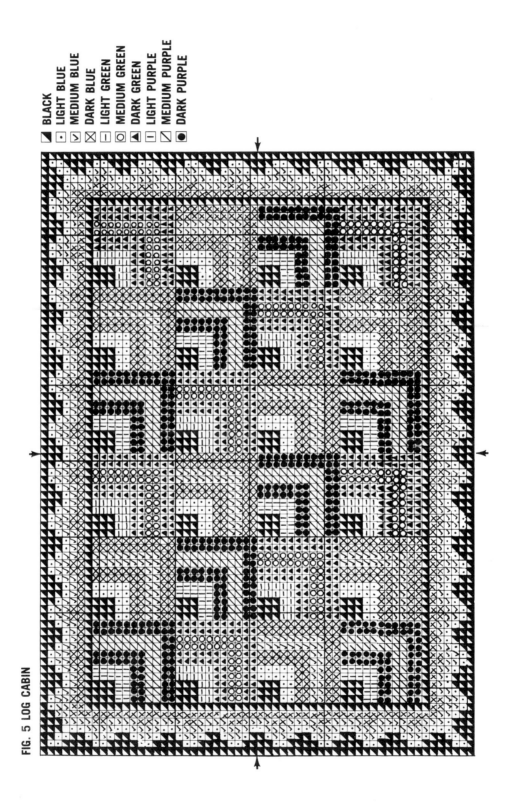

FIG. 5 LOG CABIN

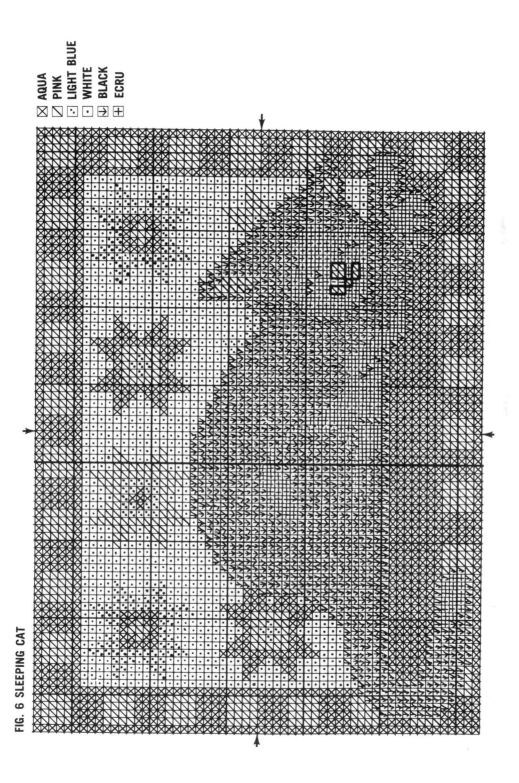

FIG. 6 SLEEPING CAT

AQUA ⊠
PINK ◿
LIGHT BLUE ⊡
WHITE ⊡
BLACK ↘
ECRU ⊞

COILED RUG

(38″ diameter)

TECHNIQUE: No-sew yarn wrap coiling.

EASY: Achievable by anyone.

MATERIALS: 90 yds. of ½″ diameter synthetic clothesline; 54 ozs. (total) of synthetic rug yarn; #16 blunt tapestry needle.

Note: To keep rug flat, work on a table top while coiling.

....

DIRECTIONS:

1. **TAPER** one end of the rope-core about ½″. Thread the needle with yarn. Catching in the yarn-end, wind the yarn around the rope-core for 1″ (*see* FIG. 7) leaving the ½″ tapered end free (wrap the yarn to cover the core but *do not* pull too tightly; *see* FIG. 7).

2. **CENTER:** Turn down the tapered end of the core about ¾″ and hold it in place. With the needle and ¾ yd. yarn, work figure-8's over and under from the core base to the tapered end, until the end is covered with yarn (*see* FIG. 8).

3. Coiling: Coil the yarn covered end around to start the circular shape (if needed repeat another figure-8 to hold the first coil in place), then work three winds around the core and attach to the previous coil with a figure-8 on the fourth wind (*see* Fig. 9).

4. Adding the Next Color: *Note: We used yarns in bright blue, gold, red, green, orange, brown and burgundy.* Continue winding until there is only a 3″ yarn-end of the first color left. Add another ¾ yd. length of color by laying yarn-ends one next to the other (see Fig. 10) and secure by winding new yarn over them. Repeat winding three times and working the figure-8 for the first 12-14 rounds of coils, then wind four times and make the figure-8 on the fifth wind. Continue winding the coils and changing the yarn colors until the desired diameter of the rug is reached.

5. Ending Off: When you have reached the desired diameter for the rug, taper the end of the core and attach it to the rug with the same color the taper abuts, using figure-8's to secure firmly. Thread the yarn back through the figure-8's, then cut it off.

FIG. 7 COILED RUG

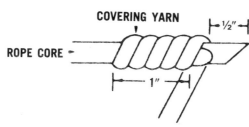

FIG. 8

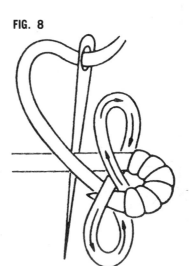

FIG. 9

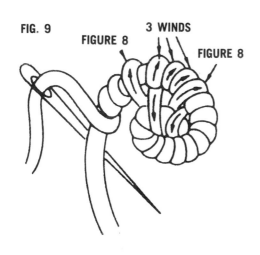

FIG. 10 CHANGING COLORS

LION BATHMAT

(24" x 36")

TECHNIQUE: Sewing.

EASY: Achievable by anyone.

MATERIALS: One 24" x 36" rubber-backed rug with rounded corners; one skein of gold and scraps of black rug yarn; two 7/8" brown buttons for eyes; a scrap of black fabric for nose; a 10" square of lining fabric; polyester stuffing; dressmaker's carbon; heavy duty thread.

DIRECTIONS:

1. **FOLLOWING** the instructions on page 294, enlarge the pattern in FIG. 11 on brown paper. Broken lines are the bathmat edges, solid lines are the cut lines and dotted lines are the fold lines.

2. **USING** carbon paper and pencil, trace all the lines of the half pattern onto the wrong (rubberized) side, flip the pattern and trace again on the opposite

second half of the rug. Trace the nose on black fabric, adding ¼" seams.

3. Cut on the heavy solid lines only.

4. Face: On the dotted lines, turn under the top edge (mouth) and side edges, in that order. Tack the front points together at the center back of the mouth; continue tacking to the upper lip for 2" each side of the center.

5. Turn under the edges of the nose ¼" and hand sew ½" above the mouth, at the center front of the face, stuffing slightly. From the lining, cut a rectangle 7" x 9". With the right side up, place the lining on the wrong side of the rug over the cut edges of the face. Turn under the lining edges ½" and hand sew to the rug, stuffing the head slightly. Sew on the buttons through all layers.

6. Mane and Tail: Cut a skein of yarn into four equal parts (lengths about 12"). Reserve thirty strands for the tail. Draw a 10" straight line on a piece of paper; center and place the mane yarns over the line and, setting your machine for a small stitch, machine stitch through the center of the yarns. Pull away the paper. Pin the mane between the circles on the head and hand sew to the head on the stitch line. Repeat (over a 3" long line) for the tail.

FIG. 11 LION BATHMAT

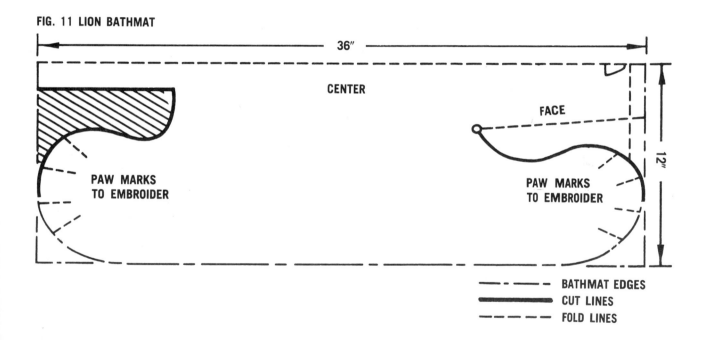

PAW MARKS TO EMBROIDER

CENTER

FACE

PAW MARKS TO EMBROIDER

36"

12"

— · — · — · — BATHMAT EDGES
━━━━━━━ CUT LINES
— — — — — FOLD LINES

PASTEL RAG RUG
AND PILLOW

RAG RUG

(*about 36" x 60"*)

TECHNIQUE: Knitting.

EASY: Achievable by anyone.

MATERIALS: 45"-wide fabric — 5¾ yds. yellow, 7 yds. pink and 3¾ yds. each of blue and turquoise, plus ½ yd. for fringes; knitting needles, one pair No. 13, OR ANY SIZE NEEDLES TO OBTAIN GAUGE BELOW; crochet hook for fringe; large-eyed blunt needle; rotary cutter, and anti-skid liquid latex for rug back (*optional*).

GAUGE: 7 sts = 3"; 8 rows = 2". TO SAVE TIME, TAKE TIME TO CHECK GAUGE.

DIRECTIONS:

1. CUTTING: Tear or cut enough ¾" strips of fabric to make, when sewn end to end, the following — 325 yds. yellow, 400 yds. pink and 200 yds. each of blue and turquoise. Roll strips (at least 5 yds. long) into a ball for each color.

2. CAST on 7 yellow stitches (3") and work in garter stitch (knit each row) for 36", tying in new strips, as needed, on the wrong side. Bind off loosely. Make six more the same. Cast on 12 pink stitches (5") and work in garter stitch for 36". Make three more strips the same; also make two turquoise and two blue the same size.

3. JOINING: Thread a ¼" strip of fabric through a large-eyed needle and weave it from one strip to another strip, long edges butting. Tie the beginning end (to fasten) and weave through every knitted stitch. Continue joining, alternating the 3" and 5" strips (*see photo*).

4. FRINGE: Cut 10" pieces of ¾" fabric. Fold one in half crosswise and, with a crochet hook, draw the loop between the first two knitted rows, at a short end of the rug. Draw the loose ends through the loop and pull up tightly, to knot. Continue across the edge. Repeat at the opposite end.

PILLOW

(*14" square*)

MATERIALS: About 150 yds. ¾"-wide fabric cut or torn in same manner as fabric for rug; ½ yd. fabric for back; pillow form or stuffing; knitting needles, one pair No. 13; large-eyed blunt needle.

DIRECTIONS:

1. CAST on 31 stitches and work in garter stitch for 14", tying in colors (on wrong side) as you choose. Bind off loosely.

2. CUT a 15" square pillow back. Seam the knitted pillow top to the fabric pillow back, right sides together, around three sides and four corners. Turn; stuff and slip stitch.

3. OPTIONAL TASSEL: Knot four 10" strips of fabric together at the centers and sew the knot to a corner of the pillow. Repeat at the other corners.

TIP

It Only *Looks* Old-Fashioned

The art of making rugs and decorative accessories from leftover fabric dates back to Colonial times. But unlike using the old-fashioned, painstaking methods, you can knit this rug and pillow quickly — and easily! Here's how:
• Tear fabrics into ¾"-wide strips; stitch end to end until strips are at least 5 yards long. • Roll strips into balls as you would yarn. (Note that separating colors into individual balls will give you more control over your finished design. Or, you can mix the colors and wind up with a random, multi-hued effect.) • Cast onto large (#13) knitting needles and, using a basic Garter Stitch, make a rug, runner, pillows or place mats. • When you finish one strip of fabric, tie on another one and continue knitting. • As finishing touches, add tassels or fringe.

•12•

CRAFT BASICS

HOW TO
KNIT

KNITTING ABBREVIATIONS AND SYMBOLS

Knitting directions are always written in standard abbreviations. They look mysterious at first, but you'll soon know them: **beg** — beginning; **bet** — between; **bl** — block; **ch** — chain; **CC** — contrasting color; **dec(s)** — decrease(s); **dp** — double-pointed; ″ or **in(s)** — inch(es); **incl** — inclusive; **inc(s)** — increase(s); **k** — knit; **lp(s)** — loop(s); **MC** — main color; **oz(s)** — ounce(s); **psso** — pass slipped stitch over last stitch worked; **pat(s)** — pattern(s); **p** — purl; **rem** — remaining; **rep** — repeat; **rnd(s)** — round(s) **sc** — single crochet; **sk** — skip; **sl** — slip; **sl st** — slip stitch; **sp(s),** — space(s); **st(s)** — stitch(es); **st st** — stockinette stitch; **tog** — together; **yo** — yarn over; **pc** — popcorn stitch. * **(asterisk)** — directions immediately following * are to be repeated the specified number of times indicated in addition to the first time — i.e., "repeat from *3 times more" means 4 times in all. **() (parentheses)** — directions should be worked as often as specified — i.e., "(k1, k2 tog, k3) 5 times" means to work what is in () 5 times in all.

THE BASIC STITCHES

Get out your needles and yarn, and slowly read your way through this special section — practicing the basic stitches illustrated here as you go along. Once you know them, you're ready to start knitting.

CASTING ON: This puts the first row of stitches on the needle. Measure off about two yards of yarn (or about an inch for each stitch you are going to cast on). Make a slip knot at this point by making a medium-size loop of yarn; then pull another small loop through it. Place the slip knot on one needle and pull one end gently to tighten (FIG. 1).

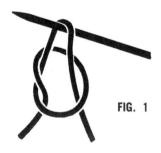

FIG. 1

• Hold the needle in your right hand. Hold both strands of yarn in the palm of your left hand securely but not rigidly. Slide your left thumb and forefinger between the two strands and spread these two fingers out so that you have formed a triangle of yarn.

Your left thumb should hold the free end of yarn, your fore-finger the yarn from the ball, while the needle in your right hand holds the first stitch (FIG. 2).

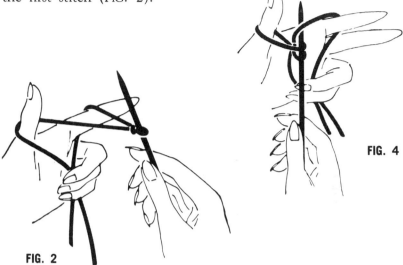

FIG. 2

You are now in position to cast on. See ABBREVIATIONS for explanation of asterisk (*).

• *Bring the needle in your right hand toward you; slip the tip of the needle under the front strand of the loop on left thumb (FIG. 3).

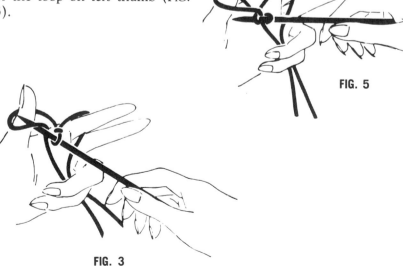

FIG. 3

• Now, with the needle, catch the strand of yarn that is on your left forefinger (FIG. 4).

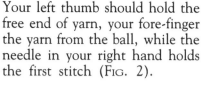

FIG. 4

• Draw it through the thumb loop to form a stitch on the needle (FIG. 5).

FIG. 5

• Holding the stitch on the needle with the right index finger, slip loop off your left thumb (FIG. 6). Tighten up the stitch on the needle by pulling the freed strand back with your left thumb, bringing the yarn back into position for casting on more stitches (FIG. 2 again).

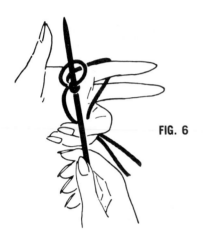

FIG. 6

• **Do not cast on too tightly.** Stitches should slide easily on the needle. Repeat from * until you have cast on the number of stitches specified in your instructions.

KNIT STITCH (k): Hold the needle with the cast-on stitches on your left hand (FIG. 7).

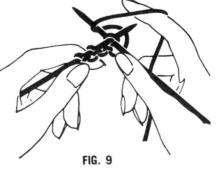

FIG. 7

• Pick up the other needle in your right hand. With yarn from the ball in **back** of the work, insert the tip of the right-hand needle from **left to right** through the front loop of the first stitch on the left-hand needle (FIG. 8).

FIG. 8

• Holding both needles in this position with your left hand, wrap the yarn over your little finger, under your two middle fingers and over the forefingers of your right hand. Hold the yarn firmly, but loosely enough so that it will slide through your fingers as you knit. Return the right-hand needle to your right hand.
• With your right forefinger, pass the yarn under (from right to left) and then over (from left to right) the tip of the right-hand needle, forming a loop on the needle (FIG. 9).

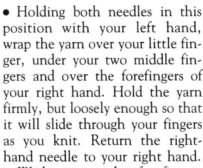

FIG. 9

• Now draw this loop through the stitch on the left-hand needle (FIG. 10).

FIG. 10

• Slip the original stitch off the left-hand needle, leaving the new stitch on right-hand needle (FIG. 11).

FIG. 11

Keep stitches loose enough so that you can slide them along the needles, but firm enough so they do not slide when you don't want them to. Continue until you have knitted all the stitches from the left-hand needle onto the right-hand needle.

• To start the next row, pass the needle with stitches on it to the left hand, reversing it, so that it now becomes the left-hand needle.

PURL STITCH (p): Purling is the reverse of knitting. Again, keep the stitches loose enough to slide, but firm enough to work with. To purl, hold the needle with the stitches in your left hand, with the yarn in **front** of your work. Insert the tip of the right-hand needle from **right to left** through the front loop of the first stitch on the left-hand needle (FIG. 12).

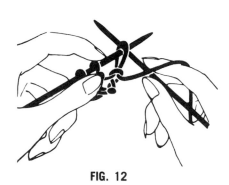

FIG. 12

• With your right hand holding the yarn in the same manner as to knit, but in **front** of the needles, pass the yarn over the tip of the right-hand needle, then under it, forming a loop on the needle (FIG. 13).

FIG. 13

• Holding the yarn firmly so that it won't slip off, draw this loop through the stitch on the left-hand needle (FIG. 14).

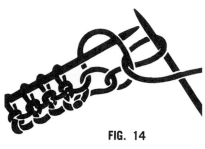

FIG. 14

• Slip the original stitch off the left-hand needle, leaving the new stitch on the right-hand needle (FIG. 15).

FIG. 15

SLIP STITCH (sl st): Insert the tip of the right-hand needle into the next stitch on the left-hand needle, as if to purl, unless otherwise directed. Slip this stitch off the left-hand needle onto the right, **without working it** (FIG. 16).

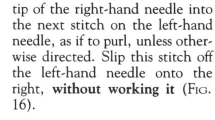

FIG. 16

BINDING OFF: This makes a finished edge and locks the stitches securely in place. Knit (or purl) two stitches. Then, with the tip of the left-hand needle, lift the first of these two stitches over the second stitch and drop it off the tip of the right-hand needle (FIG. 17).

FIG. 17

One stitch remains on the right-hand needle, and one stitch has been bound off.

• Knit (or purl) the next stitch; lift the first stitch over the last stitch and off the tip of the needle. Again, one stitch remains on the right-hand needle, and another stitch has been bound off. Repeat from * until the required number of stitches has been bound off.

• Remember that you work **two** stitches to bind off one stitch. If, for example, the directions read, "k 6, bind off the next 4 sts, k 6 . . ." you must knit six stitches, then knit **two more** stitches before starting to bind off. Bind off four times. After the four stitches have been bound off, count the last stitch remaining on the right-hand needle as the first stitch of the next six stitches. When binding off, always knit the knitted stitches and purl the purled stitches.

• Be careful not to bind off too tightly or too loosely. The tension should be the same as the rest of the knitting.

• To end off the last stitch on the bound-off edge, if you are ending this piece of work here, cut the yarn leaving a six-inch end; pass the cut end through the remaining loop on the right hand needle and pull snugly (FIG. 18).

FIG. 18

SHAPING TECHNIQUES

. . . .

INCREASING: This means adding stitches in a given area to shape your work. There are several ways to increase.

1. To increase by knitting twice into the same stitch: Knit the stitch in the usual way through the front of the loop but **before** (FIG. 19) taking the rest of

FIG. 19

the stitch from the left needle, knit **another** stitch on the same loop by placing the needle into the back of the stitch (FIG. 20). Slip the remainder of the stitch off the left needle. You have made two stitches from one stitch — **inc made.**

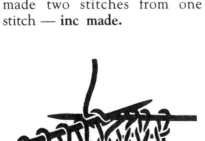

FIG. 20

2. To increase by knitting between stitches: Insert tip of right needle under the strand of yarn *between* the stitch you have just worked and the following stitch, and slip it onto the tip of the left needle (see FIG. 21). Now knit into the *back* of this new loop (see FIG. 22).

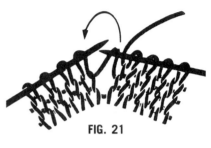

FIG. 21

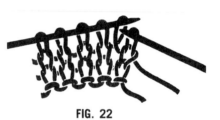

FIG. 22

3. To increase by "yarn over" (yo): If you are *knitting* pass the yarn over the top of the right needle after finishing one stitch and before starting the next, **making an extra stitch** (see arrow in FIG. 23). If you are *knitting*, bring the yarn under the needle to the back. If you are *purling*, wind the yarn around the needle once. On the next row, work all yarn-overs as stitches.

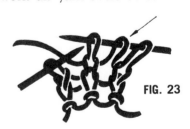

FIG. 23

Decreasing (dec): This means reducing the number of stitches in a given area to shape your work.
1. To decrease by knitting (FIG. 24) or purling (FIG. 25) two

FIG. 24

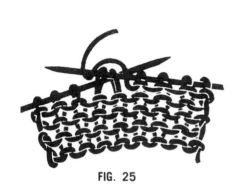

FIG. 25

stitches together: Insert the right needle through the loops of two stitches on the left needle at the same time; complete the stitch. In directions, this is written k2 tog, or p2 tog.

● If you work through the **front** loops of the stitches in the usual way, your decreasing stitch will slant to the right. If you work through the **back** loops of the stitches, your decreasing stitch will slant to the left.

2. Slip 1 stitch, knit 1 stitch and pass slipped stitch over (sl 1, k 1, psso): Insert right needle through stitch on left needle, but instead of working it, just slip it off onto the right needle (*see* FIG. 16 *again*). Work the next stitch in the usual way. With the tip of the left-hand needle, lift the slipped stitch over the last stitch worked, and off the tip of the right-hand needle (FIG. 26).

Your decreasing stitch will slant to the left. This is written as "sl 1, k 1, psso."

FIG. 26

Pass Slipped Stitch Over (psso): Slip one stitch from the left-hand needle to the right-hand needle and, being careful to keep it in position, work the next stitch. Then, with the tip of the left-hand needle, lift the slipped stitch over the last stitch and off the needle (FIG. 26 again).
Attaching the Yarn: When you end one ball of yarn or wish to change colors, begin at the start of a row and tie new yarn with the previous yarn, making a secure joining. Continue to knit or purl (FIG. 27).

FIG. 27

Work even: This means working over the stitch that are on the needle without increasing or decreasing.

HOW TO JOIN YARN

1. Never join a new skein in the middle of a row, unless it's a multicolored design.
2. To determine whether or not you have enough yarn to complete a row, carry the remaining yarn loosely over the work, back and forth, 4 times. If you don't have enough yarn, break it off, leaving a three-inch end.
3. When joining a new skein of yarn make sure to leave 3″ ends from both the new and old skeins. Begin knitting with a new skein. Knit for two rows. Tie the ends of both the old and new skeins together correcting the tension. Tie the ends again. Continue knitting, following the pattern.
4. When working on multicolored designs with bobbins leave 3″ ends when joining new bobbins. DO NOT TIE THE ENDS. When the garment is complete, weave the ends in carefully.

THE IMPORTANCE OF GAUGE:

In order to make the right size, always **gauge** your work with a test square before you begin a project. Instructions include a gauge, indicating the number of stitches and rows (or rounds) to the inch. It is very important to match this gauge. If you knit fewer stitches to the inch than the gauge, your work will be too big; more stitches per inch, and it will be too small.

With the increasing conversion to metrics, many yarn companies are repackaging their yarns in metric balls and skeins. If you haven't been knitting or crocheting recently, this means that the weight of a skein may vary slightly from the amounts you've been accustomed to. For example, much 4-ply knitting worsted is being packaged in 100 gr. (3½ oz.) skeins, instead of 4 oz. skeins. **BE SURE TO CHECK WEIGHTS BEFORE BUYING YARN!**

FOUR-NEEDLE KNITTING: Loosely cast on the required number of stitches, dividing them equally among three double-pointed needles. Being careful not to twist stitches, make a triangle of the three needles, holding the triangle in left hand, with the first cast-on stitch held close to the last stitch (FIG. 29).

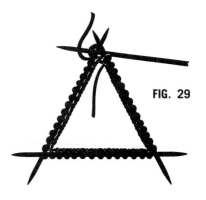

FIG. 29

• Using the suggested yarn and needles, knit a small square (about 4") sample swatch. Remove from the needles without binding off. Block the swatch (see How To Block Like A Pro, p. 296). To measure, lay the work flat. Do not include the cast-on edge but start with the first row. Count stitches and rows to see how many you have to the inch (FIG. 28).

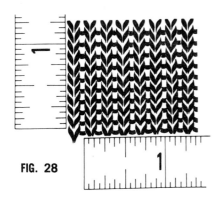

FIG. 28

• If you sample contains more stitches or rows to the inch than the gauge calls for, try to knit **looser** or use **larger** needles. If your sample shows fewer stitches or rows to the inch than the gauge calls for, try knitting **tighter** or use **smaller** needles.

OTHER TECHNIQUES

CHANGING COLORS: Always join a new color on a knit row. Start knitting with the new color at the indicated stitch, leaving a few inches of yarn to be woven in later on the wrong side. Or, you can join the two colors together with a loose knot, leaving a few inches of each color. When you have finished the work, pull the knot through to the wrong side; untie the knot and weave in the ends.

• If you are changing colors constantly, as in Argyle or Fair Isle patterns; don't break the yarn each time; use bobbins, or carry the yarn across the wrong side **loosely.** When working with two or more colors, lock the strands by picking up the new color from **under** the dropped color, or twist the new color around the previous color to prevent making any holes.

• Use the fourth needle to knit the stitches from the first needle in the regular way; then with the free needle, knit the stitches from the second needle; with the next free needle, knit the next stitches from the third needle to complete round.

HOW TO REVERSE SHAPING FOR KNITTING: Occasionally, you will come across directions which will tell you to "work Right Front to correspond with Left Front, reversing all shapings;" or, "complete as for Left Front, reversing all shapings;" or, "complete as for Left Front, reversing shaping." Here's what that means: In working a one-piece Back, directions are given for shaping the side edges by increasing or decreasing at each end of a row. As this piece is usually done first, the worker be-

HOW TO REVERSE SHAPING

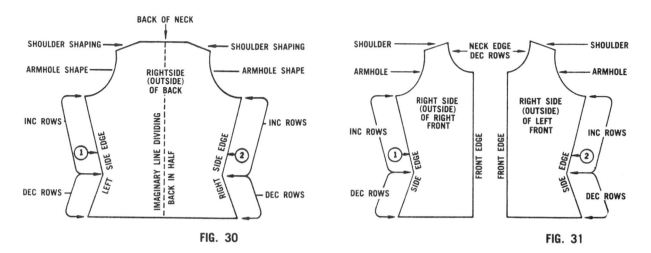

FIG. 30

FIG. 31

comes familiar with how the shaping is done at the beginning and end of a row (FIG. 30). As the **Left Front** is really half of the Back, the side shaping would be the same as the shaping done on the **right half** of the Back; the **Right Front** would be the same as the shaping done on the **left half** of the Back (FIG. 31). The same applies while shaping the neck. If while working the left neck edge the directions read "Dec one st st at **neck edge** on every other row 3 times;" it stands to reason that the same applies to the right neck edge. It also applies to armhole shaping, shoulder shaping, etc.

SOLVING PROBLEMS

Always repair a mistake in knitting as soon as you've noticed it.

DROPPED STITCHES: If a stitch slips off the needle and unravels or runs, use a crochet hook to pick it up. On the knit side, insert the crochet hook through the loop, **front to back,** of the dropped stitch. Hook the hori-

zontal strand of yarn in the row above (FIG. 32) and pull it through the loop on the hook. Continue working up until the loop on the hook reaches the knitting needle. Put the loop on the needle, being careful not to twist it. Do this in reverse on the purl side, inserting the hook through the **back** of the loop and pulling through the horizontal strand in the row above (FIG. 33).

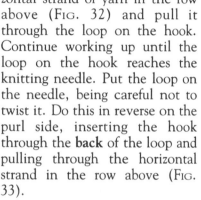

FIG. 32

FIG. 33

RIPPING BACK: If you've made a mistake and you must rip back only a few stitches, or just a row or two, it is best to do it stitch by stitch by **un-**knitting the stitches. Insert the left-hand needle into the stitch of the row **below** the stitch you want to rip while that stitch is still on right-hand needle (FIG. 34). Drop the top stitch from the right-hand needle, leaving the stitch below it on left-hand needle. Pull yarn through dropped stitch (FIG. 35). Continue as necessary.

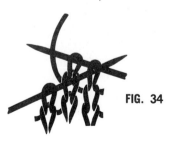

FIG. 34

FIG. 35

RIPPING BACK WHOLE ROWS: If you must rip back a lot of knitting, take the work off the needles and rip to within one row past the mistake. Carefully replace the stitches as follows: Hold the work in your left hand with the yarn end at the left. Starting at the right, and using a smaller size needle, insert the needle from the **back** to the **front** of each stitch (FIG. 36). Continue putting the stitches back on the needle until you have them all. Change to the original needle; continue as directed.

FIG. 36

FINISHING

When all parts or sections of your work are knitted, you will have to block them, put them together, and add finishing touches. Here are some of the basic techniques.

BLOCKING: Always block woolen pieces **before** joining them. Place each piece, wrong side up, on a padded surface. With non-rusting pins, pin edges of the pieces to the padding at quarter-inch intervals, following the "Finished Measurements" given in your directions. **Do not block or stretch waist or wrist ribbings.** Place a damp cloth over the knitted piece; then pass a hot iron very **lightly** and **quickly** over the damp cloth to create penetrating steam. Do **not** press

the iron down, or allow it to remain in one place. Allow pieces to dry thoroughly before unpinning.

• If you have used acrylic yarn, check the label on the skein to see if blocking is necessary. If it is, do **not** use an iron. Merely pin the pieces to the padding following the Finished Measurements, then dampen and allow the pieces to dry.

SEAMING: Thread matching yarn into a tapestry or yarn needle and join the pieces as follows:

• **TO BACKSTITCH SEAMS:** Be careful to match rows, edges and patterns; pin pieces with right sides together. Join edges with running stitches; Backstitch every inch for strength. **Do not sew so tightly that work will pucker or so loosely that there will be holes** (FIG. 37).

FIG. 37

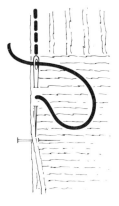

• **TO WEAVE SEAMS:** Place pieces side by side, right side up, patterns matching and edges flush. From right side of fabric take a small running stitch along the edge of one piece, then take a small stitch along the edges of matching piece (FIG. 38). Repeat until the entire seam is joined (without puckering or leaving holes between stitches).

FIG. 38

THE BASIC PATTERNS

STOCKINETTE STITCH (ST ST): When you alternate one knit row and one purl row the result is stockinette knitting. Each side is different. The knit side is the smooth side (*see* FIG. A). The purl side is the nubby side (*see* FIG. B).

FIG. A

Knit Side

FIG. B

Purl Side

• If the purl side is used for the right side, the pattern is called "reverse stockinette".

• When working the stockinette stitch on a circular needle, knit every round.

GARTER STITCH: Every row is knitted; both sides look the same and every two rows of knitting forms a ridge (*see* FIG. C).

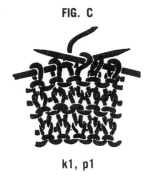

FIG. C

k1, p1

RIBBING: Usually worked on an even number of stitches, achieved by alternating knit and purl stitches on the same row to achieve an elastic texture as in k 1, p 1 ribbing (*see* FIG. D).

FIG. D

CABLES: Cables are made by twisting various sets of stitches at given intervals. Slip number of stitches specified in directions onto cable-stitch holder or double-pointed (dp) needle (*see* FIG. E *black needle*). Hold in front or back of the work, according to the directions. Work the same number of stitches from the left to the right needle, then work stitches on the cable holder.

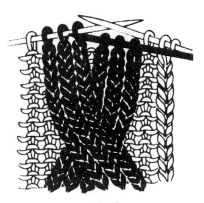

FIG. E

HOW TO
CROCHET

Abbreviations for Crochet: The box that follows is a crochet abbreviations listing, with definitions of the terms given. To help you become accustomed to them, we have repeated these abbreviations throughout stitch instructions.

CROCHET ABBREVIATIONS

beg — begin, beginning; **ch** — chain; **dc** — double crochet; **dec** — decrease, **dtr** — double treble crochet; **hdc** — half double crochet; **in(s) or "** — inch(es); **inc** — increase; **oz(s)** — ounce(s); **pat** — pattern; **pc** — picot; **rem** — remaining; **rnd** — round; **rep** — repeat; **sc** — single crochet; **skn(s),** — skein(s); **sk** — skip; **sl st** — slip stitch; **sp** — space; **st(s)** — stitch(es); **tog** — together; **tr** — triple crochet; **work even** — continue without further increase or decrease; **yo** — yarn over; * — repeat whatever follows * as many times as indicated;() — do what is in parentheses as many times as indicated.

Directions for right-handed and left-handed crocheters
Most crochet stitches are started from a base of chain stitches. However, our stitches are started from a row of single crochet stitches which gives body to the sample swatches and makes practice work easier to handle. When making a specific item, follow the stitch directions as given.

Holding the crochet hook properly (*see* FIG. 1), start by practicing the slip knot (*see* FIG. 2) and base chain (*see* FIG. 3).

FIG. 1L HOLDING THE HOOK

FIG. 2 THE SLIP KNOT (BASIS FOR CHAIN STITCH)

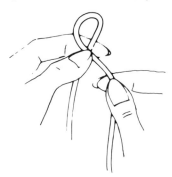

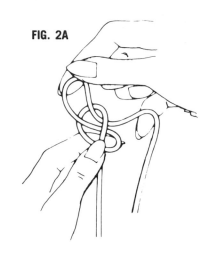

FIG. 2A

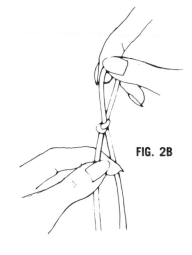

FIG. 2B

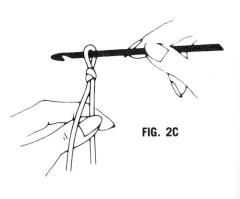

FIG. 2C

FOR LEFT-HANDED CROCHETERS
. . . .
FIGS. 1 to 3 for right-handed crocheters and are repeated in FIGS.
1 Left to 3 Left for left-handed
crocheters.

**LEFT-HANDED CROCHETERS
FIGS. 1 LEFT TO 3 LEFT**

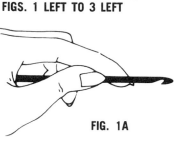

FIG. 1A

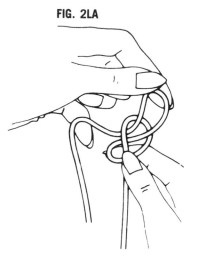

FIG. 2LA

CHAIN STITCH (CH)

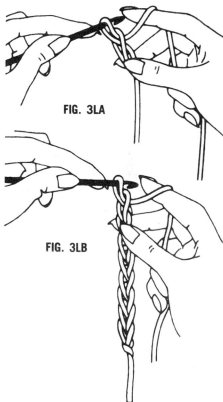

FIG. 3L

FIG. 3LA

FIG. 3LB

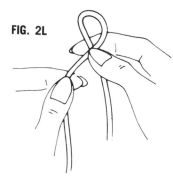

FIG. 2L

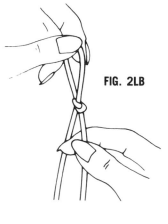

FIG. 2LB

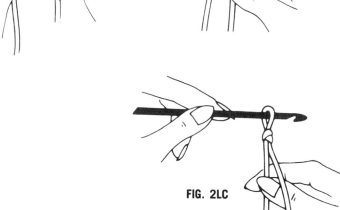

FIG. 2LC

From here on we won't be showing hands — just the hook and
stitches. Left-handed crocheters
can use all the following right-
handed illustrations by simply
turning the book upside down
and placing a mirror (with back-
stand) so that it reflects the left-
handed version.

Chain Stitch (ch): Follow the Steps in FIG. 3. As you make the chain stitch loops, the yarn should slide easily between your index and middle fingers. Make about 15 loops. If they are all the same size, you have maintained even tension. If uneven, rip them out by pulling on the long end of the yarn. Practice making chains and ripping out until you have a perfect chain.

Single Crochet (sc): Follow the Steps in FIG. 4. To practice, make a 20 loop chain (this means 20 loops in addition to the slip knot). Turn the chain, as shown, and insert the hook in the second chain from the hook (*see arrow*) to make the first sc stitch. Yarn over (yo); for the second stitch, see the next arrow. Repeat to the end of the chain. Because you started in the second chain from the hook, you end up with only 19 sc. To add the 20th stitch, chain one (called a turning chain) and pull the yarn through. Now turn your work around (the "back" is now facing you) and start the second row of sc in the first stitch of the previous row (at the arrow). Make sure your hook goes under both of the strands at the top of the stitch. Don't forget to make a ch 1 turning chain at the end before turning your work. Keep practicing until your rows are perfect.

FIG. 3 CHAIN STITCH (CH)

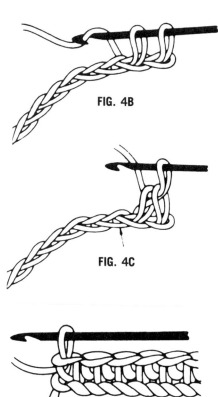

FIG. 4B

YARN OVER (YO)

FIG. 4C

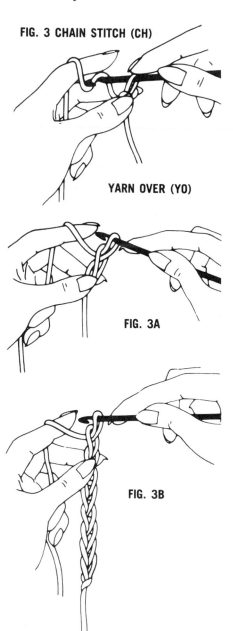

FIG. 3A

FIG. 3B

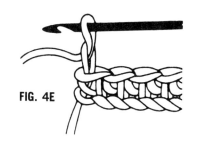

FIG. 4D FRONT OF WORK

FIG. 4 SINGLE CROCHET (SC)

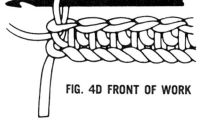

FIG. 4E

FIG. 4A

**FIG. 4F
BACK OF WORK**

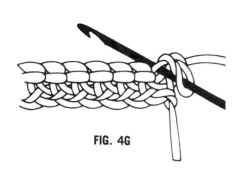

FIG. 4G

Ending Off: Follow Steps in FIG. 5. To finish off your crochet, cut off all but 6″ of yarn and end off as shown. (To "break off and fasten," follow the same procedure.)

Double Crochet (dc): Follow the Steps in FIG. 6. To practice, ch 20, then make a row of 20 sc. Now, instead of a ch 1, you will make a ch 3. Turn your work, yo and insert the hook in the second stitch of the previous row *(at the arrow)*, going under both strands at the top of the stitch. Pull the yarn through. You now have three loops on the hook. Yo and pull through the first two, then yo and pull through the remaining two — one double crochet (dc) made. Continue across row, making a dc in each stitch (st) across. Dc in the top of the turning chain *(see arrow in* FIG. 7) Ch 3. Turn work. Dc in second stitch in the previous row and continue as before.

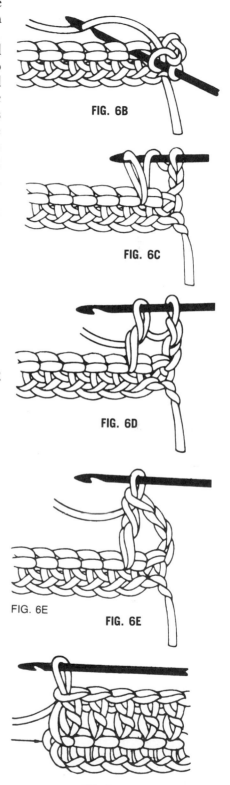

FIG. 6B

FIG. 6C

FIG. 6D

FIG. 6E

FIG. 6E

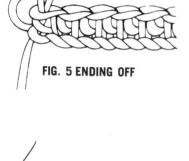

FIG. 5 ENDING OFF

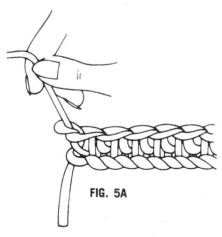

FIG. 5A

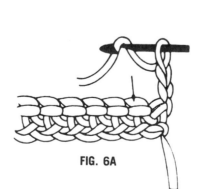

FIG. 6
DOUBLE
CROCHET (DC)

FIG. 6A

FIG. 7

Note: You may also start a row of dc on a base chain (omitting the sc row). In this case, insert hook in fourth chain from hook, instead of second (see Fig. 8).

Slip Stitch (sl st): Follow Steps in Fig. 9. This is a utility stitch you will use for joining, shaping and ending off. After you chain and turn, *do not yo.* Just insert the hook into the *first* stitch of the previous row (see Fig. 9A), and pull the yarn through the stitch then right through the loop on the hook — sl st made.

Half Double Crochet (hdc): Follow the Steps in Fig. 10 and 10A. To practice, make a chain and a row of sc. Ch 2 and turn; yo. Insert hook in the second stitch, as shown; yo and pull through to make three loops on a hook. Yo and pull the yarn through *all* three loops at the same time — hdc made. This stitch is used primarily as a transitional stitch from an sc to a dc. Try it and see — starting with sc's, then an hdc and then dc's.

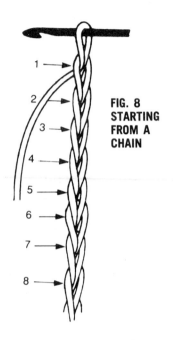

FIG. 8 STARTING FROM A CHAIN

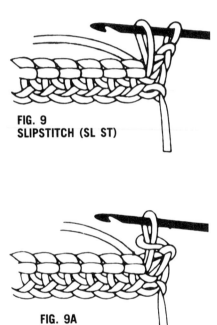

FIG. 9 SLIPSTITCH (SL ST)

FIG. 9A

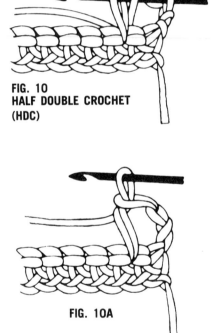

FIG. 10 HALF DOUBLE CROCHET (HDC)

FIG. 10A

The Techniques of Crocheting:
Now that you have practiced and made sample squares of all the basic stitches, you are ready to learn about adding and subtracting stitches to change the length of a row whenever it's called for. This is achieved by increasing (inc) and decreasing (dec).

To increase (inc) — Just make two stitches in the same stitch in the previous row (*see arrow in* Fig. 11). The technique is the same for any kind of stitch.

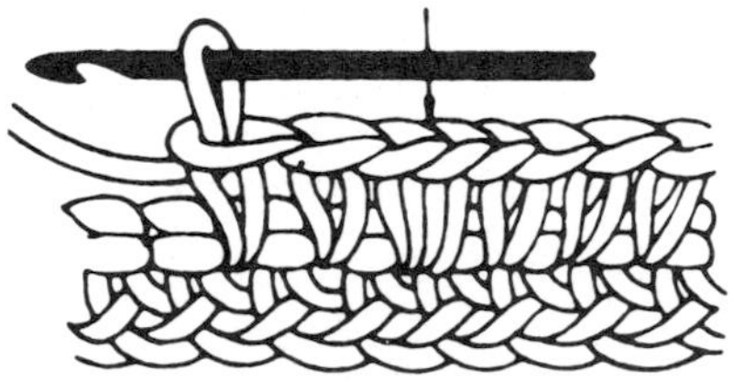

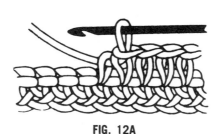

FIG. 11 INCREASING (INC) FOR SINGLE CROCHET

To decrease (dec) for single crochet (sc) — Yo and pull the yarn through two stitches to make three loops on hook (*see Steps in* Fig. 12). Pull the yarn through all the loops at once — dec made. Continue in regular stitches.

FIG. 12 DECREASING (DEC) FOR SINGLE CROCHET

FIG. 12A

To decrease for double crochet — In a dc row make the next stitch and stop when you have two loops on the hook. Now yo and make a dc in the next stitch. At the point where you have three loops on the hook, pull yarn through all loops at the same time. Finish the row with regular dc.

BASIC SHAPES

Now that you have learned the basic stitches (and the techniques for increasing and decreasing them) you should practice making basic circles and square shapes over and over — **until your tension is perfect.** The circles should be flat (not cupped), and the squares should have straight, even sides and well-defined corners.

Circle (*flat round*): To make a circle (working-in-the-round), you simply join the ends of a chain and crochet in rounds (rnds), increasing (inc) to keep the shape flat. Ch 4; insert hook through **first** loop in chain. Join ends with a slip stitch (sl st). Make 6 sc in the ring. Make 2 sc in each stitch around until you have a circle with 12 stitches. Place a safety pin as a marker in last stitch of round (rnd). Then make 2 sc in each stitch until you have a circle with 24 stitches around the edge. (Fig. 13). Move marker on every round.

FIG. 13

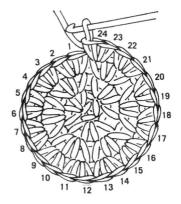

Now make a round with **only** 1 sc in each stitch of the round. That is, **work even.** Move marker. Make another round, increasing (inc) in every **second stitch.** At the end, count your stitches. You should have increased 12 times in the round and have 36 stitches. Make another even round. In the next round increase every **third** stitch. Make another even round. In the next round increase every **fourth** stitch. Continue increasing in this manner until your flat circle is the desired size.

MAKING A SQUARE: In crochet, a square is literally "a circle with square corners." It begins as a circle — but then increases (inc) are made at four equally spaced points. These four point become the corners. In each sc round you work 3 sc into 1 sc, making two increases at each of four "corners." Ch 4; join ends with slipstitch (sl st). Work as you did for the circle until you have 12 stitches in the round. Place marker in last st of rnd. Make 1 sc in next st. *In next st work 3 sc (inc two in this st). Make 1 sc in each of the next 2 sts. Repeat from asterisk (*) two times; in the next st work 3 sc; 1 sc in last st. You have now made three sts into one at four points. These will be the four corners of the square. Look at the first st in which you increased. The secret of the square is to increase two at each of the four corners on **every** rnd. Make the two increases in the middle of each group of three

sts at each corner (arrow in FIG. 14). Continue to inc in each corner until your square is the desired size.

FIG. 14

WHAT CROCHET DIRECTIONS TELL YOU

WHAT THE PATTERN DIRECTIONS TELL YOU: Crochet directions leave nothing to guesswork. First they tell you what to do, then they tell you what you've accomplished. **For instance:** To make a round of 16 sc, you aren't just told to make it. You'd read: Ch 4, join with sl st to form ring. **Rnd 1:** Ch 1, 8 sc in ring. Join with sl st to first sc. **Rnd 2:** Ch 1, 2 sc in the same sc used for joining. 2 sc in rem sc. Join — 16 sc. That **long dash,** followed by the figure, means "this is what you have made." In this instance 16 sc is a total. The long dash is also used after the directions for increasing or decreasing or changing colors — inc made, for example, or — dec made, or — color change made, or — 1 dc decreased at each end, and so on.

THE HYPHEN: You know that ch 3 means 3 ch sts, and that — 3 ch means that you have a total of 3 ch sts. But, ch-3 (with a hyphen between the stitch direction and the figure) tells you that **this is an already existing stitch,** into which you will work another stitch.

EXAMPLE: Join to top of ch-3.

THE IMPORTANCE OF GAUGE:

To assure the correct sizing or measurements of a crocheted piece, always gauge your work with a test square before you begin a project.
• Instructions include a gauge, indicating the number of stitches and rows to the inch. It is very important to match this gauge. If you crochet fewer stitches to the inch than the gauge, your work will be too big; more stitches per inch, and it will be too small.
• Using the suggested yarn and hook size, crochet a small, square (about 4") sample swatch. Block the swatch. To measure, lay the work flat. Count the stitches and rows to see how many you have to the inch.
• If your sample contains more stitches or rows to the inch than the gauge calls for, use a larger hook. If your sample shows fewer stitches or rows to the inch than the called for gauge, use a smaller hook.

ALL ABOUT YARNS

Yarns differ in size, ply, twist and fiber.

YARN SIZE: The thickness and length of yarn is given by yarn count. One indicator of the count is the number of standard lengths per standard weight. Lower count numbers mean a heavier yarn.

YARN PLY is the number of single strands twisted together. On a yarn package, the size and ply are listed as a fraction: size/ply.

YARN TWIST gives the direction and amount of twist.

YARN FIBER is the most important distinction between yarns. Fibers are either natural or synthetic. Natural fibers come from either plants or animals.

PLANT FIBERS

BAST: fibers from plant stems.

LINEN: comes from the flax plant. It is obtained after the flax has soaked in water. Linen is strong and durable.

JUTE: comes from the inner bark of the jute plant. It dyes more easily and is heavier than flax, but is not as durable.

RAMIE: a strong fiber from the ramie plant, mostly grown in China. It is similar to linen but is coarser and dyes easily. It does not shrink or mildew.

SEED/FRUIT FIBERS: are obtained from the hairlike structures surrounding the seeds or fruit of certain plants.

COTTON: is from the hair attached to the seeds of plants of the mallow family. It is smooth, lightweight and easily dyed.

ANIMAL FIBERS

WOOL: fine and thin with rough surfaces.

SHEEP'S WOOL: known simply as wool, comes from the wavy undercoat of sheep. As sheep themselves vary, so wool also varies in thickness and color.

HAIR: coarse and straight.

MOHAIR: From the angora goat, mohair is silky, stronger than wool and dyes well, but it is expensive.

CASHMERE: is the soft undercoat of the Kashmir goat. Cashmere is very expensive since each goat produces only approximately 4½ ounces per year.

ANGORA RABBIT HAIR: Angora fibers are obtained by cutting the soft hairs from this animal. Nine to 18 ounces of fiber can be produced per year. The hair is soft and short and usually combined with other fibers to create a yarn.

SILK is produced by the silkworm caterpillar. During the change from caterpillar to moth, the silkworm produces a protective cocoon. This cocoon, when soaked in hot water, unravels to produce a delicate thread. It is combined with other fibers for a strong thread.

SYNTHETICS

RAYON is made from cellulose and was first created to imitate silk. It is easy to dye, shiny and less expensive than silk.

POLYESTER is made from chemical compounds. It is very strong, crease-resistant and needs minimal care.

ACRYLIC is a synthetic fiber derived from carbon, hydrogen and nitrogen. Like polyester, it holds up even after many washings and is crease-resistant.

NEEDLEPOINT TIPS
. . . .

CANVAS: There are two basic types of needlepoint canvas. Double thread (penelope) and single thread (mono). They both come in a variety of mesh sizes (from very coarse rug canvas to the ultra fine used for petit point), and are usually made of cotton or linen. Choose a canvas mesh size which best suits the yarns you're using, and the visual effect you want to achieve. If you're not sure you've picked the right mesh size, work a small square of stitches in one corner of the canvas. Canvas showing through the threads indicates a mesh too large for the thread; when the canvas threads are squeezed together, you've picked a size too small. Even though all canvas is measured in so-many threads per inch, the only accurate way to measure it, is to count the number of threads to be covered, not the inches or feet. Sometimes the threads will vary slightly in distance from each other; this could throw off a very precisely planned design, if you haven't counted thread by thread. A third type of canvas is made of plastic. It looks like mono; it's flexible, yet rigid. It's only made in one mesh size, though, and sold in sheets, rather than by the yard. You'll find this canvas good for any article you don't want to back.

THREADS: There are many yarns to choose from when working needlepoint, but the most versatile and useful is Persian. It's adaptable to most needs, and comes in skeins of three intertwined strands of yarns. These strands can be used as one, or easily pulled apart to make one, two, or three smaller plys to use according to your needs. Other possibilities for stitching run the gamut from fine silk and metallic threads used in petit point to the very bulky rug and craft yarns. To achieve a planned effect with your threads, it's important that the thread and needle you're using match the mesh opening of your canvas. If they're not equally proportioned, you'll spend a great deal of time re-covering stitches you've already made, or ripping them out entirely. If in doubt as to the number of threads you should use at one time, pick the smaller number. It's easier to re-cover stitches than to rip.

NEEDLES: Always use blunt-tip "tapestry" needles since they'll never split the mesh threads. The needles come in an array of sizes, so you'll easily find one to fit your canvas and threads.

TRANSFERRING A DESIGN: It's easier than you think to transfer a design to canvas. First, cut the canvas about three inches larger on each side than your planned design. Then fold it in half vertically down the center, then horizontally. Unfold the canvas and lightly mark the crease lines with a pencil. Fold and mark the design in the same way as you did the canvas. Now tape the design, unfolded, to a window; place and tape the canvas over the design, matching centers, and vertical and horizontal lines. Using a **water-proof** marking pen, **starting from the center and working outward,** carefully trace the pattern onto the canvas. If you make a mistake, paint over it with white acrylic paint. Remove the pattern and canvas from window. Bind the canvas edges with masking tape so they will not ravel. Leave canvas as is, or color in design with **waterproof** paints or nylon felt-tip markers.

HOW TO ENLARGE DESIGNS
. . . .

If the design is not already marked off in squares, make a tracing of it. Mark the tracing off in squares: For a small design, make squares ¼"; for larger designs, use ½" or 2" squares, or the size indicated in the directions. Decide the size of enlargement. On another sheet of tracing paper, mark off the same number of squares that are on the design or original tracing. For example, to make your design, each new square must be 6 times larger than the original. Copy the outline from your original tracing to the new one, square by square. Use dressmaker's carbon and a tracing wheel to transfer the design onto the material that you are decorating.

HOW TO TAKE BODY MEASUREMENTS

. . . .

It's easy to determine the correct size for any crocheted or knitted garment. First, make sure the person you're measuring is wearing the usual undergarments. For all women's sizes, measure at the fullest part of the natural waistline, hips and bust. We've made allowances for ease to insure a proper fit. If you have to make adjustments between the measurements and size differential, do it during the blocking and finishing. Determine men's sizes by loosely holding the tape around the fullest part of the chest.

STANDARD BODY MEASUREMENTS

. . . .

MISSES

Size							
6	8	10	12	14	16	18	
Bust							
30½	31½	32½	34	36	38	40	
Waist							
23	24	25	26½	28	30	32	
Hip							
32½	33½	34½	36	38	40	42	
Back Neck to Waist							
15½	15¾	16	16¼	16½	16¾	17	
Across Mid Back							
13½	13½	14	14½	15	15½	16	
Shoulder							
4¾	4¾	5	5	5	5¼	5¼	
Neck							
4	4	4	4½	5	5	5½	
Sleeve Length to Underarm							
16¾	16¾	17	17½	17¾	18	18¼	
Armhole Depth							
7	7	7½	7½	7½	8	8	
Upper Arm Circumference							
9¾	9¾	10¼	10½	11	11½	12	
Wrist Circumference							
6	6	6¼	6¼	6½	6½	6½	

MEN

Size					
34	36	38	40	42	44
Chest					
34	36	38	40	42	44
Waist					
30	32	34	36	38	40
Hip					
35	37	39	41	43	45
Across Mid Back					
15½	16	16½	17	17½	18
Shoulder					
5	5¼	5½	5½	5½	6
Neck: Shirt Size					
14	14½	15	15½	16	16½
Length to Armhole					
14	14½	15	15½	16	16
Armhole Depth					
8	8½	9	9½	10	10½
Sleeve to Underarm					
17½	18	18½	19	19½	20
Back Length					
22	23	24	25	26	26½

WOMEN

Size	38	40	42	44
Bust	42	44	46	48
Waist	35	37	39	41½
Hip	44	46	48	50
Back neck to Waist				
	17¼	17⅜	17½	17⅝
Across Mid Back				
	16½	17	17½	18
Shoulder				
	5½	5½	5¾	5¾
Neck	5½	6	6	6
Sleeve Length to Underarm				
	18¼	18¼	18¼	18¼
Armhole Depth				
	8¼	8¼	8¼	8½
Upper Arm Circumference				
	13	13½	14	15

FITTING NOTE

By comparing body measurements in the size chart on this page to the finished sweater measurements given in our instructions, you can see how much ease of fit we recommend for the sweater you are making.

HOW TO BLOCK LIKE A PRO
....

For All Kinds of Needlework

Blocking is almost an art form in itself. Any piece of needlework worth doing is worth blocking well. By following the simple steps and easy methods below, your needlework will have the finished touch of a pro's.

MATERIALS:

• An absolute *must* for professional blocking is a blocking board. You can make one by purchasing a sheet of Homosote board (8' x 4' x ½") from your lumber yard. Homosote is the ideal blocking board because it is porous; needlework should always be blocked on a surface that will permit proper drying. In addition, Homosote will hold a pin, yet will easily release a firmly placed staple. Keep it in one piece if you have the storage space, and rest it on a set of saw horses, and use it to block oversized projects or several smaller ones. Or ask the lumber yard to cut the board in half so that you will have two 4' x 4' boards that can be placed on the kitchen table for blocking and then placed flat on floor for drying.

• Sufficient light-colored muslin or cotton duck to cover the board or boards. Pull the fabric tightly to the back and staple. Place the staples close together and parallel to the edge of the board. (It is not desirable to have a padded board; one thickness of fabric is all that is necessary.)

• A very hard pencil to mark 2-inch squares on the fabric, and a soft cloth to rub over the pencil lines to remove any excess graphite. (Be sure that the squares are exact and that all excess graphite is removed before using the board.)

• Rustproof T Pins and staples to hold pieces in place.

• Light-colored cotton cloth and clean sponges for pressing.

• An iron with steam and dry settings.

• Yellow soap for blocking needlepoint.

You now have a professional blocking arrangement on which to block needlepoint and crewel embroidery as well as knitted and crocheted pieces. The techniques vary depending on the type of needlework to be blocked.

TO BLOCK KNITTED AND CROCHETED ITEMS: *Note: It is possible to ease or stretch the individual pieces moderately to conform to desired measurements. This does not mean that you can turn a size 10 sweater into a size 16 or shrink a size 40 vest into a size 34.)*

• Pin pieces, face-side down, on the blocking board with rustproof T pins, pinning close together to avoid ripples.

• Wring out a cotton cloth with clear water. (Be sure that the cloth is moist, but not dripping wet.) Place your pressing cloth on the pieces to be blocked.

• Use the dry setting on your iron and a temperature setting corresponding to the fibers in the pieces.

• Move the iron in the direction of the pieces, never cross-grain. (It may be necessary to repeat the process of moistening the pressing cloth and pressing several times until the pieces are steamy and warm to the touch.)

Note: Never apply pressure to the iron. The purpose of blocking knitted and crocheted items is to align the stitches, to loft the yarn, and to straighten the pieces. This is accomplished by steam and not pressure.

• Remove the pressing cloth carefully. It may cling to the piece and you will have a damp, spongy, ripply mess. Don't despair! Pat the area gently with your hands until it returns to its desired place. This sometimes happens when a synthetic fiber is heated with steam that is too hot. No permanent damage can be done, *unless* pressure is used and the stitches are flattened.

• Permit the pieces to dry with the board in a flat position at least 24 hours, longer on damp, muggy days.

• Remove the pins; your pieces are ready to assemble.

TO BLOCK NEEDLEPOINT: The purpose of blocking needlepoint is to realign the threads of the canvas and to permit the yarn to loft and become naturally set in each stitch. The stitches should never be smashed flat, or appear to be ironed. *A Word Of Caution: You must test the color fastness of the yarns that have been used in your needlepoint. The first time you touch the iron to the pressing cloth, go over the work very lightly and then inspect the underside of the pressing cloth for any signs of color lifting from a bleeding yarn. If you have stitched with yarns that bleed,* DO NOT BLOCK. *Simply press your needlepoint on the wrong side with a warm iron. This is not going to give you the lovely appearance of a professional blocking, but it is better than the heartbreak of color streaks on a perfectly* *blocked piece of needlepoint. Check for yarn color fastness before you begin your needlepointing*

• You will need a bar of yellow Fels Naptha or Kirkman soap, the type which has been used for years in Madeira to block needlepoint. It restores a natural sizing to the canvas, doesn't harm the wool and makes the needlepoint less attractive to those bugs and insects that can cause damage.

• Place the yellow soap in a bowl of warm water and allow it to stand until the water becomes slick to the touch.

• Place the needlepoint, face-down, on the blocking board.

• Dip the cotton pressing cloth into soapy water and wring it out; place it on the needlepoint.

• Use the dry setting on your iron and the temperature setting corresponding to the fibers in the piece. Iron, but *do not* use pressure on the iron. (The soapy steam will do all the work for you.)

• Repeat dampening the cloth and pressing until the canvas is very soft and flexible, moist, but not wet.

• Place needlepoint, right-side up, on the blocking board.

• Keeping the threads of the canvas on the marked lines of the blocking board, staple about 1 inch out from the needlepoint, placing the staples close together along this line.

• Remove tape or selvages before stapling, if possible. (Staples are used in preference to tacks because they maintain a straight line and avoid the ripples caused by using tacks.)

• Staple the bottom edge the entire length of the canvas, then pull one side onto a straight line

to align it with the marked lines on the board, then continue to staple this side. Staple the top in the same way and then the second side. *Note: If the needlepoint is very distorted, it might be necessary to remove some of the staples and redo a side or two, but it isn't difficult, because the staples will pull out from the Homosote quite easily. Just keep in mind that when the sides are square, your stitching will be perfectly aligned. As you get to the third and fourth sides, you may have lumps and bulges in the center, but as the fourth side is eased into square, these will all smooth out and disappear. It is not necessary to stretch the canvas when stapling, simply place the first side down and staple it smoothly to its original size. Remember, you are not straightening the stitching, you are squaring the threads of the canvas. When the canvas is square, the stitching will be beautifully smooth.*

• Allow your needlepoint to dry 24 hours, or longer, if necessary.

• Pull the needlepoint up from board and the staples will pull out easily; your needlepoint is now ready to be framed or finished. *Note: If your needlepoint was severely distorted, it may be necessary to reblock the piece. This is seldom necessary, however, if you gave the canvas enough soapy steam and stapled it into a perfect square.)*

TO BLOCK CREWEL EMBROIDERY: *Note: All yarns and threads used in an embroidery must be tested before choosing the method, wet or dry, to block them. To test for color fastness, stitch a bit with the yarn or thread to be used on a piece of embroidery fabric. Wet the fabric thoroughly and permit it to dry. Any*

sign of bleeding or fading will warn you not to use the wet method.)

WET METHOD: Staple the dry embroidery, face-down, onto the blocking board.

• Place the staples very close together outside the stitching or framing line. Staple the bottom first, parallel to the edge of the board; staple one side next, then the top and finally the second side. (The lines on the blocking boards are your guide to keeping the threads of the fabric straight and assuring that the piece is a perfect square.)

• Moisten a clean sponge in cool, clear water. Dab the sponge gently over the entire piece to wet it evenly. (Extra dabbing will be needed to assure wetness of all yarns in the embroidered areas.)

• Allow the piece to dry at least 24 hours. As the fabric dries, a natural sizing and smoothness will restore your embroidery fabric to its original crispness. Embroidery stitches will be even and lustrous. No heat is used in this type of blocking and only clear water.

DRY METHOD: Pad the blocking board with a light-colored bath towel; place the embroidery on it face-down, and press with a steam iron set for a temperature correct for the fabric; press with the grain. This method is not preferable to the wet method, but does prevent bleeding yarns from destroying your project.

Satin Stitch

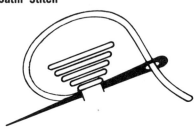

STITCH GUIDE
. . . .

Turkey Stitch

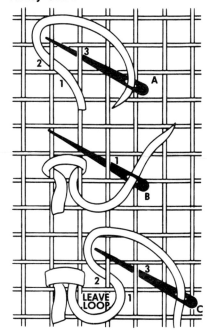

Outline or Stem Stitch

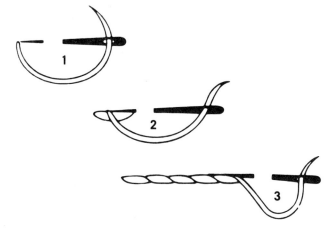

Feather Stitch

Double Straight Cross Stitch

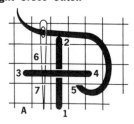

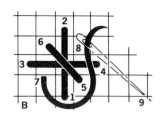

Couch Stitch

French Knot

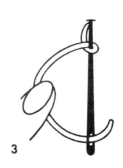

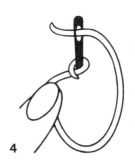

1 2 3 4

Cross Stitch

1 2

Overcast Stitch

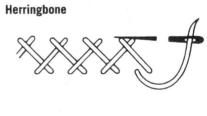

Duplicate Stitch

Herringbone

Lazy Daisy Stitch

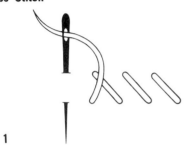

1 2

Running Stitch

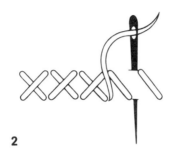

Continental Stitch

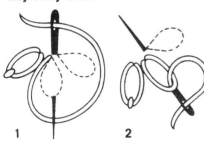

Bullion Stitch

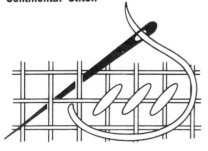

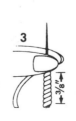

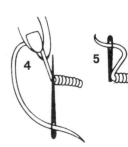

1 2 3 4 5

3/8" 3/8"

MATERIALS SHOPPING GUIDE

Susan Bates
Paton's Yarns
212 Middlesex Avenue
Chester, Conn. 06412

Bernat Yarn & Crafts Co.
Depot and Mendon Streets
Uxbridge, MA 02569

Berrocco
Elmdale Road
PO Box 367
Uxbridge, MA 48018

Anny Blatt
24770 Crestview Ct.
Farmington Hills, MI 48018

Bucilla
150 Meadowlands Parkway
Secaucus, NJ 07094

Caron International
Ave E First Street
Rochelle, Ill 61068

Coats and Clark, Inc.
Dept. CS
PO Box 1010
Tuccoa, GA 30577

Conshohocken Cotton Co.
Ford Bridge Road
Conchohocken, PA 19428

DMC Corporation
107 Trumbull Street
Elizabeth, NJ 07206

Joseph Galler, Inc.
Imported Novelty Yarns
27 W. 20th Street
New York, NY 10011

Green Mountain
Box 568
Putney, VT 05346

Lion Ribbon Co.
100 Metro Way
Secaucus, NJ 07094

Neveda Yarn Co.
199 Trade Zone Drive
Ronkonoma, NY 11779

Phildar, Inc.
6438 Dawson Blvd.
Norcross, GA 30093

Reynolds Yarn
1170 Broadway, Rm 912
New York, NY 10001

Springmaid Fabric
Springs Mills, 5th floor
104 West 40th Street
New York, NY 10018

Talon American
High Ridge Park
Stamford, CT 06905

Tahki Imports, LTD
11 Graphic Place
Moonachie, NJ 07074

William Unger Yarns
230 Fifth Avenue
New York, NY 10001

Welcomme
PO Box 300
Jamestown, SC 29453

Note: Family Circle has listed brand names in this book to correspond with the samples photographed. All materials were available at press time. Substitutions with other products may yield different results.

INDEX

Note: All *italicized* numbers refer to photographs.

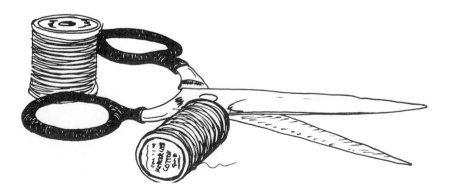

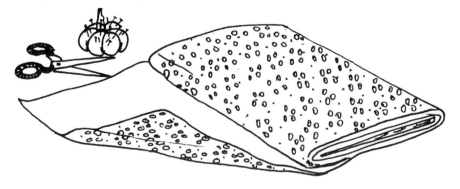

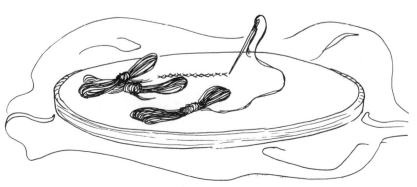

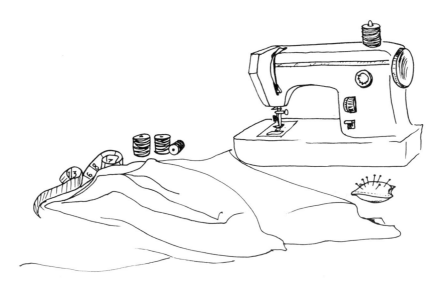

NEEDLECRAFT NOTES

NEEDLECRAFT NOTES

NEEDLECRAFT NOTES